Inclusive
GROUP WORK

Related books of interest

An Experiential Approach to Group Work, Second Edition
Rich Furman, Kimberly Bender, and Diana Rowan

Essential Skills of Social Work Practice:
Assessment, Intervention, and Evaluation, Second Edition
Thomas O'Hare

The Practice of Social Work in North America:
Culture, Context, and Competency Development
Kip Coggins

Diversity, Oppression, and Change:
Culturally Grounded Social Work, Second Edition
Flavio Francisco Marsiglia, and Stephen Kulis

Lesbian and Gay Couples: Lives, Issues, and Practice
Ski Hunter

Social Work Practice with Latinos:
Key Issues and Emerging Themes
Rich Furman and Nalini Negi

The Helping Professional's Guide to Ethics: A New Perspective
Valerie Bryan, Scott Sanders, and Laura Kaplan

Advocacy Practice for Social Justice, Second Edition
Richard Hoefer

Inclusive GROUP WORK

William Pelech
University of Calgary

Robert Basso
Wilfrid Laurier University

Cheryl D. Lee
California State University, Long Beach

Maria Gandarilla
Orange County, California

OXFORD
UNIVERSITY PRESS

Oxford University Press is a department of the University of Oxford.
It furthers the University's objective of excellence in research, scholarship,
and education by publishing worldwide. Oxford is a registered trade mark of
Oxford University Press in the UK and certain other countries.

Published in the United States of America by Oxford University Press
198 Madison Avenue, New York, NY 10016, United States of America.

Library of Congress Cataloging-in-Publication Data

CIP is available online.

ISBN 978-0-190657-09-3

CONTENTS

Chapter 10: Leadership: The Difference Offered by the Worker   127

Chapter 11: The Middle Stage of Group Work   143

Chapter 12: Advanced Skills and Conflict Resolution   160

Chapter 13: Ending a Group and Evaluation   178

PART THREE: INCLUSIVE PRACTICE APPLICATIONS   197

Chapter 14: Trauma and Intimate Partner Violence (IPV)   199

Chapter 15: Groups across the Lifespan   231

FIGURES

TABLES

PREFACE

Today's world is increasingly integrated and connected. Many communities are characterized by widespread and growing diversity, and as a result of these changing social dynamics, social work practice is increasingly called upon to work with diverse populations. Indeed, diversity underpins contemporary social life and professional practices; however, as a global community, people have not always accorded diversity with the respect that it deserves. Our collective histories are rife with the suppression of diversity in our environment and our social relationships. Hence, the concept of diversity is particularly relevant to the social work profession, which has a mandate to work toward social justice and equity for members of "non-dominant, marginalized or oppressed social groups" (Doyle & George, 2008, p. 97).

Over the past decade, literature regarding helping professions has stressed the importance of cultural competency and the implementation of different culturally based approaches by practitioners. A framework of cultural diversity is related to the ecological understandings of human interactions. A primary focus is the relative importance of ubiquitous human interactional differences and how we respond to these. A key concept extracted from this is that diversity exists in all human relationships. As such, there are important implications for how to intercept diversity and how to further develop and research these social and interactional phenomena.

Yalom and Leszcz (2005) have described groups as microcosms of the societies in which they are embedded, and thus, it is not surprising that diversity is most often encountered in group work practice. Ivey, Pedersen, and Ivey (2007) note that "multicultural issues are present in every group" (p. 372) and Wilson, Rapin, and Haley-Banez (2004) refer to an "increasing recognition that all group work is multicultural" (p. 20). Groups provide opportunities to facilitate change, growth, and development. The differences in points of view among group members provide robust material for problem solving. The group's ongoing human contact precludes staying static. As a social worker, it is vital for you to recognize that all groups are embedded in diversity and that diversity can be a positive force in all relationships. Each member of a social work group has a unique identity based on his or her biology, psychology, cultural background, life experiences, and family and social contexts (Delucia-Waack & Donigian, 2004). Respecting the myriad differences brought into a group setting is a value in group work practice, particularly as the heart of group process is exploring differences. It is the practitioner's responsibility to assist group members to understand differences along with commonalities.

This book expands the discussion of diversity and specifies how diversity provides practice with new concepts and tools for facilitating the movement of the group towards the achievement of the group's work. Over three parts, the book offers new perspectives and ways of working with the many facets of diversity that arise in groups. Part one provides a foundation for group work practice and explores various historical themes that have emerged over the years. It will focus on major concepts in group work practice, including a typology of groups, discussion of the benefits of groups, and the curative factors of groups. It will also discuss various principles of diversity informed practice, including redefining diversity and outlining its role within a strengths-based ecological framework. This part also presents an integration of diversity into a new model of inclusive group work practice. Finally, part one will discuss ethical principles and standards in group work practice. Part two will discuss how diversity can be used effectively in working with groups from preparation through the beginning, middle, and ending phases. It also presents the concept of the professional use of self and conflict resolution skills as vital components of practices for an inclusive group worker. In part three, group workers extend the application of inclusive practice in various practice settings with diverse case studies. These include groups in social service agencies; groups in mental health settings; groups that address the needs of people across the lifespan; support groups; and groups found in organizational contexts. Finally, the epilogue will explore the potential implications of this new inclusive way of working with groups as well as how the principles of inclusive group work may be applied for the benefit of our communities and society.

It is the authors' sincere hope that the information in this book will help you identify diversity as omnipresent and an integral part of the human experience. They also hope that after reading this book you will feel confident and competent to establish and facilitate an inclusive social work group. Finally, they hope that through inclusive group work, you can provide meaningful and lasting impact on consumers so that they too can work towards creating inclusive communities and an inclusive world.

ACKNOWLEDGMENTS

Cheryl Lee would like to acknowledge California State University, Long Beach for granting a Research and Creative Activity Grant to assist with time to write book chapters. She greatly appreciates the time, support, and encouragement her life partner, Zvi Plotnik, gave her to complete *Inclusive Group Work*. Also deserving acknowledgment are group work scholars and her IASWG mentors and friends who inspired her to learn more about this fantastic form of social work practice.

William Pelech would like to acknowledge several graduate students for their assistance in preparing reviews of various research topics, including Sarah LaRocque, Karen Paul, Elena Esina, and Raazia Naqvi. He would also like to acknowledge support from the Social Sciences and Humanities Research Council, which provided funding for group work related research as well as the University of Calgary and the IASWG for their ongoing support. He would like to thank various inspiring mentors, including Robert Basso, Edcil Wickham, and Norma Lang for their early guidance and support in his academic career. Finally, he would like to acknowledge the love and support of his partner, Sharon Pelech, as well as his children and grandchildren, who have taught him a great deal about the importance of valuing diversity.

Maria Gandarilla would like to acknowledge her husband, Ahmed, her mother, Lilia, and all of her family for their encouragement, love, and patience throughout this project. She is humbled by their unwavering support, their confidence in her, and their sacrifice for her success. Also deserving acknowledgment are her coauthors for the group work involved in achieving this project. She would like to give special acknowledgment to Professor Cheryl Lee for involving her in this project, as well as for giving her guidance and encouragement.

Robert Basso would like to acknowledge Wilfrid Laurier University for providing the freedom to question and probe significant questions related to diversity when such questions were not yet publicly discussed. He would like to acknowledge His wife, Jan, and son, Andrew, for providing support and enduring the writing process. Also, he wishes to remember his dissertation chairperson, Professor Norma Lang of the University of Toronto, for her early guidance.

PART ONE

Inclusive

GROUP WORK:
THEORETICAL FOUNDATION

CHAPTER 1

FUNDAMENTALS OF GROUP WORK

LEARNING OBJECTIVES

At the end of this chapter you will be able to:
- Define group work and describe its four elements.
- Explain why learning about groups is important.
- Define various forms of social organization along a continuum from aggregates to groups.
- List and describe various group attributes and dynamics.

WHAT IS GROUP WORK?

Social work with groups, which some describe as social group work, has always recognized the power of the group to bring about change. Group work is a goal directed activity with two primary uses: (1) to bring about change to individual members (as in an intervention group) or (2) to bring about change to the social conditions or environment outside of the group (as in a task group). Hartford (1971) and Middleman and Goldberg Wood (1990b), well-respected group scholars, outline four elements that constitute group work:

1. The worker's attention must focus on assisting members to become a system of mutual aid.
2. The worker must understand and respect the power of the group process, including the power of interpersonal relationships and group development to bring about change.
3. The worker enables the group to increase its autonomy and independence as an agent of change, such that the group can function without the worker.
4. The worker must facilitate the conditions in the group to enable group members to apply the group experience when the group ends.

It should be noted that although group autonomy is a main element in group work, there are some types of groups (e.g., children's groups, psychiatric groups, etc.), where the group may not be able to function completely autonomously (Lang, 1972, 2010) yet may still be successful in achieving its purpose.

WHY IS LEARNING ABOUT GROUP WORK IMPORTANT?

As a social work student, one important question that may come to mind is, "Why is learning how to work with groups important?" One of the most important reasons is that you are nearly always a member of some type of group. You were born and live your life in what Charles Cooley (1909) described as primary groups, or informal groups that include your family and friends. You also live your life in other more formal or secondary groups such as your classes at school, work in a social services agency, and involvement in the community. Then, there are the many online groups and social networks that you may be connected with via the Internet. Ultimately, all people have needs for belonging, fulfillment, praise, and approval, and a group, whether it is your family or your group of friends, is the primary means through which your basic needs are met. Because you will remain in various social groups and maintain relationships with friends throughout your life, you will always be participating in some form of group.

Another important reason why learning about group work is important is because of a group's ability to address multiple issues and needs simultaneously. When one thinks conceptually about various forms of social organization, one realizes that groups lie at the nexus of the individual and society. Development of skills in working with groups enables social workers to work effectively in bringing about change not only with individuals but also in communities. As this book will discuss, group work traditions demonstrate that groups are the vehicle through which social workers can help consumers bring about personal change as well as positive growth in communities. This is important because not all problems that consumers bring to social workers reflect individual deficits or dysfunction; often these problems reflect limitations and deficiencies situated in society.

When one thinks about all of the social change movements that have occurred over the past 100 years, one often thinks about individuals such as Jane Addams, Mahatma Gandhi, Mother Teresa, Martin Luther King, and Nelson Mandela, to name only a few. Yet, these individuals alone could never have brought about change if it were not for the actions of groups they organized. Each of these individuals needed group work skills to organize the various social movements that they led. (Figure 1.1 shows the ways individuals, groups, and communities are

Figure 1.1 Groups at the Nexus

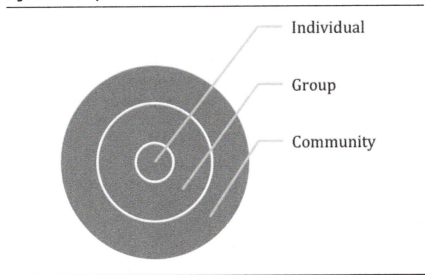

Individual

Group

Community

related.) As many of you who have participated in a successful sports team or in a class or work project can attest, groups can be creative and productive and can accomplish remarkable goals. As Susan Wheelan (2005) has observed:

> People have formed work groups in order to accomplish goals and tasks since the beginning of human history. The small group, whose members work collaboratively for their mutual benefit or survival, is the oldest form of social organization. Groups have played a major role in both the survival of human beings and the development of human culture. Some would argue that our ability to work together was, and is, the key to human survival and advancement. (p. 1)

Additionally, learning about groups is important because of their versatility, utility, and effectiveness. There are a myriad of types and purposes of groups. For this reason, not only are groups ubiquitous, they also offer great utility. There is a diverse array of purposes and settings indicative of the different types of groups that social workers must be prepared to initiate, including therapy groups, support groups, social action groups, educational groups, recreational groups, task groups, and self-help groups (Galinsky & Schopler, 1989). Some social work graduates will go on to facilitate therapeutic groups, and all graduates will take part in work groups on a daily basis. Social workers often take part in supervisory groups, project teams, and committees. As recent social science research has indicated, groups perform better than the average individual in a variety of complex tasks because groups have higher information gathering and processing capacity and accuracy (Lejarraga, Lejarraga, & Gonzales, 2014). As this book will discuss, groups are much more effective in solving complex problems than individuals acting alone. This is because a complex task requires a repertoire of diverse skills, knowledge, and experience beyond the capacity of any individual (Wheelan, 2005).

Additionally, an important reason for learning about groups is because it is a practical and effective way to address numerous clients when time, finances, and social work resources are finite. As you will find in your studies and practice, social workers are often expected to find the most cost and time effective methods to effect change. Groups allow social workers to do this in many ways. In an intervention group, a worker and the other members can affect multiple individuals within the same time frame. Furthermore, societal change has been more successful when a group brings forth the effort as opposed to a sole individual.

So, finally, if you realize that you will always be involved in groups, perhaps one of the most important reasons to learn about how to work with groups is that you can make a difference in helping a group function more effectively. Everyone has participated in groups that have not worked out well. Students often groan when a group project is mentioned, for they may have participated in a group in which not everyone contributed equally, leading to a lack of satisfaction and unpleasant feelings. Because you will inevitably need to work in groups of various types, by learning how to facilitate groups more effectively as well as understanding group dynamics, you will be in a better position to overcome challenges and realize the benefits that productive and effective groups can bring to your work and daily life.

Exercise 1.1: Group Discussion

In small groups, discuss the following:

- In what ways are you part of a group that you were not aware of or considered to be in?
- What are the potential benefits of learning about group work and how to be an effective group worker?
- Share a negative or positive experience you have had in a group. How did this experience affect your thoughts and feelings about group work?

WHAT IS A GROUP?

Now that you appreciate the value of group work, it is important that you have a further understanding of a group's important attributes. The most commonly cited definition of a group, offered by noted sociologist Earl Eubank (1932) and later modified by Wilson and Ryland (1949), is:

> two or more individuals in a relationship of psychic interaction involving an affective relationship based upon a mutual bond or we feeling. (p. 44)

However, there is much more to a group than simply two persons in some form of communication. The Canadian group work scholar Norma Lang devoted much of her career to this question of what a group is. She believed that a group is much more than a social entity, and that a group lies on a continuum of social organization.

According to Lang (2011), the most basic form of social organization is an aggregate: a temporary and accidental social gathering within a delimited geographic area that lacks any social bonds, defined boundaries, or conscious purpose. For example, individuals at a train station are an aggregate. The next level of social organization outlined by Lang (1987) is a collectivity. Lang (1987) defined a collectivity as an entity capable of becoming a group but not yet developmentally at that point, as it is "likely to be lacking in shared, common group goals, and in such essential group phenomena as group autonomy, group cohesion, and procedures for pursuing collective goals through group-directed effort" (p.9). An example of a collectivity could include a group of brand new mothers at a hospital who stay one night and learn a few things as a collective about how to bathe, change, or feed their new babies. A group to Lang (1987) is much more than a collectivity, and is part of the social organization described by Eubank (1932). (Figure 1.2 shows Lang's theory of the continuum of social organization.) Citing Theodorson and Theodorson (1969), Lang (1987) defined a group as follows:

> A plurality of persons who have a common identity, at least some feeling of unity, and certain common goals and shared norms. Further characterized by direct or indirect communication among its members, standardized patterns of interaction based on a system of interrelated roles, and some degree of interdependence among members. . . . [A] group is a more developed type of collectivity with a distinct sense of identity, and definite social structure, based upon direct and indirect interaction among its members. (p. 11).

Figure 1.2 Lang's Continuum of Social Organization

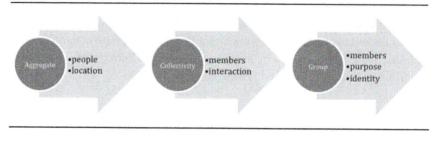

Exercise 1.2: Defining Group

Read the examples below of various forms of social organization and determine whether each is an aggregate, a collectivity, or a group. Explain the rationale for your decision.

  a. eight people waiting at a bus stop

  b. four people stuck in an elevator

  c. twelve people from different agencies meeting at a monthly community interagency meeting

  d. five employees who work in a group home on different shifts

  e. eleven people in an online chat room

  f. ten children playing on a school playground.

ATTRIBUTES AND DYNAMICS OF A GROUP

From Lang's definition, which will be used for this book, you can discern a number of distinctive attributes and group dynamics that together make a group. These include: membership, communication, relationships/cohesion, purpose, values/ group culture, norms, roles, power and status, and interdependence and mutual aid.

Membership

As suggested by these definitions, a group has been traditionally defined as having two or more members; however, most groups have more than two members. Defining membership determines a boundary between those who are members of a group (in this case the worker is included as a member) and those who are not. Some groups have open boundaries, such as a drop-in recreational group. Other groups may have rigid boundaries, such as a closed therapeutic group or a private committee meeting.

Communication

In any group, communication is omnipresent. This is true in a group because all behavior (both verbal and nonverbal) has the potential to be interpreted by others as having some meaning. Indeed, group members are always communicating. For example, in a recent class you saw one class member listening to the instructor and nodding her head, while another was sitting back in his chair with his arms and legs crossed, looking away. Neither of these classmates was verbally saying anything, but they were communicating nonetheless, and communicating what may be interpreted as very different messages. Consider the many times in a group you have heard silence. As you may recall, you could interpret the silence very differently depending upon what preceded it. It could be a thoughtful silence, a fearful one, or a shocked silence. Communication will be discussed in detail later in the book.

Relationships/Cohesion

Another important defining characteristic that makes a group a group is the relationships or bonds that arise in a group over time. The development of these bonds turns an individual's experience of an isolated "I" into a connected sense of "we" (Wilson & Ryland, 1949). Collectively described as group cohesion, this "we" feeling is what gives a group the power to bring about change in an individual, complete a variety of tasks, and transform a community. As Yalom and Leszcz (2005) observed, cohesion is a necessary yet insufficient precursor for change. That is, just as a group needs more than one person to be a group, group cohesion cannot bring about change without some other important elements. Perhaps the most important of these is group purpose.

Purpose

As Kurland and Salmon (1998a) note, the "why" of the group is its purpose. They define group purpose as

> . . . the ends which the group collectively will pursue. It describes where the group will go—the group's aims and ultimate destination. Within the common group purpose, individual group members may have specific expectations,

individual hopes, and goals that they hope to achieve as a result of their participation in the group. These individual goals are encompassed within the overarching purpose of the group. (p. 107).

Clarity of purpose is an essential feature of any effective group. It is an ally of any group worker, as it informs all of the group worker's activities from the initial conception of the group, through its design, the various stages of the group's development, through to its evaluation and ending. Clarity of group purpose enables prospective members to understand what kind of group they are agreeing to join. Clarity of purpose gives both the worker and group members a clear understanding of the ends that the group will achieve. Toseland and Rivas (2011) have identified two major types of groups arising from their different purposes. An intervention group is largely focused on meeting its members' social and emotional needs. A task group is generally focused on needs outside of the group and not directly linked to those of its members. In a task oriented group, group purpose enables group members to work together to complete a project. Although a group may have multiple objectives, the overall purpose sets the limits or boundaries as to what will be done in the group. For example, in a task oriented group it may not be appropriate for members to share challenges that they are facing in their personal relationships.

One way to assess the clarity of group purpose would be to ask the group worker and group members to explain the purpose of the group. Finally, clarity in group purpose will also enable the group worker and membership to know when their purpose has been achieved (Kurland & Salmon, 1998a).

Along with group attributes, there are also group dynamics that emerge in every group. These include values/group culture, norms, roles, power and status, as well as interdependence and mutual aid.

Values/Group Culture

Values are preferences. That is, they are "abstract propositions about what is right, desirable or worthwhile" (Northen, 2004). Values inform and are shaped by the cultural context in which the group member lives and his or her life experiences. For this reason, diverse members may possess relatively different values. Each decision made by a group will be informed by the values that each member, including the social worker, brings to the group. Finding ways in which a group can work with the diverse values is an essential part of the group's developmental tasks. Over time, a unique value system or group culture will emerge within the group, which may reflect the values of individual members.

Norms

From the values brought into the group by the worker and membership, a number of norms will emerge in the group over time. A group norm is an implicit or explicit rule that governs member behavior and choices in a group. These norms can serve to limit group member behavior and discussion. For example, norms can be liberating in terms of promoting individual self-expression or oppressive in how they suppress the expression of differences. Norms can also promote or inhibit the questioning of authority.

Roles

Roles are sets of expectations defining appropriate behavior associated with a certain membership position within the group. A diversity of roles in a group is essential to the functioning of a group. In a social work group, there are two primary roles, the role of the worker and member. A hallmark of a functional group is that roles in the group are flexible. For example, as suggested by Lang (2010), the worker's role must change as the group develops. Although he or she may adopt a more active role early in the group, as the group develops, the worker may be less active and more peripheral to the functioning of the group. Another important role is the role of leader. Social work with groups has historically differentiated between the role of the worker and leadership. Again, indicative of the worker's flexible role with the group, the worker may initially lead the group, but as the group develops, leaders will naturally emerge from the group. As this process unfolds, the worker may move out of the leadership role and play a supporting role in the life of the group, intervening only when needed. It should be noted that in some groups, such as certain task groups, roles might be appointed or elected. For example, in task groups, such as a board of directors or an executive board of an organization, roles are dictated by bylaws and the role of a chair or president remains until the person has fulfilled their term of office. In these situations you may find that although individual roles remain ascribed, tasks and responsibilities of work to be done can be fluid.

Power and Status

In most societies, there is a diverse array of power or statuses ascribed to various roles. Groups are invariably influenced by the mores of the social contexts in which they are embedded. In many social contexts, there is differential power bestowed to the perceived leader of a group. There may also be a hierarchy of power in which different members are bestowed greater or lesser status than others. There are various forms of power that may be perceived to be possessed by a member and/or role in a group (Raven 2008). These include:

- Reward power: The power to give or withhold rewards. For example, a group worker might give children stickers at the end of group for good behavior/participation.
- Coercive power: The ability to exact punishment. For example, a judge might suggest that an individual will be arrested if he does not participate in a treatment group.
- Legitimate power: Where a role is recognized to have the right to pre-scribe behavior. For example, an elected board chair has the power to assign/delegate tasks.
- Expert power: Where the role is perceived to possess greater knowledge or expertise. For example, at the beginning of the group a worker may be perceived to be an expert in problem solving and leading a group.
- Referent power: Where power comes from the psychological identifica-tion by group members. For example, in an intervention group, a specific member may model the taking of an appropriate emotional risk by dis-closing a painful personal experience that helps other members under-stand and share their own experiences.
- Informational Power: Where power comes from an individual having information other members may need or desire. The individual may influ-ence others to act or behave in a particular way through the provision of this information. An example would be a group member having informa-tion needed by other members to successfully complete the group activi-ties or homework.

These status hierarchies can affect the relative social integration present in a society as well as in a group. People's collective social histories have documented countless examples where power is used to punish, subjugate, and marginalize those who are perceived as being different or expressing a different opinion from those who possess power. For these reasons, social workers have developed ethical codes that affirm the inherent worth, dignity, and right to self-expression of consumers regardless of their diversity. These ethical codes will be discussed later in this text.

Interdependence and Mutual Aid

Another important defining characteristic of the group is interdependence, also termed mutual aid in social work group literature. As group members interact, develop relationships, and define norms, they become familiar with the different experiences, knowledge, perspectives, and skills fellow group members bring to the group. As problems are solved and tasks completed, members learn to rely upon this diversity. They realize that they are interdependent and that each member has a unique contribution to make to their shared group purpose.

Perhaps the most distinctive feature of a social work group is the recognition that it is the group that is responsible and best equipped to achieve its purpose. This purpose is achieved through the process of mutual aid wherein members help each other. The distinctive use of mutual aid has a long tradition in social work with groups, including an anti-oppressive tradition, which recognizes the strengths and self-determination of group members. In this way, social work with groups "shifts the source of helping from the group leader to the members themselves" (Gitterman & Shulman, 2005). The worker's role in a social work group is to affirm and support the group members' ability to help each other. The worker does this by helping group members engage in the group, express their differences, and form relationships that are purposeful and constructive. Understanding the various forms of social organization and the characteristics of groups enables the group worker to believe that it is possible to facilitate the development of an aggregate into this entity we call a group. How this is done is called group work.

Exercise 1.3: Identifying Power and Status

In small groups, identify and discuss different ways in which you observe the various forms of power (reward, coercive, legitimate, referent, informational, and expert) in society. Discuss how you think each form of power could affect how a group functions.

CHAPTER SUMMARY

This chapter has offered social work derived definitions of what is meant by a group and group work practice. It has also provided a compelling rationale for why learning about and being able to engage in group work practice is important. Finally it outlined some of the basic attributes and dynamics of groups.

CHAPTER 2

HISTORY OF GROUP WORK APPROACHES

LEARNING OBJECTIVES

At the end of this chapter you will be able to:

- Identify important approaches to group work that have emerged over the years.
- Distinguish how each practice model views and responds to diversity.
- Explain major concepts that have been contributed by various practice models and theories that continue to inform group work practice today.

This chapter will outline some important approaches to group work that have emerged over the years and have contributed to group work practice as it is known today. It will also discuss how these approaches and practices have responded to diversity.

The Settlement House Movement and the Birth of the Social Goals Model

Although groups and group work have been quintessential human experiences for centuries, the rise of the modern group work movement, and its response to diversity, coincides with the birth of social work in the settlement houses. Set during a time when mass immigration and increasing social problems (poverty, poor health access, unsatisfactory living and working conditions, etc.) widened the gap between social classes, the early settlement houses were intended to bridge social classes (Alissi, 2008) and to affect upward mobility. Through participation in the settlement houses, new immigrants and lower class consumers acquired access to resources and services to address the various pressing social issues they faced. Furthermore, community members from different cultural and ethnic backgrounds were given the opportunity to learn about each other and to integrate into the community. It is important to note that the vehicle through which the change occurred was group work, a process that was empowered through diversity and common need.

Through the mission of promoting social unity, the settlement houses became experts in working with diverse groups. The most notable voice in the settlement movement was Jane Addams. Addams affirmed that diversity served to enrich all members of society; thus, she challenged the assimilationist forces of her times bent on Americanizing immigrants and removing their ethnic and cultural diversity. Two enduring values directing Addams' work were democracy and reciprocity. Addams believed that with the loosening of social roles and an openness to learn from one another, reciprocal interdependence would be promoted and instilled in modern society (Pottick, 1989). One may discern many principles and themes in the settlement house movement that would later emerge in major group work approaches, including the dual focus on micro and macro change.

SOCIAL GOALS MODEL

Long before the contemporary strengths centered approaches, the social goals model focused on "problems of people, rather than people with problems" (Wilson, 1976, p. 28). Implicit in this model was the understanding that individual and community change are intertwined and interdependent. The social goals model assumed that individual growth can and does occur through collective action for the common good. Through supporting the socialization of democratic values and social conscience, the group is empowered to bring about individual growth, development, and learning in its efforts to bring about social change (Middleman & Goldberg Wood, 1990a).

In this model, there was also an assumption that leadership emerges from the group membership and is transferred from the worker to group members as leaders naturally emerge. Assessment in this model was focused on the group and understanding its unique values and behaviors. It was the role of the worker to assess and promote the development of group norms that emerged from the cultures represented in the group (Papell & Rothman, 1966). The social goals model provided many principles that continue to influence group work today. In addition to democratic principles, it placed the group in the context of agency and community influences. Some of the skills that the social goals model offered included clarification of agency policy and goals, and identification of issues suitable for collective action (Papell & Rothman, 1966). However, the group's focus on problems identified by people vis-a-vis problems experienced by people, led to the diminishment of this model as the emphasis in social work shifted from the community to clinical practice (Papell & Rothman, 1966).

In the years leading up to the Second World War, group work expanded and specialized. Although social casework was heavily influenced by psychoanalytic theory, social group workers found it challenging to translate psychoanalytic concepts to group work (Papell & Rothman, 1966). Informed by ego psychology, Robert Vinter, working with adults, and Gisella Konopka with children, developed what became known as the remedial model in social work practice with groups (Papell & Rothman, 1966).

REMEDIAL MODEL (SOCIAL TREATMENT MODEL)

The remedial model was grounded in social role theory, psychoanalytic concepts, and ego psychology. The group was viewed as both an agent and context for individual behavioral change (Vinter, 1974). In this way, the remedial model expanded and shifted the emphasis of group work away from community and societal change to the improvement of the social functioning of individuals. Influenced by the medical model and social casework, the remedial model adopted the study, diagnosis, and treatment regime for work with individuals. Treatment goals followed directly from diagnosis, and the worker used direct and indirect influences to bring about individual change (Vinter, 1974). Direct influences involved various roles managed by the worker, which included acting as: an object of identification/transference; an agent of "legitimate" norms and values; definer of individual goals and tasks; and controller of member roles (Vinter, 1974). Indirect means of influence involved the worker acting on and with the group through: group purpose (including the composite of individual members' treatment goals and the worker's purpose in meeting these); selection of group members; group size; group norms (e.g., democratic processes); and group development (Vinter, 1974).

The remedial model contributed three important concepts that continue to inform practice today. These include transference, countertransference, and defense mechanisms. A cornerstone of traditional psychodynamic approaches, transference involves the projection of feelings by group members from a previous relationship onto others in the group (Bernard & MacKenzie, 1994). Although earlier familial experiences are often the more influential source of transferential responses, other significant relationships and traumatic experiences may also trigger transference in groups. For example, the worker may be viewed as a cold authority figure by a member who experienced a similar relationship. The group as a whole may be idealized by one member as the family that they never had, or by another member in negative terms as being just like his or her family. In a sense, transferential responses reflect the past influencing the current relationships in the group.

Countertransference is a term for the feelings that emerge within the worker in response to member transferences in the group. A myriad of definitions and classification systems abound in the literature concerning the nature of counter-transference, ranging from a broad definition, where countertransference is seen as the total responsiveness to the other persons in the therapeutic relationship (Basescu, 1990) to the most narrow psychoanalytic definition as a distortion or interference emanating from the workers' unresolved issues, which impairs their understanding of the group (Goldberg, 1983).

Psychoanalysis postulates that individuals will resort to unconscious defense mechanisms (e.g., denial, projection) when they are unable to reduce their experience of anxiety to tolerable levels through the use of rational coping strategies (e.g., problem solving). Often acquired as learned behaviors during childhood, some defense mechanisms may cause an individual to misinterpret or distort reality. This distortion of reality results in the reduction of anxiety and the replacement of rational coping strategies with one or more defense mechanisms, which are used when similar anxiety-provoking situations reoccur.

As you will see, like the remedial model, many prevailing group work models have assumed that in order for the group to become an effective agent of change, bonds or cohesion between members must be promoted. These bonds are, at least initially, viewed to be based upon perceived commonalities and compatibilities among group members (Vinter, 1974). Based upon cohesiveness arising from such similarities, the group is enabled to develop social control mechanisms such that "deviation from norms often tends to be dealt with in a harsh and punitive manner by the group" (Vinter, 1974, pp. 75–76).

Although the influence of the social goals model waned in the 1950s and early 1960s as the settlement house movement weakened, there were two conceptions of social group work, one where the group was focused primarily on community change and the other focused on individual change. In the 1960s, another approach emerged, which potentially offered to integrate these two approaches to social group work.

MEDIATING MODEL AND MUTUAL AID (INTERACTIONAL) MODEL

Although social change and advocacy have long been essential components of social work competencies, those who work with individuals in clinical practice have often been accused of neglecting structural inequalities or public issues that are viewed as underlying the problems experienced by their consumers. William Schwartz (1969) attempted to resolve this false dichotomy through formulation of the mediating function of generalist social work practice. Profoundly influenced by Grace Coyle and the social goals model, Schwartz proposed that the worker serves two consumers, the individual and the larger social system(s) in which he or she belongs. This mediating function enables the group worker to transform the private troubles of individuals into public issues through bringing about policy changes at the agency or community level (Schwartz, 1976). The mediating model, introduced into social work practice with groups, has three enduring constructs: contract, mutual aid, and common ground. Contracting, which will be discussed later in the book, occurs during the beginning phase of group work. It involves agreement of the consumer, worker, and agency.

Inspired by the writings of Peter Kropotkin (1902), Schwartz (1976) conceptualized the group "as a system of mutual aid, composed of an alliance of individuals who need each other to work on common problems" (p. 266). Subsequently, Lawrence Shulman (1986) delineated nine group processes involved in mutual aid in groups. These processes include:

- Sharing data. Group members provide each other information (e.g., ideas, opinions, beliefs, facts, resources) that they have found helpful in coping with similar problems.
- Dialectical processes. Involves one or more members advancing a thesis, other members countering with an antithesis, and the group members attempting to develop their own synthesis.
- Discussing taboo topics. Includes the assistance members can give each other in discussing a taboo subject, which may have been previously avoided in the group.
- All in the same boat phenomenon. Occurs when one realizes that one is not alone and that others share similar problems, feelings, or concerns. This process is similar to a process previously identified by Lieberman, Yalom, & Miles (1973) termed universalization.
- Empathic support. Occurs when a group member, who is in emotional distress, has experienced a loss (e.g., death of family member), or discloses long repressed painful feelings, receives empathic support from other group members.
- Rehearsal. Involves helping the group member prepare to implement new ways of social functioning by trying out these new behaviors in the group.

- Mutual demand. Group members support problem solving by individual members through challenging their defenses (e.g., denial, minimization, avoidance of issues) or encouraging them to take action in their daily lives.
- Individual problem solving. Group members help themselves through the process of helping to solve a problem experienced by an individual member.
- Strength in numbers phenomenon. Group members work together to address shared barriers or unjust conditions in their community.

Schwartz believed that because the group may be viewed as a system of mutual aid, then it was incumbent upon the worker to pursue common ground between the group members and the agency. He believed that common ground was always present, and that it was the worker's responsibility to remove all barriers that served to obscure the identification of common ground (Schwartz, 1994).

The search for common ground reflected the emphasis paid in the earlier models in terms of building upon commonalities rather than integrating differences. The mediating model, as with the earlier models, did not truly harness diversity present in the group and little attention was paid to diversity and individual differences (Papell & Rothman, 1980).

Despite the popularity of group work in social work practice in the 1960s, the rise of generalist practice in the 1970s resulted in the formulation of a number of models that were intended for practice across the traditional micro, mezzo, and macro practice streams. Two notable treatment oriented approaches were built upon the work of the remedial model and the casework tradition. These approaches included the task centered and mainstream models.

TASK CENTERED AND MAINSTREAM MODELS

Garvin, Reid, and Epstein (1976) identified five steps in the task centered approach to groups, including: the preliminary interview, group composition and formation, group processes for task accomplishment, and termination. The task centered approach continued the practice introduced in the remedial approach of the preliminary interview, which has become common practice in many current intervention oriented groups. During this interview, the problems experienced by the consumer are explored and clarified prior to the start of the group. An agreement is reached as to whether the problem can be best addressed through group work, and an orientation to task centered group work is provided to prepare the consumer for the group (Garvin et al., 1976). Composition of task centered groups was also informed by the remedial model, in the groups' preference for member similarities, particularly in relation to member tasks. It was believed that increased similarities, as opposed to differences among members, made task oriented groups more effective in achieving their goals (Garvin et al., 1976). Garvin and others (1976) noted: "A task approach, however, can occur with groups with heterogeneous tasks when the members can see other similarities among themselves" (p. 252).

In group formation, the group worker helps group members find a common problem on which the group focuses. Although there is some provision for not necessarily choosing a problem that the majority identifies as a priority, this model reflects the tendency of models of this time, such as the reciprocal, of searching for commonalities relating to values, attitudes, activities, and tasks (Garvin et al., 1976). After a common problem is identified, it is further specified and narrowed in behavioral terms. The task centered approach also adopted the remedial model's use of direct, indirect, and extra-group influences to help group members accomplish their tasks.

Like many of the previous models, this model did not embrace or integrate diversity or member differences in the group. Also somewhat illustrative of its limitations was its emphasis on conformity to group norms. "When group norms exist, members discover ways to secure conformity with these norms. The worker's role is to see that group norms articulate with treatment objectives as well as professional ethics and values" (Garvin et al., 1976, p. 259).

An attempt to reconcile the differences from the foregoing models was presented by Papell and Rothman (1980) when they formulated the mainstream model in an effort to incorporate the various approaches into a model of group work. This model demonstrates the most progressive intervention of diversity up to that time. Papell & Rothman (1980) viewed each member as a social learner with the potential of making a difference in the achievement of individual goals and growth. For this reason the model also placed mutual aid as the central helping factor, where each group member is expected to participate in the work of the group (Papell & Rothman, 1980). The mainstream model also adopted many aforementioned notions of the other models, including contracting, common ground, and purpose. In keeping with earlier models, the mainstream model included a dual focus of using the group to bring about individual and social change. A distinctive element of the mainstream model was its emphasis on the development of the group as an agent of change.

SYSTEMS/ECOLOGICAL THEORY

As group work moved through the era dominated by generalist practice, two theories predominated, systems theory and the ecological perspective (ecosystem theory). Drawing from Balgopal and Vassil (1983), the ecological perspective introduced many new concepts to social work practice with groups, including: system, boundaries, environment, and diversity.

System

When one thinks systemically, one understands that the capacity of a group to bring about change in the community is greater than the sum of the resources brought by each member. The group provides a setting that can, if the conditions are suitable, enable group members to try out new ways of relating and being in the world. Moreover, given that a group may be viewed as a system of relationships, the quality of relationships within the group will inevitably affect its productivity in completing its assigned tasks or bringing about change. Thinking systemically, one realizes that as relationships form and a group develops over time, it acquires increasing capacity to bring about change. In this way, a change in one member will affect all other members, and over time the behavior of each member not only reflects his or her unique characteristics and experiences, but those of the group as well.

Boundaries and Environment

In systems thinking, boundaries are rules about who participates and how they participate in a group. Boundaries separate those who are members of a group from others who are not. These are manifested by rules around who is invited to attend group, as well as the time, date, and location of the group. For many groups, boundaries are also manifested in terms of the location of group meetings. For example, it is important that group meetings are held in places where others cannot overhear group discussions. Another example of a boundary would be the time scheduled for the start and ending of meetings. Overly flexible boundaries may result in meetings running past the agreed ending time or members often arriving late or leaving early. In most cases such boundaries would become a serious concern for many or all members. For this reason, it is often the group worker who helps the group maintain acceptable boundaries, by reinforcing the norms relating to confidentiality and the duration of meetings.

Diversity

Although it's clear that the roots of diversity have been present in social group work over the years, the ecological perspective was the first model to identify diversity as an operating principle in groups. With certain qualifications, the ecological perspective viewed diversity as a resource for groups. As Balgopal and Vassil (1983) observed, "Group environments which allow the accumulation and expression of differences in individuals facilitate an increase in the alternative choices and behaviors to its members for coping with problems and obtaining need satisfaction" (p. 125-126). Balgopal and Vassil (1983) described the total range of diversity present in the group as a product of: (1) diversity of the individuals within the group; (2) diversity of external environments brought to the immediate group environment by its members; and, (3) the diversity of characteristics found within each individual group member. However, it is important to point out that ecological theory did not always embrace diversity as a resource for the group. Indeed, like other theorists of the era, the "inhabitability" of a group for any one member was viewed as being "dependent upon the level of tolerance that the group has for his/her entire realm of individual differences" Balgopal and Vassil, 1983, p. 125). Ecological theory was also criticized by theorists who were concerned about how the ecological perspective may emphasize adaptation by diverse and marginalized groups to oppressive social conditions. Subsequently, two group work models arose that responded to this critique.

EMPOWERMENT AND FEMINIST APPROACHES

The empowerment approach shifted the focus of change back towards a balance reminiscent of the social goals movement. Breton (2004) said that the purpose of empowerment groups "is to change oppressive, cognitive, behavioral, social, and political structures or conditions that thwart the control people have over their lives, that prevent them from accessing needed resources, and that keep them from participating in the life of their community" (p. 59). Empowerment practice in groups focuses on three goals or interlocking dimensions, including: development of a more positive self-identity; increasing capacity for critical analysis of sociopolitical realities and structures; and building of resources, strategies, and competence for achievement of personal and social goals (Lee & Hudson, 2011).

Breton (2004) outlines four steps followed by empowerment groups in their collective work, which include: planning, conscientization, collective action, and embeddedness. In keeping with the democratic values of social group work, empowerment groups adopted an equalitarian stance with respect to decision making and planning. Before the group is formed, group workers and stakeholders work collaboratively to determine the purpose, goals, and membership of the group (Breton, 2004). Conscientization in an empowerment group begins with the sharing of stories, which are received with respect and legitimized as valid knowledge, relating to the group purpose by group members (Breton, 2004). From sharing and identifying common themes in member stories, the conscientization process moves onto cognitive restructuring of members' understanding of the impacts of oppression, where they challenge negative self-images and self-evaluations arising from social, economic, and political influences (Breton, 2004). The third step, collective action, involves building on their awareness and taking action to bring about the specific changes that will permit access to needed resources and opportunities (Breton, 2004). Finally, embeddedness involves the group members becoming active in the ongoing life of the community as a means of preserving and continuing changes that the group has brought to the community. Members leave the group to become involved as members of community organizations, coleaders of groups, and community spokespersons, and participate in policy development.

Feminist groups adopt a similar approach to empowerment oriented groups. Both feminist and critical theorists have long decried the blindness of systems and ecological theory in their implicit assumptions of equal power distributions. They have also criticized the clinically focused approaches as failing to address oppressive social structures underlying the social problems that consumers bring to their groups.

Lewis (1992) identified five processes characteristic of feminist oriented groups, including: development of a common consciousness, systematic deconstruction, naming, trusting the group, and community. Feminist group work includes historical and gendered analysis to redefine member identities and ways of relating to each other (Lewis, 1992). It also challenges prevailing male definitions of social reality by deconstructing and replacing them with female constructed definitions (Lewis, 1992). Naming involves identifying oppressive processes and outcomes of prevailing dominant structures and beliefs. Trusting the group involves a belief in the competence of the group process and its members to reconstruct new realities and explore new language, behaviors, and goals as well as belief in the power of the group to bring about desired changes in the members and community. Finally, a sense of community is created by members developing relationships with allies in the wider social context (Lewis, 1992).

Just as with the social goals movement, one observes how the empowerment and feminist approaches facilitate participatory competence (Kieffer, 1984) in their membership, where personal growth and competence are enhanced through the work of the group. Attention to diversity is significant in these approaches, as issues of power and oppression, which in society are often related to differences among individual and communities, are major themes. However, a similar question and limitation may also arise. One may ask if there is room for diverse perspectives under such an approach. Are members "politicized" and "liberated" to hold a diverse range of views or are they encouraged to adopt the prevailing views of the group? Are individual needs lost in the collective work of the group?

Exercise 2.1: Group Discussion

Consider how group work approaches have changed over time. Given the diverse world we live in, what are your thoughts on the level of attention given to diversity by these approaches? In a small group, discuss your thoughts.

CHAPTER SUMMARY

This chapter described the historical development of major group work practice models. As the social work profession and group work practice have evolved, it is clear that social work with groups has responded to the challenge of serving its purpose through a dual focus on individual and community needs and the use of mutual aid as a vehicle for bringing about change. Despite the value that group work has held in relation to democratic principles, and later diversity, there has been limited attention accorded to how, in this increasingly diverse social environment, a practitioner can effectively work with the strengths and challenges that diversity brings to the group. As you move forward through this text, you will continue to obtain the knowledge and the skills needed to effectively work with diversity in group work practice.

CHAPTER 3

DIVERSITY: A STRENGTHS-BASED APPROACH

LEARNING OBJECTIVES

At the end of this chapter you will be able to:

- Articulate and critique various definitions of diversity.
- Explain what diversity means in group work practice.
- Understand the relational nature of diversity in groups.
- Identify the strengths and resources that can be realized through the effective use of diversity.

Vignette: Opening Night in the Self-Esteem Group

You are one of the group workers for the opening session for your agency's ten-week self-esteem group. You are a middle aged Caucasian female. You arrive early and are seated at one side of the circle of chairs, with your younger African American coworker seated directly across from you. As you approach the starting time, group members arrive and are seated. You note that nearly all of the African American group members sit closest to your coworker, and the Caucasian and Hispanic members sit nearer to you.

What could this tell you about the relationships in your group at this point?

Although the term diversity is of fairly recent origin, member differences have always been recognized as an important resource in social work with groups. Specifically, group work has always emphasized respect for the uniqueness of each individual and the importance of democratic values in practice. Closely intertwined with this appreciation of diversity has been the recognition of the importance of individuation—that is, recognizing and affirming each member's unique contribution to the group's purpose. Summing up these values of affirming differences, Helen Phillips (1957) incorporated John Dewey's notion that effective social work groups must demonstrate "unity in variety."

Today, given the increasingly globalized world, it is not surprising that in group work there has been much discussion of the importance of cultural competence, as well as many publications that speak to different culturally based approaches to practice. Social workers support culturally sensitive practice and are required to be cognizant and responsive to diversity within the group. They recognize that being culturally competent results in better outcomes for their consumers. This chapter will critically examine contemporary definitions of diversity and research relating to diversity in groups, introduce a relational definition of diversity, and discuss the strengths that can be realized from working effectively with the diversity present in a group.

DEFINITIONS OF DIVERSITY

When one examines the literature and discourse relating to understanding diversity, it would be fair to state that, although diversity appears to be a relatively simple concept on the surface, it becomes far broader and more complex as one explores it in a deeper way. Diversity has been generally defined as the state or quality of being different, unlike in character or qualities (Diversity, n.d.). The *Social Work Dictionary* (Barker, 2003) defines diversity as "variety, or the opposite of homogeneity" (p. 126). The definition also describes the meaning of diversity for social organizations and people from minority populations as "people from varied backgrounds, cultures, ethnicities and viewpoints" (Barker, 2003, p. 126).

Definitions of diversity typically focus on demographic diversity, or the presence of differences in various characteristics among individuals and groups. Forms of demographic diversity include: age, gender, ethnic origin, race, cultural background, sexual orientation, gender diversity, nationality, language, religion or spiritual beliefs, socioeconomic status, physical or intellectual ability, marital or family status, educational level, and political orientation (Fellin, 2000; Doyle & George, 2008). Diversity also applies to deeper and less visible attributes such as values, attitudes, personality, beliefs, and behaviors (Van Knippenberg & Schippers, 2007).

Diversity is also often viewed as a group characteristic. Van Knippenberg and Schippers (2007) define diversity as "a characteristic of social grouping that reflects the degree to which objective or subjective differences exist between group members" (p. 516). Doyle and George (2008) emphasize the significance of group-based characteristics: "[T]he most relevant forms of diversity . . . are group-based characteristics, on the basis of which many, but not necessarily all, group members have been and/or are subject to marginalization and/or oppression" (p. 106). In this respect, diversity is often associated with issues of power, privilege, and social identity, which arise from broader social environments in which members of certain identity groups are perceived as "normative" and provided with certain rights and advantages. Examples of these rights and advantages include male privilege, white privilege, and heterosexual privilege (Roysircar, 2008; Smith & Shin, 2008).

At the core of these definitions, and the treatment of those who are marginalized due to their differences from a dominant majority, is the assumption that diversity is a characteristic possessed by an "other" who is perceived to be different and inferior in some way. This association between diversity and inferiority has been a tragic part of human existence, given voice in social Darwinism and the eugenics movement of the early twentieth century. Perceived inferior characteristics were viewed as a threat to human progress and were thus subject to overt suppression. Although Western societies have made some progress since that time with respect to specific groups, there remain patterns of discrimination against those who are different in some significant way. Roberts and Smith (2002) argue that definitions of diversity rarely confront social justice issues or issues of racism, homophobia, and other forms of oppression, although social work ethics involve a recognition of the impact of oppression. However, traditional definitions seem to imply that diversity is present when group members who differ in some way from the characteristics or views ascribed to by members of dominant societal groups are present.

In social work, although "diversity" and "difference" have been used interchangeably, diversity is often defined in a narrow sense, where it is reduced to a characteristic possessed by individual members. If one takes this narrow definition of diversity further, it may lead to practices that assume that members who share the same characteristics have the same beliefs, values, and experiences. As Northen and Kurland (2001) explained, "Although certain characteristics differentiate one group from another, efforts to define them may lead to negative stereotyping" (p. 164).

A narrow understanding of diversity also fails to acknowledge that it is not the outward characteristics of individual members that are important but the different perspectives or worldviews that they bring to the group that are essential ingredients to the efficacy of any group. Each member's worldview brings meaning to their experiences in groups and informs their ways of relating to others. Sullivan (2004) notes that although every human being is unique, each person is like some others in terms of their cultural and other group influences, and everyone shares common human needs. Group members of diverse groups may be asked to share their perspectives, beliefs, and values that may be consistent or differ with those ascribed to their particular group. It is here, then, in operational terms, where the concepts of "diversity" and "difference" coincide.

Just as diverse groups reflect the social world, they also reflect normative social power relationships and societal forms of oppression (Alvarez & Cabbil, 2001; Saino, 2003; Bemak & Chung, 2004; Greene, 2004; Marbley, 2004). Green and Stiers (2002) refer to "the unacknowledged and unspoken imbalance of power" (p. 233) that often exists in multicultural group therapy contexts. According to Brown and Mistry (2005), "patterns of social oppression will be repeated in social group work unless active steps are taken to counteract these tendencies and replace them with a culture of empowerment" (p. 133).

Exercise 3.1: The Debate

Over several of the past four sessions, group members of a bereavement support group have shared their struggles with coping with the loss of their loved ones and how the loss has affected their lives. The group is an open-ended group and the members are diverse in age, ethnicity, race, culture, and sexual orientation. Marsha is a new member whose partner passed away a few months ago. She begins to share her experience when another group member, Roy, interrupts her and says, "Wait, are you a lesbian?" Members begin to discuss their opinions of same sex relationships and you notice Marsha retreats to her chair as a debate ensues.

Reflect upon this vignette. What are the forms of diversity present in the relationships in the group? What are some of the commonalities that the members share? What are some of the diverse ways that members respond to powerlessness and anxiety?

How might you as a worker respond to this situation? Where would you focus your response?

DIVERSITY AS A RELATIONAL CONCEPT

As discussed above, traditional definitions of diversity have some limitations. It would be helpful to shift your understanding of diversity from differences in characteristics possessed by group members to the transactions between the members. It's important to recognize that when people meet, diversity will always be present in their relationships. With this in mind, the task of working with diversity shifts from how to work with those who are perceived to be diverse to how to promote productive relationships between group members. Diversity, thus, becomes a state that exists in the relationships between group members that is always mediated by power and status. In this way, rather than referring simply to individual or group characteristics, diversity can also be defined as an attribute of interpersonal or social relationships (Green & Stiers, 2002).

Ideas concerning diversity and difference, and beliefs about one's own identity and the identities of others, are socially constructed, rooted in interactions (Blundo & Greene, 2008). Diversity (defined according to age, ethnicity, race, gender, sexual orientation, disability, and other cultural dimensions) is a socially constructed concept, relative to the social context (Greene, 2004), and "possessing little meaning in and of themselves. The social contexts in which these are perceived, experienced, understood and defined is what renders them salient" (Greene, 2004, pp. 58–59). As such, diversity is not as significant when defined according to individual characteristics in isolation. Thus, diversity becomes apparent and significant when two or more individuals interact, enabling the more subtle aspects of identity to be revealed.

Such a relational understanding of diversity is supported and informed by a theory known as symbolic interactionism. George Herbert Mead (1934) proposed that meanings you interpret about yourself and your world arise through interactions with others through the use of symbols such as language (Marsiglia & Kulis, 2009). These meanings, including your values and beliefs about others, emerge from your relationships. Given that you are constantly interacting with others, these meanings are also subject to continual change as you interpret and reinterpret them through your interactions in relationships. Thus, your attitudes and actions are constantly being shaped by others and your beliefs about yourself (Marsiglia & Kulis, 2009).

According to Miller, Donner, and Fraser (2004), diversity "increases a person's consciousness of who they are in relation to other people" (p. 378). Thus, personal identity and self-definition are manifested in relation to other people. Less obvious or observable differences emerge in the context of relationships, as people share personal histories with others and interactional styles become more evident (Malekoff & Laser, 1999).

Redefining diversity as a relational concept shifts the perspective from one in which diversity is something possessed by another person to a condition that exists in your relationships. The benefits from this redefinition are substantial.

BENEFITS OF DEFINING DIVERSITY AS A RELATIONAL CONCEPT

First, as both practitioners and group members, a relational understanding of diversity challenges you to continuously redefine yourself by examining your beliefs, values, and perspectives rather than unconsciously accepting them as "normal" or "superior." Adopting such a stance creates opportunities for you to learn from others when you recognize that diversity is present in your relationships.

Second, adopting a relational understanding would render the oppression of others due to "their" differences as nonsensical, since the diversity would no longer be seen as being situated in others, but in social relationships.

Third, such a shift would eliminate many harmful conflicts that arise from the assumption that diversity is something that is possessed by another. When diversity is perceived as characteristics possessed by others, individuals often define their own identities against positive or negative perceptions of other individuals and groups. According to Pelled, Eisenhardt, and Xin (1999), emotional or interpersonal conflict is typically related to perceptions of one's own social "category" or identity and those of others. Conflict may be rooted in feelings of anger, mistrust, and fear, and social comparison may result in the development of negative biases and stereotypes. When you shift your perception of diversity from an attribute possessed by "the other" to a condition existing in your relationships, diversity becomes more amenable to exploration and negotiation. More concretely, a European worker cannot change her cultural heritage, nor can her Latina consumer. However, by recognizing that diversity is present in their relationship, both parties can discuss how they will work with these differences.

Fourth, a relational understanding of diversity enables you to realize that it is not the outward characteristics of individual members that are important, but the different perspectives, worldviews, and experiences that they bring to the group that are essential ingredients to the efficacy of any group.

Finally, a shifting of diversity into the relational realm fosters a discussion of power in these relationships. For example, when a different idea is proposed in a task group, whether it is adopted by the group may be influenced as much by the relative status of that individual in the group as by the idea's relative merits.

DIVERSITY AS A STRENGTH IN GROUP WORK

Earlier literature has emphasized the benefits of identifying commonalities among group members and has viewed diversity, and in particular demographic diversity, as posing challenges to the development of a productive group. Adopting such a perspective can lead to suppressing or avoiding diversity as it arises in the group. The view of the authors of this book is that adopting a strengths perspective by the group worker in relation to diversity is necessary to realize the opportunities and address obstacles that arise in diverse groups. Why is such a perspective important? A shift is important because diversity is omnipresent in groups and both workers and group members can learn how to reap the benefits of diversity.

DIVERSITY IS OMNIPRESENT IN GROUPS

Doyle and George (2008) state that "human beings are, by definition, diverse, as no two individuals are identical in all respects" (p. 106). The implications of this statement, and a fuller understanding of diversity, are that, although not always expressed or respected, diversity is almost always present in any group. As Fluhr (2005) states, "social workers are more often than not faced with the challenge of creating groups with consumers of varying backgrounds, behaviors, and attitudes" (p. 36). Even among members of groups who share a common cultural background, profound differences in perspectives may arise. Thus, "in order to avoid stereotyping, social workers must also recognize that heterogeneity within cultures is as important as diversity between cultures" (Este, 1999, p. 42). Similarly, when group members share similar presenting problems, they may still differ with respect to gender, age, culture, education, occupation, and so on (Delucia-Waack & Donigian, 2004).

The theory of intersectionality, first coined in 1989 by Kimberle Crenshaw and the feminist movement (Yuval-Davis, 2006), expands the understanding of diversity in relation to social identity. Intersectionality acknowledges the interrelated aspects of a person's identity, such as race, gender, class, sexual orientation, and the like, and how these affect an individual's perceived reality of the world, particularly in relation to the levels of oppression and social inequality experienced by an individual (Mizhari & Lombe, 2006; Yuval-Davis, 2006; Nadan, Weinberg-Kurnik, & Ben-Ari, 2015). This approach draws attention to the fact that, even though individuals within a group may share characteristics (i.e., gender, class, etc.) or are united by a common goal, other dimensions of one's identity, which may provide or deny certain privileges, factor into an individual's experience of the world.

REBALANCING DIVERSITY AND COMMONALITIES

Although many scholars have noted the importance of highlighting commonalities amongst group members early in group development in order to promote group cohesion and identification and then differences later in the group, there have been some theorists that have offered a more balanced view. William Schwartz (1971) summed up the dance of diversity in group work as a moving dynamic force, where each member is dependent on others to satisfy his or her own sense of need. For Schwartz, the interaction between members reflects both the centripetal force of common tasks and the centrifugal force of those tasks that are unique to each member. Brown and Mistry (2005) and Anderson (1997) again highlighted a convergence of diversity, where they noted that practitioners using a multicultural perspective can continually focus on the meaning of differences. Anderson (1997) suggested that this goal can be achieved by ensuring that all members have a voice. He asserted there are mutual aid expectations for the dialogue of differences. Such mutual aid processes, as they evolve, simultaneously serve members' need for autonomy and interdependence. Anderson's notions are particularly helpful in terms of understanding the construct of common ground from a diversity lens. This is evident when he states that it is not the content of the group, but rather the contract or agreement between members and the dialogue of differences that form the foundation for how members will help each other.

LEARNING TO WORK TOGETHER

If you assume that diversity is present in most groups, then it becomes incumbent upon the group worker to learn how to work with diversity from the moment the group begins. Ineffective strategies such as avoidance or suppression of differences can have adverse consequences for individual members and the group as a whole. On the other hand, by learning how to work with diversity, there will be fewer cases of group members dropping out of the group and the group will realize the potential benefits of different perspectives and experiences.

Group dynamics, processes, and outcomes are influenced by the diverse identities, attitudes, and perceptions of the members, which include the workers. Members enter the group with a frame of reference, and these values, beliefs, and prejudices, either consciously or unconsciously, become evident within the group context (Marbley, 2004). Initially, members may have increased anxiety about interactions with others that are visibly different, resulting in negative judgments. This view, known as social identity theory (Jackson, Stone, & Alvarez, 1992), posits that where demographic diversity exists, members may also favor ideas and opinions offered by similar others and reject or discount those that are different, potentially leading to conflict. According to this theory, demographic diversity, in groups lacking a skillful worker to acknowledge or address it, can reduce the quantity and quality of group communication, resulting in more relationship conflicts. Without a skillful worker, demographic diversity can also predict decreases in group cohesion and feelings of acceptance, outcomes that in turn lead members to seek alternative groups or to simply drop out (O'Reilly, Caldwell, & Barnett, 1989). "Some clients from historically marginalized groups may not feel 'safe' or fully 'trust' therapy or other groups that include members from dominant social groups" (Smith & Shin, 2008, p. 359) and as a result they may terminate group involvement early if they do not feel understood by group workers and members. The potential negative impact of diversity is not limited to morale but can also be seen throughout the group's process and performance. Donald Anderson (2007), who examined diversity processes in each stage of group development, stated that issues of power and status, a lack of empathy, prejudice, "obscure sense of identity" (p. 240), and other diversity-related issues influence initial group stages. As such, groups ought to focus on enhancing awareness, empathy, compassion, and empowerment beginning at the first stage of group development. Research has suggested that many of the threats to group morale posed by diversity weaken or disappear over time as group members learn to work with one another and even become proud of their diversity (Jehn, Northcraft, & Neale, 1999). Over time, group members may become accustomed to participating in the same group, learn about one another through frequent contact, and learn to work together, which may decrease the significance (and potential "negative" influences) of demographic diversity. These processes moderate the effect of diversity-based conflict and enhance cooperative norms within the group.

Diversity Presents Opportunities for Learning and Growth

A group can provide maximum learning opportunities because it can be representative of the world in which individuals interact on a daily basis. As Brabender, Fallon, and Smolar (2004) state, a "strength of group therapy is its power to function as a microcosm of society" (p. 232). "Differences among group members give rise to varied ideas, perspectives, knowledge, and skills that can improve their ability to solve problems and accomplish work" (Polzer, Milton, and Swann, 2002, p. 296). Member differences can also result in tension, which can "provoke a process of self-examination as members struggle to ascertain what aspects of other members are similar to and different from themselves" (Brabender et al., 2004, p. 223). Furthermore, self-defeating and other negative behaviors can best be identified and confronted in a heterogeneous group that reflects the diversity present in its immediate social context. Group members can provide direct feedback regarding those behaviors, allowing members to learn how to modify these behaviors in the safety of the group. As suggested by symbolic interactionism, individual self-perceptions evolve as a result of feedback from interactions with diverse people and, as such, diverse groups may be particularly beneficial for clarifying self-perceptions.

Diverse groups are also ideal social forums in which to examine issues related to identity- or culturally-based attitudes, beliefs, and behaviors (Abernethy, 2002;

Brabender et al., 2004), opportunities that may not be present in relatively homogeneous groups. Diverse groups offer "a corrective experience for reworking socialized stereotypic interpersonal and intrapersonal responses" (Brabender et al., 2004, p. 232). This is particularly true as a group provides members with opportunities to establish relationships across identity boundaries. Diverse groups also provide an ideal context to address issues of prejudice and oppression due to their interpersonal nature and the existence of diverse attitudes (Roysircar, 2008). These groups reflect the reality of daily social interactions, and group members are provided with opportunities to rehearse ("test") interpersonal skills within the group setting that may be applied more generally to the community setting (Fluhr, 2005).

Mixed-gender groups provide a balance of opinions, with the benefit of allowing both male and female perspectives to emerge. Women are provided with opportunities to hear and understand male perspectives, leading to corrective emotional heterosexual processes (Russell & Gockel, 2005; Yalom & Leszcz, 2005). Gender differences in a number of areas can be positively explored and utilized by group leaders and members. These areas or dimensions of gender differences include relational and communication styles, approaches to power and assertiveness, processes of self-disclosure, approaches to conflict or competition and collaboration or cooperation, and approaches to significant emotions, including anger and shame (Gearing, 2002).

Diversity Empowers Change

Diversity brings about change. Whether you are speaking about a change within an individual, family, group, community, or society, for change to occur in prevailing beliefs, actions, and policies, diversity must be present. Change and problem solving in groups is impeded when diversity is suppressed. Similarly, when a worker advocates for a change in agency policy, he or she presents a diverse and critical appraisal of the impact of the policy. Moreover, when you recognize diversity as a relational concept, you begin to appreciate how it can also be a resource leading to change in groups. The uniqueness brought to the group by each member thus represents the potential for creative change in groups.

Diversity Supports Problem Solving and Decision Making

Early social psychologists did not focus to a great extent on diversity. Rather, much of their preoccupation was on how, in a group, one's individuality was surrendered to powerful and primitive group forces. McDougall's (1920) construct of the "group mind" and LeBon's (1910) construct of a collective "crowd man" were examples of the power of groups to suppress differences. Later, Asch (1955) examined how the social pressures towards conformity affect individual cognition and judgment.

Janis (1972) coined the term "group think" to describe a group process in which there were certain group characteristics that resulted in the suppression of all differences in a group, thus limiting the group's ability to address imminent problems. However, diversity supports problem solving and decision making in groups, and lack of it can stifle the problem-solving process. In fact, diversity is important in problem definition, where different views can help to define problems for resolution in an inclusive and accurate way. Often, it is through the sharing of different perspectives that rigid or limited problem definitions adopted by individual members begin to change. New possibilities, options, and strategies become available, and in this way, the sharing of diverse approaches and disappointments empower the group to develop unique systems that promote achievement of group and individual goals.

Group members, who bring diverse perspectives and experiences, provide the group with a variety of coping strategies. Findings in organizational and social psychology (Milliken, Barel, & Kurtzberg, 2003) suggest that the presence of diverse ideas in groups provides for greater variation in perspectives, enabling group members to develop different approaches to dealing with problems and reach quality solutions. They added that divergent thinking enables a group to reduce the tendency for premature closure of discussion of different options before committing to one decision or action. Diversity, in this sense, promotes the members' shared purpose of using the group process to garner effective strategies for coping with life's problems in personal groups or agency goals in task groups.

CHAPTER SUMMARY

This chapter has examined and redefined diversity in group work practice. Since the conceptualization of diversity, it has had varying definitions. These definitions often treated diversity as an attribute, which created many challenges in the way people perceive and interact with others. By situating diversity as something that may be present in the relations between group members, you can rededicate yourself to focusing on building more productive relationships in the group. If addressed productively and sensitively, diversity in all of its forms can thus become a strength and resource to all groups.

By adopting a strengths perspective relating to diversity in groups, and learning how to effectively harness diversity in service of the group and its members, the group worker enables the group to realize the potential benefits relating to diversity, including realizing opportunities for learning and growth, empowering change, and enhancing problem solving and decision making in the group. Diverse experiences and beliefs enable group members to share diverse perspectives related to the problems they face. Indeed, if the worker is successful in creating the optimal conditions, diversity may be redefined as an emergent therapeutic factor in intervention groups.

Given that diversity is omnipresent in all groups, and that there have been mixed findings in relation to the perceived benefits and challenges posed by diversity, and that groups can work with their differences over time, perhaps the real question facing group workers is not whether diversity is a benefit or threat to a group; rather, how can group workers work more effectively with diversity to maximize its potential benefits to the group?

CHAPTER 4

PRINCIPLES OF INCLUSIVE GROUP WORK

LEARNING OBJECTIVES

At the end of this chapter you will be able to:

- Articulate inclusive practice in group work.
- Understand the importance of self-awareness and personal awareness in inclusive practice.
- Recognize the importance of anticipating diversity in group work.
- Create a safe group environment to explore diversity and taboo issues.
- Appreciate the importance of affirming diversity and acknowledging the unique contributions of group members.

Vignette: Acknowledging Diversity

You are coleading a support group for single parents. All the group members, as well as your coworker, are of African American ancestry. You are the only Caucasian person in the room. At the fourth meeting of the group, the mothers are talking about incidents that their children have encountered at school. Many of them talk about situations in which they believe school personnel treated their children unfairly. Race is never mentioned. However, you get the sense that the parents are talking about Caucasian school personnel and that they are leaving race out of their descriptions because of your presence. What would you do or say?

From Kurland & Salmon (1998b, p. 103)

WHAT IS INCLUSIVE GROUP WORK PRACTICE?

Inclusive group work practice is an approach that acknowledges, respects, and embraces the diversity that is present in the group. This approach recognizes that individual identity is complex and, in order for all members to be treated equally, their individuality must be accepted and respected. Inclusive approach encourages mutual respect and fosters a sense of belonging by recognizing that all members have common needs although these needs may be met differently. This approach engages all members and challenges issues of discrimination and inequity, particularly those that arise due to differences among individuals. Ultimately, an inclusive approach allows group members to be themselves and be accepted and embraced for the uniqueness they contribute to the group.

What are often described as effective group work practice principles and skills are also relevant to inclusive group work practice. To put it another way, effective group work practice can go a long way to creating an inclusive group. Inclusive group workers need to demonstrate authentic expression, active listening, and questioning, as well as appropriate self-disclosure or sharing of personal experiences and emotions. Effective group workers draw on personal experiences and knowledge to facilitate connections with group members and model appropriate dialogue skills (Nagda et al., 1999; Burnes & Ross, 2010). Group workers must also demonstrate norms of respect, openness, and honesty (Marbley, 2004; Smith & Shin, 2008) in their work with their groups. This chapter will highlight some of the basic principles and skills that are salient to inclusive group work practice and offer some additional practice principles.

BASIC PRINCIPLES AND SKILLS FOR INCLUSIVE PRACTICE

Self-awareness and Personal Exploration

Noted cultural anthropologist Wade Davis once declared:

> The world in which you were born is just one model of reality. Other cultures are not failed attempts at being you; they are unique manifestations of the human spirit.

Diversity represents an opportunity for change and growth. Before and during inclusive group work practice, one needs to undergo a process of continual self-exploration and expanding self-awareness. Many have emphasized the need for the inclusive practitioner to engage in processes of self-exploration with respect to personal sociocultural identities (and associated values, beliefs, assumptions, and attitudes toward other groups) (Delucia-Waack & Donigian, 2004; Greene, 2004; Marbley, 2004; Qureshi, 2005; Constantine, Hage, Kindaichi, & Bryant, 2007; Debiak, 2007; Roysircar, 2008; Smith & Shin, 2008; Parrott, 2009; Singh & Salazar, 2010). This process includes an examination of personal privilege or minority status, as these influence interpersonal relationships with group members. According to Brabender and others (2004), the worker's ability to helpfully address diversity with the group is based upon the worker's self-awareness. In addition, Delucia-Waack and Donigian (2004) emphasize the need for the workers' exploration of their personal experiences and life contexts. They state that "group leaders must understand the impact of potential biases on the kinds of issues they attend to, the potential interventions they may select, and how they respond to individual group members" (Delucia-Waack & Donigian, 2004, p. 7). Inclusive group workers also need to acknowledge their own privilege and share their own struggles, serving as role models for group members (Smith & Shin, 2008; Burnes & Ross, 2010).

Anticipating Diversity

Inclusive practitioners must anticipate how they will respond to diversity present in their groups. As Davis, Galinsky, and Schopler (1995) observe, group workers need to anticipate where and when diversity will arise in the group from selecting members for the group through to termination. Inclusive practitioners will need to anticipate potential tensions and be prepared with potential responses that will help members work through their differences and build trust.

When selecting group members, inclusive practitioners need to be aware that relationships will unfold based upon the perceived similarity among group members. Initially, these perceptions may be based upon visible similarities and differences. For this reason some theorists have called for a balance of diversity in group selection. Brown and Mistry (2005) report that group membership should be balanced (at least four nonwhite members in a group of ten), as this "makes an enormous difference to the potential for an anti-oppressive dynamic" (p. 141). They assert that isolated or outnumbered group members are more prone to stereotyping or marginalization and are more reluctant to participate and self-disclose (Brown & Mistry, 2005; Burnes & Ross, 2010).

Although it's true that there is the potential for such dynamics to unfold in groups, particularly where the sense of marginalization is compounded by members who experience isolation early in a group, many workers do not have the opportunity or resources to make changes to group membership, and indeed, may be ethically barred from doing so. An inclusive group worker would be prepared and open to discussing this situation with a prospective group member. The worker would acknowledge when diversity arises in the group, reinforce the affirmation of diversity in the group, and be prepared in the event that stereotyping or marginalization occurs.

Creating Safety to Promote Exploration of Diversity Issues

Inclusive group work practice involves an active and direct response by the group worker when diversity arises in the group. This is particularly true early in the group when group members may benefit most from modeling by the worker in terms of how best to work with diversity that is present in the group. Facilitating dialogue between members enables the group to address and clarify misperceptions and miscommunication (Ibrahim, 2010), which can otherwise escalate to an irreparable conflict later in the group. The worker must also be open to accepting differing views of what is occurring in the group in the moment and alternate ways of resolving conflict. However, in some cases the worker may need to directly confront the issues present in the group. There may also be the need for group members to de-escalate through sharing their feelings.

Group workers are responsible for modeling behaviors that promote a safe environment (Wilson et al., 2004), an environment where it is safe to be different. Constructive responses to group members' self-disclosures and to group conflict facilitate the promotion of safety, trust, and validation (Saino, 2003; Caplan & Thomas, 2004a). Abernethy (2002) also emphasizes that it is the role of the group worker to control the pace and intensity of diversity-based conflict or confrontation (for example, changing topics if necessary, or addressing persistently hostile group members).

Although group workers need to foster open discussions of diversity issues, they should also acknowledge that some degree of fear, anxiety, anger, guilt, or discomfort may be associated with such discussions on the part of group members (Abernethy, 2002; Bieschke, Gehlert, Wilson, Matthews, & Wade, 2003; Brabender et al., 2004; Marbley, 2004; Singh & Salazar, 2010). For example, DeLois and Cohen (2000) emphasize the need to recognize the sensitive nature of certain group discussion topics, the profound personal impact of those topics, and potential feelings of vulnerability on the part of group members. Group workers often have to give the group permission to discuss diversity-related issues: "[N]ot only are we acknowledging that differences exist, but also letting members know that they can talk about it in the group" (Marbley, 2004, p. 254). They also ought to ensure that all group members have equal opportunities to share their experiences and to be heard (Roysircar, 2008) and actively address issues of oppression or discrimination within the group (Davis et al., 1995).

Accordingly, some theorists emphasize the need to engage group members in creating and agreeing to ground rules to establish a safe environment and guide discussion. Ground rules can include group confidentiality, respectful speaking and listening, tolerant and nonjudgmental interactions, honoring different degrees of participation and self-disclosure, no blaming or shaming, and leaving political correctness at the door (DeLois & Cohen, 2000). The establishment of these rules, which members commit to and agree to hold each other accountable to, form a relational base among group members, laying the groundwork for future group development (DeLois & Cohen, 2000).

Miller and others. (2004) discuss the need to create environments in which conversations about identity and diversity can take place. Principles that foster these conversations include confidentiality within the group, listening carefully to others, speaking for oneself (rather than representing an entire social group), and constructively challenging ideas and behaviors. Saino (2003) noted the importance of engaging group members in clarifying group purpose and context (in creating a contract regarding ground rules, goals, and discussion topics).

It is important to acknowledge, however, that although ground rules can play a role in fostering an inclusive group experience, rules have also been used to oppress diversity. Many of the rules identified above are typical of many intervention groups. An inclusive group worker recognizes that the development of ground rules needs to foster affirmation of diversity and freedom of expression. The inclusive group worker also recognizes that group norms are always emerging and evolving and may be subject to renegotiation when new forms of diversity are expressed in a group. Traditional group work models may often be associated with cultural values regarding verbalization and self-disclosure, trying out behaviors in the group context, and other expectations regarding group participation that may not be "universal" (Delucia-Waack & Donigian, 2004). Traditional models may have to be negotiated so that they can accommodate diversity as it arises in the group.

Encounters and interactions between members of diverse identity or cultural groups may involve some misunderstanding, a lack of empathy, the development of stereotypes and prejudices, or feelings of anger, defensiveness, guilt, shame, and so on (Nagda et al., 1999). Dialogue between members of these groups is needed to address these effects (Nagda et al., 1999). Group work can play a central role in doing this and in promoting unity between members of diverse groups (Anderson, 2007). Discussions of identity issues and diversity may facilitate an understanding of shared experiences or common sociopolitical oppression (Cheng, Chae, & Gunn, 1998; Haley-Banez et al., 1999; Pedersen, 2008; Singh & Salazar,

2010). Haley-Banez and others (1999) refer to "the unifying of diverse individuals through the commonality of the human experience" (p. 406). Pedersen (2008) likewise refers to the identification of common ground between members of different cultural groups without disregarding or minimizing different aspects of identity or behavior. Moreover, discussions relating to these issues must also further the purpose of the group. In this way, inclusive group workers should balance group focus on social identity issues versus clinical or psychological concerns.

There are some other norms that inclusive group workers may wish to promote in the group. For example, group members may be encouraged to speak for themselves (using "I" statements) rather than acting as "spokespersons" for their identity groups (Nagda et al., 1999; Miller et al., 2004; Smith & Shin, 2008). Expecting one group member to "teach" other members how it is to "be" a certain person (for example, how it is to be gay) may enhance feelings of oppression (Smith & Shin, 2008). The worker should also attend to the use of language in the group. Inclusive group workers must model and encourage members to use accepting (as opposed to exclusionary) language, words, and conversation topics, which influence the creation of a safe group environment (Haley-Banez et al., 1999; Wilson et al., 2004). For example, the use of hetero-normative language may illustrate a less obvious or intentional form of oppression (Burnes & Ross, 2010). Haley-Banez and others (1999) refer to the use of words such as "married" or conversations about marriage, which in some communities may exclude gay and lesbian group members.

Addressing Taboo Issues Relating to Diversity

One distinctive group work skill is the ability to identify taboo issues (Shulman, 2015). Although identity, diversity, privilege, and oppression may be challenging and sensitive topics with which to engage group members in discussion, inclusive group workers need to recognize that working with diversity may involve raising issues that at least initially are viewed as taboo areas within the group (DeLois & Cohen, 2000; Brabender et al., 2004). By raising and helping the group to explore these issues in a transparent, sensitive, and accepting manner, the worker helps to establish group norms that promote open discussion of potential concerns and other sensitive topics.

Many group members, particularly those who come to an intervention group for the first time, experience a profound sense of inadequacy. This sense of inadequacy is compounded for those who come to the group from marginalized populations. When members realize that they share a common purpose for attending the group and also a common experience of feeling different, and that this is acceptable in the group, relationships based upon both commonalities and diversity can be forged. For example, Marbley (2004) emphasizes the importance of creating a group environment in which challenging issues can be discussed: "Groups really work when people can say difficult things" (p. 254). Similarly, Delucia-Waack and Donigian (2004) state that issues of cultural and demographic diversity ought to be raised early in the group process to assure members that the subject is not avoided as a taboo subject. The encouragement of new communication among members is an important goal of inclusive practice, and constructive dialogue about diversity may serve to enhance group cohesiveness (Delucia-Waack & Donigian, 2004). Inclusive group workers must also avoid the pathologization of individual behavior, such as labeling individuals as hostile or resistant, based on attitudes or behaviors that, for example, may be culturally rooted or associated with a disability or medical condition (Smith & Shin, 2008).

An inclusive group worker also recognizes that, just as with any conflict, denial or avoidance of diversity in a group can lead to mistrust, anger, hurt, and a lack of authenticity in interactions. The inability to talk about issues of identity and diversity may lead to feelings of discomfort, rejection, or invisibility on the part of group members who feel different, stereotyped, or marginalized. Conversely, discussions among members of diverse groups can promote an understanding of individual behavior in context (Malekoff & Laser, 1999; Smith & Shin, 2008). Ultimately, the suppression of disagreement or discussion of diversity may negatively affect group cohesion and productivity, limiting opportunities to express aspects of identity and explore and challenge preconceptions (Brabender et al., 2004; Miller et al., 2004; Burnes & Ross, 2010).

Being Curious about Diversity

Inclusive practice also asks that group workers demonstrate curiosity and an intention to learn about their consumers' cultures and worldview, and be able to empathize with experiences of sociopolitical oppression, power, and privilege (Bemak & Chung, 2004; Marbley, 2004; Roysircar, 2008; Smith & Shin, 2008). Inclusive practice demands that workers in culturally diverse groups be inquisitive about consumers' unique identities in order to understand cultural paradigms of health and healing, relationships between individuals and their family or community, and views of decision making, self-determination, and self-expression. Such an exploration can transform potential challenges faced by the group to resources for change.

Just as curiosity is a vital attribute for inclusive practitioners, it is also important that this value of curiosity to explore diversity be encouraged among group members. In this way, the inclusive group worker supports the development of inclusive groups. The purpose of discussions of identity and diversity is not simply to categorize group members, but to encourage curiosity about the influence of various cultural dimensions on one's own identity and worldview and those of others (Green & Stiers, 2002; Debiak, 2007). Discussions of diversity enable group members to gain self-awareness and understanding of one another's identities and experiences, to examine the manner in which different belief systems affect group processes and dynamics, and to understand the ways in which one's own behavior is perceived and affects group dynamics (Wilson et al., 2004).

Recognizing, Acknowledging, and Celebrating Diversity

One of the most important attributes of an inclusive group worker is the ability to recognize, acknowledge, and affirm diversity. Wilson and others (2004) emphasize the "importance of developing unity by recognizing and celebrating diversity" (p. 21). Likewise, it is through expanded self-awareness and exploration that a worker will be empowered to identify and acknowledge when diversity becomes evident in a group. Self-awareness will also enable the inclusive group worker to demonstrate comfort in discussing issues of identity and oppression, relate to members of different identity groups in a respectful and equal manner, and challenge oppressive structures and attitudes within the group (Brown & Mistry, 2005). Again, this process involves an ongoing self and group assessment (Schopler, Galinsky, Davis, & Despard, 1996).

It is crucial that inclusive group workers be prepared not only to address diversity, but to create group norms that affirm diversity in their groups. For example, Marbley (2004) states that it is important to discuss issues of diversity during the initial stages of group development, in order to address feelings of shame, fear, defensiveness, or isolation that may be associated with diversity-related attitudes and behaviors, before moving on to the next group stage. When one thinks about it, affirming diversity early in the group truly validates how group members are experiencing the group in that moment, because it is early in the group where group members are most aware of, and perhaps concerned about, their apparent differences. Consequently, the early meetings of a group offer the best opportunity to promote norms that value diversity. For example, the worker might make a simple statement such as the following:

> Early in most groups it is common for members to feel a little nervous and worried about being accepted by others in the group. Very often group members come to group with experiences of being rejected by others because they are different in some way. Can anyone relate to what I have said?

After some members respond to this question, the worker may then note:

Our hope is that together we can create a group that is accepting of all members and their different perspectives, experiences, and contributions.

Inclusive group workers must encourage the acknowledgment and exploration of diversity in the group, engaging in discussions about aspects of social identity, beliefs, and behaviors associated with diversity, and issues of oppression, privilege, and power in the group (Bemak & Chung, 2004; Brabender et al., 2004; Greene, 2004; Marbley, 2004; Miller et al., 2004; Wilson et al., 2004; Smith & Shin, 2008; Burnes & Ross, 2010; Singh & Salazar, 2010).

Affirming the Individuality and Unique Contributions of Each Member

Extending from the principle of celebrating diversity is affirming the uniqueness of each group member. Respecting individuals has been a traditional social work value. However, it has been overshadowed by an emphasis on seeking commonalities among group members. One therapeutic factor that has had a particularly profound impact on group members is the experience of universality. Given that group members come to an intervention group with feelings of inadequacy, the realization that they are not alone in their challenges can have an immensely healing effect. However, individuals who come to a group bring with them diverse experiences and perspectives and often bring a history of repeated rejections and invalidation, particularly if their perspectives do not reflect those of the dominant society. For example, in a recent group for those experiencing grief and bereavement, nearly all group members shared their experience of being told by others to get over their grief and move on with their lives. In this group, one of the most therapeutic statements offered to group members by the group workers was that everyone is free to grieve in their own way. In that moment group members realized that others shared their experience in the group and that they could grieve in their own ways in a group that would accept them.

An inclusive group worker realizes that it is not only the sense of being all in the same boat with fellow members that is beneficial, but also the freedom to be different that comes from being a member of a group that does not punish or reject them when they express their unique and authentic selves. Members in an inclusive group do not need to be the same to be accepted. Regardless of the type of group that is involved, it is difficult to imagine a group that would not benefit from acknowledging and validating the unique contributions of each member.

Moreover, it is often these unique contributions that potentially make each group a unique, creative, and meaningful experience. For example, consider some of the teams or task groups that you have been involved in over the years. Does each person in a team play the same role? Do members of a task group all bring the same skills or ideas to the table? If they did, these groups would not be very interesting or effective in reaching their goals. In sum, an inclusive model of group work behooves the practitioner to respect and value each group member's diverse experiences, perspectives, and unique contributions to the group. This deeper appreciation of diversity is expressed well by Sullivan (2004):

> All members of the human family have commonalities and uniquely differentiating characteristics across people and our various groups. Differences need to be acknowledged as contributing to the richness of society. Group membership should mean inclusion, not assimilation of differences. (p. 80)

Promoting Inclusive Empathy among Group Members

If a group is to affirm the unique contributions of each member, an inclusive group worker needs to help members to move from simply tolerating one another to learning about, respecting, and embracing differences and new ways of relating to each other (Camacho, 2001; Bemak & Chung, 2004). Pedersen (2008) states that in inclusive groups, in order to enhance connections between individuals, "inclusive cultural empathy" ought to move "beyond accommodating cultural difference to achieve an empathetic relationship toward a complex and dynamic balance of both similarities and differences" (p. 372). Indeed, obstacles that inhibit inclusive empathy in the group must be explored and resolved, and this resolution can be profoundly helpful for individuals and the group. However, in an intervention group, moving from initial negative reactions to diversity to empathy can be both challenging and ultimately profoundly therapeutic. Negative reactions to diversity can become fruitful paths of exploration that can reveal long-standing challenges experienced by group members in their interpersonal relationships.

Finally, members of diverse groups should be supported in their efforts to be actively engaged in conflict resolution processes, in order to facilitate inclusion and empowerment in the group context (Abernethy, 2002; Saino, 2003; Ratts, Anthony, & Santos, 2010). Malekoff and Laser (1999) suggest that group members be viewed as "helpers," and that they be encouraged to actively support one another. For example, "members with greater openness to a cultural focus can assist those who are less aware" (Brabender et al., 2004, p. 216).

CHAPTER SUMMARY

Inclusive group work practice offers ongoing opportunities for workers to examine their beliefs, attitudes, worldviews, and values when diversity arises in a group. Group workers need to continually increase their awareness of personal biases, values, and beliefs, and the manner in which these affect group processes, including (1) an awareness of self (of their own social identity, attitudes, and beliefs); (2) an awareness of group members' worldviews and experiences of oppression; and (3) the use of intervention strategies that are appropriate to diverse individuals and groups.

Often, it is through the sharing of different perspectives that rigid or limited perspectives adopted by individual members begin to change. New possibilities, options, and strategies become available, and in this way, the sharing of diverse approaches, failures, and disappointments empower the group to develop unique systems that benefit all members of the group. All members (including the worker) can harness and use the diversity of experiences that the group presents to achieve personal, professional, and group goals. This approach provides a new perspective in which diversity in all of its forms becomes a strength and resource to all groups. Moreover, it becomes an equally important and complementary factor with group cohesion.

CHAPTER 5

A DIVERSITY OF PURPOSES

LEARNING OBJECTIVES

At the end of this chapter you will be able to:
- Identify how formed and naturally occurring groups differ.
- Appraise the types of groups and the varieties of group activities in which social workers engage.
- Compare and contrast activities utilized in a variety of groups.

As a novice group worker, you will likely be asked to facilitate, cofacilitate, be a member of, or observe a wide assortment of groups in social agencies. Social agencies offer many distinct types of groups with a variety of different names used to advertise and promote them. This chapter will explore these different groups and will stress the importance of clarifying a group's underlying purpose and structure. The group structure should enhance the purposes of the agency and assembled group members to ensure the group's success, which is why this chapter first examines group structure and design. The chapter also alerts the group worker to the necessary harmonizing between a group member's reasons for attending a group and the publically stated purpose of a group.

STRUCTURAL ELEMENTS COMMON TO GROUPS

Open or Closed Groups

An open group is one in which membership is available to potential members at any time. Joining an open group can occur throughout the life of a group with members regularly coming and going. In these types of groups, discussions and content need to be reviewed and shared with a newly arriving member so that all newcomers know about the group's purpose and development and so they feel comfortable. Many groups have an open membership policy as a way to serve and foster new content with members entering and exiting the group. Because membership is frequently changing and current and incoming members are in different stages of having their needs or the agency's needs met by the group, open groups can expose members to various perspectives of a problem. For example, in an open grief support group, long-term members can share insight and model coping behavior to newer members who are beginning their grief journey.

Closed groups, on the other hand, have a single opening point at the start-up of the group. Only the original group members are allowed to be privy to discussions and other group content. Closed groups tend to have a more structured framework, allowing members to experience the different phases of group work. Closed groups offer a potential for members to deepen relationships over time due to the consistency in membership. Because of their nature, closed groups may better suit the purposes of group members who are dealing with trust issues, such as women who have been sexually assaulted or children who experienced severe trauma at the hands of adults.

Ongoing or Time Limited Groups

Like open groups, ongoing groups do not have a fixed end date and many times lend themselves to having new members join at any time. An example of an ongoing and open group is a substance use group. It is possible to have a closed, ongoing group as well, such as a long-term therapy group found in psychiatric centers or other agencies. In ongoing groups, members usually stay until they feel that they have achieved their goals in group.

Time limited groups have a finality of time placed onto the group sessions. Members meet only for a particular number of sessions before a planned closure. The stated time constraints can sometimes encourage group members to set goals and complete them in a more timely fashion. Examples of time limited groups can include school groups or court-mandated groups. In these examples, time constraints are placed by external factors (i.e. a court order or the school year).

Voluntary or Involuntary (Mandated) Groups

Voluntary groups are those in which individuals can decide to become members or terminate membership at their own will. Many groups tend to be voluntary in nature and thus members often join because they share a common need, goal, or purpose.

Involuntary or mandated groups are groups in which an individual is required to become a member by external forces (such as an institution or legal entity). With involuntary groups, there are typically legal or personal consequences should an individual choose not to join or participate in the group. For example, in child welfare cases, if a parent decides not to participate in a court-ordered parenting group, the parent may be at risk of not reunifying with their child. Additionally, in cases of interpersonal violence, if an individual does not participate in an ordered batterers' group, the individual could face court-ordered sanctions or incarceration. As in any other intervention group, involuntary groups have a purpose and members have a goal. However, due to the nature of the group's membership, a worker may need to address the dynamics and challenges brought forth by this membership arrangement, and in doing so, focus on engaging and empowering members early in the group process.

Conceptual Review

What could be some advantages and drawbacks of an open group or a closed group? What could be some of the challenges of working with involuntary groups?

DIFFERENT TYPES OF GROUPS

Although Catherine Papell and Beulah Rothman (1980) envisioned a mainstream or common model for group work, they acknowledged that social group work could include many diverse applications in practice. The types of groups described herein are simply frameworks that describe the patterns of meetings and lay out the member-shared responsibilities for the conduct of goal setting and goal attainment. As an introduction to understanding the variety of group types in use today, groups can be categorized as either naturally occurring or professionally created for specific purposes.

Naturally Occurring Groups

Naturally occurring groups come into existence as persons relate to others around specific interests, community locations, or shared life events. Car clubs and community and student groups are examples of this type of a naturally occurring group. Within these groups, people can share one on one interactions and close friendships. Members may also share ongoing interrelationships among themselves. The groups help to develop and sustain interpersonal attitudes, community values, and orientations. These groups potentially serve as one of the means for community socialization.

Two examples of these types of groups are interest and friendship groups. Interest groups are naturally occurring groups where members may not be connected by any other social or organizational tie. Many times group members are only joined together by a single common interest. An example of an interest group would be students who meet to form a support group to prepare for class assignments. Friendship groups are created when persons identify with others' sociopolitical attitudes, beliefs, and religious values, or simply enjoy common social activities with others. The group members meet to participate in these activities because they like each other and find a common purpose in gathering. For example, a group of employees who form a friendship group may share time together eating lunch at a favorite restaurant.

Formed Groups

A formed group refers to one that is constructed by either lay or professional persons to accomplish specific purposes. Although the principle focus in this writing is on professionally facilitated groups, the recognition of community-inspired groups will first be presented. Many of the lay, community self-help groups have proven their value in serving the community, and their utility and effectiveness is highlighted here.

Self-help Groups

Self-help groups are not conceived or led by professionals; instead, they are usually promoted and offered by group participants. The purpose of these groups is to provide peer support. Self-help groups offer members assistance through the group's interactions, which include sharing in meetings. It is common to see that established group members become group leaders, though leadership rotates as other members become more empowered to taking that role. A feature of this type of group is that members share their stories of recovery, problem solving, and coping strategies to overcome a variety of problems. Examples of the most popular self-help programs are twelve step programs such as Alcoholics Anonymous, Overeaters Anonymous, and so on.

Social workers often make referrals to community-based self-help groups as auxiliary help outside of professional contact times. A major benefit of self-help groups is that support from other members is available outside of professional services to reinforce the message that individuals are not alone in coping with their problems. One caveat is that some self-help programs present a spiritual element, which may not match a consumer's ethnocultural or religious background. In such cases other alternatives may be sought.

Community-based Help Groups

Another type of self-help group is the community-based help group. This type of group serves as an avenue for member education and empowerment with a usual focus on neighborhood and community development. Its purpose is to bring attention to local deficiencies, inequities, and shortfalls. Through membership in community groups or neighborhood associations, community residents can find affiliation and purpose. As members meet to review, discuss, and plan for changes in identified community problems, the group can begin to identify and clarify their common concerns. Developing strategies for change and deciding how to achieve this change become the group's reasons for being.

Community hope and feelings of empowerment can develop from community group membership and shared responsibility. The problem-solving process encourages broad participation when brainstorming new directions. If the community groups conclude that their situations are the result of their exposure to oppression, then the groups can assist members to collectively identify and challenge their sources of oppression.

Professionally Led Groups

These groups are intentionally formed by professionals, have clear, publically stated purposes, and focus on members' or agency needs utilizing agency programming. These groups can have different purposes and they include two primary forms of groups: task and intervention groups. Task groups are often employed and facilitated by social workers to alter environmental barriers and develop better organizational delivery of services. On the other hand, social work intervention groups are designed for the purposes of helping group members to cope more effectively, to resolve problems, and to prevent future problems.

Klein (1972) posited that professionally led groups could attend to multifaceted ways of helping and concurrently work in many different directions. He suggested eight different purposes for groups that could be combined in different combinations to best meet the needs of people. These eight concepts underlie many groups in social agencies today:

1. Rehabilitation

Rehabilitation is viewed as the restoration of a person to her or his previous levels of functioning. Rehabilitation can refer to changing values, beliefs, or attitudes. Examples of groups with this purpose include addiction-related groups and cognitive behavioral groups.

2. Habilitation

Habilitation suggests ongoing growth and development, not simply a restoration to a previous level of capacity. Examples include psychoeducational groups and seeking-safety groups.

3. Correction

Correction refers to a process of assisting persons who have difficulties with social mores and societal laws. Group members focus on difficulties with meeting societal expectations with the goal of addressing and resolving those difficulties. Examples include ex-offender and sex-offender groups.

4. Socialization

Socialization involves a group's focus to assist persons to learn how to cope and receive support from others. An example would be a divorce recovery group or a grief support group.

5. Prevention

Prevention is a process of preparing persons for new or unexpected situations in interpersonal functioning. An example would be a group for young adolescents who live in neighborhoods with gangs.

6. Social Action

Social action groups assist group members to change their living environment. Learning new roles includes presenting new information to the community and encouraging extended community participation among persons in the community. An example is a neighborhood leadership group.

7. Problem Solving

Problem solving refers to a process involving a community-wide participation of persons who become part of the decision-making process. An example includes a coalition or a task force group.

8. Social Values

The theme of social values refers to the group's efforts to develop community needs-based orientations for improving social living conditions.

Potential members are encouraged to consider joining a group based on the group's purpose and are encouraged to generate individual goals that will fit within the group's purposes. Individual goals can be thought of as simple statements of intended change that group members can monitor over time while in group.

Throughout the group's sessions, each of the members is expected to attend to his or her specifically identified goals. Group members help meet the group's purpose by contributing their own uniqueness to the ongoing and shared mutual explorations.

Conceptual Review

What is the relationship between a group's purpose and members' reasons for attending the group?

Task and Intervention Groups

As previously noted, within the realm of formed groups there are two primary group categories, usually referred to as task groups and intervention groups.

Task Groups

Task groups are described as professionally facilitated groups that attempt to improve service delivery. Task groups are established to achieve specific agency goals within a defined time frame. They are not established for members to achieve personal goals.

Task groups may be seen within agencies, organizations, and communities. They are the vehicles for institutions to modify program directions and goals. Persons are invited or assigned to a task group for the specific purpose of completing an assignment. The goals are usually defined by the convener at the start-up of the group. Common task groups include organizational ad hoc committees, specific project or program groups, or work committees. Work related groups, as seen in organizational charts, such as teams, can function as a task group with a leader or supervisor and the employees or subordinates who report to that organizational leader. An example of a work group is a group that drafts guidelines for reviewing foster home safety and is composed of a children's services supervisor and the front line workers reporting to her or him.

Task groups are useful for developing new ideas, solving organizational problems, or creating new processes. These groups are usually disbanded after they complete the assigned tasks; however, they can last longer if the task or purpose of the group addresses an ongoing need. An example of an ongoing task group would be an organization's board of directors, whose role continues as long as the agency they represent is operating. The members of a board of directors may have special skills related to the agency's needs, such as being a lawyer or accountant.

Intervention Groups

Intervention groups invite participants to bring their personal concerns into the group and specify individual goals to accomplish. These groups focus on improving members' communications, increasing interpersonal awareness and insights, and altering nonfunctional relationship patterns. Members in an intervention group can expect attention to their emotional needs, with an emphasis on personal expression and interpersonal interactions. Mutual aid is developed as members exchange perceptions and feedback with each other and explore their feelings in this group environment. Often a high level of interdependence develops among group members as the group continues to meet over time.

An intervention group is an analogue or a representative place where members can work on their everyday life issues and concerns. The group members pay attention to the here-and-now relationships inside of the group as a step towards helping members with their out-of-group relationships, problems, and obstacles. Member strengths are also reinforced through participation in the group.

Intervention groups may offer personal counseling and members may observe changes in behavior, affect, and cognition through group participation. These types of groups, called psychotherapy groups, have overarching intervention goals related to correcting deficiencies and restoring one's health and normalcy. In these groups, members examine and encourage changes in thought processes and behavior patterns through interpersonal transactions.

The causes of problems may be closely examined in group as members review, share, and comment on their perceptions of the other members. This process offers group members opportunities to improve through gains in insight and a concomitant change in their interpersonal relationships. Members also increase their emotional awareness and learn about others by sharing and working together.

Although these groups often examine past life events, the here-and-now group interactions become the primary focus for feedback and awareness building. Interpersonal counseling groups also assist group members to explore their feelings, thoughts, and behaviors to effect a deeper and lasting change, which improves spontaneity and interpersonal functioning. These groups may be ongoing or time limited and often center on a specific problem such as depression, anxiety, or the effects of family violence. For example, some specific groups center on the impact of childhood and family of origin experiences as a way to improve the capacity for human relationships.

Educational Groups

Educational groups, which encompass a subtype known as psychoeducational groups, are characterized by the presentation of information and new knowledge by the group worker to members for the purpose of growth, development, and change. Members often join these groups because the focus of the group is an identified, shared challenge by all group members. Topics for these groups are usually very specific, such as improved diabetic control, management of anxiety, and so on.

The group worker transmits content, shares resources, and describes proven techniques for addressing the identified challenge. Members also offer each other resources, ideas, and mutual aid in these types of groups. The group worker facilitates specific discussions and activities related to the teachings. Although members relate how the new content might apply to their situations, the focus is not on group members' life stories. The emphasis is also not necessarily on the members' feelings or behaviors.

Members attend educational groups for the awareness and understanding provided in group and the individual learning and acquisition of new knowledge to be used outside of the group. Ultimately, group members improve their knowledge, which supports improved problem solving.

Support Groups

Support groups are different from interpersonal counseling or therapy groups. The purpose of a support group is to assist group members to restabilize through compassionate and concerned interactions in the group. Support groups reinforce strengths, reframe problems as opportunities for change, and provide the space for group members to disclose issues related to common problems such as grief, parenting, or addiction issues. The goals of support groups are to reduce members' distress, reinforce problem-solving skills, and identify areas of hope and comfort as members continue to cope with life's sometimes unchangeable situations.

The support group recognizes the member's struggle and provides empathy and advice in a caring environment. Support is offered in group for members to consider new ways of coping and verbally expressing themselves to reduce feelings causing conflict or emotional pain. The group's steps toward support include the sharing of experiences, sharing of intense feelings, and collective responses to the information shared among all of the group members. The members come to recognize a sense of universality in that each person is not alone with his or her problem. This activity sets the stage for mutual aid among members as they discuss, review, plan, and rehearse.

A support group utilizes members' strengths as a tool of mutual aid. The variety of members' skills and abilities assists the group as a whole to lend assistance based on the cluster of strengths present in the group. The group's mutual aid supports individual members to handle difficult situations and continue to move forward in life.

Growth Groups

Growth groups offer members opportunities to discover new pathways to health and well-being and to experience self-improvement. Group members desire to alter or change themselves out of a desire for life exploration, not because of an ailment. Group members assist one another, through the group's agreement, to reach a fuller potential. Goals for this type of group include improved social competence and enriched relationships, especially through self-disclosure. Examples of this type of group include a group for couples to improve communications and intimacy, or a community group raising awareness of newly arrived neighbors' needs and strengths.

Growth groups are described as presenting opportunities to increase awareness and insights in group members' challenges. A goal of this group might be to identify and make group members aware of one's role in problem formation and problem continuation. A purpose of this type of group is to increase group members' problem-solving skills.

Cognitive Behavioral Therapy (CBT) Groups

The goal of cognitive behavior therapy groups is to address and change negative behavior by focusing on changing the group member's maladaptive thoughts and emotions that cause those behavior responses. CBT groups are often used to address depression, anxiety, obsessive-compulsive disorder (OCD), phobias, and eating disorders, among other mental health concerns. Because negative behaviors are attributed to irrational, conditional thoughts (i.e., if I eat any food, then I will immediately gain weight), CBT groups focus on helping members identify and challenge maladaptive thoughts, decrease negative response behaviors, and increase coping skills and the adaptation of appropriate behavior responses.

In the group setting, group members assist each other in identifying and exploring the cause of these thoughts in a safe and trusting environment. Group members also examine their behavior and receive feedback on how to problem solve. The group also provides members the opportunity to help each other identify triggers and risk factors that increase the likelihood of relapse to negative behavior, after changes have been made. Through this process, members learn coping skills and can share their successes and challenges in maintaining new learned behavior. In group, members receive encouragement, experience universalization, and are able to obtain various perspectives of their situation. Furthermore, members are able to role play or practice in a setting that closely mirrors society, and learn appropriate social behavior from fellow group members.

Curriculum-based Groups

These groups are often time limited and they follow a set curriculum within a specified time frame. The curricula used by these groups are often evidence based and can include set objectives and goals. The groups can cover various topics such as social skills, parenting, anger management, interpersonal violence, empowerment, and the like. Curriculum-based groups tend to share components of other groups, often using a mix of an education and support group component. For example, an anger management group may educate members on how to identify anger triggers and coping skills and also ask members to share in group the challenges and successes they have had in managing their anger.

Because these groups are time limited, are evidence based, and often mix education and a support component, curriculum groups are often used in schools and the community. Court-mandated groups (empowerment, parenting, intimate partner violence, etc.) also use curriculum groups.

CONNECTING INDIVIDUALS TO GROUP PURPOSE IN THE GROUP START-UP

As previously noted, you are almost always a part of a group throughout your life, whether they be social or professional groups. Persons who approach professional social work group efforts may hesitate to join or work in a group for various reasons. Potential members bring interpersonal histories and life experiences from their own group experiences that may be positive or negative. Group members' feelings about joining a professionally led group may be influenced by these or other experiences or by the fact that joining the group was mandated. Group workers can assist potential group members by presenting a clear statement of the group's purposes, the frequency of sessions, and the layout and design of how the group can work, as well as by reviewing the potential risks and benefits of group membership. They can also assist by listening to members' concerns. Group workers can facilitate expectations by clarifying the members' opportunities for sharing communications in group. Members would also benefit from a description of the work to be done in group over the time period set aside for the group. These steps will help to assuage a potential member's fearful or resistant feelings at the outset of the group. The group worker should also introduce the idea that group members will be working on similar—not the same—concerns and that all who attend will participate in a common discovery process.

Despite these efforts to acclimate potential members to group, the worker should be cognizant that some individuals may not be ready to engage in group work or may not benefit from group intervention. For example, individuals who have social phobias and are not ready to interact with others, individuals who are an immediate risk of harm to self or others, or individuals who have experienced recent severe trauma, to name a few, may not be appropriate candidates for group activity. In these cases the worker should make appropriate referrals to ensure the individual has access to treatment and services.

DIVERSITY PRACTICE CONSIDERATIONS

Shulman (2011) indicates that social workers need to connect the mission of a sponsoring agency and the consumers' needs to the design type of a group in order to maximize the potential for a successful group outcome. This addresses a matching process that a social worker should employ when designing the group model. Special care needs to be paid to the group's structure meshing with expectations of talking and activities in the group.

Extra care also needs to be paid to the diversity of members who might attend the groups. Although diversity is often described in demographic terms, this is not a substitute for diversity of thought and experiences. Groups should invite and incorporate members via inclusivity; this means all group members agree to a mutual adaptation process, not just assimilation and tolerance of their differences. Some of the group types require more frequent or ongoing attention to this point. Groups that are short term and open ended will be admitting members and releasing members rather quickly, even before full relationships among members can be fostered in the group. The social worker needs to attend to the diversity and inclusion issues routinely as new group members arrive. All groups should offer relevant experiences and opportunities for members to engage with others while giving and receiving mutual aid and support.

CHAPTER SUMMARY

Overall, there is an array of group types and purposes that can be utilized by a social worker to best meet members' needs. Many groups' purposes include providing opportunities to learn about self through group interactions or working towards accomplishing a particular task. Group members can also learn how to give and receive feedback, how to organize others into a concerted effort, and/or how to support changes in self and community. By knowing the diversity of group purposes, you will be able to identify and bring forth a group that will best meet the needs of individuals and the community.

Group Work Practice Scenario

1. *Consider that you are a social worker in a hospital and that you want to plan a group for adult patients recovering from a myocardial infarction or a heart attack. What type of group would you examine and choose?*

2. *As a group worker in a child and family counseling center, you identify a need for foster parents to meet and connect with other foster parents regarding parenting and authority issues as foster parents raising other people's children. What type of group would you recommend?*

3. *While working as a community social worker, you become aware of the problems that a neighborhood association is facing regarding crime and delinquency problems. What type of group would be appropriate for potential members? Describe the group outreach and how you would choose to assist them.*

CHAPTER 6

PLANNING A GROUP WITH A FOCUS ON DIVERSITY

LEARNING OBJECTIVES

At the end of this chapter you will be able to:

- Articulate the purpose of planning a group with consideration of social work with groups' ethics and standards.
- Demonstrate the ability to plan an inclusive group using the ten keys to planning.
- Apply the planning checklist to analyze if you have properly planned a group.

In order for a group to succeed, it is critical to plan (Kurland, 2008). Planning is the first aspect of a worker's involvement in the group and consists of many interrelated responsibilities. The worker will have to consider: the need for the group; its purpose; group and individual goals; agency and community support; recruitment; membership; structure; location and time; content; process; activities; ethical, legal, and safety concerns; evaluation; and costs. This chapter will give the reader a comprehensive understanding of the group planning process for either a task or a personal intervention group. Although this chapter discusses the planning process under ideal circumstances, as a social worker in the community you will find that circumstances are rarely ideal. The intent is to give you a foundation of best practice for planning a group, so that you, in consultation with a supervisor when possible, can adapt these to meet your agency and community circumstances. A checklist with ten key aspects of planning will be provided at the end of the chapter.

REASONS FOR PLANNING

There are many reasons to plan groups, a major one being to meet the needs of individuals, communities, and society. People often join groups seeking solutions, strategies, support, motivation, education, and resources for serious concerns they have. By planning, group workers are preparing themselves psychologically, culturally, and educationally for a journey with members to ensure progress toward meeting important goals.

Exercise 6.1: Planning?

Can you think of a time when you were part of a group, project, or event that was poorly planned and/or disorganized? Now think of a group, project, or event that was well planned. Which of those turned out more favorably and for what reasons? In what ways do you think poor planning could affect the success of a group? Meet in a small group of peers to discuss.

Planning Neglect

The social worker or human service professional, for a variety of reasons, may not carefully plan a group. When this occurs, the group is usually not successful. Both the members and the group worker are frustrated with the experience as individual members' or an agency's needs are not met. Members quickly lose interest in the group, are bored when attending, and/or fail to attend. The group worker begins to lack confidence in what he or she is doing and begins to feel it is not productive to work within groups.

What are some of the reasons careful planning does not occur? At times newer social workers have a passion for starting a certain type of group based on personal experience and begin a group without first completing a thorough needs assessment to learn what type of group will be productive. Experienced workers might also not plan, relying too much on their past group work experiences. Doing this may neglect the fact that newer practices may be more appropriate and thus need to be utilized for a different group of members. Another reason planning may be neglected rests with the social work ethic of self-determination. The National Association of Social Workers (NASW) includes self-determination as one of the ethical responsibilities of social workers to consumers (NASW, 2008). A concern may be that if the group worker determines the purpose and goals of the group without member input, the members' self-determination is ignored. Conversely, consumer self-determination is strengthened when careful planning takes place. With careful planning of the group, the group worker can meet with consumers prior to the group's start to ensure that members agree to join the group with knowledge of the group's purpose and goals. The worker can also plan time in sessions where members discuss the group's purpose and goals to see if modifications are warranted and to determine personal goals in intervention groups. In task groups, careful planning will allow the worker to create and utilize tools (i.e., agendas, meeting calendars, meeting minutes, etc.) to keep the group organized and on task.

Northen and Kurland (2001) asserted that when there is a structure in place and members feel the environment is safe, new and creative ideas emerge. In a mandatory group, planning is crucial, as these members are usually more skeptical about the group's benefits. The astute worker will plan a first session that allows involuntary members to vent and thus negative feelings can be tended to in the group (Gitterman, 2005). Finally, lack of planning can result if an agency exerts pressure on a social worker to start or continue a group without giving the worker enough time to plan.

Planning for Diversity

In the group composition process, one important concept that may have been neglected in prior literature about planning is purposely composing a group that is diverse in nature. In fact, theorists have discussed the difficulties of a heterogeneous group because the members have different values, desires, and perspectives (Toseland & Horton, 2008). Basso, Pelech, and Wickham (2014) make a cogent case for the value of diversity in groups. Diverse members in groups are able to share different values and perspectives related to the issues and varied ideas on how problems may be prevented or solved (Basso et al., 2014). In planning a personal intervention group, the worker can seek out diverse members from religious institutions, community centers, advertisements in public libraries, and other organizations in order to strengthen the group. The prudent worker will plan how diversity will be addressed in the group, such as role modeling the practice of cultural humility (Ortega & Faller, 2011). This practice involves the worker asking members to explain cultural nuances to the group and can be planned for the beginning stage of a group.

In task groups, planning for diversity is critical. Diverse members can provide different experiences, skills, and knowledge to help task groups succeed in their intended goals. The community or agency from which the task group emanates often includes diverse members. The proposed changes will be more readily implemented if the members represent the community or the agency's diverse employees and consumers. Exercise 6.2 relates to the strengths of planning for diversity in a group.

Exercise 6.2: Strengths of Planning for Diversity

Meet with peers in a group with one person acting as the group worker. As the group worker, engage the group members in a discussion of the diverse perspectives that they might bring to a university student support group.

TEN KEYS TO PLANNING A GROUP

There are ten interrelated keys to planning a group. The details of the ten keys may vary depending on the type of group, its purpose, and the target population. Several steps may be completed concurrently or modified when new information is obtained. When the group will have coworkers, the planning needs to be done together in order for both to become fully engaged in the group from the beginning.

Planning Key 1: Conducting a Needs Assessment

A needs assessment is an exploration and analysis of the needs of members for whom the worker plans a group. It includes learning from an agency or community what they believe is needed, and if they will support the group. Group workers or human service professionals may have good ideas about types of groups that might help a particular population or are needed in order to create an agency or community program. It is critical to conduct research to see if the group could be valuable and, if needed, what components will inspire success. To conduct a thorough needs assessment, the group worker studies the professional literature, communicates with agency administrators and staff, and obtains input from potential consumers and community members.

Group workers begin the needs assessment by locating and reading current professional and scholarly literature about the concept of the group. For example, if workers want to facilitate a group for consumers who suffer from depression at a mental health agency, they will want to read current literature regarding depression, evidence-based practices that have worked for consumers with depression, and groups that have been conducted with people who suffer from depression. The group worker will want to use research studies to become as well informed as possible about current evidence-based theoretical frameworks and practices. The same would be true of an agency or community task group. For example, a task group to prevent adolescent sex trafficking was developed in the community of one of this book's authors, and the group began with a review of current research-based articles about this topic.

Meeting with key agency staff to learn if a group is of interest to the agency is also important. The worker would want to assess if the purpose of the group aligns with the agency's mission. Then, the worker would need to research the agency's data to learn, for example, how many children the agency serves, for what reasons children are referred and by whom, and what the demographics of the consumers are. To gather further relevant information, the worker would have to make inquiries in the community that surrounds the agency. For children's groups, the worker would contact local school personnel to learn what types of groups would help children who attend the school. It is also recommended that other community organizations such as children's medical groups, the local child protective agency, and the local Boys and Girls Clubs be approached regarding needs. For the task group to prevent adolescent sex trafficking, diverse professionals in the community were asked about their perceptions of the problem. For example, information was sought from local law enforcement agencies, youth shelter staff, and child protection agency personnel.

Kurland (2008) recommends talking with potential consumers about what is needed when planning a group. The worker needs to contact consumers who are diverse in culture/race, socioeconomic status, gender, and other ways for input. Service consumers may have different ideas of needs based on varied demographic factors, life and work experiences, and personal values. In the task force for the prevention of youth sexual trafficking, it was important to talk with past victims to obtain information on what they believed could have prevented the problem. It was also important to recruit former victims for the task force.

When conducting a needs assessment with consumers for a children's group, the worker can ask children questions such as, "How are you doing in school? How do you feel about joining a group of other children? What do you think would be fun things to do in a group?" The worker can also ask the children's parents or caregivers, "Would you like a group in which you can learn effective ways to manage your child's behavior? What types of content would be helpful to you and your family? Would you like to gain support and resources from other parents who have a child with similar difficulties? What would make the group convenient for you, such as scheduling, location, childcare, or other accommodations?" An example of a needs assessment for a relational group is documented below.

Example: Needs Assessment

A bilingual social worker, Cecilia Rodriquez, was employed at a child guidance center that primarily serves Latino consumers in a diverse urban community. She noticed that she had many children in her caseload diagnosed with attention deficit hyperactivity disorder (ADHD). From reading articles about ADHD, she learned that in addition to medications, children with ADHD benefited from social skills groups that teach them how to get along and communicate better with their peers. She also read many articles that discussed how parents/caregivers benefited from psychoeducational support groups that teach about ADHD and strategies to better manage their children's behaviors. The parents also reported that receiving support and resources from other parents was especially beneficial. After reading the literature, she felt that her child consumers diagnosed with ADHD would benefit from a social skills group, and their parents or caregivers could benefit from a psychoeducational support group. She discussed her ideas with her supervisor and the agency director who provided her with statistics, the number of children and families served by the agency, how many of the children had an ADHD diagnosis, the children's ages, the families' ethnicities, and who referred the families to the agency. The social worker was encouraged by the agency administrators to pursue her ideas for the groups. She communicated with principals, teachers, and school staff at the nearby elementary and middle schools to see if they also believed that this might be a needed group in the community. They were interested and advised that they would refer children and parents to the groups.

A thorough needs assessment, including a comprehensive review of the literature and communication with diverse consumers and professionals, takes time and effort, but it is important in order to find out if the group is a viable endeavor. A thorough needs assessment will lead to a valid group purpose. After information is gathered for the needs assessment, the worker can use the information to write the first part of a written group proposal when developing and proposing a group.

Planning Key 2: Developing the Group's Purpose

If the needs assessment indicates that a group is needed for a particular issue, the second key planning element is developing a group's purpose. If you were developing a group, what would your group's purpose be? Should the members always know what the group worker's purpose is? How does the group's name relate to the group's purpose? These are important questions relating to purpose.

A social work group's purpose must be transparent to its members and potential members. For example, Alcoholics Anonymous is a popular self-help group whose purpose is to assist members in stopping their use of alcohol (Alcoholics Anonymous, 2001). The word anonymous in the name implies that the group is not interested in members' personal identifiers. The name of the group reflects the group's purpose. In another example, a social worker in an elementary school held a children's group for children of recently divorced and separated parents. The group had the following purpose: help children cope with their parents' divorce/separation, feel better about themselves, and support each other. The group was called "the Banana Splits." This is a humorous way of conveying that the group is for children of divorce or parental separation without stigmatizing the children. It is essential that a group's title conveys its purpose, attracts people, and does not stigmatize. The following exercise will assist you in creating purpose statements for groups.

Exercise 6.3: Creating a Group's Purpose

Develop and write a purpose statement for a task or intervention group. In addition, name the group with a title that conveys the group's purpose. Meet in a small group of peers and share the purpose statement and the name you created for the group. The members of the group will give you feedback about the transparency of the purpose and the appropriateness of the name.

Having completed the needs assessment and purpose statement, the worker is ready to plan the group's structure. However, prior to moving on to discussing structure, a separate key on cofacilitation will be reviewed because oftentimes a group worker will be working with a cofacilitator.

Planning Key 3: Working with a Cofacilitator

Certain groups will benefit from cofacilitation. This may be due to the size of the group, population served, or the content. For example a group for adolescents with mental illness at an inpatient hospital facility may benefit from having two workers, one who can attend to the group, and the other who can assist an adolescent who is having a serious behavioral outburst. Also, field supervisors often place interns in groups as cofacilitators with a more experienced group worker.

When cofacilitators are involved, it is imperative that the planning involve both of them so they can discuss all aspects of the group's plan prior to beginning the group. For example, it is recommended that the facilitators agree on theoretical frameworks and evidence-based practices that will be utilized in the group to prevent conflict in the facilitation process. For task groups, agendas and/or timelines for task completion need to be determined by cofacilitators. They need to plan recruitment and member prescreening, agreeing on criteria for selecting members. They should discuss the group's evaluation. The structure and content of the group should be collaboratively planned along with the roles each will play in the sessions and/or meetings. They need to decide when they will meet to process the group sessions and how supervision will transpire. Additionally, cofacilitators should discuss how diversity and any themes or conflict around diversity will be approached and used throughout the group. Cofacilitator power imbalance and how this will be addressed within the group should be discussed as well. Clear and honest communication is vital during the planning process, as it will set the stage of how work is done and issues are resolved throughout the life of the group. Unresolved conflict between the group workers will affect the group's success, hamper members' progress toward meeting goals, and affect the coworkers' attitude and approach. This does not mean coworkers will always agree about the group plan, but negotiation and compromise must occur in advance of starting the group. The next exercise will allow you to imagine planning with a coworker.

Exercise 6.4: Planning with a Cofacilitator

Pair with another person and discuss how you would go about cofacilitating a task or personal intervention group. What are issues that you will discuss? Will you discuss your diverse beliefs, perspectives, and group work methods? Do you foresee any conflicts arising? How will you deal with conflicts?

Planning Key 4: Creating a Group Structure

After the need for the group and its purpose are established, the worker needs to plan the group's structure. Having a flexible structure will allow the group members not only to feel safe in the group environment but also be creative. For example, if an unusual event occurs during the life of the group, such as one of the members having an automobile accident, the group worker can process the event with the member and the entire group rather than moving on with the planned schedule. This also applies to task groups and gives members additional opportunities to engage and build cohesion.

The worker will also need to determine logistics, such as how long the group will meet for each week, the structure and activities of each session, how many sessions will be necessary to cover the content and achieve goals, and whether the group will be open or closed to new members after its inception. Group logistics will depend on many factors, including the demographics of the group's members, the type of group (task, education, support), the group's purpose, and the content.

The worker will want to consider the group members' demographic diversity in the planning process and structure the group to minimize hurtful conflict due to diversity. Anderson (1997) recommended composing a group with at least one demographically similar member when there are differences such as race or sexual orientation to prevent feelings of isolation or scapegoating. He called this recommendation "pairing" or the "Noah's Ark principle" (Reid, 1991; Anderson, 1997). Levi (2007), when writing about organizational teams, advises that surface characteristic attraction and bias can be strong in the beginning of a group but can change as a member's identity with the group and its overarching purpose and goals develop. Inclusive group work practice strongly supports diversity of group membership. Regarding structuring of the group's sessions, the worker will want to plan to have an early session regarding diversity of personal and/or professional perspectives and complete research about cultures of group members that most likely will be represented in the group. The next exercise will assist you in planning for diversity.

Exercise 6.5: Planning for Diversity

Meet in a small group of peers and discuss your planning for diversity in both task and intervention groups. Would you employ the Noah's Ark principle in task and intervention groups? How could consideration of diversity affect the way you would plan a group?

Another component of group structure is size. The worker will plan for the size of the group to maximize progress and have everyone participate. Children's groups, for example, will include fewer members due to children's greater need for attention and discipline as compared to adults. In a task force group attempting to solve a community-wide problem (i.e., human trafficking, homelessness, etc.), a large group may be ideal, as you want as many stakeholders as possible to be represented and present. The structure of the group will also be different if it is open or closed to new members. There will be a need to continually orient new members if the group is open. In planning the group's structure, the group worker needs to develop icebreakers and activities that will fit the content at the different stages of the group and/or that meet the population's needs (Middleman, 1982; Lang, 2010). This may also be beneficial in task groups to keep members motivated and to promote relationship building and group cohesion. Also, time needs to be set aside for processing and evaluating. The following is an example of how a social worker planned a group's structure:

Example: Planning the Structure of Group Sessions

A social group worker, Aneesa Rogers, is employed at a community center in a diverse urban area, and planned a group for older adults. The purpose of the group was to educate older adults in the community about the normal aging process and to encourage healthy coping strategies. The worker planned a six-week closed group with two-hour sessions held each Wednesday morning for ten older adults. The first hour of each session would consist of a presentation of educational content, such as content on loss, followed by discussion of the group members. The second hour was dedicated to mutual sharing of members, beginning with an icebreaker activity related to the educational theme of the day. For the third session on coping with loss, Aneesa planned the following icebreaker activity. She would give each member a beautiful fall leaf. Group members would then take turns holding up the leaf. When looking at one side of the leaf, the member would disclose a loss that he or she had experienced as an older adult. The group worker would then ask the member to turn the leaf over and give a healthy coping strategy to deal with the loss. The worker would encourage the other group members to also suggest coping strategies for the member.

Prior to beginning a group, it is excellent to tend to other logistics related to group structure and to have a skeletal outline of sessions with exercises. For example, a pleasant environment will support the group's structure and will be discussed in planning key 5.

Planning Key 5: Establishing Location and Time

The group worker needs to plan a location for the group that is conducive to member attendance. The group's location needs to be convenient, accessible, private, safe, clean, and comfortable. For example, you may want to consider a location that is accessible by public transportation for members who do not have a car. The location also must fit the developmental needs of the particular population being served. For example, a young children's group location would be different from a location serving adults with substance misuse challenges. Appropriate locations may be found in social service agencies, schools, religious institutions, healthcare agencies, and community centers. Some members who come to the group to learn healthy coping strategies for personal concerns may be more comfortable in a community setting than a social service agency or mental health agency due to stigma. The worker can make the location more comfortable and convenient for members by offering amenities such as childcare, transportation, refreshments, and other incentives. Safety of the group members is a primary consideration. A security guard may need to be present in the building during the group, and the parking lot will need to be well lit if the group is held in the evening. For a community task group, the location must also be convenient for members. When one author of this book coordinated a task group to create mandatory classes for divorcing and separating parents focused on their children's needs, she was able to secure a large conference room at the superior court in downtown Phoenix, Arizona. This location was centrally located so that diverse members of this large task group could attend.

Besides considering the physical space, the worker needs to schedule the time of the group to maximize member attendance. As part of the needs assessment, canvassing potential members about when to schedule the group is helpful. The group worker may need to schedule groups in the evening or weekends for working members or during the day for older adults because of available transportation. Group workers may plan Internet or telephone support groups for members who cannot leave their homes due to caregiving responsibilities or disabilities. Teleconferencing or videoconferencing may also be used to include members who cannot physically attend a task group meeting. If these types of arrangements are needed for the group's success or member inclusion, it is important that the worker plan properly to accommodate for these equipment or technology needs.

Planning Key 6: Recruitment and Pre-engagement of Members

Nobody wants to plan an awesome party and then have no one come. The group worker sets the stage for recruiting members of groups during the needs assessment. While interviewing potential members, agency personnel, or community members, the worker stirs up interest in the group. Other important ways to advertise the group are: posting flyers in diverse venues, making phone calls, initiating in-person contact with potential members or referral sources, talking with professionals about the group, making presentations at meetings, and using the media (radio, TV, the web, and newspapers). It is important when one plans a group to advertise and locate members who could benefit from the group. It is also important for the group worker to advertise for members in diverse community venues, and select members who will bring different values, ideas, and perspectives. In-person contact is usually the best way to recruit members, followed by telephone contact, posting/distributing flyers, and mailings.

Some agencies or institutions have many consumers who might benefit from groups, and these can be a great referral source. For example, teachers can refer children to appropriate groups at their school or a nearby agency. Child protective service workers often refer consumers to parent education groups in the community. Groups are often the main interventions in outpatient or inpatient substance use programs. Even when there are potential members who receive services at an agency, the group worker needs to advertise the group and reach out to colleagues for additional members.

Recruitment for task groups may be somewhat different than for personal intervention groups. The group worker will want to recruit members who have expertise, skills, political power, motivation, and other attributes that assist in accomplishing a particular task. Many of the members will be experienced professionals or stakeholders. For example, in the youth trafficking prevention task force previously discussed, it was important to recruit diverse members who were motivated to assist with this problem and who had expertise and credibility in the community. The group worker recruited school administrators; lawyers who represented young people; former victims; religious leaders; a city council member; social workers and youth leaders from agencies serving adolescents; and members of the probation and police department. Youth leaders from the YMCA were also important to include as they had different perspectives on the problem and could recommend creative solutions.

Exercise 6.6: Member Recruitment

1. Create a radio advertisement for a personal intervention group and practice broadcasting the advertisement.
2. Make a flyer with all the relevant information about a group that you would plan. Show your flyer to peers and receive feedback.
3. Identify a community project that interests you. Who will you recruit as members to assist in accomplishing the goals of this project? What are the attributes the potential members will bring?
4. With a peer, take turns role playing a television/radio broadcaster or a newspaper reporter and a group worker discussing the formation of a new group.

After potential members are recruited for a personal intervention group, the group worker may pre-engage members in person or by telephone so that the person can determine if the group is appropriate for their needs or interests. Also, the group worker can assess if the group will be able to meet the needs of the potential member. The pre-engagement process involves a dialogue between the potential member and the group worker in order for the potential member to explain hopes and goals for the group, and the group worker to explain the purpose, rules, expectations, and plans for the group. It is recommended that the group worker ask the new member to sign an agreement or contract for group membership. In the case of a children's group, the parent/guardian would give authorization for the child to attend the group, and the child would also sign an agreement. (A sample permission slip is included in appendix A.) Members who are not appropriate for the group at times are referred to the group. For example, a person who is extremely depressed and suicidal may benefit more from intensive individual therapy and medicine prior to joining a group. It is critical to not make the member feel rejected but to explain the reasons the group may not be appropriate at this time and to make sure the person is referred to professionals who can offer help. There may be other reasons that a person is not a good match for the group being planned but could benefit from another type of group. If the potential member is not appropriate for the group, the worker needs to refer the person to another source of help.

Planning Key 7: Content and Activities

Besides reading journal articles and books about types of groups one is planning to facilitate, it is important to have a thorough understanding of substantive content and theoretical frameworks that will be applied in the group. For example, if offering a breast cancer support group, the group worker will need to become thoroughly knowledgeable regarding up-to-date information about this disease and whether support and educational groups have been helpful to this population. The group worker will also need to talk with professionals who are knowledgeable about breast cancer. These experts may include physicians, nurses, and group workers who have facilitated breast cancer support and education groups and who regularly work with this population. The group worker would want to talk with potential diverse group members who have breast cancer to learn what they would find helpful in this type of group and what they would expect from such a group.

The worker will also want to plan activities that will further the group's purpose. These activities may be different for intervention groups and task groups. For example, in the beginning meetings of a task group, the group worker will want to develop and provide brainstorming activities that give the diverse members a chance to participate and lend their expertise before embarking on a path to meeting the task group's goals. In addition, the worker may have to plan strategies for addressing power imbalances or other obstacles such as cultural norms that inhibit full participation.

Becoming knowledgeable about the culture of members can be done through reading and discussion with potential members or professionals prior to the group. For example, in a group for gay, lesbian, and transgender young adults who want to learn more about the coming out process, the group worker would want to become knowledgeable about the population's and subpopulations' cultures.

Planning Key 8: Evaluation

It is important for the group worker to plan how a group will be assessed and evaluated. The worker will plan to conduct an evaluation during each session and a formal evaluation at the end of the group. In a personal intervention group, the group worker plans an evaluation that will demonstrate if the group's purpose and individual goals of members have been accomplished. For example, if a group worker plans to facilitate a psychoeducational support group for adults experiencing depression, the overall purpose might be for members to develop coping strategies to alleviate depression and offer mutual support and resources to each other. The group worker could plan to administer a reliable and valid depression instrument to members at different stages of the group, including the group's termination session, to measure if the group has been successful in meeting its purpose. When planning a community task group, the group worker would also plan for an evaluation. For example, for a task group whose purpose is to prevent youth gang involvement, the group worker might plan to use varied measures to measure attainment of goals, such as police reports, a focus group of stakeholders, and school reports. In addition, the group worker might plan to evaluate the group's process using Macgowan's (1997) Group Engagement Measure (GEM) or the Cross-cultural Counseling Inventory (CCCI), which measures sensitivity to diversity in a group (LaFromboise, Coleman, & Hernandez, 1991). More information about assessment and evaluation can be found in the assessment/evaluation chapter in this book as well as in the chapter on the ending stage of group.

Exercise 6.7: Planning the Group's Evaluation

Meet in a small group of peers. Decide on a task or intervention group that you would want to evaluate. List the overall purpose of the group and two objectives of the group. How would you plan to evaluate this group?

Planning Key 9: Budgeting

Like everything else, groups cost money. It is important to consider the financial aspects of a group as a separate planning item and prepare a detailed budget. The budget will include all the items necessary to facilitate a group as well as a budget narrative explaining what the costs will cover. In the planning process, a group worker who carefully considers a budget will be in a much better position to get a group proposal approved by an agency or to apply for outside funding to support the proposed group.

There will be direct costs for facilitating a professional personal intervention group, such as the salary of the group worker if the group is not part of the group worker's regular work or volunteer tasks, rent of the room, an evidence-based curriculum, supplies, advertising costs, refreshments, and an outside evaluator, when evaluation is not done by the worker or hosting agency. There may be indirect costs associated with the group, such as agency insurance and administrative costs such as supervision or payroll costs. The agency may financially support the group with in-kind donations of space, equipment, or postage. Also, fees for service may offset some of the expenses. There will also be costs associated with developing and implementing a task group in an agency or a community. The costs may be borne by one agency or by multiple organizations in a community. The budget is a key element in the planning process. By completing the budget and submitting it for agency approval, the worker becomes more aware of the entire group planning process. The following exercise will assist you in creating a budget and budget narrative for a proposed group.

Exercise 6.8: Creating a Group's Budget and Budget Narrative

Create a budget for a group that would be offered at a social service agency. Create a list of possible budget items and then create a budget and budget narrative that is realistic for a group.

Planning Key 10: Writing a Group Proposal

It is highly recommended that you create a complete written group proposal prior to starting a group. The proposal will be tailored to the specific group that is being planned. For example, a proposal for an agency task group will be very different in purpose and member composition than a proposal for a personal intervention group offered by a mental health agency. The commonality is that it is a written group proposal and covers most aspects of the ten keys for planning of a group. The group planning checklist in appendix B outlines the ten keys for planning a group that have been discussed in this chapter and will ensure that important aspects of group planning are considered. The written proposal can be used for several purposes: to obtain agency and/or community support and approval; to promote and advertise the group; and to apply for internal or external funding. In addition, the group worker will find it useful to have a written plan, which can serve as an outline or blueprint for the group. The written proposal can also be used and modified for future groups that are planned.

The written proposal includes: a needs assessment, including background from the literature, qualifications and experience of the group worker or coworkers, the group's purpose and objectives, recruitment strategies, group structure and logistics, a description of the group sessions and activities, an evaluation plan, a budget and budget narrative, and an implementation timeline. The timeline may be in the form of a table and may include items such as: hiring of group workers, planning of the group, timing of recruitment, evaluation benchmarks, and final reports about the project.

Exercise 6.9: Written Group Proposal

Create an outline of what you would like to put in a written group proposal. Discuss your outline with a peer and obtain feedback.

CHAPTER SUMMARY

This chapter covered a rationale for group planning, reasons for planning neglect, and ten keys for successful planning of personal intervention or task groups. It emphasized the importance of planning for diversity in groups in order to achieve greater success in accomplishing the group's purpose and goals. The ten keys include: reviewing the literature and obtaining data demonstrating the group's potential; creating a transparent purpose; planning with a coworker, if applicable; organizing a structure for the group; establishing logistics such as location, time, and accommodations; recruiting and engaging diverse, appropriate members for task and intervention groups; researching content, theories, evidence-based practices, and relevant activities; creating an evaluation plan; completing a budget and budget narrative; and producing a written group proposal using the group planning checklist (appendix B).

FURTHER READING

Alcoholics Anonymous. *Alcoholics Anonymous* (4th ed.). New York, NY: A. A. World Services, 2001.

Anderson, J. *Social Work with Groups: A Process Model.* White Plains, NY: Longman, 1997.

Basso, R., Pelech, W., and Wickham, E. "Harnessing the Promise of Diversity in Group Work Practice." In *Social Group Work: We Are All in the Same Boat: Proceedings of the International Association of Social Work with Groups, Long Beach, California*, edited by C. D. Lee. London, England: Whiting and Birch, 2014.

Gitterman, A. "Group Formation." In *Mutual Aid Groups, Vulnerable and Resilient Populations, and the Life Cycle* (3rd ed.), edited by A. Gitterman, and L. Shulman. New York, NY: Columbia University Press, 2005.

Kurland, R. "Planning: The Neglected Component of Group Development." *Social Work with Groups* 28, no. 3/4 (2008): 9–16.

LaFromboise, T. D., Coleman, H. L. K., and Hernandez, A. *Professional Psychology Research and Practice* 22, no. 380 (1991), doi: 10.1037/0735-7028.22.5.380.

Lang, N. C. *Group Work Practice to Advance Social Competence*. New York, NY: Columbia University Press, 2010.

Middleman, R. *The Non-verbal in Working with Groups: The Use of Activities in Teaching, Counseling and Therapy*. Hebron, CT: Practitioners Press, 1982.

Reid, K. E. *Social Work Practice with Groups: A Clinical Perspective*. Pacific Grove, CA: Brooks/Cole, 1991.

CHAPTER 7

ETHICS AND STANDARDS

LEARNING OBJECTIVES

At the end of this chapter you will be able to:

- Define ethics and provide examples of how you will apply ethical behavior to your practice of social work with groups.
- Identify standards from the International Association of Social Work with Groups (IASWG).
- Analyze ethical issues and group work standards in social work with groups.
- Apply critical thinking skills when analyzing ethical dilemmas.
- Contrast how the ethic of confidentiality differs in individual work with a consumer and work with members in a personal intervention or a task group.

Vignette: The Survivors' Group

After working at the local community hospital, a new social worker encounters several patients from the oncology unit inquiring about support groups. This inspires her to begin a support group for women cancer survivors. Because she lives close to the hospital and feels involved in this community, she opens her home to the group that meets every Wednesday night from 7:00 to 8:30. It will be an open group and members are welcomed from all stages of recovery. What are ethical dilemmas the group worker may encounter?

This chapter focuses on ethics and standards that apply to social work practice with groups. *The National Association of Social Workers (NASW) Code of Ethics*, which is used to guide ethical social work practice in the United States, advises: "Professional ethics are at the core of social work" (NASW, 2008, p. 2). This implies that social workers who are not steeped in the ethics of their profession are deficient in their practice and may harm consumers. The Standards of the International Association of Social Work with Groups establishes guidelines for quality social work practice with groups (IASWG, 2010). These guidelines, which will be referred to in this chapter as "the standards," were created and reviewed by experts in social group work (Abels, 2012) from several different countries. According to the standards, group workers, in addition to utilizing the IASWG standards, should use the code of ethics of the country in which they are practicing social work or group work, as there will be cultural nuances. This chapter will define ethics and standards, review the NASW Social Work Code of Ethics, the Canadian Code of Ethics, the international code of social work ethics, and the IASWG standards. It will also present ethical dilemmas for further exploration and consideration of ethics in practice.

DEFINITIONS OF ETHICS/VALUES AND STANDARDS

The Social Work Dictionary defines ethics as "a system of moral principles and perceptions about right versus wrong and the resulting philosophy of conduct that is practiced by an individual, group, profession, or culture" (Barker, 2003, p. 159). The dictionary further defines a code of ethics as "an explicit statement of the values, principles, and rules of a profession, regulating the conduct of its members" (Barker, 2003, p. 84).

NASW has established and continues to update the ethics or values to which social workers in the United States are expected to adhere (NASW, 2008). For example, one of the ethics for social workers is integrity, which means social workers are required to be honest with consumers and act responsibly when making commitments to them.

A standard is: "a level of quality, achievement, etc. that is considered acceptable or desirable" (Merriamwebster.com). IASWG created a set of standards in 1996 that were revised in 2006 and 2010 (IASWG, 2010; Abels, 2012; Macgowan, 2012; Topor, Grosso, Burt, & Falcon, 2013). These principles are guidelines for social work intervention, task, community, or advocacy groups. One of the core standards is that group workers encourage mutual aid among the members in the group. There is overlap in the tenets set forth in the NASW Code of Ethics and the IASWG standards, and many are complementary; yet, there are differences because the standards are entirely focused on social work practice in groups whereas the NASW code applies to social worker practitioners in their work with systems of all sizes (i.e. individuals, families, groups, communities, and organizations).

NASW CODE OF ETHICS AND SOCIAL WORK ETHICS OF OTHER COUNTRIES

There are many different ethics or values set forth in the *NASW Code of Ethics* (NASW, 2008), which is seventeen pages in length. Social workers and students of social work in the United States need to thoroughly study the *NASW Code of Ethics* in order to ensure ethical behavior in their work and internships. The next sections review many of these ethics with examples of how these values apply to inclusive social work with groups. The core values in the *NASW Code of Ethics* are: service, social justice, dignity and worth of the person, importance of human relationships, integrity, and competence (NASW, 2008). The NASW ethics as well as the Code of Ethics of the Canadian Association of Social Workers and the International Federation of Social Workers Ethical Principles are also discussed below. The ethics of these three documents are similar.

Service

Service means to help people in need and elevate service to others above self-interest (NASW, 2008). Examples of this ethic have occurred when there are natural and man-made catastrophic events, and social workers facilitate support groups, often with little or no remuneration. Many groups were formed by social service agencies after the bombing of the World Trade Center on September 11, 2001 (Malekoff, 2004; Cohen, Phillips, and Hanson, 2009). Social workers facilitated many emergency groups for youth, adults, and older adults in the New York City area, as people of all ages were traumatized and suffered losses. These types of service support groups also transpired in Japan in 2011 after the earthquake and tsunami. Group workers facilitated activity groups with people of all ages to distract them and help them move forward with their lives after suffering tremendous losses (Nagai, 2012).

The Canadian Association of Social Workers (CASW) also has a code of ethics. Similar to the NASW code of ethics, service to humanity is one of its six core values. This code states the social worker is to put personal interest or gain aside when serving others (Canadian Association of Social Workers, 2005).

Social Justice

Social justice is a prominent value in social work professional ethics codes, including the Canadian Code of Ethics, NASW's Code of Ethics, International Federation of Social Workers' (IFSW) *Statement of Ethical Principles*, and the IASWG standards (CASW, 2005; NASW, 2008; IASWG, 2010; IFSW, 2012). Social workers are mandated to assist in the empowerment of vulnerable and oppressed individuals and groups of people. They are to increase understanding of social and ethnic diversity in their practice and promote "access to needed information, services and resources, equality of opportunity, and meaningful opportunity for decision making for all people" (NASW, 2008, p. 3). The tradition of social group work is grounded in democracy (Northen & Kurland, 2001; Northen, 2004); therefore, group workers are to include all members of the group as equal participants and decision makers. In addition, according to Breton (2004), all groups are required to have a social justice component where even members who are vulnerable themselves can assist others within the group and/or in a community project related to the purpose of the group. The IASWG standards make it clear that if a member of the group is acting in a prejudicial or discriminatory way, the group worker or another member is to confront this behavior (IASWG, 2010).

Exercise 7.1: Vignette: A New Group Member

In a small group, read and discuss the vignette below. In what ways does the value of social justice apply to this scenario? How could you address the situation in a way that adheres to this value?

You are a group worker for an open-ended group in a day treatment hospital setting. The group has the aim of providing experiences that will prepare clients for community life. You are a member of a treatment team that has focused much effort on preparing a client named Jane to enter the group. However, when you approach the group to inform them that Jane will be joining the group, you learn that the group adamantly opposes her entry, despite your strenuous efforts, and votes not to accept her because she has been consistently disruptive in other activities. No other potential member has been opposed in this way before.

As noted earlier, the value of social justice requires group workers to advocate for others and to confront group members when they are acting in a prejudicial or discriminatory way. There are several ways that the dilemma posited in the vignette in exercise 7.1 could be addressed, and the following are some suggestions. It may be useful for the worker to identify and validate the underlying emotions and fears that are involved in the group's strong opposition. Are members concerned that her previous behavior may disrupt the group dynamics or the work of the group, among other things? By exploring these further, the worker can also challenge members to explore whether they are willing to make compromises or come up with alternate solutions, such as allowing Jane to join the group if a plan (i.e., contracting of behavior expectations and consequences) is set in place to address their concerns.

Can you think of other ways social justice can be incorporated into inclusive group work? Examples are asking members to explain cultural traditions to each other to increase understanding of diverse values and solutions, implementing an advocacy group to eradicate environmental hazards in a neighborhood, facilitating a support group for undocumented immigrant youth who do not have access to higher education, and offering a friendship group for older adults in their native language. Applying this value to the vignette at the beginning of this chapter, one might question whether offering the group only to women with cancer is implementing the value of social justice.

Dignity and Worth of the Person

The Canadian Code of Ethics, the IASWG standards, the IFSW Statement of Ethical Principles, and the NASW Code of Ethics are completely congruent on the ethics of respecting the dignity and worth of each person and encouraging a socially just society. Value 1 in the Canadian Code of Ethics is "respect for the inherent dignity and worth of persons" (CASW, 2005, p. 4). The NASW Code of Ethics requires social workers and group workers to treat each person with respect, being mindful of individual differences and cultural and ethnic diversity (NASW, 2008). The International Federation of Social Workers (IFSW) states: "Social work is based on respect for the inherent worth and dignity of all people and the rights that follow from this" (p. 2). The International Association of Social Work and Groups (IASWG) lists two core group work values: respect for persons and their autonomy and social justice.

Group workers are to promote members' socially responsible self-determination, formulate goals in partnership with them, and empower them. In addition, social workers are to enhance consumers' capacity and opportunity to change and to address their own needs (NASW, 2008). Group workers are to be cognizant of individual needs in the group and help members form goals to increase members' competence within the scope of the group's purpose. In a task group or intervention group, it is critical for the group worker to treat each member with respect and dignity and to establish, as well as reinforce, this group rule for all members to adhere to from the start of the group

Regarding the value of respect for all individuals, group workers need to be mindful of the group's agency and/or community contexts and support socially responsible self-determination among members. For example, if a member advises that she wants to hurt someone outside of the group, the group worker must report this type of threat to the proper authority in the community. Another way group workers demonstrate this value of giving respect is to identify and encourage indigenous leaders in the group to assist in furthering the group's work. The standards state that in the middle stage of the group, members are to feel empowered by the group worker, which relates to this value (IASWG, 2010).

Exercise 7.2: Vignette: Keeping Safety

In a small group, read and discuss the vignette below. In what ways does the value of dignity and worth of a person apply to this scenario? How could you address the situation in a way that adheres to this value and promotes the safety of George and his ex-wife?

You are the worker for an outpatient group for adults coping with depression. George, a moderately depressed group member, shares how angry he is with his ex-wife, whom he blames for his depression, and discloses that he intends to physically harm her.

As noted earlier, adherence to the value of dignity and worth of the person includes reporting a threat of harm to self or others to the proper authority in the community to ensure the safety of the threatened individual. In maintaining this value, it is important that the worker, when appropriate, refer the individual to additional service and supports so that any concerns can be addressed.

Importance of Human Relationships

"Social workers understand that relationships between and among people are an important vehicle for change" (NASW, 2008, p. 4). Social workers are to strengthen relationships in order "to promote, restore, maintain, and enhance the well-being of individuals, families, social groups, organizations, and communities" (NASW, 2008, p. 4). As previously noted, the NASW Code of Ethics is concerned with how social workers work with systems of all sizes whereas group workers concern themselves primarily with groups.

One of the main reasons for using a group to assist a consumer is to increase the number of people supporting the change. In individual work with a social worker, the consumer and the worker may be the only ones involved with the change process. The relationship value has a strong fit with group work because a group worker's promotion of mutual aid among members is the prominent group work standard, and is the one accredited with promoting positive change in behaviors and movement toward reaching goals (Steinberg, 2004; Gitterman &

Shulman, 2005; IASWG, 2010). Mutual aid cannot be accomplished without the development of good relationships among group members. Another example of the relationship ethic in social work with groups is when the group worker engages consumers of services as partners in accomplishing desired changes (NASW, 2008; IASWG, 2010). When working in groups, social workers enlist member input at every stage of the group. For example, in the beginning stage of a mandated group for perpetrators of interpersonal violence, the group worker will ask members the reasons they might not want to be a part of the group in order to deal with negative feelings. This discussion may free members to move forward. In the middle stage of groups, the members are involved in making decisions concerning the group's progress. For example, in a task group, members might suggest different strategies to reach the group's goals. In the ending stage, the group worker may help members by asking them about other supportive relationships they will seek outside of the group.

Integrity

"Social workers act honestly and responsibly and promote ethical practices on the part of the organization of which they are affiliated" (NASW, 2008, p. 4). The Canadian Code of Ethics states, "Social workers maintain a high level of professional conduct by acting honestly and responsibly. . . ." (CASW, 2005, p. 6). Under the principle of professional conduct, IFSW (2012) states, "Social workers should act with integrity. This includes not abusing the relationship of trust with the people using their services, recognizing the boundaries between personal and professional life, and not abusing their position for personal benefit or gain" (p. 4). One way this ethic has application in group work is when the group worker is transparent about the purpose of the group with participants. It would also have application when working with mandatory members. For example, if there are consequences to probationers if they do not attend the group or participate, then they need to be advised of this at the beginning of the group. In every aspect of the group, the group worker is expected to act responsibly and with integrity. For example, if a group worker is leaving the agency prior to ending the group, the group worker must advise the members and give them adequate time to process the group worker's departure and the facilitation of the group by someone else. Furthermore, if reportable abuse (i.e. elder or child) is disclosed, it is important that the worker act with integrity when dealing with this, as the members may need to review the limits to confidentiality and process how any resulting consequences to the member from the mandated reporting of this disclosure affects group members' feelings of safety and trust in the group.

Practice Integration

What are examples of integrity (honesty and responsibility) issues that you might encounter in facilitating a group? What could be potential consequences of a worker not having integrity in group work practice?

Competence

The NASW Code of Ethics (NASW, 2008) and the Canadian Code of Ethics (CASW, 2005) state that social workers need to be competent to do their work, seeking out updated professional resources and evidence-based practices when available. In addition, social workers are required to contribute to the knowledge base of the profession. The IFSW's *Principles of Professional Conduct* states: "Social workers are expected to develop and maintain the required skills and competence to do their job" (IFSW, 2012, p. 4). This social work ethic requires that group workers be trained to work with at-risk populations in groups, and that they keep abreast of current research and evidence-based practices. Maintaining professional competence is also an IASWG standard with the same mandates as in the aforementioned codes of ethics. The codes of ethics and the standards imply that social work students and interns should be receiving theoretical and practice training about social work with groups and be supervised by experienced group workers. Student interns are expected to advise the group members that they are students of group work, and that their work is being supervised.

Codes of Ethics (CASW, 2005; NASW, 2008) and the IASWG standards (IASWG, 2010) require social workers to contribute to the knowledge base of the profession; therefore, group workers are expected to evaluate what theories and activities are working in their groups and which are not and to disseminate these findings in professional venues (i.e. conferences and refereed journals). In this way, the practice of social group work is enhanced. Other aspects of professional competence are: informing human subjects of research and maintaining confidentiality. How will you maintain competence as a professional group worker?

Exercise 7.3: Vignette: To Lead or Not to Lead?

In a small group, read and discuss the vignette below. In what ways does the value of competence apply to this scenario? How could you address the situation in a way that adheres to this value?

Felicity is a second year undergraduate social work intern at an inpatient mental health hospital. Felicity was tasked with cofacilitating a support group with her agency's licensed clinical social worker (LCSW) as part of her internship project.

A day before the group was scheduled to start, the LCSW suddenly left her job, leaving Felicity to facilitate the group on her own. Felicity has recently started her group work class and she does not feel she has the knowledge and skills necessary to lead a group. Felicity speaks to her internship supervisor about her concerns and is told that the start of the group can be delayed for one week so that she can prepare but due to a shortage of staff, she is still required to facilitate the group with minimal to no supervision.

As held in the value of competence, social workers (including social work students) have a professional and ethical responsibility to practice within their scope, skills, and abilities. As a student, it is possible you may find yourself in a similar situation as Felicity in the vignette in exercise 7.3. Felicity's response to speak to her internship supervisor was appropriate and promoted the value of competence. As this conversation did not result in a solution that would be ultimately beneficial to the consumers, it is important that Felicity take other steps to prevent any harm to her consumers. As a student, this may mean that you consult with your school internship liaisons so that the best possible solution can be reached.

Additional Social Work Ethics or Values

There are many other ethics in the three codes of ethics that were not discussed thus far in this chapter. These include: guarding against conflicts of interests, not exploiting consumers, charging reasonable rates, carefully protecting human subjects in practice, evaluation, and research, and offering resources to consumers upon termination. There is no substitute for reading the *CASW Code of Ethics*, the *IFSW Statement of Ethical Principles*, and the *NASW Code of Ethics* yourself, as these will ground you in professional social work ethics. Social group workers are expected to follow the code of ethics within the country in which they are practicing social work, as well as the IASWG standards, which will be discussed in the remainder of the chapter.

Exercise 7.4: Applying Ethics

Meet in a group of four group work peers and make a list of the values from the CASW Code of Ethics, the IFSW Code of Ethical Principles, and/or the NASW Code of Ethics that you will apply when facilitating social work groups. For each value that you list, give an example from a group you have experienced or plan to experience.

THE IASWG STANDARDS

Brief History of the Standards

Although scholars wrote about group work standards in the social work profession during the twentieth century, it was not until 1999 that a small book, *Standards of Social Work with Groups*, was published. Scholars and practitioners affiliated with IASWG created the standards, which consisted of IASWG's position on the values, knowledge, and skills required of competent group workers (Cohen, Macgowan, Garvin, & Muskat, 2013; IASWG, 2010). The IASWG professional organization's membership mostly consists of social work academics and practitioners (including students), but IASWG prides itself on inclusivity and diversity and welcomes group work professionals from other disciplines as members. Thus, the standards could be applied to groups facilitated by other professionals (i.e. psychologists, masters in counseling, nurses, teachers, psychiatrists, art therapists, etc.). The standards were revised in 2005 and copyedited in 2010 (Cohen et al., 2013). Although the standards can be obtained at no charge on the IASWG.org website, it is frequently not an integral part of social work academic group work courses, and the existence of this short book of group work standards is not widely used by group workers (MacGowan, 2012). MacGowan (2012), a social work group scholar, recommends that the IASWG standards be taught to social workers and used when they are involved in groups. The eighteen-page document created and published by IASWG is based on group theory from the social sciences, the codes of ethics for social work in diverse countries, the historical roots of social group work (which largely derive from the settlement, recreation, and education movements of the early twentieth century), principles of democracy, and current practice and research (Northen and Kurland, 2001; Northen, 2004; IASWG, 2010).

Core Values

As mentioned previously, the two core values in the IASWG standards are: (1) respect for persons and their autonomy, and (2) the creation of a socially just society. The standards advise the worker to compose the group of members with differences and not to exclude people based on their diverse characteristics. The standards place a high value on diversity of all kinds in groups (i.e., culture, ethnicity, gender, sexual orientation, physical and mental abilities, and age) (IASWG, 2010), which supports inclusive group work practice.

Another standard states that members or legal guardians should give informed consent for joining the group. This includes contracting regarding the group's purpose and expectations. Confidentiality and its limits (harm to self or others, disclosures of abuse, subpoena by the courts, etc.) is a value as stated in other social work codes of ethics. A discussion of the rule of confidentiality should include information regarding the lack of control a group worker has over members' maintenance of confidentiality. Also, safeguarding social work records has additional nuances when applied to group work. Group work records should not identify other members in individual progress notes, and a group worker must take care to not identify individual members by name in a group record. Technology is still a largely undocumented area in the social work ethical codes and in the standards, but both advise social workers to keep abreast of research and best practices in working with technology mediated interventions. Many professional groups are conducted online and by telephone, and in those cases social workers and group workers must consider issues of privacy and confidentiality as well as other ethics and standards.

Exercise 7.5: Vignette: A Broken Promise

In a small group, read and discuss the vignette below. How does this vignette present the challenges of maintaining confidentiality in a group setting? In what ways could this incident affect the group? How could you address the situation in a way that addresses these challenges and allows the group to move forward in its work?

You are the worker in a men's violence prevention group. One member named Ted, who was separated from his partner but who had expressed a desire to reconcile his relationship, disclosed several weeks ago that he had gotten drunk and had an affair. Another group member, Fred, disclosed this affair to his partner, who was a close friend of Ted's ex-partner. Fred's partner told Ted's partner and now Ted's partner has filed for divorce.

As noted earlier, confidentiality in the group setting requires other considerations that may not be present in one-on-one counseling. Breaches of confidentiality, such as the one presented in the vignette in exercise 7.5, can present a critical point in the group and thus must be dealt with in the group setting as soon as possible. It is important for the group worker to encourage members to share and explore their thoughts, emotions, and concerns regarding the breach of confidentiality and its implications on the group process. The group worker should also review confidentiality and its limitations and reaffirm the group rules and contracts of expected behavior. Through this discussion, the group worker attempts to reaffirm a safe and trusting environment. When members are ready, the group worker should engage them in a discussion of a plan to move forward. This may include the establishment of new group norms or rules.

Knowledge of Individual and Group Behaviors

One different aspect of the IASWG standards in comparison to the aforementioned codes of social work ethics is that it recognizes the importance of knowledge of individual behavior within the group as well as knowledge of group behavior. Regarding individual behavior, the group worker is to have "knowledge of individuals within their familial, social, political and cultural context that influence members' social identities, interactional styles, concerns, opportunities, and attainment of their potential" (IASWG, 2010). The group worker must understand members' strengths, capacities for change and giving help to others, and risks and protective factors, including an appreciation of the diverse backgrounds they bring to the group.

The expected knowledge of behaviors within groups includes: a group's unique culture, an appreciation for the power of mutual aid, and the importance of member and group empowerment. The worker must understand that the group will have group and individual goals and that achievement of these goals will depend on the stage of group development. The group worker should be able to recognize the different stages of a group and use skills that are appropriate for the different stages. In addition, the group worker must have knowledge of group dynamics, which include: communication, integration factors such as norms and roles, expressions of affect, and how conflict can be mediated. Knowledge about the agency where the group is housed, the type of group, and the group's purpose must also be obtained by the group worker.

Responsibilities of the Group Worker

The IASWG standards specifically lay out the major responsibilities of the group worker. These responsibilities include: encouraging individual and group autonomy, helping the group and members arrive at purpose and goals, and employing flexibility, creativity, and sensitivity in group facilitation and assessments (IASWG, 2010). The group worker is responsible for assessing the group with member input and using reliable and valid evaluation measures to denote the group's progress. The group worker is to follow ethical codes, reflect on practice, and seek consultation and supervision (IASWG, 2010).

Knowledge and Skills Specific to Different Group Stages

The IASWG standards list and explicate the knowledge and skills that are utilized by group workers in different stages of groups (i.e., pregroup/planning, beginning, middle, and ending stages). The knowledge and skills are fully elaborated on in the other chapters in this book that pertain to the aforementioned group stages or to group worker leadership skills. Just as you are strongly encouraged to review original social work ethical codes, it is highly recommended that you read and review the IASWG standards yourself.

CHAPTER SUMMARY

This chapter covered three different social work codes of ethics and described how these values apply to social workers practicing in groups. In addition, it reviewed the IASWG standards. It is very important that you read the code of ethics for the country in which you practice social work as well as the IASWG standards. Grounding yourself by reading these documents will prepare you for competent and ethical inclusive group work practice.

CHAPTER 8

GROUP DEVELOPMENT AND ANALYSIS

LEARNING OBJECTIVES

At the end of this chapter you will be able to:

- Explain how groups develop over time.
- Identify and describe various models of group development.
- Understand the role of diversity in promoting group development.
- Employ various techniques and criteria to assess the functioning and development of a group.
- Use assessment information to formulate interventions aimed at improving the functioning of your group.

GROUP DEVELOPMENT

Evident in early group work literature was an appreciation of how a group develops over time and is akin to a living organism. A significant role of the worker is to support the process of group development. Thus, one of the most important theoretical frameworks for any group worker is an understanding of how groups develop over time. This enables group workers to anticipate the feelings and behaviors of group members at different points in the group, and this perspective can enhance response.

Often the idea of designing a group is conceived by social workers in an agency, upon the realization that the needs of individual consumers may be better served in a group rather than on an individual basis. After the group is conceived and sanctioned by the agency, the planning or pregroup phase begins. During this phase, all of the necessary planning and recruitment of group members occurs. After the pregroup phase comes the arrival of group members for the first meeting. This first meeting is when the potential of a group is born. As time passes and relationships are formed, members may have the desire to deepen connections and/or challenge limits. These changes in the dynamic of the group mark the transition from the beginning phase to the middle phase. In the middle phase, the group reaches its maturity and becomes a fully functional entity. This maturity is a product of the learning that has occurred by group members by working through the earlier phases. During this phase, the group relies less on the group worker and more on itself. Finally, the group comes to an end as the group's purpose and goals are completed. Endings are not only an event, but also a process that becomes more prominent in the group as members become aware of termination prior to the last meeting.

In table 8.1, you will find some of the most widely known models of group development. The first model, by Tuckman and Jensen (1977), is drawn from the field of social psychology. The popularity of this model may be because it captures the feelings associated with each phase of group development. Each group needs to move from an assemblage of persons or collectivity to something more than the sum of its parts. Thus, in the model, the phases of storming and norming are interrelated.

Storming refers to the onset of conflict over roles, power, and authority in the group. Challenges to the worker's authority and ground rules are common at this point. In negotiating and clarifying the rules and roles in the group, norms are created for the group (the process of norming). It is important to note that these norms can act to support or undermine the therapeutic goals and tasks of the group. After the group has acquired the skills and awareness to work through obstacles, and has sorted out how members will work together, it moves into a more mature (and its most productive) stage, performing. During this stage, the group works to achieve its purpose and accomplish the intended tasks of the group. Finally, in the

Table 8.1 Models of Group Development

Model	Tuckman & Jensen	MacKenzie	Corey & Corey	Garland, Jones & Kolodny	Schiller
Beginning	Forming	Engagement	Forming	Preaffiliation	Preaffiliation
	Storming	Differentiation	Initial Stage	Power and Control	Establishing a Relational Base
	Norming	Individuation	Transition		Mutuality and Interpersonal Empathy
Middle	Performing	Intimacy	Working	Intimacy	Challenge and Change
		Mutuality		Differentiation	
Ending	Adjourning	Termination	Ending	Separation	Separation

adjourning stage, the group has achieved its goals and members terminate their experience. This stage is often associated with mourning and loss because the feelings that one associates with the loss of a loved one are also associated with the adjourning phase. Although Tuckman's model is informative in relation to understanding how groups develop in general, the model was not created from the observation of therapeutic groups (Tuckman, 1963).

Next, there is MacKenzie's (1990) model of group development. Mackenzie's model is a six-stage model that was derived from observation of short-term psychotherapy groups. Although his model is similar to others, he added an additional stage termed individuation. Individuation reflects a transition from the ambivalence and conflict associated with storming, to increasing openness, to individual exploration (interpersonally and intrapsychically).

The next model, which comes from Gerald and Marianne Corey (Corey, Corey, & Corey, 2013) and the field of counseling psychology, outlined an intervention oriented, five-stage model that parallels that of Tuckman and the other five-stage models.

The next two models are variations of what is now referred to as the Boston model (Garland, Jones, & Kolodny, 1965). The Boston model is a model empirically formulated through direct observation of groups. It is also the most prominent group development model in social work with groups. The five-stage Boston model is similar to the Tuckman model with one notable difference; the important stage of differentiation is added to the middle phase. Although much of the emphasis in the early phases is devoted to focusing on building relationships and affirming commonalities, in differentiation, the group task is for members to be free to disagree or to offer different opinions. It is here that the group as an agent of change reaches its potential, as members offer different perspectives and observations in the spirit of mutual aid.

Last, there is the seminal work of Linda Yael Schiller (2007), whose work with women's groups led her to question whether the other models were a good fit for this population. Schiller noted that the conflictual and challenging phases of other models did not emerge until much later in many of her women's groups. This was because a relational base needed to first be established before conflict could emerge. Similar to the Boston model differentiation phase, Schiller's model acknowledges that challenge and change may be part of a member's differentiating from previous socialization and expectations concerning what is acceptable behavior for women in social settings. In a way, Schiller's model supports and enhances the Boston model.

The next section will more fully examine the Boston model and the role that diversity plays in promoting group development and mutual aid.

DIVERSITY AND GROUP DEVELOPMENT

A full appreciation of the value of diversity in group work can be obtained only through an understanding of how diversity plays out over the life of a group. As with all other models, the Boston model is based upon a number of implicit and explicit assumptions about how groups change and develop over time. As noted by Garland, Jones, and Kolodny (1965), the model assumes that closeness is a central theme or ingredient in group development. There are also several other implicit assumptions unstated by the authors of the model. First, as noted above, the model assumes that group members must learn to be close before they can accept their mutual differences. In this way, exploration and acceptance of diversity is often delayed until the later stages of the group, where intimacy exists and members are more willing to take risks and engage in such discussions. This view has also been accepted by other traditional group work theorists (Trecker, 1972; Henry, 1992; Northen & Kurland, 2001). However, it is important to note that diversity is also a central theme throughout group development, and an instillation of diversity as a therapeutic factor earlier in an intervention group enables members to benefit from their differences throughout the life of the group. Contrary to being a threat to group cohesion, diversity in its broader sense can form the basis for individual and group change. Although agreeing that full appreciation of the therapeutic value of diversity may take some time in group, this book's authors believe that the benefits of diversity transcend all group stages and indeed play a pivotal role in effecting the individual change and group transition between stages.

Another implicit assumption of the Boston model is that group development begins at the first group meeting. Although there is some validity to this view, there has been a long-standing appreciation that group development begins with a planning or pregroup phase (Hartford, 1971). Pregroup planning and, in particular, preparation of members for group participation must also be recognized as the beginning of group development. For this reason, this discussion of diversity over the stages of group development begins with pregroup preparation.

Pregroup

In the past, group workers in intervention groups have utilized prescreening of members in order to maximize the commonalities and homogeneity among prospective group members. This was based upon an assumption that greater commonalities would result in a more successful group. On the other hand, in a task group, selection of group members is based upon choosing potential members who offer diverse skills and knowledge necessary to enable the group to successfully complete its tasks. Consequently, it is important to question the need, in intervention groups, for an exclusive focus on creating commonalities through group composition beyond an assessment of the extent to which the group is likely to meet a prospective member's needs. Such a preoccupation fails to recognize the contribution that diversity could make to group development. Of more concern is the risk that an overemphasis on homogeneity in intervention group composition may have in the past served to exclude diverse members from service provision. Moreover, if diversity is reframed as a beneficial therapeutic factor, an exclusive focus on the commonalities of prospective members may be seen as counter therapeutic and potentially destructive to the capacity of the group to facilitate change. In real terms, it is difficult, if not impossible to select or create a truly homogeneous group; even the most homogeneous groups contain a fair amount of diversity (Caplan & Thomas, 2004a). Thus, diversity is both desirable and unavoidable in group membership.

The pregroup assessment by workers and potential group members may be viewed as a shared activity and an invitation for change. Pregroup assessment provides an opportunity for the worker and prospective members to explore the purpose, possible goals, and activities of the group. The effectiveness of the pregroup stage will in large part determine whether the necessary conditions of psychological safety are met. In an inclusive approach, the worker must be aware of the value and benefits of diversity. He or she must know how diversity will be affirmed and used in the group process. In an inclusive approach, workers would shift their assessment to include what new perspectives and experiences each prospective member might bring to the group. Further, each member would be viewed as an expert in their understanding of their circumstances. Adopting a diversity focus would involve helping prospective group members to understand and deal with the many faces of diversity that each member is likely to bring to the group. Potential members may be afraid of the unknown or have participated in previous negative group experiences, where it may have been unsafe to express diversity. Thus, of particular salience to an inclusive assessment would be to explore each prospective member's experiences with diversity in previous groups. The worker needs to assess how members are likely to respond to diversity in the group.

As noted, in a task group, the focus of selection is shifted from the needs of individual members to the needs of the group. When considering whom to recruit for group membership, one must keep in mind the needs and characteristics (e.g., cultural, geographical, socioeconomic, etc.) of the community, as well as the organizational mission, needs, and goals. From these elements emerges a list of attributes and competencies that can inform selection of task group members. For example, in recruiting members for an agency board, one should consider the demographic characteristics of the community and the agency consumers. Next, the board should consider what general attributes (e.g., commitment, leadership, integrity, expertise, critical thinking, and communication) it requires for all board members and what specific competencies it needs to fulfil its responsibilities (e.g., financial management, evaluation, legal consultation, governance, community outreach, etc.). Diversity plays an important role here, not only to ensure a variety of competencies but also so that the board includes those who are able to engage with and understand the needs of the diverse populations in the community.

Beginnings

The practitioner's goal in the beginning phase is to build in safety for member participation. All models acknowledge that members commonly experience some uncertainty and ambivalence towards initial involvement in groups. Most human beings experience apprehension and fear when they are expected to discuss their problems and concerns with others, particularly strangers. Members may also fear the uncertainty of whether they will be able to work together successfully to achieve the group's purpose, particularly in task focused groups. Uncertainty and previous negative group experiences are likely to further heighten the anxiety of members and, in some cases, such fears will become obstacles to enabling members to test the waters and reduce anxiety associated with taking risks.

Effective pregroup preparation in a task or intervention group allows for exploration of prospective member concerns. Coupled with a firm commitment to respecting diversity, this can reduce the anxiety often associated with beginnings in a new group. At this point, an inclusive approach encourages the worker to reaffirm his or her understanding of the value and benefits of diversity for the group by conveying to each member that he or she has a unique and indispensable contribution to make to the group. Each member's previous experiences and perspectives about the group experience are to be respected and valued as important sources of information. Negative experiences may also serve as important issues that can be utilized to promote safety within the group. Thus, the worker's effectiveness may depend on the ability to help the group to accept diversity, develop a climate of safety and trust so that members are not penalized for taking risks, and, at the same time, promote interaction and honest sharing among all members of the group.

Due to the natural commonality brought by members sharing in relation to a shared purpose, during the beginning phase the worker needs to promote norms that acknowledge the value of different perspectives and experiences. In this way, group members will begin to gain a sense that they are not alone in their experience and that they will not be rejected for expressing different ideas and perspectives. Through promotion of norms that highlight respect for each member's humanity and diversity, group members are also encouraged to listen to each other. In this way, diversity can and should be used to help the group become cohesive, thus ensuring that the worker and members can progress towards achieving the group goals through the human need for approval, understanding, and fulfillment. Group members can also be helped to recognize that their goals will be similar to others but how they approach them will be different. Ultimately, as important as the instillation of hope is the instillation of an appreciation of diversity in the group.

A strengths perspective is also helpful, particularly in an intervention group, in enabling the worker to acknowledge that each member is an expert in their life and their problems. In keeping with the member's need to test out the group, the worker may also note that group members should offer their perspectives to others tentatively for consideration. Through normalizing member affect, actively promoting the value of diversity, encouraging tentative participation, and reframing inadequacy into competence, it is likely that member anxiety will be reduced, allowing members to take manageable risks in the group. Then, if members experience acceptance, they will take measured steps towards change through acceptance of their differences and those of others. As a result, this inclusive process will foster therapeutic norms of acceptance and mutual aid.

A number of theorists (such as Garland et al., 1965; Shulman, 2015) observe that, as the group moves on, members will demonstrate different responses to authority themes. In an inclusive approach, these authority themes, like early ambivalence, will be greatly diminished. Respect for diversity in the group will reduce the need for members to dominate the discussion or withdraw from involvement. Where diversity is valued, there will be less need for members to question the abilities of the group worker. However, where such themes arise, how the worker responds to the diverse concerns expressed will serve to support or suppress the expression of differences in the group.

Later in this stage, the interactions in the group shift from polite conversation to expression of differences among group members. Although earlier in the group the worker promotes a belief in the values of diversity and mutual aid and establishes a contract relating to acceptance of diversity in the group, it is at this point where group members may test out the contract and the group through expression of diverse opinions, core beliefs, and attitudes. Here, members check the responses and reactions of the group worker and other members to see if their different thoughts, emotions, and behaviors are understood, accepted, or rejected. The focus on diversity goes beyond simply identifying options but also affects how members experience each other, what each member might say in group, and how each member could be helpful to another.

There are several common phenomena that have been described in groups where diversity is not reinforced. In some cases, certain stories and voices may be given greater authority, while others may be devalued, dismissed, or silenced. This diversity negating process can degenerate into scapegoating. Scapegoating behavior occurs in groups where some differences are found to be unacceptable by a majority of group members. Members who appear to be different in some way (e.g., demographic characteristics; lifestyle; power differentials; and expression of unpopular views, experiences, feelings, or ways of relating) may be scapegoated by the group. Where the expression of such behavior (e.g., stereotyping, scapegoating, etc.) serves to undermine group diversity norms, the worker needs to intervene to reinforce group norms affirming acceptance of diversity and self-exploration.

As Toseland and Rivas (2011) have observed, many developmental models identify a conflictual/transitional phase early in the life of a group. Kurland and Salmon (1998a) have articulated several notions that are of particular salience for this stage of group development. They note that differences need to be respected and that members need to come to terms with acceptance, even if one does not agree with another. Members can accept that others have a right to their opinion and that disagreement is not the same as personal dislike. Most important, they note that the worker must also instill a sense of confidence in the group that it will be able to eventually integrate differences to the benefit of all members (Kurland & Salmon, 1998b). Ultimately, the way in which the group resolves conflict also serves to promote or diminish the ways in which diversity is utilized in the group.

How the group and the worker respond and learn to work with aspects of diversity early in the group will profoundly shape each member's experience of acceptance as well as willingness to take further risks. In short, acceptance of diversity promotes the expression of differences and, accordingly, provides greater freedom for further member participation. This may affect member participation and retention in groups, particularly in open-ended groups, where membership may be constantly changing. Membership change has been found to affect the transition past the beginning group phase and the completion of tasks (Schopler & Galinsky, 1990).

Middles

At this point, members will have learned how to negotiate diversity arising amongst the group's membership and will have developed a clear understanding of the tasks to be accomplished and how the group will proceed with these tasks.

In an inclusive model, this accomplishment leads the group to the point where there are norms and structure affirming the value of diversity. These norms and structure provide the group with a sense of safety and trust, even though there may be some discomfort for the individual member.

Facing the difficulties of beginning and the struggles related to the earlier stages often provides the group with affective rationales for wanting to be close. The evidence of group cohesion indicates to the group worker that members can now be encouraged to deepen their level of risk taking, caring, and sharing. The concept of interdependence and the need for mutual support and responsibility should be stressed and encouraged. If the group has been able to establish sufficient cohesiveness and norms that promote the acceptance of diversity, conflicts arising during this phase may be beneficial. On the other hand, if expression of difference was not permitted earlier, cohesiveness in the group may suppress the expression of differences.

With this sense of common purpose, the content of members' presentations becomes much more personal and less censored. The diverse themes presented at this time usually revolve around relationship issues such as trust, adequacy/inadequacy, dependence/independence, feelings of low self-esteem, and the myriad of feelings, thoughts, and behaviors related to these issues. In task groups, similar issues (trust, adequacy/inadequacy, dependence/independence, etc.) are present. Several affective themes seem to arise for discussion at the same time. The group worker's task is to help members to identify the many themes presented, prioritize them, and then systematically explore the chosen themes.

Like group members, the worker may also experience a sense of comfort and closeness that arises during the middle phase of group life. He or she may feel drawn to join the group as a member and may be tempted to use the group for his or her own personal needs. In an inclusive approach, the practitioner must avoid falling into the trap of joining and potentially colluding with group members in avoiding differences and contentious issues. Although the worker will move into and out of the group as needed, she or he must continue to reach for diversity among group members. Although group members may be enjoying each other's company, the practitioner must be willing to express difference during intimacy by supporting group members in challenging the illusion of progress and making a demand for more work (Shulman, 2015).

As the group reaches maturity, members fully realize the value of diversity and the importance of each group member's unique contributions and efforts towards individual and group goals. This realization arises with each member experiencing the value that diverse perspectives and opinions have had in the problem-solving process. A major objective of task and intervention groups is to help the individuals as members of the group to acquire problem-solving skills. There is growing recognition that diverse experiences and beliefs enable group members to share different perspectives related to the problems or issues they face. Diversity is also vitally important in problem definition, where different views can help to define problems for resolution in a much more inclusive and accurate way. Often, it is through the sharing of different perspectives that highly rigid or limited problem definitions adopted by individual members begin to change. New possibilities, options, and strategies become available, and, in this way, the sharing of diverse approaches, failures, and disappointments empowers the group to develop unique systems that benefit all members of the group. As the group goes through this problem-solving sequence, members gain knowledge and understanding of a method that they can use to solve current and other problems.

In an inclusive approach, many of the characteristics that are identified as indicators of "differentiation" (Garland et al., 1965) may unfold earlier in the relational development of the group. In a sense, these characteristics become process goals that the worker continually works towards throughout the group. For example, as noted, the worker can continually help members understand and actualize the fact that they can be close and yet different. The worker can affirm that even with their separateness, they can support each other and provide realistic feedback to each other and the worker. Moreover, each of them can use their differences to find new interpretations of the problem, and by extension, new ways of resolving problems. Consequently, as time goes on in the group, the group will become better able to utilize diversity in service of individual goals.

The safety and trust developed earlier also empower members to try out new behaviors in their interpersonal relationships. Other members are quick to give honest and realistic feedback in a sensitive and caring manner. Challenge is counterbalanced by support. Interdependence is highlighted, while dependence is minimized. Clarifications are sought and are often readily given. In this way, in an intervention group, the individual's intervention goals may be achieved with group support, and the group may achieve one of its primary objectives, namely individual change through the group process. Often, during this stage, there is excitement about personal and group achievements.

Not only is each member encouraged to try new roles in the group, but members are encouraged by each other and the worker to take their insights and learning from the microcosm of the group into the macrocosm of their larger social environments. Members are encouraged to examine all aspects of their social and personal relationships and at the same time look at other relationships outside of the group. There must be support and encouragement for trying new behaviors outside of the group and seeking the group's response to these efforts after they have been tried. Such support and encouragement serve to heighten constructive criticism among members.

The capabilities of group members will influence the development of the group (Lang, 1972; Lang, 1987). For example, the maturity (e.g., children's groups) and social functioning (e.g., groups with members with severe mental illness) of group members may require that the worker remain in an active leadership role throughout the group. However, in most groups, the worker will adopt a more peripheral position at this stage. As the group tends to run itself, the worker plays a pivotal role in the transitions during this stage. In an inclusive approach, these transitions can be achieved by noticing and amplifying diversity. The worker must be prepared to challenge group members to acknowledge differences present in the group. As the interactions unfold around diversity, the worker facilitates mutual empathy among members and continues to reinforce the value of diversity and acknowledge the importance of each group member's unique contributions and efforts towards individual and group goals.

It is through the unique contributions of individuals that members gain personal insights into their own situations as well as those faced by the group. With the awareness gained, members can be challenged by each other and the practitioner to change their ways of thinking, feeling, and behaving. The practitioner also assists with the clarification and interpretation of the process as it unfolds and can expect that the discussion or activity during this stage will revolve around the themes of identity and interdependence. The worker can help members to normalize their feelings of ambivalence regarding the proposed change, to realistically evaluate the advantages and disadvantages of the change, and to take action in keeping with their intervention goals. Finally, as the group moves into and through this stage, members will begin to realize that the group is not going to last forever and will begin to express concern over its ending. These concerns herald the onset of the final stage in the group.

Endings

As the group comes to an end, diversity will arise in service of individual and group needs. During this stage, members will again display different responses as a way of dealing with the pain associated with ending or loss. Garland, Jones, and Kolodny (1965) described the diversity often present in the group:

> The approach of group termination appears to set off a number of reactions, the diversity of which is reminiscent of the range of approach-avoidance maneuvers displayed in Stage 1. (p. 57).

These responses have been identified as flight, denial, regression, a need to continue, recapitulation, and review and evaluation (Garland et al., 1965). Through accepting and working with these diverse responses, the worker can help group members acquire a deeper, more balanced, and realistic appraisal of the meaning of their group experience.

Such a valuing of diversity can be challenging for both the worker and group members. For example, respecting diversity at this point may involve accepting and exploring negative comments and member disenchantment. If the practitioner or group members react defensively or allow punitive responses to such differences, they impair the group's ability to realistically appraise the achievement of individual and group goals and to gain insight into the personal meaning of the ending for each member. Indeed, by dismissing negative appraisals or feelings, an important opportunity is lost. Adoption of an inclusive approach empowers the group to utilize different perspectives shared by members to appraise their group experience realistically. For example, disenchantment expressed by one member can be useful in helping others who have idealized the group experience to appraise its limitations more realistically. Conversely, those expressing disenchantment may be challenged by others to further explore what they have learned or how they have changed during the group.

The worker's primary aim during this stage is to help members to put separation in a realistic context and to make connections with the ending of the group and their own endings in other social situations. This stage also provides opportunities for members to share their fears, desires, and concerns so that there is a sense of ending and not an overwhelming feeling that there is or will be unfinished business. The more ably individuals handle their terminating processes in the group and consolidate their learning, the more likely they will be able to handle similar processes outside of the intervention group.

As groups and individuals anticipate the end of their social interaction with each other, they often try to reenact and review in great detail various parts of the group experience from earlier sessions (Garland et al., 1965). This provides an opportunity for the group worker to ask the group what the specific reenactment or review meant, what insights were gained, and how these insights may be used outside of the group. Again, acceptance of diversity will enable group members to gain additional insights and meanings.

Members should be asked to examine what insights, experiences, skills, and strategies they can take from their group experience. In an inclusive approach, it is hoped that what they take from the experience will be an awareness that it is acceptable to be different and express differences as well as the ability to use diversity in solving problems and in relating to others. In this way, an inclusive approach will further the social goal of promoting acceptance of diversity in groups, communities, and societies.

GROUP ASSESSMENT

Assessing the phase of group development is one of the most important group work skills. In group work, assessment involves a continuing series of observations over time. In this way, assessments are like photographs, as they provide a snapshot of the current functioning of a group. Assessment helps a practitioner in determining the relative position of the group in its developmental journey. This is important because groups are not necessarily functioning at their full capacity at their first meeting. Time is required for relationships to form and tasks to be accomplished. How you as a group worker respond to your group will be determined, in part, by your assessment of its development and functioning.

In addition to assessing the development of a group, there are several other important elements that should be included in a group assessment. These include assessment of group: (1) membership; (2) purpose and goals; (3) communication; (5) cohesion; (6) roles; (7) decision making; (8) critical events and themes; (9) worker interventions; and (10) strengths and obstacles. For intervention groups, one additional assessment criterion would be the extent to which therapeutic factors have been promoted in the group.

Membership

Membership refers to those individuals who have joined the group for a definite or indefinite period of time. In most groups, members have voluntarily chosen to become group members. However, in some settings, those who are mandated by courts or other authorities may experience harsh consequences if they choose not to attend. In a task or intervention group, the worker records who is present and absent, as well as late arrivals, early departures, and who arrives with whom. This recording is important because absences, as well as repeated late arrivals, may be indicators of some reluctance or obstacle that is impairing a member's engagement with the group. In some cases, repeated late arrivals or absences may be due to issues such as transportation difficulties or childcare responsibilities. When these issues are discussed in the group, fellow group members or the agency may be able to assist members experiencing such challenges, enabling them to more fully participate. However, frequent absences or late arrivals may also be indicative of a member's ambivalence about participating in the group. Again, as with the earlier example, raising this issue in the group may enable the group to address these concerns and respond in a way that enables the reluctant member to engage more fully in the group. Similarly, in an inclusive group, the worker will be particularly sensitive to these issues and will address them as appropriate.

Group Purpose and Goals

Another important assessment criterion is an assessment of the group purpose as well as group and member goals. Clarity in group purpose is both an operational and ethical imperative for successful groups. Informed consent is not possible where the group purpose is unclear. In addition, the group purpose must be assessed in relation to the agency and/or program mandate and mission. A misalignment between group purpose and the agency mandate often will jeopardize the sustainability of the group. When designing a group, the worker will specify a number of group goals. These goals are expressed tentatively, as group members will bring their own goals. Intervention group goals may need to be modified to accommodate the diverse goals of group members. Group and member goals will need to be assessed by the acronym SMART. That is, are they specific, measurable, achievable, realistic, and time limited? In a task group, it is also important to assess if group members share similar goals and appear to be working towards a common purpose.

Communication

When assessing verbal communication, the group worker needs to assess the distribution and frequency of statements by group members. This assessment addresses questions such as: Which group members and workers verbally participated in a group meeting and how often did they participate? Was there a relatively equal frequency of statements by each member or did some members verbally participate more than others? Were most of the statements to and from the worker(s) or between members or were they to the group as a whole? A worker-centered distribution may be typical of early group sessions, but may signal that there is an obstacle to group functioning later in the group, where members typically will interact freely with each other as the group develops. By assessing which group members respond to other members, the worker may be able to understand the nature of the relationships in the group. For example, when the group workers observe that some members interact with only a select number of other members in a group, they know that a subgroup has formed in their group.

Although only one member can effectively speak at one time, group members can and do communicate through their nonverbal responses. One of the most informative aspects of nonverbal communication is seating position. In a task group, most often group members are seated around a rectangular table. When one joins a more formal board or committee meeting, where does the chair or leader normally sit? Typically, the leader or authority figure will sit at the head of the table. Group members are most likely to sit with those who they perceive are similar to themselves or with whom they have previously developed friendly relationships. Conversely, group members are more likely to sit farther away from those they perceive as less like themselves or with whom they have a conflictual relationship. Seating position can reveal a great deal about the patterns of affiliation and power present in any group.

In an intervention group, how members situate themselves with respect to the group's workers, particularly in the early sessions, may communicate how they are responding to the authority represented by the workers. Those who adopt a more dependent stance toward authority may sit close to one of the workers, while those who are more inclined to challenge authority may be seated farther away. It is also important to watch for those members who sit outside of the circle, as this may signal some reluctance with respect to engaging with the meeting.

An inclusive approach also recognizes that nonverbal communication and group participation may be profoundly influenced by culture. A member who refrains from making prolonged eye contact may be assumed to have self-esteem issues in one cultural setting and in another may be viewed as being polite. It is vital for group workers in diverse groups to avoid making assumptions about the meaning of nonverbal communication and be open to exploring what each member is attempting to express to others in the group.

Cohesion

Defined as the "resultant of all forces acting on all members to remain in the group or the attractiveness of the group for its members" (Yalom, 1995, p. 48), group cohesion encompasses the prevailing group climate or atmosphere and includes such elements as warmth, belongingness, acceptance, and a sense of group identity or *esprit de corps* among group members. The relative cohesiveness of a group will in large part determine whether the group will be able to work through conflict and whether members will be able to work together to accomplish group goals.

Roles

As Shulman (2015) has observed, member roles are a product of group needs, individual personality characteristics, and social relationships. (See figure 8.1 for

Figure 8.1 Sources of Member Roles

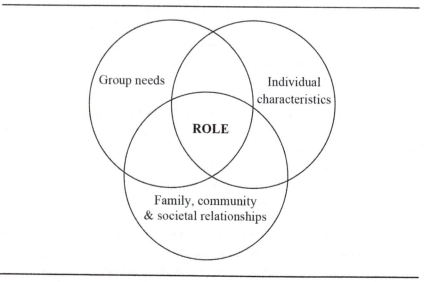

sources of member roles.) Group intervention represents the interaction of these elements. Member roles are thus emergent properties of any group and may be viewed as the way a group has organized to achieve its goals or create a solution to a problem. Role negotiation and conflict may be seen as both inevitable and normative as a group learns to work together. Though there have been a myriad of role descriptions identified, there are, by virtue of the pervasiveness of social roles and power structures, similarities in role descriptions in the literature. As Shulman notes, it is wise to view member roles systemically and individual behavior as expressing something for the group. From a systems perspective, member roles interlock and are affected by shifts made by other members. For example, for there to be a scapegoat role, there must be persecutors; for a monopolizer to continue, there must be quiet members. From a systems perspective, then, it is important for the worker to bring awareness to the group concerning the presence and impact of these maladaptive roles. By raising maladaptive group functioning to member awareness, the worker opens the door for the group to examine the impact of these patterns on the group and find new ways of dealing with their problems. Of course, there are numerous helpful roles that emerge in a group, not the least of which is leadership. Chapter 10 will address various skills and attributes of leadership. Many of those aspects would be important considerations when assessing the leadership in any group.

Decision Making

It is also important that one assesses what decisions are made and how they are made. It is essential in any group that all decisions made by the group are recorded. Frustration often ensues when a task group must revisit a previous discussion in order to confirm a decision that was previously made by the group. Also of importance in one's assessment is how the group makes decisions. Are decisions made by the worker or by one or more influential leaders? Is the decision-making process one based upon consensus, voting, or authority? As will be noted later, the process of decision making can have considerable impact upon the relationships and cohesiveness of a group. Each process has its advantages and disadvantages, and various approaches may be appropriate depending upon the circumstances faced by the group.

Critical Events and Sessional Themes

It is important to record a summary of critical events during the session. These events may include important disclosures or discussion topics, progress achieved toward individual or group goals, and other important events (e.g., conflict) that occurred during the meeting. The worker may also identify where she or he senses that there are taboo issues that have been addressed or avoided in the group, as well as the group members' responses to these and other issues. Emerging from an understanding of group purpose, member needs will be group themes. Themes emerge from the linking and exploration of interactions that occur in the group. For example, although different members of a group of sexual abuse survivors may share their respective frustration with getting insurance and medical benefits, financial settlements, and challenges in obtaining support from their employers, they are all speaking about a sense of powerlessness they are experiencing relating to the impact of the abuse they experienced. Recognizing and revisiting such a theme can have tremendous therapeutic benefit in deepening future group discussions. In task groups, themes can also be present. For example, when a task group has a history of identifying problems but no efforts to solve these problems are ever made, the group worker can identify this theme, encouraging and challenging members to address this.

Worker Interventions

A summary assessment also requires a summary of the major interventions utilized by the worker as well as the worker's perceived impact of these on the group. It is important to note how the group uses the worker. For example, does the group turn to the worker for advice or decisions? The effectiveness of worker interventions can be assessed in terms of their relative immediacy and focus. Interventions that are more immediate (i.e., they are process oriented, address present vs. past events, and are empathic in nature) tend to be more effective than those that offer less immediacy. Also, the focus of the intervention (i.e., individual, interpersonal, or group) will have differential impacts on the group and its members.

Group Strengths and Obstacles

Every group possesses strengths and encounters obstacles. It is important that the group worker acknowledges and records emerging strengths and obstacles. From both strengths and obstacles come recommended strategies for utilizing the strengths and addressing the obstacles in future group meetings.

INTERVENTION GROUPS— PROMOTION OF THERAPEUTIC FACTORS

A therapeutic factor is an element of therapeutic process that contributes to individual therapeutic change in group intervention and is a function of member-member, member-worker, and member-group relationships. Therapeutic factors may be observed in most intervention groups; however, their perceived value or helpfulness is often relative to the specific group focus, design, and developmental stage. Research has identified significant differences in how group members and workers rate the helpfulness of various therapeutic factors. Moreover, different theoretical standpoints also influence the relative importance placed upon particular therapeutic factors. For example, some psychoanalytic group models would downplay the value of cohesion as a therapeutic factor. Corsini and Rosenberg (1955) developed the first major classification system of therapeutic factors, which included: acceptance, altruism, universalization, intellectualization, reality testing, transference, interaction, spectator therapy, ventilation, and miscellaneous factors. Yalom (1970) later made a major contribution by adding interpersonal factors (e.g., interpersonal learning, instillation of hope, guidance, existential factors). Yalom and Leszcz's (2005) factors included the following:

Cohesion

This is considered by Yalom and Leszcz (2005) to be both a precondition and a therapeutic factor essential for individual change. Cohesion has been consistently selected as one of the most important factors by members, and is often under-valued by clinicians. The relative importance of cohesion as a therapeutic factor in promoting positive intervention outcomes (Bednar & Kaul, 1994) has resulted in it being considered as important as the consumer-worker relationship in case-work (Yalom & Leszcz, 2005). Moreover, it has come to be regarded as a neces-sary precursor for the development and influence of other therapeutic factors (Yalom & Leszcz, 2005).

Catharsis

Catharsis is a therapeutic factor that occurs when members discharge pent-up feel-ings, self-disclose previously withheld personal information, and learn how to express their here-and-now feelings about other group members or the worker(s).

Instillation of Hope

This occurs when group members gain confidence in the efficacy of group inter-vention and realize that improvement in their social functioning and personal lives is possible. This factor is often an important determinant in whether members remain in the group and is increased when members observe improvement in themselves or other group members.

Universality

This factor occurs when a group member's sense of isolation is reduced through increased awareness that his or her problems, feelings, or experiences are shared by others.

Guidance (Imparting Information)

Guidance occurs when group members receive useful information or instruction (e.g., psychoeducational information) from the worker or obtain advice or sug-gestions from other members.

Altruism

This occurs when members offer their support, reassurance, or comments to help other members. Members benefit both in terms of what they learn in the process of helping and in discovering that they possess skills and other strengths that enable them to assist others.

Family Reenactment

This therapeutic factor occurs when the group provides a setting for the exploration, reenactment, and correction of early familial relationships and conflicts.

Identification (Imitative Behavior)

This factor can be found when members learn through observing the therapeutic experiences of other members and by modeling the interpersonal behavior of other group members or the worker(s). The presence of this factor may range from simple vicarious observation to the use of psychodramatic techniques.

Interpersonal Learning

Yalom conceptualized the group as a social microcosm in which members improve their way of relating by attempting new, potentially positive behaviors or by responding to other group members (e.g., accepting/giving feedback). Yalom and Leszcz (2005) combined several previously separate factors under this category, including: (a) interpersonal learning-output, where members learn through trying out new behavior in the group; (b) interpersonal learning input, where members receive feedback from other members about their behavior; and (c) self-understanding (transference and insight), where members work through interpersonal perceptual distortions and generate new meanings about their behavior, motivations, and experiences.

Existential Factors

Here members demonstrate greater willingness to accept responsibility for their behavior, choices, and lives. Existential factors are also present when members struggle with major life transitions, developmental crises, and loss.

ASSESSMENT AND RECORDING

Recording is essential in the assessment process. Because there are many elements, interactions, and changes over time to be assessed, workers cannot expect to hold this information only in their memories. Records provide permanent accounts of the process, interactions, goals, objectives, and outcomes of the intervention process. Recording should be built into the procedures that the practitioner ordinarily uses in his or her work with the group. There are several types of recording. Verbatim recordings involve the transcription of entire audio or video recorded sessions. It should be noted that audio or video recordings may present issues to confidentiality and, therefore, should be explored with group members prior to their use. Somewhat less time consuming are process recordings, which include all significant events during a group session. However, given the time constraints faced by group workers and agency staff, the most common form of recording is the summary recording, which provides a summary of main sessional events.

The primary purpose of recording is to enhance the quality and effectiveness of group functioning. In group work, assessment is ongoing and is often incorporated into brief reports. All group workers need to have a format for recording important elements of each group meeting. Recording is more than simply describing what has occurred in a group meeting; it can and should include an assessment of the functioning and development of the group. As will be discussed, a group recording often includes a sociogram and a brief one- to two-page summary.

Sociogram

There are many charting and assessment instruments that have been designed over the years to assess various elements of group functioning. The most widely used instrument for assessment of interpersonal attraction and interaction patterns is the sociogram. The sociogram, developed by Jacob Moreno, offers a single page snapshot of each group meeting and is useful for assessing both task and intervention groups. The sociogram can include information about attendance (including late arrivals and early departures); the distribution and frequency of member verbal communication (e.g., Who speaks most often? Who appears isolated?); relative seating position; interpersonal relationships; and the presence, membership, and relationships of subgroups. One can also include important verbal and nonverbal communications.

For most groups, a brief summary of the group meeting and a sociogram are all that are needed for the effective recording of a task or intervention group meeting. To complete a sociogram, place the members and worker's names or initials in the center of the circle that reflects their relative seating position in the group. Figure 8.2 shows some of the standard symbols utilized in sociograms.

The standard symbols include an arrow, which demonstrates a statement directed toward a group member as well as attraction or engagement. Statements made by members/worker to the group as a whole are shown as lines or arrows extending towards the center of the circle. Dotted lines indicate indifference, and

Figure 8.2 Standard Symbols for Sociograms

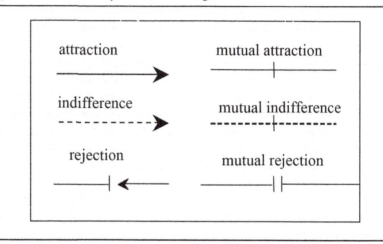

a t-shaped line indicates rejection or disengagement. Small hash marks on lines or arrows near each member indicate the relative frequency of interactions during the group meeting. In addition, identifying the various roles played by each member during the session can enhance a sociogram. It is also useful for you to create your own symbols to reduce the amount of writing that will be needed for the summary. It is important to include their meaning in a legend so that coworkers or supervisors will be able to interpret these symbols.

As a snapshot, the sociogram is meant to capture the major aspects of the group meeting. It is a summary, and so the worker does not need to capture every interaction or member statement. It is beneficial for coworkers to collaborate in the completion of a sociogram and summary after each group meeting. If this is not possible, it will be helpful for coworkers to share their sociograms and summaries with each other before the next meeting.

To provide an example of how to use sociograms to capture group meetings, figures 8.3, 8.4, and 8.5 show three sociograms from a group for men who have experienced problems with intimate partner violence (IPV). What do the different sociograms tell you about the group's process from one session to another?

Group Summary

Summary recordings provide a summary of main sessional descriptors (e.g., group name, session date, workers' names, session number), events, and a number of

Figure 8.3 Men's IPV Process Group Session 1

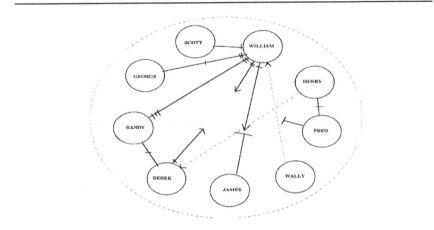

Figure 8.4 Men's IPV Process Group Session 3

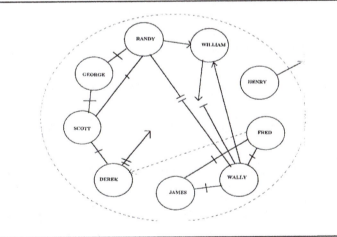

important elements. In addition to assessing the general development of the group described earlier, there are a number of group characteristics that need to be included in any assessment and the group summary. These characteristics should be included in a brief summary report. The summary recording should end with a number of proposed interventions that logically flow from the assessment, aimed at improving the functioning of the group.

Figure 8.5 Men's IPV Process Group Session 5

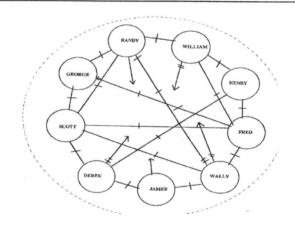

CHAPTER SUMMARY

This chapter explored how groups develop over time and how diversity is present throughout the group phases. It discussed how attention to diversity could be given throughout the group process to enhance the group experience and support the achievement of individual and group goals. It is hoped that group workers can begin to incorporate an inclusive group work approach to their practice and, in doing so, begin to utilize the diversity within the group to benefit group members and as a tool to help the group process. This chapter also discussed assessment, different elements of importance when assessing group members, and several aspects of group development.

PART TWO

Inclusive
GROUP WORK PRACTICE

CHAPTER 9

BEGINNINGS

LEARNING OBJECTIVES

At the end of this chapter you will be able to:

- Identify the different components of a beginning stage intervention or task group.
- Explain applicable ethical issues for a mandated group (or a group with some mandated members) and demonstrate how a worker will engage mandated members in the beginning stage of a group.
- Demonstrate facilitation of a beginning stage intervention or task group and analyze what processes occurred.

A Case Study

Social work students are meeting for their group "Serenity Seekers" for the first time. It was proposed to be a closed group for currently enrolled undergraduate students at the university. The facilitator is a social work graduate student who recruited members and has already prepared an outline of group sessions for the following year. In previous years, students requested and helped coordinate this group to address common concerns students had with ongoing stress felt during the academic year. In the past, the group members discussed how they managed homework, balanced their social lives and academia, made career decisions, and planned work and school schedules. The facilitator intends to address the same topics in group meetings.

What other issues will need to be addressed during the first couple sessions related to group members and sessions? What are some ideas for icebreakers the worker can implement with the students to help them feel more comfortable within this type of setting? What are potential concerns students might have that the worker could address in the first meetings?

According to the IASWG standards, the tasks to be fulfilled in the beginning stage of a group are: (1) establishing a beginning contract, (2) cultivating group cohesion, and (3) shaping norms of participation (IASWG, 2010). The knowledge that the group worker is required to have includes (1) an understanding of the interaction among the community, agency, group, and individual members; (2) knowledge of theories and evidence-based practices regarding human development and psychosocial needs of members (for an intervention group) and organization theory (related to a task group; (3) the group type and associated technology; and (4) special consideration relating to the beginning stage of a group, such as working with mandated members, replacing a previous worker, and entry of new members into an ongoing group (IASWG, 2010). This chapter will address each of these standards.

SETTING THE STAGE

The beginning of a group sets the stage for the rest of the group. It is like the beginning of a newspaper article, movie, song, or relationship. If done well, it engages the new members, builds rapport, and makes them feel they made a good decision to come to the group. In many instances, members are required or mandated to attend a group and have little or no motivation to attend. In this case, the group worker in the beginning sessions will want to engage the members, allow them to discuss their feelings, and offer hope that their time will not be wasted in the group (Yalom & Leszcz, 2005).

The first step in the beginning stage is for the group worker or workers to greet people as they arrive at the first meeting, provide them with name tags or name placards, and then facilitate a way for people to begin to know each other through introductions or icebreaker activities. Many new members will feel anxious or fearful because they may not know the other people, are not sure what they are getting themselves into, and have their guard up because the group purpose may be very sensitive, such as recovering from addictive behaviors or learning new ways of coping with past abuse and grief. It is important for members to feel they are in a safe and trusting environment if they are expected to reveal sensitive issues about themselves or their families. Similar to the members, the group worker may also have feelings of anxiety and fear. These feelings are normal and are to be expected, particularly for a new group worker. By acknowledging and attending to these emotions as they arise, the group worker can engage in self-exploration and increase self-awareness to be better equipped to deal with other emotions that may be present from the group experience.

The group worker may want to do the introduction in a formal way, such as asking members to give their name, what their job is, and what they might expect to accomplish in the group. Even formal introductions might have an element of fun to help people relax, such as asking participants to share about an enjoyable activity they did the prior weekend. Another way to introduce members is through icebreakers. For example, the worker might ask members to meet with one other person (a dyad) who they do not know and find out some information about them (name, where they were born, and what they like to do for fun, etc.). Then, each member of the pair will introduce their new acquaintance to others in the group, which takes the spotlight off of oneself. This is a good method because some people will be shy about introducing themselves in the larger group. Group workers will want to introduce themselves first to the group so that they can give the group's purpose, information about the agency that is sponsoring the group, and their credentials. They would then introduce themselves with the same information they are asking members to give so that the group worker serves as a role model for the introductions.

Introductions can be accomplished through the use of other creative icebreaker activities or games so that members begin to know each other and the group worker, as well as further the purpose and cohesion of the group (see appendix C for a list of icebreakers). The introductory activities should fit the type of group, the age and developmental stage of the members, and the group's purpose. For example, children might prefer a game such as passing a bean bag around and giving bits of information about themselves, whereas adults might enjoy a game of signature bingo where they collect signatures of members who speak French or Spanish, are left handed, or who like to read novels. Round robin communication, where the group worker goes from person to person in a circle giving each member an opportunity to give out information about himself or herself, can also be a form of check-in in all group meetings. It is a great way to build cohesion in a group (Furman, Bender, & Rowan, 2014), as well as to ensure input from all members. As the members' brief backgrounds are expressed in the group, the group worker attends to commonalities among the members and comments on them in such a way that members begin to see there are others with similar interests, issues, and challenges. Furthermore, an inclusive group worker can begin to recognize, acknowledge, and affirm diversity, demonstrating and setting the tone for how diversity can be embraced and utilized in the group. Icebreaker activities are a way to move the collective (not yet a group but a gathering of individuals) toward a cohesive entity with a shared purpose and goals (Lang, 2010).

Most people will have some anxiety about joining a new group. Perhaps they will be excited to be part of a new experience, but will also wonder if they will be accepted or whether the endeavor will be worthwhile. The important thing to remember is that people want to feel that: (1) they will be recognized and engaged; (2) they have something in common with the other members and will be accepted by them; (3) the group's purpose fits with their needs; and (4) the group feels like a comfortable place to be and is trustworthy. For these reasons, new members will expect an orientation to learn the purpose of the group and how it will function.

Exercise 9.1: Creative Introductions

Meet in a group. Each person pairs with another member of the group. First, one member will ask the following questions of the other member in the pair: In what region did you grow up? What are your hobbies? Who is in your immediate family? What is one of your expectations for the group? Then, each person will introduce their new acquaintance to other members of the group.

THE PURPOSE OF THE GROUP

In the first session of the group, the group worker will want to introduce the purpose of the group that was carefully crafted during the group's planning stage after a thorough needs assessment of the agency, potential members, and the community. It is important for members to understand the purpose of the group, which will be the overarching theme of the group, so that they can enter into a contract with the group worker with knowledge about what to expect from the group. In task groups, this discussion can help members understand the main tasks and goals they are expected to accomplish. Individual members could have been informed of the purpose of the group during pregroup interviews; however, discussing it with the group as a whole is very important because the group becomes a system of its own with its own culture (Coyle, 1948; Toseland, & Rivas, 2011). During the discussion of the group purpose, the group worker will want to solicit feedback from each member to make sure that there is a common understanding of the purpose. Although this may sound simple and logical, it is worth spending time in the first couple sessions to ensure that members are on the same wavelength as far as the group's purpose.

In the case example at the beginning of the chapter, the group worker explained that the purpose of the group was to relieve stress of the undergraduate social work students who were members of the group. One member said she was relieved that she could come to such a group, as she was having trouble sleeping. She had so much to do for school that she was not able to spend much time with her young son. Another member asked if the group worker was going to teach them how to meditate in order to relieve stress, and a different member wanted to know if group members were going to study together. The group worker explained that each individual member would develop goals they hoped to achieve in the group, and that the goals would relate to the overarching purpose of the group— reducing their stress.

Members who are ordered or mandated by the court system to attend a group in lieu of serving jail time or suffering other serious consequences, such as severance from their children, might not believe the group's purpose relates to them. For example, in a group for people who have received "driving while intoxicated" citations and are ordered to attend a twelve-week substance misuse group to learn better coping strategies, some members may deny that they have a drinking problem. In the beginning stage of mandatory groups, it is important for members to discuss any frustrations they might feel about attending the group. The group worker will point out that the overall purpose is for members to understand the consequences of alcohol or substance misuse and to find healthy ways to cope with problems. The group worker will also inform members that they will have the opportunity in the first couple sessions to formulate individual goals to accomplish in the group. The group members need to have the opportunity to ventilate in the beginning stage of groups, but it is also the group worker's responsibility to inform members of any consequence for not attending. For example, the group worker might state that attending the group each week is required by the courts, or the person might be placed in jail for a period of time.

Exercise 9.2: Integrating Information

Meet in a group of peers, and practice giving purpose statements about a group that you might want to facilitate. Obtain feedback from the members of the group as to whether the purpose seems clear to them.

Exercise 9.3: Role Play to Integrate Information

Imagine that you are the group worker for a group of adolescents (your peers will play the roles of the adolescents) who are having behavioral and academic problems in their high school classes. The purpose of the group is to help the adolescents improve behavioral and academic problems. They are being mandated to attend the group or risk being suspended from their regular high school and sent to an alternative high school. Role play the group's first meeting.

ORIENTATION TO THE WAY THE GROUP WILL FUNCTION: RULES/NORMS AND ROLES

As the IASWG standards state, one of the main tasks for the group worker in the beginning stage of groups is to hold a discussion of how the group will function (IASWG, 2010). The group worker might begin this discussion by explaining that groups function best when everyone participates and/or completes assigned tasks, attends each week, and arrives on time, because everyone has strengths and ideas to further the group's purpose and goals. Another rule the group worker would recommend, especially for intervention groups, is confidentiality. It is crucial to have rules regarding confidentiality so that people feel they can be open and honest about what they say or do in a group. Without members' openness and authenticity in a group, it will be difficult to reach therapeutic goals. A third rule to establish is that people act in a respectful way to each other so that members feel comfortable attending the group. After the group worker suggests these three basic rules, she or he would want to get feedback from the group as to how they feel about these rules, whether they wish to add other rules and norms, whether any should be modified, and whether the members believe they could sign a contract that they would abide by, which would include the rules. It would be good to involve the members in establishing the rules for the group, as this is empowering, and perhaps one member could write the rules down for all to see. These rules can then be posted for future meetings and may be used to remind members when rules are neglected. Basic rules give the group structure and help the members trust what will happen in the group.

ROLES AND STATUS OF THE GROUP WORKER AND MEMBERS

In addition to covering the rules and norms of the group, the group worker will want to discuss the roles of the group worker and the members. Many members will expect the group worker to be the leader of the group, especially if they are from a culture that expects authority figures and professionals to dominate in a group. They will want the group worker to take on a directing role, give the preponderance of information and advice, and exert more power. The beginning stage meetings give the group worker an opportunity to discuss the idea that social work groups are democratic groups in which the members each have an equal role and status and that each member is expected to give and receive mutual aid.

The group worker has a leadership role. Responsibilities include: arranging the meetings, providing information, and facilitating the meeting. Of all the stages of group development, the group worker takes the most dominant role in the beginning stages. However, the group worker also expresses from the beginning the fact that often the most useful information shared in group comes from fellow members, their experiences, and even mistakes. Eventually, when the group reaches the middle stage, members will have just as pivotal roles as the worker. Leadership roles can be shared in a task group where different members with specific talents and tasks will take on significant roles in the group. Both in intervention and task groups, the group worker should reach for the group members' perspectives on how the group will function and what the roles of members and the group worker will be, and propose a statement to be part of a written contract along with the group rules.

Negative feelings and perspectives can emerge in the discussion of roles. For example, in an older adult group, a member might state that she did not feel that they were all equal because some members had a great deal of education and distinguished professions, such as being a chief executive officer of a large corporation or a retired judge. If such a statement is made by a member, the inclusive group worker can take the opportunity to model healthy norms about respect and equality for all members of the group regardless of their differences and status/power outside of the group. These beginning group discussions are important, as they set the norms for the group, such as respecting diversity and related issues that may arise in later sessions. It is recommended that the group worker devote a session or a portion of a session in the beginning stage of group to discuss diversity of the membership.

In some groups, during the beginning stage, participants may question the authority of the group worker. Members will want to know how committed the group worker is to the group and to helping them reach the group's and/or individual goals. The group worker can use this as an opportunity to explore these and other underlying concerns, as well as to affirm early on the group worker's commitment to being an invested member of the group.

Trust is sought in all groups, and trust is a critical element for the group to reach its full potential. If members do not feel a sense of trust and respect in the group, it is likely that they might not continue to attend or that they might tune out. Confidentiality, respect, inclusiveness, and authenticity will have to be discussed in the group in the beginning stage.

The functioning of a group will depend on its type, membership, and purpose. The group worker must have knowledge of human development and theories, group dynamics, and how other systems affect the group in order to facilitate the group. With this knowledge, the group worker can help members formulate beginning goals in an intervention group and group goals in a task group.

GOAL SETTING

An important aspect of the beginning stage of group is goal setting. In a support, psychoeducational, or therapy group, there would be individual goals tailored to each member as well as group goals. For example, in a divorcing parent support group, one of the group's goals might be to discuss common issues of divorcing families, and individual members' goals might be: to learn how to live on a reduced income; to make new friends; to develop a business-like relationship with the ex-spouse or partner; or to build self-esteem. The individuals in the group, with the assistance of the group worker and the other members, formulate goals. In a social work group, the group worker is always working in partnership with members, and individuals' goals are created in this way. In addition, feedback is sought from group members about the individual's goals.

In task groups, the group goals must be clear in order for the group to reach its purpose. For example, when author Cheryl Lee was a program director for the Arizona Supreme Court's Administrative Office Domestic Relations Division, she created and facilitated a task group to work on legislation to help parents who were divorcing or legally separating focus on their children's needs during this difficult life transition. The purpose of the group was to create and lobby for legislation that would create a psychoeducational program for all newly divorcing and legally separating parents. There were many interim goals that had to be met in order to create good legislation and then to pass it. Some of these goals were: draft legislation; meet with the state's stakeholders to get their feedback and support; educate legislators about the bill; and secure media support (Lee, 1997).

After preliminary goals are formulated, a contract can be completed. Over the life of the group, goals can be modified to meet the members' needs within the scope of the group's purpose or in a task group to reach the group's purpose.

Exercise 9.4: Task Group Integration

Meet in a group of peers and develop goals for a task group for a task in which your friends and you have an interest.

Exercise 9.5: Role Play on Goal Setting for an Education and Support Group

You are a facilitator for a group of people who were recently laid off and are worried that they cannot support themselves or their families. Your peers will role play the members of the group.

CONTRACTING WITH MEMBERS

Following welcoming and introductions, a discussion of the group's purpose, the creation of rules/norms, an orientation to the group's functioning, and preliminary goal setting, the members and group worker are ready to complete a written contract (Corey, Corey, & Corey, 2010). All social work groups involve contracting in the beginning stage, but many group workers only facilitate an oral contract with members and do not go the extra step of asking members to sign a written contract. A written contract is recommended, and in research on AIDS groups in Canada, members found it to be beneficial in ensuring confidentiality, a prerequisite to a trusting, safe, and productive atmosphere (Olivier, 2009). The contract should include the purpose of the group, basic rules, member and group worker responsibilities, and goals. See an example of a contract in appendix D in the back of this book.

The group worker can distribute a template contract appropriate for the group with standardized language for all members to sign. There can be blanks for individualization of the contract, such as a section on individual goals for an intervention group. For children's groups, contracts can be written in simple language and children's authorization to participate should be sought. For all groups involving minors, parents or legal guardians must give authorization for group participation unless there are legal exceptions.

CHAPTER SUMMARY

The beginning stage of a group is a time for welcoming new members, building rapport, and orienting members to how the group will function. The group's purpose and goals are clarified with feedback from participants, and members create preliminary individual goals in intervention groups. Members may be anxious and fearful in this stage; thus, the group worker needs to attend to each member and help to create an environment of trust, positive norms, and an inclusive culture where all members are shown respect. For task groups, individual goals are not formed, but it is important to have an open atmosphere so that creative ideas can be generated by all members prior to finalizing group goals. A contract, preferably written, which includes the purpose of the group, basic rules/norms and roles, and goals of the group and/or individuals, is generated between the members and the group worker in the beginning stage. A checklist (appendix E) that group workers can use to ensure they are covering essential aspects of the beginning stage of group can be found in the back of this book.

Exercise 9.6: Group Beginnings

In small groups, role play a beginning stage group in class. At the end of the group, process the group, and report back to the class as a whole about the strengths and weaknesses of the group and what was learned from the experience. Discussion questions are:

1. How was welcoming of group members achieved?
2. How were group members oriented?
3. What was the purpose of the group and how was it clarified?
4. What were group and/or individual goals of members?
5. How did the contracting process go?

An alternative assignment is: Students observe or facilitate a group in their internship and answer the above questions.

CHAPTER 10

LEADERSHIP: THE DIFFERENCE OFFERED BY THE WORKER

LEARNING OBJECTIVES

At the end of this chapter you will be able to:
- **Outline characteristics of effective group leadership.**
- **Demonstrate a variety of content and process oriented skills.**
- **Appraise the benefits and challenges in working with a coworker.**
- **Work with diversity as it arises in coworker relationships.**

UNDERSTANDING LEADERSHIP IN GROUPS

Qualities of Group Leadership

One of the defining characteristics of social work with groups is that the group, and not the leader, is the agent of change. For this reason, the worker's role in the group is to assist the group to become an effective agent of change. For nearly a century, social work with groups has favored a distributed form of leadership and recognized that, for most groups, leadership is a role that is optimally shared by members of a group. Indeed, one indicator that one is working in a functional and empowering group is that the group provides opportunities for each of its members to undertake a leading role when needed by the group. For these reasons, this chapter will reframe the content found in many contemporary group texts and speak about the attributes of group leadership as those qualities that one wishes to promote and affirm in each group. Although there is a multitude of qualities that may become important in a specific group, this chapter will outline twelve qualities of group leadership. There are a number of ways in which these attributes can be promoted in any group. One way is for the worker to model these qualities. Another way is for the worker to promote a group climate and norms that affirm and encourage these qualities among group members.

1. Presence

Being present in the group is more than simply being physically present. It also means allowing oneself to experience in the moment thoughts and feelings evoked by discussion and events happening in the group. It means being attentive and vulnerable to the feelings and thoughts shared by group members. Sometimes these feelings may be in the form of anger directed to you. In this way, being present means being able to hear and acknowledge difficult feelings towards you.

2. Transparency

At the heart of transparency is self-disclosure, when the group worker reveals aspects of self to the group. In most cases, these disclosures relate to the worker's thoughts and emotional responses to what is happening in the group in the moment. For example, a worker may disclose at the end of a group just how much he or she learned and appreciated the group. In some cases, the worker may share some personal information about himself or herself to group members. However, workers must always reflect on their intentions, including whose needs are being met when they reveal aspects of their lives outside the group. For example, in a group for adolescents, the worker disclosed that he too struggled but was now in recovery. The worker's intention was to demonstrate to the group members that he was just like them. Following his disclosure, the group discussed how he managed to recover and what he did to be successful. His intention to join the group, however, was unsuccessful, as he became an expert in the group. What might have been more helpful was for the worker to use his experience to acknowledge the thoughts, feelings, and challenges faced by group members. Another example of helpful transparency would be when workers at the beginning of the group use their own anxiety to acknowledge that other group members may be feeling a bit uncertain and anxious at this point in the group. By using their anxiety in this way, the workers are able to promote transparency by other group members.

3. Self-reflection

If workers or members are present and transparent in a group, there will be many points where they will need to reflect on how the group has affected them and how they have affected the group. There will be many points where intense feelings may be evoked. As noted earlier, diversity affirming practice requires that the worker be aware of his or her own cultural values and mores. He or she will need to explore emotions and thoughts that are evoked in the group. Have they been triggered by an earlier event in life? For example, in a group for male survivors of sexual abuse, a worker was triggered by the anger of a group member who resembled the person who had assaulted him. Intense anger was triggered. In this case, the worker was no longer present in the group, and an emotional response to the group member would have damaged his relationship with him. However, he would not have experienced this realization without self-reflecting.

4. Integrity

Integrity is walking the walk and talking the talk. It is demonstrating congruence. It is not sufficient to establish rules and tell others in the group how they can promote an effective group; it is much more helpful to model these behaviors. Credibility and trust are eroded when a worker does not do what is promised or behaves contrary to what he or she is telling others. Indeed, often it is important that group members point out when others in group are saying one thing and doing something else.

5. Courage

Being present and vulnerable, confronting issues in the group, and taking risks in terms of sharing oneself with a group of people require a certain degree of courage and self-acceptance. The worker, by modeling these behaviors and encouraging and affirming others to do so, helps to establish norms in the group that will promote more openness and risk taking by group members. The simple acknowledgment that it requires courage to share one's thoughts and feelings with others can set a positive tone for the group.

6. Trusting and Trustworthiness

Trust is like a currency that is earned and grows with time to become a major resource for any group. Perhaps the most important element of trust in group work is learning to trust the group. Group members are experts in their own experience. They each bring resources, strengths, experiences, and insights that can, if permitted, benefit others in the group. By continually demonstrating confidence in the group's ability to address problems and obstacles and complete tasks, the worker promotes trust in the group and its abilities. Likewise, by modeling and affirming presence, transparency, integrity, and courage, the group worker becomes trustworthy, and so too do the other members of the group.

7. Consensus Driven

An inclusive group is one that is consensus driven. In a democracy, there are always winners and losers. When consensus is achieved, everyone is a winner, as everyone is included. Of course, there may be times when a decision that is made by consensus may not be, from the worker's view, the optimal solution. However, although it may be beneficial to point out limitations of any decision, and in some cases to note where there is potential harm to group members or others, trusting the group involves trusting that a consensus decision is often the best one. In many cases, to reach a consensus, members in a group must be encouraged and supported to make compromises.

8. Curiosity

Being curious, particularly when diversity is present in the group, can represent an opportunity to explore and deepen group members' understandings of each other and build constructive relationships. Thus, curiosity is an invitation for members to get to know each other. It is the opposite of making judgments and assumptions that cut off communication and stifle opportunities for learning. By promoting curiosity in the group, the worker opens doors for members to share things with others that they may not be able to do outside of the group.

9. Acceptance

Curiosity helps to deepen understanding of others in the group, providing a foundation of acceptance. In countless groups, each member realizes that the first impression of others may not always be accurate. Early in the group, the worker may need to challenge judgments and assumptions made about others in the group in order to help members come to this realization. Through learning about each other, members gain a deeper understanding of why others behave and relate to others in the way that they do. From understanding comes acceptance, and from personal exploration each member gains insights into how they have become the person who they are. In this way, members learn to accept themselves and others in the group. The worker can promote acceptance in the group by modeling, such as acknowledging mistakes that one has made in the group.

10. Compassion and Empathy

Natural consequences of curiosity and acceptance are compassion and empathy. When a group member comes to understand and accept another in the group, they are empowered to care for that person. Although they may not always fully understand the experiences of another member, they can certainly express compassion for them and their situation.

11. Humor

There are moments in a group where tension can be relieved by humor. Humor can be a powerful ingredient that all group members may contribute to any group. Humor can be used in many ways. Perhaps most beneficially, it may help members to reduce worries and fears. It can also be helpful in reducing some of the punitive self-criticism that some group members experience. However, it should never be at the expense of the self-esteem of any member.

12. Flexibility

Perhaps the most important quality the worker must model and promote in a group is flexibility. For example, when needs of a group member or something in the outside world has changed, group workers and members may need to discard their agenda for a particular meeting and tend to those needs. Being flexible also means taking on a different role when needed by the group.

GROUP WORK SKILLS

Middleman and Goldberg Wood (1990a) outlined a number of criteria to differentiate social work with groups from other forms of group work. In keeping with social work groups' appreciation of the power of the group to effect change, they observe, "As we see it, social workers do not run groups. They help groups to organize, develop, and run themselves. They help the participants to develop a system of mutual aid" (p. 92).

In order to promote the development of the group as a system of mutual aid, the worker must "think group"—that is, have group concepts as a mindset or frame of reference for looking at and making sense of what is happening in group. The worker must consider the group first and the individuals second when working in a group (Middleman & Goldberg Wood, 1990b). Recognizing and actively facilitating the development of the group as the agent of change, the worker must strive to promote the autonomy, where possible, of the group to function independently. In essence, the worker must have the attitude that he or she will work himself or herself out of a job.

As Middleman and Goldberg Wood (1990b) pointed out, a group worker needs to develop skills for working with both individuals and the group as a whole. There are also a number of requisite skills that must be present in order for a group to reach its goals. These skills may be categorized into content and process oriented skills.

Content oriented skills are those skills that enable the group to complete its tasks. Content is about what is being stated and the tasks that are completed in the group. Process oriented skills include skills that build and maintain constructive interpersonal relationships in a group, enabling it to become a system of mutual aid. As with leadership qualities, these skills, although most often offered at least initially by the group worker, can and optimally should be implemented by any group member.

CONTENT ORIENTED SKILLS

Initiating

In order for the group to begin, someone needs to start the discussion. Often it is the worker who performs this task, particularly during the initial meetings of a group. This skill may involve helping to define problem(s), addressing tasks, or raising a relevant topic for discussion. Of course, later in the life of the group, a group member may initiate the discussion based upon an event or experience over the past week. Indeed, later in the group, initiation may involve saying only, "Let's get started."

Imparting Information

This skill simply involves providing information to the group. Schwartz (2006) identified imparting information as an important group work skill aimed at helping members develop alternative courses of thinking or action. However, there may be times where the workers may be asked their opinions on a particular subject. Here, the workers must be cautious. One might state that the worker should avoid providing information if she or he believes that group members may reasonably possess this knowledge. Often a wiser course is to first turn to the group and ask if anyone can respond to the question posed in the group. Why? If one believes that the group is the agent of change and group members are the real experts on their experience, it makes sense to encourage group members to turn to the group for answers.

Elaborating

Elaboration helps to keep the group moving. After a group member has shared information or feelings, it is often helpful to ask members to add to and expand upon this content. Sometimes elaboration may involve assisting members to openly express fears and expectations by simply acknowledging how difficult it may be to talk about a taboo subject. One may also invite members to further explore statements, behavior, or relationships using "what" or "how" questions to heighten self-awareness and understanding of what is currently being discussed in the group.

Identifying Themes and Summarizing

One cannot overemphasize the value of an effective summary statement. Summarizing involves identifying group meeting themes, and may also include linking past meetings with the current meeting. In an intervention setting, the worker needs to also interpret and then summarize the latent or underlying emotional meaning of verbal and nonverbal messages shared in the group. Such a summary can serve to deepen the discussion and uncover beneficial insights.

Evaluating

How does one know when a group has accomplished its tasks or if the group members have achieved their goals? How does one know when the group is on the right track? This calls for the skill of evaluation. Here, the worker (or a group member) may need to reiterate the group purpose in order to get the group back on track. There may also be the need to conduct a periodic review with group members. Such a review in a task group could involve reviewing past meeting minutes and discussing how many tasks have been completed and how close the group is to achieving its goals. In an intervention group, it may involve reviewing scores on clinical scales and reviewing with group members the progress they have achieved towards their individual goals. Evaluation also involves celebrating gains, affirming risk taking, and monitoring progress toward individual and/or group goals. Middleman and Goldberg Wood (1990b) stress the importance of verbally expressing appreciation of group progress and achievements.

PROCESS ORIENTED SKILLS

Tuning In

Tuning in was identified by Shulman (2015) as a skill where the worker attempts to anticipate what needs, feelings, and experiences members will bring to the group. For example, think about your first day of classes. How did you feel when you entered your first class? Were you feeling excited and yet a bit anxious? Now think about a violence prevention group for men who have abused their partners. How do you imagine they may be feeling about their first group meeting? Is it possible that they may fear being judged or criticized? As noted above, when group members come to a first group meeting they may experience some fears about being judged by others. Your ability to tune in to these potential feelings of ambivalence can be used to promote an early atmosphere of acceptance and respect that can help the group form supportive relationships. Reading about the needs and experiences of those populations from which your group members are drawn can also be helpful.

Scanning

This skill involves being present, looking with "planned emptiness" (Middleman & Goldberg Wood, 1990b, p. 94), and looking with a wide angle lens to take in the whole group by making eye contact with each member. As the worker scans a group, he or she accepts and interprets internal cues and external cues from group members. This is a vital skill, as members may respond very differently to what is being discussed in a group at a particular time. For example, your scanning may inform you that some members may not be in agreement with (shaking their heads) or may lack understanding of (puzzled facial expression) what other members are saying.

Amplifying

This skill occurs when the worker acknowledges and draws the group's attention to unacknowledged, subtle, or incongruent messages. From scanning, you may be able to note when a group member smiles when he or she is speaking about a painful memory. By extension, as noted under scanning, you can inquire when you notice a member who demonstrates body language that appears to communicate that they disagree with or do not understand what is being discussed. It is also important to use amplifying to draw attention to and reinforce norms that promote group functioning or promote group development. For example, in a task group, the worker would amplify a diverse opinion offered by a group member as the group is identifying various options when it is attempting to solve a problem. In an intervention group, the worker would amplify a statement by a group member that questions a taboo issue, challenges the authority of the worker, or offers a different opinion about the helpfulness of the group.

Clarifying

Many intense and intractable conflicts begin with a simple misunderstanding. Indeed, what later erupt as destructive interactions may have started by a simple misunderstanding of what has been stated by a group member. Sometimes, a group member may intend to say one thing but, because of challenges they face in self-expression, it comes out quite differently. Accordingly, what someone has said may be interpreted quite differently by those who have listened. An inclusive group worker does not assume that what he or she understands has been said is necessarily the same for all group members. The worker checks out his or her understanding of recent member statements, explores underlying intent of statements, and promotes a clearer and consensual understanding of member statements.

Harmonizing

Harmonizing involves mediating conflicts between members, relieving tensions, highlighting member similarities, and reframing or reducing the affective intensity of potentially destructive statement messages so that they can be heard and accepted by the recipient(s). The worker helps to clarify the member's statement and intent and then asks that the message be rephrased or repeated.

Blocking

Particularly during the early stages of a group, as group norms and ground rules are being negotiated and tested, workers may need to block certain member activities, such as questioning, probing, gossiping, invading privacy (Corey et al., 2013), and giving put-downs, without undermining the personhood of the members involved.

Confronting

The worker may need to intervene with members whose behavior is disruptive or may need to point out incongruent statements and behavior. As Shulman (2015) noted, to be effective such interventions should be balanced; offering a challenge concerning specific member behavior and expressing care and concern for the member.

Linking

This is a distinctive and vital group skill through which the worker links members together and promotes group cohesion by noting when two or more members have expressed similar thoughts, feelings, or experiences in the group. The use of information linking assumes that the group members are experts in their own experiences (Middleman & Goldberg Wood, 1990b). After a member shares a specific feeling, thought, or experience, it is often important for the worker to reach for links between members by exploring if other members share similar thoughts, feelings, or experiences. The linking of feelings assumes that members share some similar experiences and are able to empathize with each other.

Modeling

By demonstrating effective communication skills, the worker helps members to learn improved ways of relating and enhances the group's capacity to serve as a system of mutual aid. Some of these skills include concreteness, appropriate self-disclosure, immediacy, giving and receiving feedback, and nondefensiveness.

Regulating

The worker ensures that member and group activities are congruent with (a) individual and group goals, (b) the capacity of members to participate, and (c) the stage of group development. He or she monitors the pace of group activities to ensure that members do not become confused, frightened, or overwhelmed. Regulating also involves a number of other skills identified by Middleman & Goldberg Wood (1990b) including:

Encouraging Balanced Participation
The worker needs to encourage balanced participation by group members. Inclusive group work practice recognizes that how group members participate may vary depending upon their cultural backgrounds, previous group experiences, and preferred styles of communication. Also, the purpose and the tasks of the group may influence when and how various group members participate. For example, in a task group planning a youth program, different group members with different expertise may participate more frequently, depending upon which aspect of the program is being discussed (e.g., activities, advertising, risk management, budget). However, balanced participation means that each member must have opportunities to participate fully in a manner that works for them. The worker can promote balanced participation by structuring participation in a way that is appropriate to the group purpose, size, and cultural preferences (e.g., maypole with violent offenders, talking circle for groups with indigenous members, agenda controlled in task groups).

Redirecting Messages to the Member(s) for Whom They Were Intended
This involves asking a member whose message is intended for another member to direct his statement or feeling to that person, whether that person is present or not. It is seldom helpful for a group member to speak about another member as though they are not present in the group. When a group member is absent, it may be beneficial for group members to speak about their concerns about the missing group member and the impact of the absence on the group. However, it is important that this discussion is revisited upon the return of the absent group member.

Assisting Members to Give and Receive Feedback Effectively
It has been known for some time that feedback offered by peers is much more influential than feedback offered by the worker. Often group members enter group with a history of challenges in their interpersonal relationships. The group can become a place for learning new, more effective interpersonal skills. One way in which this can occur is through learning how to give and receive feedback in a constructive way. Constructive feedback needs to focus on what can be changed—that is, behavior, not personality traits. It must be offered as an invitation to change as opposed to issued as an ultimatum. Constructive feedback must also include the impact of the behavior on the one who is giving feedback, involving the use of

"I" statements (e.g., "I felt sad when you talked about your partner leaving you" as opposed to "You didn't deserve her."). As the example indicates, constructive feedback avoids making any assumptions about the motives or judgment of the member to whom it is directed. The worker may need to explore how the receiver interprets the feedback by asking them to restate it in their own words.

Softening Overpowering Messages

Sometimes, particularly when one or more group members are agitated, statements may be made that are so raw, exaggerated, or absolute in nature that they cannot be heard by others in the group. For this reason, the worker may need to reduce the intensity of affective messages so that they can be heard by asking that the message be repeated using more helpful words or by repeating it.

Ensuring that Interpersonal and Group Issues Are Worked through before Facilitating the Group's Movement into New Issues

Unresolved conflicts and incomplete tasks can often grow into major barriers, resulting in group members bringing up old issues or linking current disagreements to earlier unresolved conflicts. More problematic is when unresolved conflicts result in an escalation of tensions and anger over what appear to be relatively minor disagreements. In most instances, it is important that the group resolve issues as they arise before moving on.

Helping Group Members to Maintain a Here-and-now Orientation

This involves encouraging the group to refrain from going back to revisit previously resolved issues, conflicts, or decisions. Although there may be some groups, such as psychodynamically oriented groups, where working through past individual traumas is essential, for other groups revisiting old conflicts or decisions can become a barrier to moving forward.

Monitoring Adherence to Agreed Group Norms and Discussing Group Behaviors That May be Detrimental to a Member or the Group

This involves calling attention to group norms (e.g. agency, ground rules) when they have been ignored and are creating a negative impact on the group or naming deleterious covert norms.

Turning Issues or Problems Back to the Group

As indicated with imparting information, the worker can empower the group and its members by asking members to use their own experiences and strategies to deal with speculations, problems, and plans that are shared by group members.

Reaching for Consensus

As noted earlier, inclusive practice is consensus driven, as it works towards including all voices in group decision making. However, the worker can sometimes err in the assumption that silence by group members represents agreement with what is occurring in the group. Workers need to periodically check to see if members are in agreement with how things are going, particularly after heated/divisive conversation or when only a few group members have spoken during a discussion.

Reaching for Difference

An inclusive group worker recognizes how different perspectives can help members see experiences and problems from various perspectives. Particularly in the group, when group members may fear negative evaluation by other group members, the worker must invite and affirm members for sharing different views and ideas.

Adopting the Metaphors of the Group

This skill is intended to promote group identification and group cohesiveness. This means that in order to build group identity, the group worker needs to use "we" instead of "I" when speaking to the group and to adopt the metaphors that emerge in the group. For example, in a violence prevention group, which contained several men who rode motorcycles, themes relating to "the road" and "the ride" emerged in the group. The group worker adopted these metaphors when speaking about progress made (e.g., it has been a long hard road) and the obstacles that group members had encountered (i.e., rocks and potholes).

COWORKER RELATIONSHIPS

The choice of with whom and how to work together is often one of the most influential early decisions a group worker makes in planning a group and determining its composition. It must be a fully informed decision and one made with the group purpose and needs of prospective group members as preeminent considerations. As several theorists have pointed out (Kahn, 1996; Wickham, Pelech, & Basso, 2009; Corey et al., 2013), there are advantages and disadvantages associated with working with a coworker in a group. Some of the advantages of working with a coworker include:

- Shared responsibility for the group: Sharing responsibility reduces the chance of burnout, especially with low-functioning groups.
- Dual focus on individuals and group as a whole: When intense emotions are expressed by one member, one worker may stay with that member while the other monitors reactions by other members.

- Preserving continuity of group sessions: Having coworkers enables the group to continue if one worker is unable to attend.
- Opportunities for emotional support for learning and growth: A worker strongly affected by countertransference and the emotional impact of the group can explore reactions with their coworker.
- Opportunities for modeling: Workers can model effective communication, conflict resolution skills, and expression of different perspectives.

Use of the male-female cofacilitation model is particularly effective when the intervention goals include:

- exploring transference reactions to the presence of a parental dyad
- observing opposite-sex individuals engaging in a mutual, nonexploitive relationship
- interacting and identifying with two different-gender role models
- observing and experiencing flexible role enactments by members of the opposite gender
- identifying and working through gender distortions that occur in group.

Beyond the potential monetary cost associated with having two paid workers in a group, the major disadvantages associated with having coworkers in a group is the time required in developing and maintaining an effective working relationship. Most problems and disadvantages cited in working with a coworker may be associated with circumstances in which coworkers are not able to contribute the time, openness, and honesty necessary to establish and maintain a clear contract and working relationship. Such problems may lead to distrust, competition, and rivalry between coworkers. When these problems arise, they can interfere with the group dynamics and processes. If coworker conflict is evident and interferes with the group, group members may feel the need to choose a side.

Though the advantages of having coworkers in a group generally outweigh the disadvantages, from the authors' experiences, having one worker in a group is often preferable and more effective than having coworkers who have not committed themselves to developing and maintaining a good working relationship.

Developing Effective Coworker Relationships

Just as with any personal or professional relationship, developing and maintaining an effective relationship with a coworker requires mutual respect, acceptance, time, and commitment. In order for two workers to collaborate effectively in service of a group, each must respect and trust the other. Mutual respect must extend to finding ways in which each worker's different styles and personality character-istics can complement one another. Perhaps most important is a clear contract that defines how coworkers will work together. This contract must include a commit-ment to take the time to sort things out before and after each group session. Both workers must also be willing to take the time to work out inevitable conflicts that will occur between them and to evaluate their work, group progress, and plans for future sessions.

Developing a Contract with a Coworker

Long before workers prescreen prospective members, coworkers must determine whether or not an effective working relationship can be established with each other. The major factor determining whether two workers can form an effective team is their ability to relate honestly and openly with each other. Openness and honesty are the foundation stones of a viable contract for working together. Some of the things commonly identified as important issues to sort out between prospective coworkers include:

- previous experiences, theoretical orientations, philosophy, and approaches to group work (e.g. structure, responsibility)
- each worker's concerns about working with the other, including perceived obstacles, and how different types of skills/complementary talents can be harnessed in service to the group
- individual strengths and weaknesses and their potential impact upon the ability to work together with the group
- values and principles of ethical practice
- roles and responsibilities to be assumed by each worker
- conflict resolution and problem-solving strategies.

COWORKER RELATIONSHIPS OVER THE STAGES OF GROUP DEVELOPMENT

After two coworkers have agreed on a contract, both should have equal responsi-bility in forming the group and getting it started. Of course, both need to be clear and agree on the purpose, goals, and design of the group. During the early stages of the group, an effective working relationship will enable coworkers to model trust, respect, authenticity, sensitivity, and directness with each other. Just as with the members, coworkers may search for and identify similarities and differences during these stages. Status differences are usually denied at this stage and are avoided by agreements to divide the leadership tasks and establish role differences. In the early stages of group development, group members will often attempt to recruit the workers in ways that are familiar to them. For example, male members may seek validation from and an alliance with the male worker in relation to what they perceive as "male" experiences, while seeking support and nurturing from the female worker. Here both workers must be willing to acknowledge and explore member needs, as well as avoid colluding with these stereotypical role enactments. However, avoidance of acknowledgment of diversity may lead to tension between the coworkers and undermine the coworkers' relationship. The strength of the coworker's relationship will often be most directly tested during the middle stage. Here both workers must be clear on how they will respond to challenges and confrontations by group members. Though an empathic response by both workers to a member challenge is preferable, when one worker is challenged by a group member, the other worker must not take sides or defend his or her coworker; rather, he or she must serve in a mediating role and assist the group to explore and resolve the conflict.

Later in the group's life, members may attempt to align themselves with a particular worker or to split the worker dyad in ways that reenact their family of origin experience. Here again supervision and an open coworker relationship are essential. Coworkers must be able to step back to observe and share both their perceptions and feelings associated with the projections occurring in the group. If the workers are unable to address and explore these projections within the group and their relationship, then the growth of the group, its members, and the coworker relationship will be hindered. In termination it is common for one or both workers to have difficulty in acknowledging and dealing with their own feelings concerning ending the group. Mutual support here will assist coworkers with dealing with such feelings and thereby free them to work more effectively with group members.

Exercise 10.1: The Men's Group

You are one of the workers assigned to work with a violence prevention group for men who have abused their partners. The group has two components: a four-week psychoeducational component, followed by eight weeks of process oriented sessions. The large group of approximately sixteen members has been separated into two groups of eight. One worker is an experienced male worker and the other is a slightly less experienced female intern who has just joined the group for the process oriented component.

During the first process oriented session, the male members constantly defer to the male worker whenever they are speaking. They seldom engage visually with the female worker and are generally unresponsive to whatever questions/interventions offered by the female worker.

After group, you usually spend a few minutes to debrief the session. Taking on the role of the male, and then the female worker, reflect on what you have observed and experienced in the group. What do you sense is underlying the men's deferential behavior? Develop a plan as to how you will deal with this behavior in the group next week.

CHAPTER SUMMARY

This chapter has outlined some of the characteristics of effective leadership. It has emphasized that in an inclusive group, where diverse perspectives and expertise are embraced, leadership is a role that is distributed or shared by different group members who offer what the group needs at various points in its work. The chapter also briefly examined the first and most influential relationship present in many groups: the coworker relationship. The chapter identified the relative benefits and challenges that arise in coworker relationships and outlined steps for workers to prepare and work with differences that arise in their relationships.

CHAPTER 11

THE MIDDLE STAGE OF GROUP WORK

LEARNING OBJECTIVES

At the end of this chapter you will be able to:

- Describe the group worker's role in this stage, and incorporate a group work contract and a set of goals.
- Work collaboratively with group members to achieve helping through decision making and problem solving.
- Demonstrate an understanding of key practice activities and their application to further the group work during this stage.

Vignette: Working with Nonverbal Behavior

In the sixth group meeting, Frances shows impatience when Thomas shares his story. The group worker picks up on Frances' nonverbal behavior and inquires about her "gut reaction" to what is being shared in group.

Frances: "I don't know. . . . We keep hearing the same stories every week and there seem to be no efforts from any of us to try out ideas that were shared in our group. . . . Is this the way groups are supposed to work?"

Group Worker: "There are really two parts to your question. First, do groups work this way? And the answer is yes, sometimes we review past content before we are ready to move on. The second part is potentially more significant though. Are we exploring or incorporating anything from the group into our lives, especially related to what brought us to group in the first place?

The middle stage in group work is the one in which members work towards either task completion or changes in self and in relationships with others (Jacobs, Harvill, & Schimmel, 2009). The middle phase of group work is characterized by a group that presents and responds to content and attends to and comments on its own processes. Content refers to the information shared among the members, as well as the feelings associated with this information. Process refers to how group members share the direct verbalizations and indirect communications (i.e. eye movements, body language, utterances, and facial expressions) that are evident in the group. Both content and process are necessary components to a group's helping relationships. The help available in groups is the result of the care and cooperation of group members as they listen, comprehend, ask, and respond to the group's content and processes.

As the group progresses towards sharing and deepening relationships among the members, the group members also become keenly aware of the tensions and clashes among themselves. Members see, hear, and feel the closeness and disconnects among them, leading to a range of emotions from hope to apprehension, doubt, and/or uncertainty. The group worker attempts to reinforce the relationships among all members and at the same time recognize that differences exist and that these ultimately will be viewed as strengths. Open identification of group members' uniqueness and differences can assist in the group's development of better, alternative communication skills.

ROLE OF THE GROUP WORKER

The role of the group worker in the middle stage includes a process function, which is to maintain group focus as the group meets over time, to value emerging self-disclosures, and to respect group members' apparent or subtle differences. The worker monitors expressions of distrust or alienation in the group and brings these forward for the group's consideration. The group worker stimulates a further discussion about how the different worldviews present in the group might be affecting the work that members are doing together (Sciarra, 1999). Issues of privilege should also be considered and discussed. Although the worker's role is ascribed by virtue of the fact that he or she assembled the individuals for a group experience, the functions of the role are meant to be shared with and distributed among the group members. In the middle phase, group members can assume parts of the worker's role over time.

The initial power and control of the group attributed to a group worker by members in the earlier stages may elevate the helper to a role of an expert. Group workers need to recognize that this is only a temporary power position. Although it may be appealing to some group workers, their continued use of power sets the stage for group members' dependencies and expectations that the worker will do all of the work. In a well-functioning group, power and control over group events is redistributed among the members over time as the group is able to accept this shared responsibility.

Exercise 11.1: Group Leadership Scenarios

In the fifth group meeting at an alcohol intervention facility, members begin to tell jokes and not attend to the purpose of the group. What is happening and what might you choose to do about this?

As a group worker in the community who asks neighborhood groups to identify needs and set priorities for municipal projects, you encounter a community group that wanders from the planning task as they keep returning to topics of sports, camping, cooking, and so on. What is happening and what might you choose to do about it?

GETTING STARTED IN THE MIDDLE PHASE

Group workers plan for the use of time in the group, thereby creating a structure for meetings that follow. In task groups, the worker incorporates ideas and agenda items for the group to work on. The group worker recaps the work done in the previous meeting and brings forward discussion items for that group session. Many intervention groups also include a check-in of how each member's week has unfolded. In order to prevent the check-in from overtaking the entire group time, it might be advisable to limit a check-in procedure to ten minutes, or about a minute for each group participant. In this time frame, each person can identify a positive or negative feeling about what happened to him or her during the preceding week and indicate if there is a request to further discuss this in group.

In task or intervention groups, the group worker assists members to decide if new content fits the purposes and goals of the group. Members agree on the work to be done in that particular session, making the group's start-up each week a joint responsibility among members and the social worker. The shared exercise in setting the group's agenda reinforces empowerment as members may soon realize that they have a chance to direct and structure their mutual time together.

Group members give and receive feedback with each other in this phase. Some members may need assistance to provide helpful, not hurtful, comments to others. Pejorative comments have no place in group. Comments based within the group's immediate context, sometimes referred to as the here and now, are valued when based upon behaviors and comments shared in group. Assumptions about others are not welcome and should be challenged by the group worker or other members as they occur. Members are encouraged to address one another rather than talking about the other group members. Trust is reinforced through direct inquiry, genuine comments among the group members, and no interpretation of others' experiences.

Trust does not have to be strained in a group when group members deal with issues related to differences and diversity. Members who come from places of privilege such as higher socioeconomic status or dominant community memberships can be encouraged to listen for the others' oppressive life events or situations and offer comments that do not minimize the other members' distress and pain. Simply stated, time and effort are necessary for a group to succeed in this sometimes difficult personal learning. Lack of attention to these seemingly small but potent details may yield mistrust and contribute to group attrition. Some members may have difficulty with the unfolding subject matter of the group and then display anxiety or intolerance. Framing this group activity as part of the expected dynamic uptake of group content may help (Northen & Kurland, 2001). Trust is fostered within a context of differences when the group affirms the common purposes, goals, and tasks among all of its members.

GOAL SETTING, CONTRACTING, AND HELPING IN GROUP

In the middle phase of group work, the understanding of purpose and goals is a "continuous process of definition and redefinition of both the long range and immediate purposes as these become more specific as they undergo gradual changes" (Northen, 1988 p. 232). The members' goals evolve from the more general statements of concern in the beginning of group to more specific and concrete statements of desired change in the middle phase of group work. The group leaders strive to clarify and assist members to restate their goals as the group continues to meet. The contract among group members also becomes clearer as members agree to listen and respond thoughtfully to others who are struggling with the wide array of challenges and obstacles that may be perceived during this stage.

The group worker encourages members to engage with each other in group. The engagement is based upon creating an understanding of the challenges that are presented in group. The group strives to obtain any additional information that might explain or clarify the presented challenges. The group worker assists by guiding group discussion into specific content areas. Individual members show an increased motivation to inquire and offer interpersonal support when others share data in group.

The group constantly assesses any new information as it comes forth and examines earlier shared statements, looking for new ways to understand challenges. The group members and the group as a whole begin to explore potential tasks that might assist in goal attainment. With the group worker's help, the group discusses alternative actions to consider before taking action. The tasks might be in-group activities such as role playing or activities assigned to complete outside of the group. Individual group members can be helped to achieve their goals through discussions of potential keys for change and obstacles blocking change.

MUTUAL AID IN GROUP

The concept of mutual aid has been a most important foundation in understanding how groups can be helpful. Yalom and Leszca (2005) noted that a group offers valuable aid to all of the members. Helping is reciprocal in nature, as members offer assistance to others and at the same time receive assistance from them. Mutual aid represents the potential of group members to receive help and to assist one another as they work on their needs, concerns, challenges, or problems. Shulman (2011) notes that simply bringing persons together will not yield helpful behaviors among members. The group worker must exercise care to generate and reinforce openness and feelings of goodwill among members. In order to do this, a group worker needs to face "his or her own feelings and . . . stereotypes" in order to successfully facilitate group processes (p.23).

Help results from group interactions that foster mutual aid among members. The members adopt any number of roles that facilitate the helping process. Bales (1950) first conceptualized "role" to be an important part of the life of any group. He specifically noted that group members support particular tasks in groups that assist the group to get its work done. Examples of contemporary group roles might include:

- the enabler: who assists others
- the information broker: who offers data and makes connections for others
- the mediator: who offers conciliation between parties
- the advocate: who speaks loudly on behalf of another person
- the teacher: who instructs with details and meanings.

A role initially adopted by an individual may be based on previous interpersonal relationships and/or family history. A goal of helping may be to assist a person to expand the number of roles that he or she can fulfill in relationships. For example, a woman who comfortably helps with assisting others but makes no time for getting her own tasks completed might benefit from a group process that encourages her to value her own needs as equal to others. With assistance, she might attempt to place a priority on her own need to accomplish self-supporting tasks and minimize her role of a "supporter" to others.

Exercise 11.2: Refining Group Goals

- In the early group meetings, all of the members identified some aspect of communications with loved ones as problematic in their lives. In the middle phase, nobody is discussing communications, but members instead are focused on individual wants, needs, and rights. What would you do to highlight the interpersonal communications problems first presented?

- In a group meeting at the city mayor's office, all persons speak in favor of a particular motion, but nobody votes in favor of the motion. What could be potential causes for this outcome? How could you address this in the group?

MEMBER DECISION MAKING AND PROBLEM SOLVING IN GROUP

In the middle phase of group work, it is expected that group members commit to working together on the concerns, situations, problems, or challenges identified in group. Groups survive and thrive when they recognize and establish a common purpose and a commonly held meta-goal that represents the direction in which the group members are headed together. All groups need to have a purpose and a meta-goal. A well-functioning group supports the overarching group goal as well as the differing individual efforts to attain unique personal goals.

In this phase, group members feel that relationships with others in the group are in place and they begin to work with the connections that they established with other members. Cohesion is the traditional concept used to describe the "all in the same boat phenomenon" (Shulman, 2011, p. 27). Feelings include interpersonal comfort and a sense of a developing trust that is essential in order for the members to present their problems or reasons for seeking help and to ask others in the group for assistance. After the group agrees to try out the group process, some may need clarification regarding the risks inherent in sharing personal and emotionally laden significant stories. It is common that some group members may need opportunities to openly discuss their fears related to the group's closeness and intimacy.

During this phase of group development, members engage in interactional exchanges with the other group members, including the group worker. Sometimes members criticize the group's efforts and progress. The group worker must realize that some group members are asking for the opportunity to speak up about changing some aspect of the group (i.e., the topics being discussed, the ways that members respond to one another, or the need for a new direction). Stresses in interpersonal exchanges usually indicate that the group needs to discover and clarify meanings and features of others' messages. Egregious behaviors in group may elicit the creation of new norms as the group progresses in its work. The group's ongoing examination of members' exchanges contributes to assessing existing norms and lays open the groundwork for evolving group norms.

Trust is an essential requirement for a group to progress in this stage. When members represent differing belief systems or points of view, the group is more often than not fully aware of these obstacles. The social worker must address the differences in group as real life representations of the differences among members and communities and then reframe the differences as potential contributions to new understandings or ways of relating. It is at this point that individual members, especially persons representing some aspect of diversity, may need support from the group worker or other members to ease into an interactional comfort level as the group strives towards deepening feelings of connectedness. As group members share more expressions of emotion over time, there may even be a drive towards interpersonal conformity as they learn the limits of how to communicate with each other (Lakin, 1988).

Conformity may endanger the future participation of some group members who might begin to feel that they are on the outside of the group. A leader's task in the middle phase of group work is to be alert to in-group expressions of dominant ideologies that may be oppressive in nature. Members' assumptions and attitudes are worthy of closer examination, especially if related to cultural meanings, nontraditional ways, and invisible identities. A group worker brings forward to the group any previously unattended or disregarded diversity elements so that the group attends to them and builds awareness of the contributions of all of its members.

Questions from the worker to the group invite members to reflect on cultural, ethnic, gender, and other unique qualities or differences in the group. Members are asked to comment on how each thinks that the uniqueness and differences might influence individual participation and affect the group as a whole. Members are encouraged to meta-talk: to share their perceptions of how they might engage one another in conversations and share personal information in group. All members are asked to affirm respect for all others in that process.

Group members learn through shared group experiences of empowerment to deliberate alternatives and to select their next steps from the range of possible choices. Although the concept of cohesion suggests that group membership is based on similarities among individual members (Toseland, Jones, & Gellis, 2004), the individual group members maintain character uniqueness representing a diversity of members and life experiences in a group. By respecting differentness among its members, the group can then encourage individual problem solving without threatening group members' connections.

The group worker's tasks are to maintain focus on the diversity of individuals and their problems and the variety of potential solutions to the problems presented in group. As Shulman (2011) noted, members start with nonexact statements of problems and when they trust the process, move to share deeper dimensions of the problems.

The group's strength is to offer alternatives and choices for the individual member to consider. The group accepts the differences of members and assists in the description and development of individuals' concerns or issues and explores the depths of these in group. It is during this phase that group members become aware that the leaders are not going to provide answers.

The group worker also prevents "sudden closure" or quickly choosing a solution within the group context. Members are reminded to take time to reflect on the impacts of decisions throughout the week. These steps thwart a development of "group think" where members decide upon the superiority of a particular course of action either for an individual's or a group's final solution to a common problem.

The group member's shared experiences have the potential to become an educational tool. As the group participants share information about themselves, respond to another's situation, identify with feelings, or offer support through personal accounts, the problem sharing and decision making progresses for members.

Structure of Group Problem Sharing and Decision Making

Decision making follows a pattern of sharing, finding common bonds, and contemplating the alternatives. In the group, an individual's statement of his or her concern, problem, or challenge is followed by information that verifies this. Group members offer other statements that corroborate or challenge the perception held of a problem. Group members may contribute their related life experiences as well. The presenter of the challenge may acquire support and new directions for handling the situation. During the following week, there is an opportunity to work on the problem with new insights or confirmed perceptions of the problem. The group does not make decisions for any person who presents a problem or a social situation.

Exercise 11.3: Case Examples

- A woman who was abused shares with group members her deliberations of leaving or returning to a partner who batters. The group members share their related life experiences and discuss potential choices, but then leave the decision making to her at the individual level. As a safety precaution, the group worker points out that at times victims are most at risk for harm by the abuser when they consider leaving. What more would you consider doing?

- An agency team of social workers must decide on whether to recommend returning a child to the natural parents or a foster home. The child's background information and interviews with parents, teachers, and police are reviewed numerous times with the team split on a final decision. How would you facilitate this situation?

DECISION MAKING IN TASK GROUPS

Groups have been generally shown to be more effective in completing tasks or solving problems than individuals, particularly when dealing with complex tasks or problems. What makes groups superior to individuals is their ability to delegate tasks to group members and to generate more potential options (Fatout & Rose, 1995). Decision making is an integral part of the problem-solving process. Originating with John Dewey in the 1930s, the problem-solving process involves the following steps:

- Identify the problems, issues, or concerns, and rank them.
- Collect data on the problems, issues, or concerns.
- Critically analyze the data.
- Examine the options, including the available resources.
- Select the most appropriate options and attendant consequences and rank them.
- Decide on the options to be explored.
- Choose and implement an option.
- Devise procedures for evaluation and feedback in relation to the choice of option (Wickham, Pelech, & Basso, 2009, p. 9).

Brainstorming

As suggested in the problem-solving process, an important part of solving problems is the generation of sufficient diverse options that will enable the group to make an effective decision. In some groups, member apprehension about potential ridicule or judgment by others may inhibit their sharing of different ideas. However, an inclusive approach would establish norms that affirm and celebrate diverse ideas. Brainstorming is a strategy that can be employed to generate many diverse ideas or options relating to a specific topic or question. Effective brainstorming requires the following:

- Each member shares one idea at a time and continues sharing ideas until they have shared all of their ideas and have run out of new ideas.
- Each idea is recorded as given by group members.
- Evaluation of ideas is delayed until after all of the ideas have been shared. No member should be asked to justify any idea that is shared during brainstorming.
- Members improve upon, modify, and link ideas that are shared by others.

Following brainstorming and the creation of a list of ideas, the group evaluates the relative merits of each idea or option. Reverse brainstorming is a technique that may be used to reduce the number of ideas to a more manageable number. Coined by Richards (1974), reverse brainstorming asks that group members brainstorm the limitations of each idea or the negative consequences of its selection for implementation.

As suggested, the problem-solving process involves making decisions about which options are most likely to be effective in solving the stated problem. For this reason, the outcome of this process hinges on effective decisions. In many task groups, there are more formal and explicit procedures utilized in making decisions. Table 11.1 lists a number of decision-making methods that are commonly

Table 11.1 Decision-making Strategies

Method	Strengths	Challenge
By a person in authority without discussion	Speed	Does not use member expertise
By a person in authority after discussion	Allows everyone to express opinion.	Members may not be committed to the decision
Decision by expert member	Good decision if really expert	May be difficult to identify an expert
Average members' opinion	Speed	Members may not be committed to the decision
Majority control	Speed	Minority may be alienated
Minority control	Can be useful if not everyone can attend	Members may not be committed to the decision
Consensus	Members will be committed to the decision	May require considerable time, skill, and energy

found in task groups. Each method presents its own strengths and challenges. As noted earlier, research has shown that groups are generally better than the average individual in making the best decisions; however, groups are not better than the best individual when it comes to decision making (Fatout & Rose, 1995). The worker must consider a number of variables when selecting a decision-making method. Important considerations are:

• Time: How much time is available to make the decision?
• Expertise: Who possesses the knowledge and expertise to make an effective decision?
• Impact: How will the chosen method affect the group and its members, particularly if the group will continue or is needed to implement the decision?

Role Playing

One of the primary advantages offered by intervention groups over individual counseling is that intervention groups offer a realistic social microcosm for members, not only to act out their maladaptive coping strategies, but also to enhance their social functioning by trying out new ways of relating to others (Yalom & Leszcz, 2005). One technique that harnesses these interpersonal benefits of group work is role playing. There are a number of ways in which role plays can be used to enhance member interpersonal skills.

First, a member who is facing a challenging interpersonal problem or issue with someone outside of the group may rehearse how they will address this issue with that person by role playing the encounter in the group. For example, in a youth group for gay teens, one member, Miguel, who had not yet disclosed to his parents that he was gay, practiced ways that he could come out to his parents with group members who had already done so. After two group members were asked by Miguel to play the roles of his mother and father, Miguel then further described his parents to assist the two group members to play the role of his parents. Next, Miguel tried out different ways of coming out and the group members who played his parents (as well as other group members) responded to each approach by providing feedback and suggesting new approaches.

Second, role playing can be used to reverse roles, enabling group members to gain insights into the thoughts, feelings, and responses of significant others in their lives. For example, in an interpersonal violence group for adult males, one member, Sam, wished to understand how his behavior had affected his partner,

Jason. After Sam described a specific incident when he became abusive, including both his behavior and that of his partner, one group member was asked to role play Sam, while Sam played the role of Jason. From this experience, Sam gained a deeper understanding of how his behavior affected his partner and a sense of empathy for Jason's experience in their relationship.

Third, although there are other more elaborate role playing techniques (e.g., sculpting, family reconstruction), a very simple form of role playing allows group members to express thoughts and feelings for those who are unavailable to them. For example, Joan, in a grief support group, wanted to say goodbye to her twelve-year-old son, Michael, who had been killed in a motor vehicle accident. In the group, an empty chair was used to represent Michael. Joan then shared her feelings of guilt over not being able to protect him and talked about how much she missed and loved him.

GROUP WORK INTERVENTIONS IN THE MIDDLE PHASE

Helping in group work involves the twin activities of assisting an individual and the group as a whole. The focus is always on group process and how this facilitates individuals to consider personal change. Members' self-disclosures usually supply the group with specific information. Members' general responses and direct feedback provide group members with both challenges and support over time. Receiving and integrating feedback can be a difficult task for members. Group workers openly discuss the potential difficulties that hearing feedback can produce. Members are reminded not to quickly assume that their perceptions are always correct. All members are reminded to ask questions to clarify understandings before offering their perception of events. This step provides a way to either ask for more details or to confirm one's perceptions before verbalizing them.

Although some individual clarifications may be necessary with a group member, this brief individual work is woven back into the tapestry of the purpose of the group and related to the goals of the group. A group worker would rarely conduct long individual interviews with separate members as others passively watch. In its simplest form, the group is an opportunity for members to interact with one another. In the shared exchanges in group, members give and receive questions, feedback, and support from other group members. The establishment of interpersonal relationships assists in the group's formation of trust and members' willingness to accept diverse, alternate ways of perceiving and acting. This process is based upon healthy interpersonal connections in group that support members to be honest and empathetic with each other. (See exercise 11.4 for intervention activities.)

Exercise 11.4: Interventions

Individual Member Interventions

- Ask a group member to elaborate on his or her feelings related to discussion points.
- Encourage self-examination of individual cognitive process related to problem discussion, paying close attention to "self-talk" or an individual's internal messages.
- Invite a group member to try out new behaviors in group.

Interventions for the Group as a Whole

- Invite all members to identify feelings related to a situation being discussed in group.
- Encourage others to reflect on their own similar experiences when dealing with the problem.
- Ask members to respond to a member's attempts to try out changes within the group context.

KEY PRACTICE ACTIVITIES

Listening, Questioning/Confronting, and Responding as Basic Skills

A safe group environment is created when group members practice listening to others' presentations of thoughts and feelings. Questions that emanate from the shared content usually begin to show others that members are thoughtfully hearing and comprehending what is being shared. Questions elicit clarity among the group members. Confronting others simply refers to the sharing of an honest and constructive assessment of another group member's situation using content and behaviors shared in group. Responding, especially with empathy, can demonstrate to a speaker that others care, are moved emotionally, and/or understand the content and processes as presented in group. The group moves towards empathic listening skills so that members can begin to respond to others' feelings. The group worker may have to model this initially so others learn how to verbally and nonverbally respond to feelings when these are presented in the group. Members may learn to be more aware of their facial expressions and tone of voice when giving others feedback.

Demanding that Members Work

A group worker continuously focuses on the group members' concerns as they meet over time. These focal points provide members with opportunities to delve deeper into aspects of their issues and concerns. Although groups may wander from the stated reasons for meeting, group members can be reminded of the group's purposes and asked to attend to their goals. Throughout the process, group members can be invited to comment on what is happening in the group. As the members share their personal perceptions, they potentially receive positive feedback regarding their personal expertise in the social environment. As they share their perceptions, they can be rewarded for sharing authentic feelings in the group as well.

Dealing with Anger

Working with people means that the anger they have as a part of their human life will also be present when meeting in a group. Group members may need to present information in group related to their angry feelings. It is an irony that groups designed to aid with the expression of feelings usually chill with the expression of anger, especially when anger presents to some as an unexpected, volatile, and often frightening experience. The group contract usually sets important agreements and guidelines for exploring members' feelings, and the contract can be reexamined or clarified during a group in order to facilitate the inclusion of anger. The group worker needs to make it clear that anger is a human expression and that aspects of anger presented can be safely reviewed in the group.

Dealing with Disruptive or "Off Task" Behaviors

The group focus is on the group's purpose, meta-goal, and individual member goals. Sometimes group members engage in activities that block progress in the group. These activities include personal storytelling, intellectualizing, and distancing oneself from others by adopting a role of advice giver or associate group leader. Storytelling is the disclosing of personal details and/or information about others that is not germane. Intellectualizing is a member's exclusive focus on thinking without much integration of his or her feelings about a topic. The group is encouraged to integrate thoughts and feelings related to the content being developed. Distancing oneself occurs when a member adopts the role of a leader who gives advice, who asks, probes, and comments on dynamics without sharing anything personal about himself or herself in group. When these behaviors occur, it may be beneficial to redirect the member or group. Attention should be given to possible underlying causes of such behavior for further discussion in group.

Monitoring Group Progress

The ongoing evaluation of the group's achievement of goals should be undertaken throughout the life of the group, whether done in a weekly, biweekly, or monthly format. The members can contribute written anonymous comments that can then be shared in group the following week; doing so reinforces members' strengths and mutuality in group. Member completion of progress indicators can demonstrate on a Likert scale how far along an individual's goal attainment is progressing. Process indicators can qualitatively ask how well the group facilitates an individual's attainment of his/her goals.

When Groups Stop Working

When a group is not working, the group worker and the members know it by a lack of focus on the group's purpose and assorted goals. The characteristics of a non-working group include: avoiding important issues, attending to extraneous minutia, and evading agreed upon tasks. Group members may complain of confusion, mistrust, helplessness, dependency, or other feelings that signal a loss of direction or lack of understanding of group priorities and problems to be shared in group.

Capturing the group's commitment again can be accomplished in a number of ways. One would be to recap the group's previous foci and invite members to briefly evaluate those activities. Another route would be to recall where the group's work ended and cite the goals not yet achieved. In any strategy, the group worker tunes in to the feelings of the members, listening for fatigue and their willingness to continue to self-disclose in group.

When Resistance Appears in Group

The concept of resistance appears in many different sources of professional helping texts. A popular understanding of resistance is that a person refuses to accept or comply with something. Yalom and Leszca, (2005) refine this understanding and view resistance as a person's ability not to be affected by something and that the resistance is deeply ingrained. In the first instance, a person actively brushes aside criticism, caring, or suggestions. In the second instance, interpersonal interactions simply bounce off of the individual with no apparent impact or meaning to him or her. Resistance, seen as indifference, can impede the progress of an individual and the group as a whole towards their stated goals.

A reason for resistance may be that the group does not match one's expectations of helping. Other group members do not provide what codependants in life provide to an individual. Resistance in group appears as a lack of connection between or among group members, but what it signals, Epstein (1992) suggests, is a lack of congruence in motives among group members to work together on problems that are meaningful to them.

Epstein (1992) further suggests that, when resistance appears, the best response is to return to asking about the group member's self-interests. This provides members a way to reinvest in the group process. The group worker facilitates open discussions around the apparent resistance that forge interpersonal links and make connections that reopen a potential for helping. Successful interventions "were those in which the client's motivations were directed toward what the social workers were attempting to provide" (p.47).

Resistance may actually represent group members' real but unspoken concerns. Used appropriately, the group worker's ability to illuminate his or her own misunderstandings of the group's or member's content and assumptions about the group's process is an important step to clarification of the issues. Group workers are encouraged to examine these misunderstandings and assumptions throughout the existence of a group (Gitterman & Germain, 2008; Corey, Corey & Corey, 2010).

When Ambivalence Appears in Group

Ambivalence is seen when individual group members hold opposing feelings, beliefs, or attitudes towards others, the concerns presented, or the group's process. The appearance of ambivalence represents an approach-avoidance conflict as the group member identifies his or her own internal polar opposite reactions both for and against the issue. Nonverbal behaviors usually indicate the internal struggle that the member is going through, and an attentive group worker or group member should recognize the hesitation, grimace, or discomfort. Simply recognizing this usually sparks follow-up discussions, and group members can share their similar experiences of ambivalence.

When Inappropriate Self-disclosure Occurs in Group

Each member brings to group his or her interpersonal boundaries, and these set important and significant limitations on the sharing of personal information. In the middle stage of group work, it is expected that members will attempt to reveal deeper understandings of their concerns. Two concerns may become evident requiring intervention. The first is when some members offer more personal information than is required and present many private and unnecessary disclosures in group. Members can be reminded of the purposes of the group and asked how the disclosed information relates to the goals that they chose to work on, thereby emphasizing some limits to what is shared. The second is when members from a different background struggle to disclose any information. It may not be within the cultural norms of members to share so openly. These group members may have difficulty understanding how self-disclosure promotes a fuller understanding of one's problems. Group workers need to sensitively encourage sharing and confirm the appropriate confidentiality from all members, which reinforces trust in the group.

Exercise 11.5: Group Work Practice Examples

Review these cases and think about how you would manage the situations described.

- In the third meeting at a community-based service office, community members and government officials assemble an agenda but fail to follow the items on the distributed agenda. What is happening and what are your options to intervene and get the group back on track?
- As a group worker in a family counseling organization, you encounter a group member who wanders from the agreed group focus. What elements will you consider before you intervene and how will you intervene?

CHAPTER SUMMARY

The middle stage of group work follows the initial stage of developing relationships and exploring common ground and purposes along with unique individual problems and goals. This chapter discussed the role of the group worker in the middle stage and how the worker can promote the group process through the reaffirming of diversity, the helping relationship, trust, and the group's goals. The chapter also provided considerations and tools for effective decision making and problem solving. Finally, it discussed key practice activities for this stage and inclusive strategies a group worker can utilize to address obstacles that may hinder the group process.

CHAPTER 12

ADVANCED SKILLS AND CONFLICT RESOLUTION

LEARNING OBJECTIVES

At the end of this chapter you will be able to:
- Explain the elements of the professional use of self.
- Apply the professional use of self to a practice vignette.
- Articulate the benefits of working effectively with conflict.
- Apply an inclusive model of conflict resolution to a practice vignette.

This chapter will discuss two advanced skill sets that are essential for effective group work practice. These include the professional use of self and conflict resolution. The chapter will explore these two skill sets through the use of two practice vignettes.

THE PROFESSIONAL USE OF SELF AND DIVERSITY

In social work with groups, there has been a long tradition that spoke to the professional use of self or, as it was previously called by many seminal social group workers, the conscious use of self (Wilson & Ryland; 1949; Phillips, 1957). It is here where the worker offers an essential difference that is not available in self-help or peer led groups. In this sense, and in addition to any other attributes, it is the worker's professional use of self that embodies the worker's diversity in the group.

Phillips (1957) believed that feelings were reactions to the worker's self, group members, and the content of their shared experience. Feelings were also conceptualized as representing the strength and quality of the connections between members and the worker. The worker disciplined his/her feelings by acknowledging their presence and then separating empathic responses from personal reactions.

Phillips (1957) asserted that feelings may be disciplined for conscious use or be denied and removed from conscious control. Denied feelings are subject to unconscious projection through forms of expression such as nonverbal facial expressions or gestures. Through disciplining his/her feelings, the worker frees his/her empathic sensitivity for the experiences of individual members and the group as a whole, thereby promoting stronger interpersonal connections. Because blocked or pent-up feelings withheld by group members also have negative implications for interpersonal relationships and group development, the worker uses his/her empathic skills to help members acknowledge and take responsibility for their own feelings. Moreover, Phillips (1957) implied that the worker's feeling connection served a vital role in sense making, helping the worker to translate observation and knowledge into helping. She asserted that although professional training provides a worker with a bag of techniques and also informs the worker as to *how* to assess a social work group, it is the worker's connection that provides the *when* of worker intervention.

Lang (1994) described a sense-making process in qualitative research that provides a more elaborate understanding of the professional use of self. This chapter has adapted Lang's model, integrating some of the skills discussed earlier in this text to create a process that involves four elements: (1) observing, (2) exploring, (3) conceiving, and (4) transforming. This model will be explored through the use of a vignette that will enable the reader to apply the model to an actual practice situation.

Exercise 12.1: Professional Use of Self in Groups

Vignette: Just a Student?

You are a Caucasian, middle class, female social work student placed at a local community counseling agency. One of your learning assignments is to cofacilitate a twelve-week group for men who have exhibited intimate partner violence. Your African American, middle class, male coworker has a few more years of experience with this type of group. You and your coworker begin the group by welcoming the members and stating your names, the purpose of the group, and your role. You also note that you are a social work graduate student, who has been placed in the agency on a practicum. You then ask the members to introduce themselves and invite them to describe their reasons for coming to the group. All of the members are working class males; five out of the ten members are African American; three are of Hispanic ancestry; and two are Caucasian. Several members introduce themselves; then one African American member, Michael, perhaps feeling concerned to hear that you are only a student and do not appear to have anything in common with him, states, "Just a student?"

Picture yourself in this scenario. Where would you focus your attention? Would you reflect on your position in the group? Would you glare at your coworker, hoping for a response?

Observing

The activity of observing implies two elements: positioning and scanning. In other words, the worker must adopt a position and orientation to the group in order to engage in scanning self and group phenomena.

Positioning involves knowing who you are in the group and focusing your awareness in the here and now. Each worker brings to the group his/her own diversity, capacities, values, and ethics, which may be differentiated into personal and professional aspects. By staying in the here and now, the worker can avoid the negative consequences of focusing on previous negative personal experiences or an excessive preoccupation with success or task completion. Positioning also requires that the worker be conscious of the setting of the group session and of his/her physical positioning and posture with respect to each member. Another positioning element is the contract or working agreement negotiated between the worker, group, and agency. A clearly understood and negotiated contract provides parameters within which the worker may freely use himself/herself. Finally, positioning involves preparing to enter into the feelings and thinking of group members (i.e. tuning in, preparatory empathy, and projective imagination).

Next, the worker scans with all his/her senses the group and his/her internal responses, gathering as much information as possible. There are several distinctive elements involved in scanning. First, this scanning is broad (expanding to as far as the group's social context), deep (detecting underlying feelings, meanings), and multidimensional (engaging at various communication levels, e.g., verbal, nonverbal; individual, interpersonal, and group). Scanning also involves heightened sensitivity and detachment, enabling the worker to freely shift from one object or level to another. Scanning is oriented to discovering uniqueness and novelties presented by the group. Scanning also manifests a reaching out quality, whereby the worker identifies and forms feeling connections with other members.

Exercise 12.2: Observing ("Just a Student?")

Thinking back to the vignette in exercise 12.1, would you scan the rest of the group? Would you attend to your internal responses? If you decide to observe your internal responses, what might be some of the feelings and thoughts that would arise in your mind when you hear the words, "Just a student?"

Exploring

To explore involves searching through or into and examining minutely. The term also connotes leaving or separating from the familiar to search out new territory. Arising from the skill of scanning are internal responses within the worker. Just as in the group when diversity arises, an inclusive approach is beneficial here. In order to raise these responses to a fully conscious level for identification and use, the worker must acknowledge, accept, and describe these diverse internal responses. The worker must also suspend his/her immediate and familiar reactions and judgments in order to work effectively with his or her diverse internal responses. Moreover, he/she must stand aside from himself/herself, demonstrating sufficient detachment to note what has happened or been recorded with his/her senses. Several writers have noted the potentially damaging consequences of the worker denying these responses, ranging from incongruity (where the workers' words do not fit with their actions) to the unconscious projection of these feelings onto the group.

Going beyond simple description, the worker's exploration involves the separation of personal feelings and thoughts from subtler and finer professional empathic responses, intuition, and intelligence. Such a screening out process requires two related forms of self-awareness. First, the worker must be aware of his/her own biases, prejudices, attitudes, and needs. Second, he/she must have awareness and sensitivity in order to discern how different feelings or sensations manifest themselves internally. Through examining inner responses, the worker is then able to free his/her perceptions and compare them with other data (Lang, 1994).

Exercise 12.3: Exploring ("Just a Student?")

Thinking back to exercise 12.1, let us say you choose to explore your internal responses before responding. Would there be any judgments present? Let's say that you begin to feel a little inadequate, fearful, and defensive. How might you respond internally to these feelings? Might you defend against them by denying your feelings and rejecting them? Or would you choose to accept these feelings and explore them?

Conceiving

While exploring involves the separation of self and responses, conceiving entails an inner dialogue serving to connect together the worker's experience to create meaning and identify forms of intervention. Just as the worker attempts to build relationships in the group by linking members who share similar ideas or experiences, conceiving involves linking by comparison external events with internal responses and searching for patterns and commonalties. These linkages assist the worker in verifying the accuracy of his/her inner empathic and intuitive responses and related inferences. They also help maintain the vital connection between the worker and the group. However, in the same way that the worker can deny his or her inner responses and perceptions, the worker may also defend himself/herself from making these linkages, effectively separating her inner self from the group and preventing verification of his/her own subjectively derived meanings.

Upon confirming his/her internal responses, the worker continues the process of linking by connecting his/her current experience with his/her group work knowledge and previous group work experiences. In comparing the new with the known, the worker makes use of his/her conceptual framework to derive meaning and identify appropriate interventions from his/her behavioral repertoire. When considering the potential interventions, the worker must now ask what implications his/her meanings have for the state of group development, his/her role, and the group's movement toward its purpose. Of sole consideration by the worker should be what form of intervention would be most beneficial for the group and its members.

Exercise 12.4: Conceiving ("Just a Student?")

Again, think back to the vignette in exercise 12.1. After exploring your feelings, you may begin to become open to reflecting on how Michael may be feeling. What might be some of the ways that Michael and other group members may be feeling at this stage of their group experience? Is it possible that they may be feeling some ambivalence at this point? Is it possible that Michael may have already been judged by others as being abusive and that his normative ambivalence and reluctance may have been heightened by the situation he finds himself in as someone who has been labeled as abusive?

You may also realize that because of the diversity present in the group, including your position as a Caucasian female authority figure in the group, he may be concerned that you will judge him without understanding him. Perhaps you also realize that Michael may be stating something that is shared by other members of the group. However, if you choose to focus on your personal feelings and defend against them, how might you respond? Is it possible that you may become angry or feel threatened by Michael?

Transforming

Identified by Lang (1994) as a single multifaceted element involving the return-ing of the worker to external reality to implement a chosen action, transforming as outlined here includes the activities of intending, acting, and evaluating. Intend-ing speaks to the motives of the worker in choosing and implementing the inter-vention. Within the literature, there are two motivational aspects; one is based upon meeting the needs of the group and its members in a way that is consistent with the worker's service providing responsibility, and the other is driven by the worker's personal needs for approval, ego-gratification, or anxiety reduction.

The first choice the worker needs to make is whether to respond or simply contain their response. This choice may take very different forms depending upon which aspect of motivation the worker has adopted. An intervention is any worker behavior intended to enhance the functioning of a group. The worker's choice of how to act is also guided by his/her connection with the group. However, if the worker feels that he/she may be likely to act from a personal egoistic basis, he/she may demonstrate self-control by containing his/her reactivity and seeking super-vision after the session has ended, or he/she may react (as he/she may have throughout the earlier activities) to control or escape.

As complex systems, groups are particularly influenced by initial conditions and early developmental stages. Interventions occurring at critical points in group development have a significant impact on the effectiveness of the group. Workers should also be prepared for unsuccessful results even when their actions are well-timed and appropriate. Interventions may be evaluated in terms of four dimensions:

1. Focus

Worker interventions may focus on different group aspects. Worker interventions may be aimed at individual members, interpersonal interactions, or group level processes. In general, different foci elicit different member responses. For exam-ple, often interventions focused on group processes are less likely to elicit defen-siveness than are interventions focused on a single member.

2. Immediacy

Interventions may also be evaluated in terms of how they orient group discussion toward further exploration. Interventions that respond to the feelings evoked by what is currently happening in the group (group process) have more immediacy for the group than do those that respond to content or facts. Interventions with high immediacy tend to free up group interactions and heighten group vitality. Interventions with low immediacy tend to dampen group interactions.

3. Responsibility

Interventions vary in terms of the degree of responsibility for growth put on the group itself. Excessive interventions by the worker may promote member dependency and impair development of the group as a system of mutual aid. Thus, interventions may be evaluated in terms of the degree to which they promote leader centered responsibility and encourage leader-member interactions or group centered responsibility in terms of promoting member-to-member interactions.

4. Relevance

Another way to evaluate interventions is in terms of their relevance to the stated group purpose and the needs and intervention goals of group members. Awareness of common issues and themes experienced by group members (e.g. powerlessness in a survivors' group) may be most helpful in assisting the worker to harness events, interactions, and discussion in service of member intervention goals.

Finally, after intervening, the worker returns to an observational form of self-reflection to evaluate his/her motivations and to what extent his/her action, and its impact on the group, matched his/her intentions and predictions. Further, he/she must assess the implications of the group's response in terms of his/her subsequent positioning. Ultimately, the worker must evaluate whether his/her use of self has contributed the vital difference necessary to move the group toward its goals. Where no difference has been shared with the group, the worker, through supervision and self-examination, may enhance his/her self-awareness and conceptual framework, increasing his/her effectiveness in subsequent group sessions.

Exercise 12.5: Transforming ("Just a Student?")

Recalling exercise 12.1, how do you decide to respond? Do you continue to contain your response and wait for your coworker to say something? Or you do respond by asking Michael to share his concerns? For example, "Yes, Michael, you are right. I am a student. I sense that you may be concerned about that. Would you like to tell me more about that?" Such a response would enable Michael to share this ambivalence about being in this group. He may state that he is concerned that you may not understand him or be able to help him with his challenges. In response, you could say, "You know, Michael, you may be right. I may not have all the answers. How about others here? Are you also concerned that my coworker and I may not be able to help you?" As the others respond with their concerns, there will be an opportunity for you to acknowledge their ambivalence and clarify your roles as workers. You might add that everyone brings different strengths and challenges to this group, but together you can make a difference. You might even finish by thanking Michael for sharing his concern in the group.

DIVERSITY AND CONFLICT EXPLORATION

Conflicts in contemporary life are continually changing and are complex. Group members bring with them intimate knowledge of conflicts and tensions related to social living.

Webster's dictionary ("Conflict," 2015) includes in its full definition two aspects of conflict that bring together our foregoing discussion of diversity and the use of self. Conflict may be experienced externally in the group among group members or internally in the thoughts and feelings of group members. In this way, conflict can be multilevel in nature. More specifically, in keeping with the earlier discussion on the professional use of self, conflict may arise as a mental struggle resulting from incompatible or opposing needs, drives, wishes, or external/internal demands. As noted earlier, it may also manifest as antagonistic states or action arising from divergent ideas, interests, or persons.

If one accepts that diversity is present in every group, then conflict is likely to be present as well. Although conflict is often perceived as something negative, conflict can prove beneficial for a group, and what is more important is how conflict is addressed when it arises. Conflict in a group can lead to critical incidents that help the group move towards achieving its goals. Some research in task groups has shown that a moderate level of task conflict is more productive for team performance than a very low level of task conflict (Bang & Park, 2015). Whether or not conflict is acknowledged and addressed (that is, whether it is expressed overtly or covertly) will have profound consequences for the group. Unresolved conflict can lead to reduced commitment of group members towards the group decisions (Janssen, Van de Vliert, & Veenstra, 1999), early departures by group members, and the eventual disintegration of the group (Northen, 2003).

Exercise 12.6: Conflict, Anyone?

Think of the last time that you worked on a group project with other class members. Think about a point in the group where you experienced a conflict with one or more group members. How did you feel? Did you choose to address the conflict or avoid it? If you chose to address this conflict, how did you address it? How did the way in which you addressed it affect your group? If you chose to avoid the conflict, how did you feel and how did avoiding this conflict affect the group?

Group workers often experience some reluctance in addressing conflict. Just as many people have experienced negative repercussions for being different in some way, for many, the experience of unresolved conflict often has been at best unpleasant and at worst traumatic in nature. So, although it is understandable that many group workers might desire a conflict-free group, the absence of the overt expression of conflict is not always indicative of a group that is well functioning.

As with the presence of any form of diversity, when conflict arises the group worker's initial reaction will either hamper the work of the group or set the stage for future exploration of challenges in group. The multilevel nature of conflict often signals that there are core issues and dilemmas that group members can examine. Particularly early in the group, when members may not have experienced the successful resolution of conflict, it is the responsibility of the group worker to field these issues and bring them to the attention of group members. The variety of issues and the meanings attached to these conflicts can become discussion points among the group members. It is also important to note that group members see conflict around them through the lens of their cultures, social context, and interpersonal relationships (Avgar & Neuman, 2015). Group members can outline their common interests and directions only after they recognize and examine their differences.

As suggested, diversity in groups usually means that members have conflicting values, power relationships, and personal agendas when they enter group. Some group members might advance personal interests over those of other members. Initial self-interest exhibited by group members may be a form of cultural hegemony. Cultural hegemony refers to a cultural and ideological oppression employed to maintain societal rules and social structures (Gramsci, 2011). Cultural hegemony is sustained by the tacit or overt agreements by people to follow prevailing social norms and support socioeconomic structures devised by the powerful in society. Such a regime serves to suppress the expression of diversity. At the local level in group work, the unquestioning adherence to these norms and expectations can be very evident, as group members likely have assimilated core beliefs. In an inclusive group, members are encouraged to examine these beliefs during their work in the group.

Diversity may fuel conflict in groups because of group members' initial inhibitions and negative interpersonal interactions, but in the end diversity can lead to healthier group functioning. Diversity-fueled conflict can be sharp and very uncomfortable in the moment. As group members share their different identities and perspectives, conflict likely will arise. This may impede the group's work and task completion in an early stage of group development. Responding to diversity-fueled conflict begins with focusing attention to perceptions of inequality plus recognizing the group members' different identities. Discussions of differentness among the members can lead to potential gains for the group members. Working through the conflict(s) can lead to recognition of the group members' shared fate, shared group identity, and ultimate reconciliation among members.

Every group has to respond to the types of conflicts that surface and the reasons for the conflicts. Conflict resolution that settles personal or organizational disputes is necessary—and yet many times difficult to achieve. Further, the purpose of the group and the contract that is established between the agency, worker, and group members will direct the process and content of conflict exploration.

Social workers can establish group norms that assist in the development of the exploration of diversity and conflict in groups by encouraging members to do the following:

- View differences among themselves as opportunities to bring different worldviews into the group.
- Understand that disagreements among members are to be expected.
- Recognize that group discussions of differences contribute to group progress.
- Grasp that constant agreement with one another is not realistic and that disagreement among members does not equate to dislike or disrespect.
- Build hope that the group is strong and can withstand conflicts (Kurland & Salmon, 1998b).

Special attention must be paid to group members' cultural preferences for expressing not only conflict but emotions in general. Verbal and nonverbal communications will vary among diverse group members. Western ways of expressing oneself may not match the expectations of all in the group. For example, Camacho (2001) noted that for collectivist cultures, interdependence and group harmony may be highly valued by group members. Such a value orientation may result in viewing conflict as a violation of group norms. On the other hand, individualistically oriented cultures may see the direct expression of conflict to be an appropriate means of resolving differences. Group discussion of how to openly discuss subjects, issues, and themes would help to establish a group norm that is distinct and apart from members' backgrounds (Ringel, 2005). Moreover, an inclusive approach asks the worker to negotiate a process with group members that empowers them to work with diversity as it arises in the group. Such a process may involve delineating principles for conflict resolution that are viewed by group members as being beneficial, and negotiating strategies on how conflict will be addressed when it arises in the group (Camacho, 2001).

Lewin's (1997) early work demonstrated how social groups attempt to amass status, wealth, or privilege, leading to conflicts with others. He also showed the potential for creating new relationships or repairing established relationships through dialogue and negotiation. Conflict exploration and potential resolution suggest either an amelioration of social problems within existing social structures that maintain social values and norms, or a transformative experience whereby all parties change values and norms to some degree. Conflict resolution utilizes problem-solving methods to accomplish these ends. Problem solving engages group members in multicultural and multidisciplinary content with analyses of helpful, explanatory theories and grounded practice examples (Ramsbotham, Woodhouse, & Miall, 2011). Successful outcomes might include reductions in stereotyping, prejudicial feelings towards others, fears of differentness, and an increase in trust among group members. Northen (1988) described the benefits of effective conflict exploration as follows: "The successful resolution of conflicts strengthens the consensus within the group and enables the members to move forward toward the accomplishment of their goals" (p. 41).

Conflict exploration will be examined in both task and intervention groups, adopting the process outlined for the professional use of self: (1) observing, (2) exploring, (3) conceiving, and (4) transforming. As you will see, the internal processes involved in exploring and resolving conflict in the observing and exploring phases are similar. However, differences do arise in the conceiving and transforming stages for task and intervention groups. As with the section above, this section will explore working with conflict through a vignette (see exercise 12.7).

Exercise 12.7: The Violin

Over several of the past four sessions, group members have shared their struggles with depression and how it has affected their lives. Tony and Roy have shared the steps that they have taken in trying to fight off its effects. They have stated that they will never give in. Others have noted how it has been difficult, but they have tried to take small steps. Up to this point, the group has been supportive of their mutual efforts and challenges. One member, Cindy, has repeatedly described how she has been victimized by her illness. Cindy feels that no one (e.g., parents, partner) can understand how she feels, and she feels powerless to change herself and her life. Next, Roy and Tony repeatedly offer suggestions to Cindy to help her deal with some of the problems that she has shared. In response, Cindy states that she appreciates their suggestions, but that she does not think that what they have offered is helpful. She continues to share her victimization, and later in response, Roy says, "Does anyone have a violin?" Cindy becomes visibly upset and moves to the edge of her chair. She states, "You and the others are just like my partner. I don't know why I come to this group." As the tension continues to build, others in the group jump in to support Cindy or Roy. Cindy stands and threatens to leave the group. How might you as a worker respond to this situation? Would you defend Cindy? Support Roy? Where would you focus your response?

Observing

Conflict does not signal that something is going wrong in the group. Given the ambivalence evoked regarding conflict, it is not uncommon for group workers to avoid conflict, deny it, or fail to notice that it is present. Group workers who avoid conflict provide a signal that the group cannot handle important divergence and disagreements. Distrust and disengagement from group process can occur when conflict is not openly identified and brought forward for the group's consideration. However, there are often some very clear signs of conflict present in a group, including: verbal disagreement, lack of overt communication, and double messages (statements that veil hostility or resentment, such as gossip). Internal cues may include somatic responses such as tension or tightness in one's chest. It is important that the worker in a task group understand the difference between healthy and unhealthy debates. Table 12.1 displays the difference between healthy and unhealthy debates in task groups. In this table you can see how the characteristics of an inclusive group foster diversity through openness, listening, and efforts at understanding the views of others. In a noninclusive group, diversity is suppressed through the assumption that one member is right, speakers are cut off, and no one is interested in seeing how others view the situation.

Table 12.1 Healthy vs. Unhealthy Arguments

Healthy Debates involve . . .	Unhealthy Arguments involve . . .
• Openness to hearing others • Listening and responding • Efforts to understand the views of others • Objective & factual focus • Problem-solving approach	• Assumption of being right • Speakers are cut-off or others respond without responding to the speaker's ideas • No one is interested in how others see the situation • Personal blame or attack • Lack of a structured approach

Resolving conflict requires only one of the parties to have awareness of the conflict and to be willing and able to explore their momentary state (e.g. feelings and position) in the conflict. During this observing phase, the worker needs to ask: "What am I feeling and doing, and where am I with respect to my position in this conflict (which side or neutral)?" In addition to the aforementioned approaches to inclusive practice, to be able to work with conflict effectively, the worker needs to adopt a position that includes neutrality and detachment. Adopting a neutral position means that the worker must avoid taking sides in the conflict. It is from this position that the worker will be able to support all sides to explore the conflict. The worker also needs to remain detached from the conflict, in terms of being able to maintain awareness in the midst of group chaos and confusion, by letting go of identification with an issue, responsibility, fears, projections, or the need to win or protect self.

In the vignette, would you have some difficulties in remaining in a neutral position? Some might be tempted to jump in to defend Cindy and chastise Roy for his comment. Others, who were similarly affected by Cindy's tales of woe, may jump in to support Roy. Where would you position yourself?

Exploring

After the worker has acknowledged that a conflict is present and is able to adopt a position characterized by detachment and neutrality, he or she is then able to explore his or her own feelings and motives for addressing or not addressing the conflict. The feelings that are evoked may greatly influence the intention underlying the worker's response to conflict. Feelings of powerlessness may trigger feelings of anger. Identification with one member in the conflict may result in a response that serves to protect that member. From a neutral and detached position, the worker can also tune in or empathize with the feelings of each side of the conflict as well as other group members.

In the vignette (exercise 12.7), what would you be feeling? What do you sense would be some of the feelings that Cindy and Roy may be experiencing in the group? How about the others who are present?

Conceiving

In the conceiving phase, the worker matches his or her internal experience with what is happening in the group. After the worker has confirmed the presence of conflict, he or she must assess the impact of the conflict and the group's ability to work towards a resolution. Sometimes tension or uneasiness experienced by the worker may be a result of his or her own past experiences with a situation that has arisen in the group. In other cases, there may be evidence of escalating anger or hostility in the group that matches the worker's feelings of tension and discomfort. By assessing the impact of the conflict, as well as the group's ability to manage the conflict, the worker is able to make a conscious choice of if and how to intervene in the group. For example, intervention may be necessary when a conflict is producing prolonged or escalating bad feelings, gossip, absenteeism, or a sense of hopelessness. The worker must immediately intervene and stop interaction when neither party is willing to examine the conflict or adhere to group ground rules, or if one or both people are clearly out of control (e.g., rage response). Like workers, some groups may avoid conflict, deny it, or simply not be able to productively work with it. There is a greater likelihood that group members will avoid conflict during the early meetings in a group. As a result, such conflicts may fester and build up until they erupt later in the group.

If the worker decides to intervene, he or she must be prepared with strategies for working with the conflict and the agreement of at least one member to address the conflict. As with all interventions, the way in which the worker intervenes when conflict arises in the group will be determined by the group purpose. In most groups, workers have to search for mutually beneficial gains so that all group members acquire even a small sense of achievement towards a desired goal (Ramsbotham et al., 2011). The group worker attempts to value the group's acceptance of diversity by exploring differences and relating how these strengthen the group as it goes about its tasks (Northen & Kurland, 2005). Dealing with conflict in an open manner demonstrates to group members that their cohesive bonds can endure through difficult conversations with each other, ultimately reinforcing the members' relationships.

There are a variety of conflict strategies that are widely used in task groups, each of which varies in its effectiveness. Some of these include:

- Competing: involves the use of authority or status to make points and quell conflict
- Accommodating: involves asking members to accept each other's views or simply agree to disagree
- Compromising: involves looking for the common ground between views where each side may have to give up something.

Each of these approaches has some major limitations. In competing, the person with the strongest or most popular view (including the chair or most powerful member) will carry the day, simply by imposing his or her resolution on the group.

Such a strategy may suppress the overt expression of conflict, but conflict will continue to linger, serving to divide the group and further marginalize those who lack power. In accommodating, although the group may realize that different views will be respected, the conflict is simply left without resolution, little progress is achieved toward group goals, and members may drift further apart. In compromising, each member gains and loses, there may be some progress toward group goals, and members may be brought together through the identification of common ground. Task groups that use a cooperative approach to conflict management rather than a competitive approach enhance group member relationships, which increases group productivity and member commitment (Tjosvold, Poon, & Zi-You, 2005). However, what these strategies share in common is that, in adopting any of these strategies, the opportunity to integrate diverse views and perspectives is lost.

Another and more collaborative approach to working with conflict in task groups was proposed by Middleman and Goldberg Wood (1990b). This approach involves (a) confronting situations—making a "civil presentation" of descriptive information to work through diversity; (b) validating angry feelings—enabling group members to de-escalate or cool down so that they are able to think about the conflict; (c) focusing on facts—engaging in mutual problem solving after de-escalation has occurred; (d) converting arguments into comparisons—reiterating different sides of an argument as differences of opinion about the way to accomplish a goal and presenting options for rational consideration; and, finally, (e) proposing superordinate goals—large, important, basic goals to which all parties can subscribe and which can encompass dissenting views.

However, the most effective approach of all is an inclusive strategy that parallels the worker's professional use of self and the following model. Essentially, it is a parallel and dialectical process adapted from the work of Mindell (2014) in which the worker assists the group members to work through observing (acknowledging the presence of conflict), exploring (fully exploring their experience in the conflict), conceiving (exploring the experience of the other side), and transforming the conflict in the group.

Acknowledging the Conflict

In this first phase, the worker acknowledges the presence of the conflict. He or she can use the skill of transparency to share what he or she has observed and experienced in the group and then assist the group members to share what they have observed and experienced in the group. The worker will also share reasons for raising and trying to resolve the conflict. In a task group, this may include helping the group to overcome this obstacle to its work. In an intervention group, it may include helping group members explore the deeper meaning and gain insight from the conflict. In any group, the reasons for intervening must be related to the group purpose. The worker must also ask the group members to state or restate their position with respect to the conflict—that is, which view they support—while leaving space for additional unspoken views to emerge. Unlike the position of the worker, the group members are not required to adopt a neutral or detached position with respect to the conflict in order to participate in its resolution. During exploration, it is essential that members share where they stand with respect to the issue, including whose side they are on or if they have their own position or are indifferent. Finally, the worker should also ask the members for their consent to explore the conflict and outline the strategy that will be used.

In the vignette, the worker could start with asking the members to share what they have been experiencing in the group. Roy, and those who identify with his position, could start by sharing their frustration with Cindy's "victim stance." Cindy, and those who support her, would likely share their frustration with being offered advice instead of group members simply listening and accepting her feelings.

Fully Experiencing the Conflict

In the exploration phase, each group member, starting with those who are most intensely affected by the conflict, needs to fully express and experience their position in the conflict. In a task group, this may involve fully expressing their ideas and, where appropriate, their feelings about the conflict. In an intervention group, the exploration of experiences and feelings may go further and deeper, and could include feelings that may be repressed or disavowed. Where appropriate, they may also explore past situations and experiences that relate to the conflict that has emerged in the group. It is important to note that ways in which conflict is explored may vary. As Von Glinow, Shapiro, & Brett (2004) concluded, in culturally diverse groups, artwork or other forms of aesthetic expression may be more effective ways of exploring conflict than talking.

In the vignette, Roy and his supporters would be encouraged to explore the underlying feelings associated with his feelings of frustration. He would likely share how difficult it was for him to listen and feel so powerless. He might be tempted to share a moment in his life where he too felt powerless and how he has chosen to fight his depression and not be a victim. Cindy might share that she too has felt powerless in her experience of depression and in having people listen and respond to her needs.

Exploring the Other Side

When members fully explore their perspective or side in the conflict, they may find that they begin to feel less attached to their own positions. For example, as Roy explores and expresses his own thoughts and feelings concerning the conflict, his need to defend himself from anxiety by attacking Cindy may also diminish. With exploration, affect experienced by each group member will also de-escalate. De-escalation is usually signaled by lowering of voices, moving or looking away, or tension reduction. When noticing signs of de-escalation, the worker should explore what changes members are experiencing in how they are feeling. Then members, if they agree, may be asked to move to a neutral or more detached stance to look at the conflict. At this point, they may be asked how they see themselves and their opponent. Exploration continues with each party exploring the perspectives of their opponent. In moving from one's own side to the opponent's, members need to be assisted to look at them to see how they look, respond, and feel. Here members develop empathy and compassion for each other. How successful each member is with respect to taking the other's perspective will be signaled by their opponent's body language (e.g., relaxation, sitting back) and emotional response. Exploration continues until members have explored all remaining perspectives arising in the conflict. The culmination of this phase of the process is members sharing their insights and new understandings about the nature of the conflict.

In the vignette, the worker may explore: What are some of the diverse ways that members respond to powerlessness and anxiety? What are some of the commonalities that the members share? As the process unfolds in the vignette, Roy and Cindy will feel less angry and be able to reflect on the conflict. As they move to a more detached position, they may be able to recognize that they share a feeling of powerlessness in relation to depression. They can then be encouraged to explore how the other is experiencing the conflict and gain new insights into how depression has affected their lives and their relationships.

Transforming

In transforming, the worker will first decide whether to intervene in the conflict by adopting a strategy. If the worker adopts an inclusive strategy, such as the one outlined above, each group member and the group itself will be transformed by the conflict. They will likely be in a different position than they were when the conflict arose. They will also have achieved a deeper understanding of the issue and their fellow group members. They will at this point be able to resolve the substantive issues included with the conflict through problem solving. In some cases, before leaving the conflict, each member may wish to offer apologies and for-giveness or make amends in some way. It may also be helpful for members to iden-tify some new ground rules or norms about how they will address conflict when it arises. In an intervention group, it is essential to have members explore what they have learned about themselves and others. Members may be encouraged to trans-fer what they have learned in the group to their external relationships.

Regardless of which intervention strategy is employed, the group worker should always evaluate the impact of the strategy in the group. Was it relevant and effective in resolving the conflict and supporting the expression of diversity in the group? Was the intervention focused appropriately and immediately in terms of addressing the affective elements surrounding the issue? Finally, did the inter-vention promote greater responsibility and autonomy of group members in work-ing together to address conflicts as they arise in the future?

CHAPTER SUMMARY

This chapter has explored two advanced group work skills, the professional use of self and conflict exploration and resolution. Given that diversity is always present in a group, conflict is simply another way in which it can be expressed by group members. An inclusive group embraces conflict just as it embraces diversity. Just as an inclusive practitioner would encourage the expression of diversity in a group, he or she must anticipate, acknowledge, and respond effectively to conflict. Through the professional use of self and inclusive conflict strategies, the worker may effectively harness the benefits of diversity and conflict. Conflict becomes an opportunity for group members to learn more about themselves and other group members. Through the inclusive resolution of conflict, group members will be brought together, interpersonal relationships will be enhanced, and group members will be empowered to resolve conflict should it arise again in or outside of the group.

CHAPTER 13

ENDING A GROUP AND EVALUATION

LEARNING OBJECTIVES

At the end of this chapter you will be able to:
- Formulate a well-organized plan that incorporates an end point for group membership and an evaluation of group progress.
- Articulate professional coping strategies when confronted with difficult group endings.
- Reinforce group members' changes and recognize unmet goals.

Practice Scenario: A Stressed Group

A group of coronary patients contracted to meet at a local hospital for a fifteen-week group experience following major heart surgeries and procedures. The group focused on lifestyle education and change. Each of the men and women in the group expressed somatic pains in the week or two prior to the last group session and each was advised to check with a medical doctor. At the last group session, a number of them complained of feelings of heaviness on their chests— classic signs of cardiac distress. The nurse practitioner who coleads the group with a social worker encourages each group member to identify strengths learned or reinforced during the group. As members engage in descriptions of personal changes, the social worker asks each to also identify personal feelings that they are experiencing in the group right now. The group members collectively speak about their fears of dying, loss of sociopersonal supports with the group's ending, and fear of the future. All agree that the discussion on feelings helps to reduce feelings of tension, and most report a lessening of chest distress. What are your thoughts about this group's ending?

GROUP WORK THEORY AND ENDING

All groups, whether centered on social activities and community needs or personal assistance within the group, come to an end. Many group work theorists present models of group development with the last stages or phases representing the end of a group. Northen and Kurland (2001) present stage IV as separation-termination. In the Boston model, Garland, Jones, and Kolodny (1973) portray the last stage as separation. Tuckman's (Tuckman & Jensen, 1977) last stage, which describes the conclusion of tasks and the cessation of interpersonal relationships, is called adjourning. As noted by these theorists, group development is not always serial or simply sequential, though. Groups may fluctuate and return to an earlier stage, especially when group members leave or new members join in an open group format. As a member enters or exits the open group, the remaining group members must reorganize the group and reaffirm their commitment to the purposes of personal growth or task completion.

CLOSED AND OPEN GROUPS

Closed groups end for reasons related to the completion of a specific time-limited contract, the achievement of goals, or a group reaching an impasse in its work together. Because all members end at the same time, the group worker can assist all to deal with common ending issues. Group workers can invite members to review and reconsider the gains they made in group. In task groups, members can be invited to review gains made towards the group's purpose and lessons learned from the work together. Group members can examine the changes in perspective that they have made, especially related to self-awareness and trusting others, successfully dealing with conflict situations, and giving and receiving feedback in group. Although this examination and discussion is not necessarily always done in group for task groups, task group members also benefit from this exploration, as lessons learned through the group experience can be applied to future experiences. The group worker can reinforce the message that opportunities exist for members to connect to others outside of the group and replicate some of the experiences by utilizing the skills learned in group. The main message from the group worker is that the interpersonal skills that they learned in group are transferable to other social situations.

Open groups experience a different rhythm, as members enter and leave the group over time. Individual members attending open-ended groups present a challenge for the group worker and members because they have differing needs and are at different phases in working through their goals. Members entering and leaving the group can signal a gain or loss of certain skills, perspectives, or experiences. Patience and goodwill among group members is a necessity. A member who leaves the group patterns the ending that all will eventually experience.

From the initial contact to the member's or group's final meeting time, the ending of the group should be a part of the group's awareness and dialogue. Each group session has an ending so the group can practice its weekly endings. In task groups, members can be reminded of the ending of the group as they regularly review the progress made towards achieving their task and the work that still needs to be done. In this way the group can become oriented to the final ending, which will be established on a known and comfortable pattern associated with ending work in the group.

To facilitate this further, the group worker's role at the midpoint of a group is to begin a countdown to remind members and to encourage members to work on their stated goals. A brief and simple comment such as "We have four weeks left together. Are you finding time to bring your concerns to group?" signals the group's ending to all members and reinvites all to engage in the group's process. The group worker also often encourages members of the group to examine their goals and levels of accomplishment of those goals.

Before the formal ending, the last few weeks begin to mark the transition to leaving the group and a return to everyday living or movement toward other supports or counseling. In preparation for the last group meeting, members are asked to reflect on their collective goals and personal time in group. This is an invitation to think about the accomplishment of their goals, any unfinished business, and whether the group commitment was time well spent. It is advantageous to ask members to assess what they have gained as individuals so that their achievements can be recognized and reinforced in the group context.

PERSONAL FEELINGS ABOUT ENDING THE GROUP

Ending a group can activate many feelings not only in group members but in the group worker as well. As group members work on a number of tasks together, they develop a group character and share qualities, including elements of a shared emotional life. Many members exit a group experience with mixed emotions, feeling ambivalence in their grief yet a sense of release in the group's ending. In groups where individual members and the group as a whole assisted others in the work of facilitating goals, the ending means closing the many relationships that were begun and fostered in the group context. The feelings associated with the attachments to others and the anticipated losses of support can be difficult and stressful for the members. The group worker's capacity to deal with feelings associated with personal loss and anxiety emerges as a necessary skill to facilitate the group's ending. A self-aware group worker is better able to help group members openly examine and discuss feelings related to the ending's sadness and celebration, attachments and dependencies, as well as fear of relapse and hope in the members' optimism for the future.

Exercise 13.1: Practice Consideration

Why do you think it is important to identify your own feelings as you approach the ending of a group? How will putting your own feelings in order help you and the group?

In the final group session, group members can be invited to get in touch with their *in situ* current feelings and reflect upon the significance of the shared group experience. Common feelings and reflections will likely emerge as members begin to disclose these. The group worker can capitalize on the shared recognitions and acknowledgments by summarizing and connecting similar thoughts and feelings among the members. At this point, the group worker can also invite members to comment on their interactions with the group worker and note any positive help or drawbacks. As a result, group members can learn that authority figures can be approached and they may modify their perspectives of them when seeking assistance in the future.

Exercise 13.2: Practice Scenario: What Would You Do?

In a final group meeting, one of the members adamantly states that she does not want the group to end and that she wants others to meet again next week. What would you explore with the group? How would you address her issues?

TASKS ASSOCIATED WITH THE GROUP WRAP-UP

The social worker's tasks while ending group processes is described in a helpful way by the International Association for Social Work with Groups. The tasks include:

- identification of members' reactions to the conclusion of the group
- sharing of the group worker's feelings about ending the group

- uncovering of members' feelings about finishing with others
- solidification of members' gains and changes they have made resulting from their participation in the group
- the application of new knowledge and skills in group members' daily lives
- an invitation to members to provide feedback to the worker
- an exploration of honest evaluations of the members' work together
- if needed, a plan for care or help for members beyond this group
- an assessment of progress of individuals and the group as a whole
- a critical overview of the group experience on individuals and their external environments.

These tasks can be modified to be covered, as appropriate, in group during the anticipated departure of a member of an open-ended group and in task groups where some of these elements may not be a focus (i.e., exploration of feelings).

CHANGE, GROWTH, AND LEARNING

The group worker encourages members to discuss their thoughts and feelings about applying the group-supported concepts and problem-solving skills beyond the group experience. At the group's ending point, group members set out to discover if they can continue in a meaningful direction on their own without the mutual aid and diverse perspectives offered from other group members. Because group members will no longer have the group's support for trying out new behaviors, exploring ideas, or making changes in their lives or community, they must find ways to sustain their efforts.

Group members can receive reinforcement of their new skills by recognizing, sharing, and discussing the members' perceptions of gains made throughout the group sessions. Areas of personal growth to highlight might include improvements in emotionally connecting with others, identifying one's needs, speaking up for one's rights, utilizing feedback from others to modify one's own behaviors and/or thoughts, and recognizing and managing interpersonal conflict situations in everyday life. The hope is that group members can continue to move forward and relocate newly learned skills and abilities from within the group context to members' lives outside of the group. The goals attained in a group context must be applicable in real life situations in order to qualify as successful.

Exercise 13.3: Practice Scenario: Moving Forward

In the final meeting, a group member suggests that everybody should attend a "graduation party" at his restaurant the following week instead of meeting at the agency during the designated group time. Everybody seems interested. Should you be concerned about creating dependencies and potential backsliding? How will you weigh your response to stress the importance of their gains towards their goals and their abilities for finding assistance in the community to meet their needs beyond the group?

PRACTICE IMPLICATIONS

In brief, a successful ending is a process that covers key group practice elements. Although these will be discussed in the context of time specific groups, these elements can also be covered in group when a member prepares to end their participation in an open-ended group. The first element is an exploration of the emotional impact of the group's work on the group's members. The second is an integration of topics, themes, and issues shared during the group's time together. The third is the conveying of what was learned by group members during the group and what each will take from the learning experience. The fourth is the intellectual and emotional closure of the group's work. Group members are asked to critically analyze the meanings, impacts, and importance of the work of the group.

A successful ending is a closure process that wraps up and reinforces what people have learned. In this stage, it is hoped that members understand that they leave with increased skills and altered views of presenting problems and persons in their environment. This can provide them with a different problem-solving orientation in everyday living and empowers them to choose alternatives from among an expanded repertoire of choices. The group worker assists group members to exit the group and continue their life journeys by asking each member to recall significant assistance and aid received during the group. Members are asked to identify what they will take from the work of the group and utilize in their own lives. The group members share their unique individual reflections of the group's accomplishments and unfinished work. Group members share their plans for the maintenance of changes made and plans for future work. Group members are asked to think about an action plan that lays out plans to advance their goals beyond the group. A goal of the group's ending is to assist the group members to utilize what they learned about endings when experiencing future closures and changes in their lives (Dion, 2000; Furhman, 2009).

Exercise 13.4: Practice Scenario: Loss of Group Supports

Group members may experience a level of ambivalence about the group ending. They may want to try out new skills but be fearful that they cannot succeed without the group's support. A group member states that she has become attached to all of the group members and will miss them. She openly expresses sadness and mourns the imminent change that arrives with the termination of the group. How can you help the group to see strengths in this moment?

Discussion in the last group meeting usually includes multiple recognitions for all group members' contributions. Individual group members' achievements are openly identified. Group members have a last chance to state personal responses and to identify what it was like to be a member of the group. They can catalog the persons and activities that were helpful or harmful during the group. They can also reflect on the sharing among members that contributed to personal change. The ending of a group includes members' reviews and recognition of changes in the group members.

The group worker's goal is to facilitate task completion and assist in the interpersonal disengagement among the group members. The disengagement can be an apprehensive time. The last group meeting is the time in which individual group members have opportunities to personally say their goodbyes to others. The group ending highlights the finale of group support and inclusion.

The final group meeting also provides an avenue for presenting other resources if members need this supportive information. The group leader can share with members any future opportunities that they may have to meet again (e.g., agency refresher courses or check-ups and/or social events if the sponsoring agency has them). Many group members express a desire to exchange personal contact information, and this activity is best guided by the sponsoring agency's guidelines and group contract (Shapiro & Ginzberg, 2002).

The following guide provides openings for discussions among the group members who may want to focus on one or more issues that may be vital to them.

Group Ending: A Group Worker's Guide

- Review positive and negative aspects of the group experience.
- Recognize progress made by self and others.
- Consider anything that you learned about yourself and others.

- Describe how you might utilize this learning in everyday living.
- Assess goals that you achieved and goals that were not reached.
- Anticipate how to handle stresses and problems.
- Discuss your plans following the ending of the group's interpersonal connections.
- Identify strengths and supports in one's life.
- Talk about what the group interactions meant to members. Who cared for whom? How was this demonstrated?
- Inquire if anybody wants to say something that he or she may regret if left unsaid.
- Ask what group members will remember most about the group.

It is not uncommon to have group members inquire about the last group meeting and the sharing of food or other traditional or cultural exchanges. Group workers might consider balancing agency directives and the universal expression of sadness with the human need to affirm helpful relationships. The endorsement of a warm group ending might prevent negative feelings and represent a new expression of ending that members can use throughout their lives. If agencies allow the sharing of food, members may choose to bring diverse samples of food items for sharing with others. Different but tasty food serves as a reminder of the diversity of group members who attended. Also, the symbolic gift sharing among members can be a significant reinforcement of changes that each member made throughout the term of the group. Ultimately, the inclusion of group members in planning an ending process affirms their partnerships among the group members and group worker.

DIFFICULT ENDINGS

The ending of a group is often presented in the literature in the best possible framework, but sometimes groups end in less than ideal ways. Real group endings may be characterized by denial, regression, or other negative experiences such as angry feelings and incriminations that the group was not helpful. Denial may surface as group members decline to acknowledge improvements in their lives and/or deny that they have a continuing problem. Regression may be seen in the group members' return to behaviors related to earlier problems or concerns. Anger may be central to group members as they cope with the anticipated loss and potential grief. Statements that the group was not worthy and helpful are designed to ridicule all of the group members' hard work and group worker's efforts. The closing of a group can reactivate previous feelings of anger, loss, or abandonment.

A variety of feelings are expected to surface during the ending phase. The group worker's task is to spotlight the reality of ending the group, focusing on the connection between the group's ending and their feelings. The group workers can and should highlight the humanness of ending relationships, drawing upon the strengths of group termination as being similar to ending relationships outside of group. Group members' comments that are full of emotion can be identified as connected to the imminent group ending. The group worker can offer assurances that members are more capable because of the time shared in group.

The group can be steered to discussions that review their individual accomplishments and their movement towards goal completion in group. The group can assess their common history of where they began and where the group is now ending. The contract provides a structure to guide the review process. Nonaccomplishment of goals can also be reviewed. Group members can be asked to restate what they wanted to attain, and then discuss their perceptions regarding the lack of goal accomplishment. Ask members for a future commitment to pursue areas needing further exploration and development.

Exercise 13.5: Practice Consideration: Endings

The contract sets the stage for a group helping process. How can you utilize it in the process of ending a group?

Ending the group suggests a finality that can be recast instead as a fresh launch for group members. Although members will not feel the potential safety and reassurance offered by the group, they are living in the world again but with the knowledge that it is a transition or new start in life. In the closing meeting of the group, ask each member to consider the following questions. While in group, what did you change? How did you feel about it? Do you now relate differently to others? What are you going to do beyond the group? Their recognition of their learned behaviors and thoughts reinforced by group experiences can help to alleviate intimidating or sad feelings.

Each group member can be encouraged to create an action plan to use outside of the group. The action plan asks each person to draft specific steps to continue to grow and develop after the group ends. Each step should identify what behaviors or thoughts will be attempted by the member as she or he returns to everyday life without the group's support. If agencies permit it and members will contract around it, group workers may arrange a single group contact three or six months after the group's ending as a follow-up to check on the group members' progress. These contacts can provide data collection points as well.

Exercise 13.6: Practice Scenario: A Difficult Departure

In a group organized to assist persons with depression, a member arrives to the closing group with a sad countenance and falls into his chair, wiping a tear from his cheek. Group members immediately attend to him, inquiring about his feelings. He then announces that his life is simply worse now that he has been to the group and that he is sorry that he wasted everybody else's time. Members try to encourage him to see some positives. As the group worker, what might you say and plan to do in this situation?

COWORKER RELATIONSHIPS AND ENDINGS

As with any part of the group process, whenever there are coworkers it is imperative that a thorough discussion be had about the ending of the group. Coworkers should consider common termination issues and determine how these issues will be addressed in group. The ending provides an opportunity for the workers to provide feedback to members. The coworkers should have a thoughtful discussion in order to provide congruent messages to members. Any concerns about individual members should be discussed, along with referrals that may need to be provided.

The ending of the group also signifies the ending of the coworker relationship, in relation to this group. It is important for coworkers to discuss their feelings about ending the group. Coworkers should also engage in an evaluation of their work together and of each other as coworkers. Coworkers may want to assess their leadership styles, techniques, and skills. Coworkers will want to reflect on the entire group process, noting critical turning points and what skills, activities, or techniques facilitated those important junctures. Finally, feedback on ways to improve the group for the future is also beneficial.

ASSESSING/EVALUATING GROUP PRACTICE

Evaluation is an essential component of all group work, and it is a process that occurs throughout all stages of group work. Prior to the beginning of the first session, it is important for the worker to have a clear evaluation plan. This plan includes establishing, articulating, and documenting clear goals and outcomes to be achieved by the group. Additionally, there may be other aspects of the group that require measurement and evaluation. For example, in a task group, it is important that the worker and group members monitor progress achieved as the group completes its assigned tasks. In an intervention group, it is important that progress towards each member's intervention goals is monitored, including such variables as the individual's affective, cognitive, and behavioral growth. The complex process of evaluation cannot be carried on in a vacuum but must be done within the context of the sponsoring organization, the referral source (if one is involved), the environment, the consumer, the worker, and the group.

Recent practice expectations are that group outcomes be assessed in order to substantiate meaningful changes (Burlingame, Fuhriman, & Johnson, 2002). Contemporary group practitioners must view the requirement to assess the work done in groups as a necessity, as many funding sources are not prepared to continue funding these practice efforts unless accompanied by data to support these efforts. Although some may view the need for data collection related to practice activities as intrusive, it is better to view this as a professional opportunity to demonstrate group work viability.

The assessment and evaluation of group practice are now part and parcel of contemporary services and are often referred to as evidence-based practice or EBP (Gambrill, 2000). Evidence is collected in a variety of data sets that capture the changes that group members make as a direct result of group participation. EBP suggests that groups follow the steps in a manual to ensure the efficacy of group procedures (Gambrill, 2000). The creativity utilized in many groups to reach out to a diverse membership may not align with this assessment expectation. Emphasis then must focus on the assessment of the effectiveness of the group.

In many helping groups, the collection of pregroup data allows for a comparison with postgroup data. Data collected are conceptually related to the measurable goals contractually selected by the group members. Work groups can be evaluated by assessing the successful completion of tasks or specific group activities such as the social action goals completed.

Several purposes have been identified for evaluation in group work (Garvin, 1997; Toseland & Rivas, 2005, 2011). First, evaluation is conducted to monitor changes in group conditions and processes. Monitoring can be conducted both by members and the worker(s). Members may monitor the group through use of behavioral counts, checklists, logs, journals, and periodical reports of their feeling states. The worker may monitor the group through the use of conventional process, summary, or problem-focused recording. Second, evaluation may be conducted to improve future groups in terms of developing, testing, evaluating, modifying, and reevaluating intervention methods on an ongoing basis as new groups are offered. Finally, as previously noted, the most common reason for evaluation is to monitor individual change and the effectiveness of a group in achieving group and member goals.

Monitoring Individual Change

In planning with and for the group, the worker(s) and members should clearly identify aspects of their individual, interpersonal group functioning that they wish to change. Specific criteria that will be used to monitor change should be shared with members. Both members and workers may be involved in recording and monitoring this change. Although there are a number of checklists that measure global individual change, one's choice of instruments may be largely informed by the purpose and intervention goals of the group. For example, a measure for depression, such as the Beck depression inventory, may be adopted for a group designed to assist those experiencing depression. Some other global measures of individual change include:

- behavioral counts: the number of times a member engages in a desired act (e.g., goal oriented, therapeutic)
- goal attainment scaling: a measurement of member progress in achieving goals on a five-point scale
- self-ratings on emotional states: self-reported ratings of emotional states (e.g., depression, anxiety)
- value clarification ratings: used in values clarification exercises to measure change in member values
- ratings on skills in understanding self and situation: scales used to evaluate member ability to perform specific tasks or demonstrate particular skills (e.g., problem solving)
- task accomplishment: an instrument adapted from a task centered casework instrument, developed by Garvin (1997) to rate member task accomplishment
- psychological instruments: a list of psychological instruments applicable for measurement of individual change in groups (Fischer & Corcoran, 2013).

MacKenzie (1990) suggests that, in evaluating individual member change, the worker should develop a change-measures battery or series of tests that meet the following criteria: (1) multiple measures that gauge different aspects of functioning; (2) both subjective and objective behavioral measures; (3) individual reports and standardized measures; and (4) assessment information from several sources. MacKenzie (1990) also provides a basic summary of some of the most common instruments and strategies and lists the following measures or data sources:

- demographic data sheet: a sheet that includes the usual demographic variables relating to age, gender, class, education level, and so on
- outcome questionnaire (OQ 45.2): a forty-five-item questionnaire designed for use in busy service settings to provide a global measure of distress, including subscales for subjective discomfort, interpersonal relationships, and social role performance
- symptom checklist 90 (SCL-90-R): a ninety-item self-report symptom inventory that provides an overall measure of symptom status
- social adjustment scale: a sixty-item self-report instrument that assesses members' functioning in a number of social roles (developed for use with depressed outpatient populations).

More recently, the American Group Psychotherapy Association has developed a series of instruments that can be utilized to support group member selection, as well as measurement of group outcomes and processes. The CORE-R offers a tool kit of resources for use in intervention groups (Burlingame et al., 2006). As suggested by the above measures, anticipated member change can be stated in specific terms that are observable and measurable. The goals and outcomes for each member and for the group should be as concrete as possible. During the early group sessions, the worker must assist members to identify the necessary steps to operationalize the behaviors, feelings, and thoughts to be changed. The data resulting from these operationalized goals can then be observed, measured, and analyzed by all members. In task groups, although individual goals and personal change are not the focus of the group, measurement of individual change may also be beneficial for members. It serves to evaluate member progress and to help members recognize that no matter what type of group one participates in, the group will always have some type of impact on the individual. Whether it is learning confrontation and conflict resolution skills when members are unreliable or learning how to communicate and relate with others, individual change and impact can be a product of group involvement in task groups also.

At the midpoint of time together, group members can be asked to begin reviewing their progress towards goal attainment. Most will likely focus on the reasons for attending group and their stated goals, but a few members may shift away from earlier stated goals and refine them at this time. As the time shared in group increases, members' awareness of their problems and any necessary changes grows so that some may choose to alter their chosen goals.

In a very simple process framework, the group workers can ask members to rate their progress towards goal completion by rating each personal goal on a scale of one to five, with one representing minimal progress and five maximum progress. Members can be asked to identify what might be helpful to move them closer towards the attainment of their specific goals. Individual members can be encouraged to make note of the steps that may be needed to reach these goals. This can also be done with task groups; however, a focus may be on the overall group task completion or members' rating of their efforts toward assisting in the group's task completion.

The group as a whole can comment on the perceived helpfulness within the group. If the group identifies helpful processes operating within the group, then the group worker can invite them to further relate how individuals were assisted in group. If the group struggles to recognize helpful processes, then discussion can center on what has to change in group or happen differently in order to allow the group to move in new directions. Often, group members share a mix of positive and negative comments that assist the group to keep some activities and adopt new ones. In task groups, this discussion may involve the appraisal of techniques and tools used to keep the group organized or to make progress toward completions of tasks.

Exercise 13.7: Practice Scenario: An Adjustment

In the last few weeks of time together in the group, some members state that the check-in used at the beginning of group is frustrating because not everybody gets to check in when some other members consume so much time. As the group worker, how do you reconcile this information? What might you state to the group to elicit further comments?

ASSESSMENT FOLLOWING THE FINAL GROUP

The assessment of group work practice can examine one or two key components. These inquiries demonstrate whether groups have successfully completed the group's stated purposes and goals or examine the group work members' knowledge and skill attainment as a result of participating in the group. Assessments facilitate group members' thinking about what the group was all about with specific emphasis on the group's goals and how members met their goals. Assessment verifies results that can be utilized for funders and for advertising group services in the community.

The assessment plan needs to be based upon clear goals and objectives from which specific questions can be drawn. Examples of pertinent questions that can address group activities include:

- Has participation in the group changed behaviors, thoughts, or feelings?
- How satisfied are participants with their group experiences?
- Did the group assist members to track changes and accomplishments?
- What do members consider to be strengths of the group?
- How is diversity represented within group and among group members?
- If members leave group in an unplanned manner, why do they leave?

After selecting the principle questions to be asked, choose the methods that can provide answers to the inquiry. Consider process measures, which provide data regarding what the group did to facilitate members' goals, and outcome measures, which provide specific results. There is a broad selection of methods to obtain answers to the questions, including: group members' surveys of satisfaction with goals, group members' responses regarding satisfaction with individual and group outcomes, surveys measuring behaviors, and key participant interviews that focus on individual changes.

Some methods include the collection of journals from consenting group members. In the journals, group members begin by responding to the question, "How do you think you will do regarding meeting your goals or (in a task group) the group's goals?" During the group, members are asked to journal their estimates of how they think that they are doing regarding reaching their own or the group's goals. This uncovers group process, especially if you ask members to specify what is happening in the group that is helping them reach the goals. At the conclusion of the group, group members are simply asked, "How do you think that you did?" Their answers identify outcomes. All three inquiries at the different data points lead to a more comprehensive understanding of the group's accomplishments.

Past group members can serve as key informants for data collection purposes. Interviewing them after the group permits the completion of updated information on the significance of the group. To improve the group direction, key informants can be asked to share their insights and the elements that assisted them to succeed in their own goal attainment. Their information can be collected as qualitative data that can be presented in a written narrative format with simple descriptive statistics highlighting percentages or proportions.

Goal attainment scaling is another method for assessing whether group members achieved their goals. At the beginning of group, members catalog and prioritize a select number of goals. At the conclusion of the group, members assess the level of personal change and goal achievement. Their responses are most helpful if documented as Likert scales. These allow a simple arithmetic calculation showing change.

Behavioral surveys provide another type of data. Personal risk assessment and harm reduction may be a part of this approach if a member wants to reduce potential harm to self and others. A behavioral survey can help to assess the types of risky behaviors group members continue to engage in at the conclusion of the group. Pretest and posttest surveys can show changes over the life of the group.

For each of these approaches, identify all measurable outcomes or indicators. This is a most important yet likely forgotten phase in considering a group assessment. This can be a difficult step because a relatively undefined practice construct has to be transformed and made into a measurable concept (e.g., increasing self-awareness or increasing assertiveness in social situations). Sometimes proxy indicators have to be selected to stand in for the principle concept. The identification of relevant information that is necessary to conceptually validate the chosen indicators takes careful consideration. For example, if a group member desires an increase in social contacts, this can be surveyed relatively easily. If a group member wants to experience a decrease in negative social interactions, tracking both positive and negative interactions may show a change in the proportion of negative exchanges with an increase in more positive exchanges. This balanced approach can yield a more insightful and complete picture of the group members' changed behaviors.

Exercise 13.8: Practice Consideration: Measuring Outcomes

How prepared and comfortable are you with the task of collecting data on group work practice? How would you go about planning for the assessment of a group's activities? What preparations do you need to accomplish this task?

EVALUATING AND ASSESSING THE WORKER

Another important aspect of evaluation is the evaluation of the group worker's practice. Due to confidentiality, evaluation of the worker is often completed through self-evaluation/self-report, observations of the actual group process (when approved by the agency and/or the group), from coworkers' evaluations of each other, or from member feedback. Chapter 7 discussed the IASWG standards for group work practice and encouraged use of this document as essential to guidance in group work practice. Consequently, one important measurement is that of a group worker's behavior and adherence to the IASWG standards. The IC-SWG is an inventory that measures, through the worker's self-report, how confidently a worker was practicing and how clearly, during the different stages of group, the worker demonstrated the items listed in the standards (MacGowan, 2012). This measure is a reliable, validated measure and is considered evidence-based practice in group work. The measure can be used after each and all stages of the group development and process as a comprehensive assessment of self-rated group worker competence.

Exercise 13.9: Practice Consideration: Evaluating Competence

Why is it important to evaluate your own competence in practicing group work? In what ways can evaluation help group workers develop in their own practice?

Exercise 13.10: Evaluation Strategies

Select one of the following groups, and suggest some evaluative strategies that you would employ to monitor progress and achievement of outcomes.

• an anger management/violence prevention group for adult males
• a sexual abuse survivors' group for women
• a support and educational group for new immigrants
• a support group for caregivers of children who experience a chronic illness
• a life-skills group for youth seeking employment
• an intervention group for adults who experience depression
• an advocacy group for people with intellectual or physical challenges
• a support group for single parents
• an intervention group for adults who abuse substances
• a grief support group for adults who have experienced the loss of a loved one.

CHAPTER SUMMARY

In this chapter, the ending phase of a group was explored with directions for the group work practitioner. The ending of a group provides members with opportunities to celebrate accomplishments and say adieu. Group members can recognize and comment on each other's changes and growth. In task groups, members can reflect on the group's growth and change as they worked together to complete their tasks. A group ending process may also tap into group members' previously dormant feelings related to their losses and grieving, which can be addressed in this ending.

The group worker is advised to encourage members to reflect on the group's process. The group worker can reframe group members' shared personal disclosures in group as investments in their future social interactions outside of group. Workers can also invite members to comment on what each will "take away" from the group. A discussion of the goals achieved can help to cement the accomplishments of the members with special emphasis on what each group member learned about himself or herself. This conversation with task group members can help members recognize that no matter what type of group one participates in, the group will always have some type of impact on the individual group members. Members can be invited to recollect both positive and negative parts of the helping process that was shared among all of the members When appropriate, focus on grieving the end of the relationships and time together but point to the future opportunities that will be forthcoming. When there is a coworker relationship, special considerations in the ending and evaluation process must be given so that coworkers can process and evaluate their work with the group and their work together.

As an integral part of ending a group, the group worker and the agency need to ascertain if the group has been helpful and has achieved the stated objectives. Multiple evaluations may be more informative than a single assessment. Group workers and agencies have to account for the funds utilized in the delivery of group services. Group workers can draw upon a range of evaluations over time to improve their own group skills as well as plan for improved group services. Assessments immediately following a group provide relevant information on the apparent changes recognized by the group members. Delayed data collection a few months after the group can point towards continuous changes being made by members who utilize resources within their sociopersonal environments as they apply skills and knowledge learned and reinforced in group. For task groups, delayed data collection or data collection in multiple points after the group can determine and identify whether the intended macro change was effective and sustainable long term. Ultimately, the evaluation of any group is vital to determine whether the group was an effective investment of time and resources toward addressing the group's purpose and whether changes need to be made to ensure lasting effects. Just as the group is evaluated, it is equally important that the group worker evaluates himself/herself.

Inclusive
PRACTICE APPLICATIONS

Part three presents twelve case studies, which span a diverse range of practice settings and populations. These case studies have been organized into four chapters. In chapter 14, Trauma and Intimate Partner Violence (IPV), you will find three case studies that focus on trauma, including intimate partner violence. One case study in this chapter describes an IPV group in Ireland, another describes a group for Aboriginal males in Canada, and the third case study describes a mixed gender group that includes a substantial number of military service members. In chapter 15, Groups across the Lifespan, you will find five case studies that focus on the needs of children, youth, and parents, with a particular focus on groups serving diverse populations, including African American children and youth as well as Native American parents. In chapter 16, Supportive Groups, you will again find a diverse range of innovative groups, including supportive groups for exotic dancers, adults who experience bipolar disorder, and women in relationships with men from an Arab country. Finally, chapter 17 closes part three with an example of a task group serving Native American children and families.

To promote comparison and contrasting of these diverse groups, contributors organized their case studies using a similar structure. Generally, each case study includes a description of the needs of the population served by the group/organization, the organizational and community context, group purpose and goals, group membership and structure, activities, evaluation, and implications for practice. Particular emphasis is devoted to how the group worked with diversity over time, during pregroup, beginnings, middles, and endings. Also included is a description of critical incidents where diversity arose in the group and how the worker and group responded to these events.

It is important to note that these case studies are neither intended to be regarded as perfect examples of group work practice nor pristine applications of a model of inclusive group work. These case studies, like all group work, are meant to promote reflection, learning, and insights, particularly into working with diversity. To this end, you can use the following discussion questions to compare and contrast these case studies. These questions can serve as the basis for class discussion as well as individual learning and assignments.

Discussion Questions for Case Studies

1. How and where was diversity present in this case study?
2. How was diversity defined or identified in this case study?
3. How did the worker and group respond to diversity when it arose in the group?
4. What leadership attributes and skills were demonstrated in this group?
5. How did the worker evaluate the group? What would be some ways to improve the evaluation of the group?
6. Evaluate the extent to which the case study modeled the principles of inclusive practice by doing the following:

    a. Provide examples where the group workers in the case study demonstrated inclusive practice.

    b. Offer suggestions about how, if you were an inclusive group worker, you could have applied the principles of inclusive practice to improve the group.

CHAPTER 14

TRAUMA AND INTIMATE PARTNER VIOLENCE (IPV)

MEN WHO ABUSE:
AN INTERVENTION GROUP FOR FIRST NATIONS MEN
Steven Thibodeau

Needs of the Population Served by the Group

In this case study, the terms Aboriginal and First Nations will be used to describe classes of Native persons in Canada. The term Aboriginal is used to describe Native Canadians generally and includes such groups as First Nations, Métis, and Inuit people. First Nations people possess a special fiduciary relationship with the federal government under the Indian Act. The term First Nations has been adopted to recognize the original inhabitants of Canada, and the special relationship they hold with the federal government through treaties and agreements.

First Nations females are twice as likely to suffer from partner abuse as are other Canadian women (Moyer, 1992). This phenomenon has caused government agencies and First Nations communities to allocate resources to address this concern. First Nations communities in southern Alberta, and the Blackfoot Confederacy in particular, have been instrumental in establishing treatment groups for men who batter their intimate partners. However, such treatment groups require special consideration. Kiyoshk (2003), an accomplished researcher and practitioner with men having assaultive issues in Aboriginal communities, states, "Assaultive men's counseling in the Aboriginal community is a lot different than in mainstream programs. This is because the history, dynamics and circumstances affecting the aboriginal populations are quite different" (pp. 238–239). Kiyoshk (2001) asserts, "Domestic violence statistics in Canadian general population figures show high degrees of domestic assault occurring nationally, while Aboriginal figures show astoundingly higher rates of domestic assault and other forms of family violence" (p. 10). The magnitude of this social phenomenon is conveyed in the 1999 Canadian General Social Survey (GSS), which compares the aggregate Aboriginal population to the aggregate non-Aboriginal population. According to the authors of this study report, "20% of Aboriginal people reported being assaulted by a spouse as compared with 7% of the non-Aboriginal population" (Family Violence in Canada: A Statistical Profile, 2000, p. 28). Perrault (2011) noted that First Nations people were almost twice as likely as non-Aboriginal people to report being a victim of spousal violence in the five years preceding the survey. Although such reports are of significance when examining treatment initiatives in Native communities, they have been admonished for their tendency to ". . . objectify and quantify abuse without really getting down to the reality of the oppression and its long-term effects on aboriginal people" (Kiyoshk, 2003, p. 239).

Organizational and Community Context

Planning for the delivery of meaningful and effective treatment groups is particularly important in the First Nations community. When developing treatment groups to address family violence, the group facilitators can expect to devote as much as six months to a year in the developing and planning of this service. Group facilitators are required to understand the sociopolitical structure of the community as well as the influence of extended families and clans. Such knowledge enables group facilitators to anticipate potential concerns held by community members. Time must also be made available for group facilitators to visit and consult with influential family and clan members and community elders (Hart, 1996). Furthermore, First Nations treatment groups must contend with many of the practical issues faced by mainstream models. Confidentiality is a sensitive issue and must be discussed thoroughly with group members. Group members are advised that standardized records are kept on each session and those records are stored in a secure place. Only the facilitators have access to them, unless directed by group members.

A further factor affecting community context is that First Nation communities are fairly impermeable to nontribal members, resulting in few newcomers from off the Native reserve gaining entry. When family violence initiatives are held in a member's home community, it is possible that the group may include the member's father, uncle, brother, nephew, brothers-in-law, or other close family members. Often these men deeply value family loyalty regardless of how misguided or misplaced that loyalty may appear. This becomes a particularly poignant clinical issue, as family violence prevention initiatives are based on the principles of confrontation and accountability (Perrault, 2011). The presence of strong family loyalties may thwart the group facilitator's and elder's efforts to promote such principles.

Group Goals

The group facilitated was titled "Men in Relationships: A Group for Blackfoot Men." A broad goal of the group was to assist men in learning healthy, nonviolent ways of relating to their intimate partners and other significant people in their lives. Men learned this goal from open, frank, and honest interaction and confrontation within the group. Topics included: improving communication skills; strategies for strengthening relationships; anger management skills; assertiveness and coping tools; and discussing attitudes, values, beliefs, and spirituality in the context of relationships. Empathy for their significant other was a critical and consistent theme throughout the group process.

Several fundamental group goals included:

- understanding the safety needs of the abused woman/partner and other family members
- accepting responsibility for their violent behavior
- stopping the use of violence, which has been used to maintain power and control in the relationship
- influencing the men's behavior so that they do not reoffend
- understanding the historical and political factors that contribute to family violence
- understanding that partner abuse is perpetrated by women's political, social, and economic inequality and is supported by culturally based sexism (Dobash & Dobash, 1992; Kiyoshk, 2003; Perrault, 2011).

Group Membership

The group was open to all First Nations men who wished to improve their intimate relationships and enhance their interpersonal skills, who had a history of family violence, and who were able to demonstrate a reasonable level of mental acuity. Men were excused from the group if they were intoxicated, violent, incoherent, or disruptive. There was no restriction to membership if men were related.

Group Structure

The group convened one evening a week for one and a half to two hours. Often groups would be offered over a six-month period. However, groups were ongoing and were always open ended, resulting in group members leaving the group for a period of time, only to return several weeks later. The setting was made as comfortable as possible by providing soft chairs in quiet, private surroundings. Often, indigenous artifacts by local artisans were tastefully displayed in the meeting room. As these groups were open sessions, members entered at any time, making it difficult to control the number of participants at times. On average, about five members attended each group, which appeared to be ideal. The role of the group facilitators was to foster a climate of nonshaming attitude, acceptance, and confidentiality. The sessions would often start by providing general themes leading to open conversation, discussion, and vivid storytelling. It was not the role of the group facilitators to lead the session, but to gently influence the direction of the themes discussed and the stories told so that treatment goals were adequately addressed. On occasion, a group facilitator was needed to support an individual group member who got triggered or unduly distressed by the content of a session. The elder augmented the role of the group facilitators who cofacilitated the group process. The elder had a distinct role, which included opening and closing each session with an agreed upon ritual, such as a prayer, song, and/or a smudge. The elder would add richly to the storytelling and contribute to the stories mentioned by others in the group. There was a fine balance between the roles of the elder and the group facilitators. The elder brought traditional wisdom, indigenous experiences, and customs, while the latter brought a clinical understanding of group process, family violence, and interpersonal trauma. It was expected that each would be respectful and appreciative of the other.

Group Activities

Normally, each weekly session began with a check-in round, where men discussed their experiences and challenges that they experienced between sessions. Incidents of violent behavior or potentially violent behavior were identified and discussed. In keeping with traditional Native norms, the check-in proceeded in a clockwise fashion. Often group members passed around a rock, feather, or some sacred object as they recounted their experiences to the group. The check-in also provided an opportunity for new members to introduce themselves. In a similar fashion, each session ended with a check-in round, where members were asked to share what they had found most helpful about the session. The closing check-in was particularly important in reducing and defusing agitation or arousal associated with interactions during the session. Past clinical experience, which is supported by research, indicates that group members who leave a group session in a state of heightened arousal are at significant risk to reoffend (see Perrault, 2011).

The group facilitators, in close partnership with the elder, facilitated the group by suggesting a series of themes, including: (a) the impact of violence on one's partner, (b) violence in one's family of origin, (c) strategies to arrest violent behavior, (d) male entitlement, and (e) cultural and historical factors leading to violence in First Nations communities. Throughout the sessions, these themes were identified, and ample opportunity was given to group members for spontaneous discussion and poignant storytelling. The elder played a key role by maintaining the focus of the group discussion on healthy themes through his/her storytelling and remembrances.

How the Group Worked with Diversity over Time

Pregroup

A potential member was required to state his readiness and willingness to participate in the group, willingness to refrain from alcohol and drug use for two days prior to the day of the group, and ability to identify some degree of conflict in his relationship with his significant other. The standard prescreening offered the treatment team the opportunity to determine if the potential participant was ready for the treatment, to assess his strengths and areas of concern, and to understand his purpose and interest in the group. Issues discussed at the prescreening phase included the participant's expectation of the group, his specific goals, and the group's expectation of him. Efforts were made to encourage members to discuss intergenerational issues, particularly those related to Indian residential school experiences and the suggested corollary of increased family violence. Older and veteran members (those who had attended several cycles of the group) served as mentors and role models for younger or newer members. Veteran members were described as forming the four foundational poles of the group teepee, while the contributions of new members were portrayed as adding new poles to strengthen the structure. In this way, each member's contributions and support were viewed as a form of service to the group. The use of a male/female and/or Native/non-Native cofacilitator team offered special advantages for this group. Members' responses to the female group facilitator provided opportunities for further exploration of their attitudes towards women. Although it is noted that female group facilitators could not speak on behalf of the men's partners, they could validate the impact of abuse, as witnessed by a female. The presence of a healthy and engaged First Nations group facilitator provided an immediate validation of accepted Native behaviors, values, and traditions. When there was more than one facilitator, it offered group members an opportunity to observe a relationship between group facilitators where power was shared equally and where decision making and roles were products of negotiation.

Beginning

Unlike groups convened in urban areas, all members of the First Nations group were generally known to each other. The session began with the elder taking on a unique role as a spiritual and/or cultural leader, while the male and female facilitators welcomed each member to the group. The elder often opened the group with a ritual and explained the importance of the ceremony. Small talk centered on the various familial relationships that existed between members of the group and led to a discussion of each member's goals, and how these goals might be achieved through the use of the group's processes. New members were asked to identify an important female in their life and explain why she was important to them. The remaining group members were asked to share their past experiences in the group with new members and to identify their individual goals. This served as a reminder to all men in the group of their goals and modeled to new members a clear articulation and ownership of one's treatment goals. It also fostered a sense of common purpose and connection among group participants. During the early sessions, the facilitators and elder also normalized feelings of anxiety, advising new members that they could say as much or as little as they wished. The group facilitators and the elder stressed the fact that the group represented a safe place for members to discuss their feelings and behavior, but that all men in the group would be held accountable for all of their behaviors. Occasionally, troublesome alliances emerged between members that supported disparaging comments and views of women. When these attitudes emerged, the female group facilitator advised members of the group of the expectation that all women be treated in a respectful and honorable fashion. The elder supported this position and indicated that their comments were not in keeping with the Native way of treating women. There was often a reiteration of the purpose of the group, which was to enhance and promote healthy and respectful relationships. The facilitators then redirected the conversation to the theme of taking personal responsibility for one's own behavior. Members of the group were reminded that it was important that they be supportive of each other; however, it was more important that they help each other see their "blind spots" in their relationships through confrontation. In this way, socialization of new members was largely achieved through the work of veteran group members. The elder was supportive of these concepts and would tell traditional stories that focused on taking responsibility for one's behavior and the need to be frank with each other. The elder shared a sentiment at the end of his narrative, stating, "We all have to pull together as a clan; otherwise we can do much harm to each other." Both facilitators encouraged open discussion of these comments, which led to greater cohesion and the instillation of group norms that included taking personal accountability for one's actions, having respect for each other in the group, and gaining a better understanding of the use of confrontation as a tool for the therapeutic leverage. These norms encouraged members to be appropriately confrontational without undermining the self-esteem or respect of fellow members.

Middle

As the weekly sessions progressed, members commented on how the group felt like a family. In this atmosphere, several members were able to disclose their experiences of being abusive with family members and friends. In each instance, members supported each other while discussing strategies for handling the various situations that arose. The elder helped the group members talk about the shame brought to First Nations people when members of the group are abusive. Throughout these sessions the men were acknowledged for their brave disclosures, and were encouraged to stay focused on their treatment goals of bringing safety and respect back to their wives and girlfriends. After a number of sessions, members actively questioned and challenged each other about their use of violence as a way of resolving difficulties with other family members. Moreover, members were less defensive when challenged about their behaviors. Some sought the opinions of others when resolving issues of insecurity, anger, and suspected infidelities by their partner. Although members openly questioned and challenged each other, the elder was able to bring historical context to issues by exploring intergenerational themes within their respective families. As a further strategy, members acknowledged having valuable role models within their families and extended families to draw upon when developing new approaches of relating to their partners.

Ending

As the group approached the last week of its time together, many men began to wonder how they would spend their Monday nights. Participants made plans for the final session, which involved a sweat lodge. One participant reported that he was not sure if he could attend the last session. This caused a few men to react negatively, and lingering feelings of separation and endings surfaced, which in turn were discussed and normalized. On the final session, a late-night sweat lodge was arranged. Before the ceremony began, men gathered around the fire and each spontaneously shared an incident from the group sessions that was meaningful to him. There was much levity and ease among the men. During the sweat lodge, themes related to relationships, self-control, and respect for loved ones were discussed. For many of the men, their personal goals were brought to this spiritual place for review and reflection.

Evaluation

Evaluation is optimally an ongoing process. Throughout all group sessions, members identified what they had learned or gained from the experience at the end of each session, often by an open questionnaire. The evaluation process also included meeting with each member's partner and/or possibly other family members for a report on the progress made since the commencement of group therapy. Their view of the situation was significant, as they often provided a critical and more objective analysis of the changes made by the group member (see Dobash & Dobash, 1992).

As is customary with most groups, summary recordings were made following each session. The twenty-five-item partner abuse scale (Attala, Hudson, and McSweeney, 1994) was also administered for evaluative purposes.

Implications for Practice and Policy

There are a number of implications that can be gleaned for group facilitators and administrators. It is important that considerable time be allocated in the early stages of developing an intervention group that includes meeting and conferring with community members. The structure of the groups must include a role for a community elder, and every effort should be made to include a male and female facilitation team, preferably with First Nations facilitators. The program should have clear treatment goals that include promoting an attitude of safety and respect for women in the community and also include a cultural and historical context of violence in the community. The operation of the group should be based on storytelling and memories that focus on key aspects of recovery. The role of the elder and the group facilitators is to facilitate focused group discussion and process new insights as they emerge. It is also important that the group end in a way that reflects the traditions and customs of the community and those of the men in it. Such closing traditions should be decided through consensus among group members and with the support of the elder and facilitators.

FURTHER READING

Dobash, R. E., and Dobash, R. P. "The Therapeutic Society." In *Women, Violence, and Social Change*, pp. 242–250. New York, NY: Routledge, 1992.

Kiyoshk, R. *Family Violence in Aboriginal communities: A Review*. Ottawa, ON: The Aboriginal Nurses Association of Canada and Royal Canadian Mounted Police, 2001.

Kiyoshk, R. "Integrating Spirituality and Domestic Violence Treatment: Treatment for Aboriginal Men." *Journal of Aggression Maltreatment and Trauma* 7, no. 1 (2003).

Moyer, S. "Race, Gender, and Homicide: Comparisons between Aboriginals and Other Canadians." *Canadian Journal of Criminology* 34, no. 1 (1992): 15–34.

Perrault, S. *Education Groups for Men Who Batter: The Duluth Model.* New York, NY: Spring Publishing Company, 2011.

DIVERSITY AND VULNERABILITY: GROUP WORK FOR WOMEN WHO HAVE EXPERIENCED IPV, CHILDHOOD TRAUMA, AND SUBSTANCE USE
Sarah Morton

Intimate partner violence (IPV) remains a major social issue, with a growing recognition of the intersection of violence, substance use, and childhood abuse in women's lives (Elliot, Bjelajac, Fallot, Markoff, & Reed, 2005; Tucker, Wenzel, Straus, Gery, & Golinelli, 2005; Covington, 2008). In the United States, 28.9 percent of women experienced physical, sexual, or psychological IPV during their lifetime, according to one study (Coker et al., 2002), while a similar study in Ireland found 15 percent of women experienced severe emotional, physical, or sexual abuse in their lifetime (Watson & Parsons, 2005). Women experiencing IPV have a range of emotional, practical, and physical needs in relation to themselves and their children when accessing IPV services. Service delivery responses can include shelter, advocacy, counseling and court support underpinned by qualities such as empathy, empowerment, and individualized care planning (Kulkarni, Bell, & McDaniel Rhodes, 2012).

In recent years, there has been greater exploration and recognition of how IPV may be related to further complex presenting issues in women's lives, such as problematic substance use (Bennett & O'Brien, 2007). It has been theorized that women will seek help for their issues based on immediacy or the potential for life threat (Brown, Mechoir, Panter, Slaughter, & Huba, 2000), suggesting the need for an integrated service response. Where there is an intersection of problematic substance use (for the survivor or the perpetrator) and IPV, harm reduction and risk assessment in relation to the patterns of violence, control, and substance use are required (Wright, Tompkins, & Sheard, 2007). Covington (2008) also maintains that it is important to explore women's substance use as a coping method and response to trauma. Group work approaches for IPV survivors have been identified as being particularly useful in addressing women's isolation, recognizing mutual survivorship, improving self-esteem, and contextualizing women's individual experiences within a wider cultural or social context (Goldberg Wood & Roche, 2001). Group work programs for IPV also offer the potential for positive mutual aid between participants (Liu, Morrison-Dore, & Amrani-Cohen, 2013). This case study considers the issue of diversity in a group work program for women who have experienced IPV and possibly substance use and childhood abuse.

Organizational and Community Context

Cuan Saor is an IPV agency based in a large town in a rural area of Ireland. The agency provides a range of services to women experiencing IPV, with additional dedicated services for the children of these women. Services include shelter, counseling, advocacy, helpline, court accompaniment, children's support, supervised child access provision, and a group work program. In recent years, the organization has developed a coordinated response, across their range of services, to women experiencing IPV and problematic substance use. Working from a harm reduction approach, the coordinated substance use and IPV response includes: accommodations in the shelter for women who are actively using substances, an outreach clinic to the substance use service, on-site substance use counseling, and integration of harm and risk minimization into all support and advocacy services.

As part of its wider service delivery, the organization also delivers a psychoeducational group work program based initially on the pattern change program (Goodman & Fallon, 1995) for female survivors of IPV. In line with the development of a coordinated response to IPV, substance use, and the emerging issue of childhood sexual abuse, this program has been developed to encompass and respond to these intersecting issues in women's lives.

Group Purpose and Goals

The psychoeducational group work program delivered by Cuan Saor seeks to address the impact of IPV by recognizing and building key life skills in relation to understanding rights, boundaries, and assertiveness (Goodman & Fallon, 1995). Working from a gendered perspective in terms of how IPV is understood and responded to by society, the program is strengths-based, exploring how women may be supported to recognize their own skills and abilities and to advocate for their own protection. The program seeks to provide a unique group-based space for women to understand and address the impact IPV has had on them, their life patterns, and the lives of their children (if they have them). This approach of the program is to balance emotional support, education, and sharing of experience.

Program content includes four main areas: (1) a contextual focus on gender-based violence (GBV); (2) exploration of childhood legacies of abuse or neglect; (3) consideration of the intersection of substance use and IPV; and (4) development of healthy sexuality for survivors of childhood or adult sexual abuse or violence. The program seeks to "future proof" participants from further abusive relationships by exploring childhood legacies and adult experiences, as well as focusing on education and skills in developing and maintaining healthy relationships. It is never suggested or implied that women are responsible for their own victimization, but rather that they may have had some vulnerabilities that made them targets for an abusive or manipulative adult relationship. The diversity aspects are present in terms of some degree of: cultural diversity; diverse experiences of violence; diverse experience of substance use (some women have used substances to cope, others had partners who used, or both); and diverse experiences, attitudes, and (often emergent) identities in regard to sex and sexuality.

Group Membership

As the program aims to address the impact of IPV and related issues, rather than the immediate safety and risk from IPV, the program is targeted at women who are no longer in an abusive relationship. Referrals are drawn internally from the range of Cuan Saor services, as well as from related agencies, including social work, drug and alcohol, and mental health services. All of the participants are female and have a history of IPV. They may have substance use issues and may have experienced childhood sexual abuse or neglect. The participants are screened to ensure that they have been or are receiving appropriate support and intervention to deal with IPV and/or substance use. If this is not the case, they are offered alternative supports and intervention. Additionally, the content and focus of the program is discussed with all applicants so they are aware of how the content may relate to their personal experience. The program offers a maximum of fifteen places.

The ages of women attending the program have ranged from nineteen to sixty-five, with most falling into the twenty-five to forty-five age range. The majority of women in the program have children. The majority (90%) of the participants are white and Irish, with small percentages of women from different ethnic backgrounds, including Irish Traveler (an ethnic group characterized by people with a nomadic lifestyle and their own dialect and cultural customs) and Asian. In a usual intake, around 50 percent of women will have used substances problematically during their lifetime. Substances used problematically have included alcohol, prescribed medication, and illicit substances, most often cannabis. For around 80 percent of the participants, their abusive partner will have used substances problematically, and in at least 50 percent of cases, there will have been problematic substance use in their family of origin. Around half of the women in each intake will have experienced mental health problems at some point in their lives, with one or two participants in each program dealing with an enduring mental health issue, such as depression or an anxiety disorder.

Group Structure

The program is delivered over a twelve-week period, one session per week. Ten of the sessions are three hours in duration and two are full days. The full day sessions cover the intersection of IPV and substance use and the development of a healthy sexuality in the wake of sexual abuse or violence. Six practitioners are involved in delivering the program, with two facilitators and one support staff member present for each session. The support worker provides in-session or immediate follow-up support to any of the participants if required, and also follows up with participants between sessions if required. The facilitation of the program is deliberately shared across four practitioners to enable best use of expertise and continue to develop capacity and expertise in group work within the organization. Full wrap-around services are provided, including counseling, court accompaniment, advocacy, twenty-four-hour helpline, and shelter accommodation if required. The program is delivered in a community building with disability access and free parking. Childcare and transport costs are covered for participants, if required, for the duration of the program.

The program facilitators seek to position themselves in ways that allow for emotional vulnerability and promote mutuality and consumer-based progress (Caplan & Thomas, 2004a). Particular attention is paid to the risk of either positioning themselves as "superior" to the women in the program or of falling into the role of "rescuer," based on the belief this would hamper the collaboration and trust with the women in the program (Caplan & Thomas, 2004b; Liu et al., 2013). They therefore balance maintaining safety, delivering content, and facilitating exercises while not reinforcing patriarchal concepts of hierarchy and control (Caplan & Thomas, 2004a). They position themselves carefully in relation to their own histories or experiences, some of which may have been abusive. Personal disclosures of IPV experiences are deliberately not utilized in order to avoid binary categorization of themselves as either abused or not abused. They do, however, use examples from their lives of dealing with violence or abuse, operating from a belief system that all women are subject to or at risk from some form of violence or abuse in their lives (Kelly, 1988).

Group Activities

The program content is a mix of education, mutual support, and exercises that seek to both build life skills and make sense of previous life experiences. The program is underpinned by a belief in women's strength and resilience, as well as a belief in women's capacity to resist violence and abuse and to recognize their own personal agency. A number of different methods are used in the delivery of the program, including group discussions of theory or ideas, small group work, case studies, and individual written or reflective exercises. Participants are invited to share their understanding or meaning they derived from a given exercise if they wish. From the start of the program, focus is given to the women making sense of their experiences rather than personal disclosure of details of abuse, violence, harm, or substance use. The program works from the stance of considering the impact of the woman's experience, rather than reinforcing systems that push her to keep retelling her story if this is not useful.

Exercises that tend to highlight the diversity within the group are: creative exercises that map each woman's life story, exercises on family of origin and impact of childhood legacies, and exploration of problematic substance use. For instance, one exercise asks each participant to map her life history utilizing pictures, color, and symbols and then, if she wishes, discuss this process with the other women in the group. Participants are asked to pay particular attention to the dominant narratives in their life stories; what narrative they tell themselves, other people in their lives, and their community; and how they might construct a narrative that highlights their resilience and strengths (Epston & White, 1990). An exercise such as this tends to amplify the differences and diversity in the group, in terms of cultural background, education, class, abuse experiences, and substance use.

Use of Diversity over Duration of the Group

Diversity and its possible generative impact for women in the group are considered on a practical, individual, and social level at all stages of the group planning and facilitation. At the planning stages of the group, ethnic origin, physical and mental disabilities, learning difficulties (such as dyslexia), literacy issues, and known mental health issues are noted, as well as whether women have English as a first or second language. Focus is also placed on diversity of experience, including histories of childhood abuse or neglect, type of IPV experienced, family status, economic status, and substance use history. On a practical level, the facilitators discuss and agree on any supports or additional resources that may be necessary to enable full participation of the women, such as childcare, language support, and literacy support as well as any facilitator skills or knowledge required to ensure cultural competency (Marrs & Fuchsel, 2014).

At the planning or pregroup stage, all of the women are pre-interviewed. The program aims and content are explained and discussed. Any of the diversity issues raised during the referral stage are discussed with each woman in terms of how her participation and safety can be promoted within the group. Each woman is also asked if there is anything she feels may hinder her participation or anything she feels she would like in place to support her. The majority of women referred to the program have already accessed other support services, such as substance misuse, shelter, counseling, or mental health services, and are openly able to discuss this history and the impact of their life history on their potential to engage with group work.

In the very early stages of the group work, great attention is paid to contracting with the participants, agreeing on ground rules and ways of working together that recognize and promote both shared and different experiences, life histories, and diverse backgrounds. This would include, for example, identifying difficulties some participants may have in comprehension if English is not their first language. The group is then asked to brainstorm ways to ensure everyone in the group understands the content and discussion. As outlined by Caplan and Thomas (2004b), group practitioner interventions can progress the work of the group by establishing global themes, while also validating the experience or context of individual members. This in an approach used throughout the program by the facilitators to respond to issues of diversity.

In the case of English not being a first language, for instance, this individual experience of a few group members is linked to the global theme of isolation. So practical solutions are sought to address language comprehension, on the basis of the group agreeing to challenge feelings of isolation within the group. This can be particularly powerful and positive for the participants, as isolation of the victim is a key underpinning to perpetrating abuse, and all of the women would have experienced social, family, and community isolation to some degree. The aim in the early stages, therefore, is not to negate difference and diversity, but to recognize and address it in a way that encourages mutual aid (Liu et al., 2013) and affirms wisdom and agency (Goldberg Wood & Roche, 2001) for the women. This is also modeled by the workers, who deliberately highlight differences and diversity between each other in terms of cultural background, language, education, and life experiences, illustrating how these diverse elements have helped in developing knowledge and skills in regard to IPV, substance use, and childhood abuse.

As the group progresses into the middle stages, both positive outcomes and challenges can arise in relation to handling diversity in a generative and positive way. As all of the women have themselves experienced isolation, guilt, and shame, they will often work hard to ensure inclusion and participation of all of the women in the group. They will often listen to each other and draw comparisons between their experiences, highlighting differences in culture, economic background, or education, then highlighting that the outcome in relation to IPV was similar. For instance, one woman may state that she was brought up to believe marriage was forever and had internalized this cultural belief. She may add that she had no economic means to support her to leave her relationship. Another woman might respond that she had support from her parents to leave the relationship and had her own income, but still stayed because the perpetrator controlled her through emotional abuse. In the middle phase of the program, these types of interactions are generative, building cohesion, collaboration, and trust among the participants.

Diversity can be a challenge to this cohesion, and has tended to arise in relation to experience of IPV, substance use, and childhood abuse and in how women have dealt with these issues in their lives. This often manifests as a woman responding in a dictatorial way to another woman voicing her experience. It often happens where a woman still has unresolved issues in relation to a particular type of experience; she therefore responds with judgment or a degree of criticism when another woman speaks of something similar. As Caplan and Thomas (2002) point out, practitioners must develop the awareness to manage their own counter transference to enable participants to explore difficult moments to derive meaning. They must also help participants to manage their own counter transference, in order for meaning-making to flourish in the group.

The facilitators are quick to respond to this dynamic, reminding the participants of the diversity of women's histories and responses to issues in their lives. If appropriate, a discussion is opened on how women can be triggered by listening to another woman's experience if it relates to a global theme. Women often feel pain or insecurity around such themes as intimacy, grief, or betrayal (Caplan & Thomas, 2004b). The middle stages of the group work can often, then, have a heavier focus on balancing the psychodynamic and social aspects of diversity.

At the ending stage of the program, diversity naturally arises in terms of the participants' journeys, life stages, and the degree of vulnerability they may be feeling in their lives. Some participants are still involved in lengthy court processes in regard to separation, divorce, or child custody. Others are dealing with immigration status issues subsequent to the ending of their relationship, while others are going on to further education or work opportunities. Often the women will reflect through the evaluation and ending exercises on how their new knowledge and skills would have helped them earlier in their lives and also changed their experiences of substance use or mental health services. The reality of this mix of shared experience of IPV and diversity of life paths and experience is utilized by the facilitators to highlight the importance of each woman's unique experience. To recognize and celebrate this diversity, group exercises focus on each woman's future path, aspirations, resilience, and changes she has experienced as a result of undertaking the program.

Critical Incidents

Two examples of critical incidents arising in regard to diversity will be explored. The first example centers on the disclosure of an experience of sexual violence by a participant in the group. The participant was from a different ethnic and cultural background from the majority of the group and, over the preceding six weeks in the program, had often commented on issues in relation to how they were thought about or acted on within her culture and country of origin. The group was discussing a general topic about how women are often socialized into taking responsibility for their own safety and protection from gender-based violence (GBV), along with the belief that the greatest risk is from strangers. The participant, Rosa (pseudonyms are used throughout this case study), gave the example of how when she was a student they were always told not to go across the park in front of their accommodation, as it was dangerous for women to be alone in the park. The atmosphere suddenly changed in the group, as a feeling of fear crept into the room. "I did not listen to that," said Rosa. "I did not want anyone telling me where I should go in case I would be attacked by a man," she added. "Then," she said, "one day I crossed the park and I went up to my room. And it was there that I was raped, there in my own room, on my own little bed, by a man I knew, from my building, not in the dangerous park, from some stranger. And after that," she said, "I never walked across the park again."

There was silence as Rosa finished her sentence. She had disclosed her own history of sexual violence victimization and also provided a poignant example from individual experience of the social dynamic being discussed by the group. She had also, with her story, brought into the room the feeling of risk many women experience in their daily lives.

The worker left a short pause, then spoke, knowing the importance of minimizing the impact of Rosa's disclosure on the group, but utilizing it to further the understanding and knowledge in the group. There was a risk that women in the group could distance themselves from both Rosa and experiences of sexual violence because of her ethnic difference and the fact the incident had happened in a different country. The facilitator validated Rosa's personal experience and linked it to the global themes, then invited the rest of the participants to engage with that discussion. One of the women responded to this input from the facilitator immediately, "Your story reminds me, Rosa, of how scared I get if I even start to think about how vulnerable I am, living on my own." A full discussion on vulnerability and resilience then followed. The impact of Rosa's disclosure became generative rather than destructive, with the possibility that Rosa felt understood and believed, but also that disclosing her experience had supported other women to discuss themes of safety and risk. The group contains both women who used drugs and alcohol and women whose partners used drugs or alcohol, so addressing this diversity can be key in building respect and understanding in the group, as well as understanding the many complex ways women cope with threat and violence in their lives. The second example relates to the use of drugs and alcohol by women in the group and/or by their partners who were the perpetrators of IPV.

A number of women were discussing how their partners used alcohol and drugs as an excuse when they perpetrated violence. The discussion had a slight tone of judgment against anyone who used alcohol or drugs, with one woman commenting, "I just never drink, not after I see how he used it to make excuses for his behavior and the impact it has had on our kids." At this point there was a risk that any use of drugs or alcohol associated the person with abusive behavior or harmful impact on children. Another woman, Jenny, interceded, "Well, I did drink and for me it was a way of coping with his control and violence. It did really affect my daughter. I have been through treatment and it is still a struggle, every day."

One of the facilitators responded to Jenny's comment, highlighting that women may use drugs and alcohol as a way to cope with violence and some may experience guilt and shame about both their use and the impact on their children. This response by the facilitator aimed to draw on global themes of coping, guilt, and shame, rather than allow Jenny to feel judged or isolated within the group because of her substance use. Two women responded to these comments. One stated that, although she had never used drugs or alcohol, she still felt huge guilt in regard to the impact on her children of the IPV. A second woman turned to Jenny and said, "I know what you mean. I used to drink with my partner because I knew what was coming and it was easier to deal with if I had drink on board, and also sometimes if I drank with him, he would not be so violent." This then opened up a conversation about how the women used different strategies to manage the risk of violence from their partners. This second example again illustrates how the diversity of experience can be utilized within the group to develop conversations and shared understanding in relation to global emotional themes such as safety and grief (Caplan & Thomas, 2004a).

Evaluation and Outcomes

The program is evaluated on completion utilizing both process and outcome measures. Attendance and completion rates are analyzed, and participants are invited to complete an anonymous outcome evaluation questionnaire. The questionnaire asks them about: the relevance and effectiveness of the content, personal outcomes they experienced as a result of participating in the program, whether they would recommend the program to a friend, and what changes they would like to see in the program. At the final session, women are invited to verbally reflect on the value, content, and any changes they would like to see in the program. This evaluation structure has resulted in ongoing development and change in the program, including the introduction of modules on drugs and alcohol, on women's mental health, and on sex and sexuality.

Between twelve and fourteen women commence each cycle of the program, with attendance rates averaging 80 to 100 percent and completion of the program averaging above 90 percent. In the majority of cases, women who leave the program do so in order to access other program services, usually counseling. This is usually because undertaking the program has highlighted an emotional issue or issues, such as childhood sexual abuse, that they feel is best suited to one on one counseling. Identified outcomes are linked directly to program objectives and include elements such as: understanding the impact of abuse; realizing how other factors, such as childhood legacy, community responses, substance use, and sexual violence, may be related to abuse; knowledge about maintaining healthy boundaries and being assertive; confidence in identifying healthy relationships; and life skills for living life well.

In all of the evaluations to date (Morton, 2014), women have reported change in relation to the emotional, practical, or life skill issues as a result of completing the program. Women have also highlighted the importance of the group work approach, commenting on the value of realizing "you are not alone" and also of the importance of mutual aid (Tutty, Bidgood, & Rothery, 1993; Tutty, Bidgood, & Rothery, 1996). One participant summed up the impact of the program in her final comment: "Whoever comes into my life as a future partner will have to be of a high standard. He may not even exist! But I still want to be sure I don't settle for 'less bad than the last guy'."

Implications for Practice

As noted by Caplan and Thomas (2004a), even the most seemingly homogenous group contains diversity. At first glance, participants in this group work program appear relatively homogenous, beyond obvious markers of cultural or ethnic difference; however, diversity exists in terms of experience, family status, income, education, substance use, and mental health. Utilizing these differences to widen participants' understanding of the global themes that affect women's lives is a key feature of the program. This approach of relating individual experience to wider community and social contexts requires nuanced facilitator skills. One of the most important of these is to relate women's experiences and relationships to those of other women in the group and to utilize the latent diversity to widen and deepen participants' experience, mutual aid, and life skills. As understanding of the intersection of complex issues of abuse, IPV, and substance use emerge (Tucker et al., 2005) there are implications for workers in terms of knowledge of the interplay of these issues, as well as the skills required to facilitate group work that is generative and positive.

FURTHER READING

Bennett, L., and O'Brien, P. "Effects of Coordinated Services for Drug-abusing Women Who Are Victims of Intimate Partner Violence." *Violence against Women* 13, no. 4 (2007): 395–411.

Brown, V., Mechoir, L. A., Panter, A. T., Slaughter, R., and Huba, G. J. "Women's Steps of Change and Entry into Drug Abuse Treatment: A Multidimensional Stages of Change Model." *Journal of Substance Abuse Treatment* 18 (2000): 231–240.

Caplan, T., and Thomas, H. "The Forgotten Moment: Therapeutic Resiliency and Its Promotion in Social Work with Groups." *Social Work with Groups* 22, no. 2 (2002): 5–26.

Caplan, T., and Thomas, H. "If This Is Week Three, We Must Be Doing 'Feelings': An Essay on the Importance of Client-paced Group Work." *Social Work with Groups* 26, no. 3 (2004a): 5–14.

Caplan, T., and Thomas, H. "If We Are All in the Same Canoe, Why Are We Using Different Paddles? The Effective Use of Common Themes in Diverse Group Situations." *Social Work with Groups* 27, no. 1 (2004b): 53–73.

Covington, S. "Women and Addiction: A Trauma-informed Approach." *Journal of Psychoactive Drugs* 40 (SARC Supplement 5) (2008): 377–385.

Elliot, D. E., Gjelajac, P., Fallot, R. D., Markoff, L. S., and Glover Reed, B. "Trauma-informed or Trauma-denied: Principles and Implementation of Trauma-informed Services for Women." *Journal of Community Psychology* 33, no. 4 (2005): 461–477.

Epston, D., and White, M. *Narrative Means to Therapeutic Ends*. New York, NY: Norton, 1990.

Goldberg Wood, G., and Roche, S. E. "Representing Selves, Reconstructing Lives: Feminist Group Work with Women Survivors of Male Violence." *Social Work with Groups* 23, no. 4 (2001): 5–23.

Goodman, M., and Fallon, B. *Pattern Changing for Abused Women: An Educational Program*. Thousand Oaks, CA: Sage, 1995.

Kelly, L. "What's in a Name? Defining Child Sexual Abuse." *Feminist Review*, 28 (1988): 65–73.

Kulkarni, S., Bell, H., and McDaniel Rhodes, D. "Back to Basics: Essential Qualities of Services for Survivors of Intimate Partner Violence." *Violence against Women* 18, no. 1 (2012): 85–101.

Liu, S, Morrison-Dore, M., and Amrani-Cohen, I. "Treating the Effects of Interpersonal Violence: A Comparison of Two Group Models." *Social Work with Groups* 36 (2013): 59–72.

Marrs Fuchsel, C. L. "Exploratory Evaluation of Sí, Yo Puedo: A Culturally Competent Empowerment Program for Immigrant Latina Women in Group Settings." *Social Work with Groups* 37 (2014): 279–296.

Morton, S. *Cuan Saor Strategic Review*. Cuan Saor: Clonmel, Co Tipperary, Ireland, 2013.

Morton, S. *Cuan Saor Pattern Change Program: Report on the Support and Outcomes for Participants*. Cuan Saor: Clonmel, Co Tipperary, Ireland, 2014.

Tucker, J. S., Wenzel, S. L., Straus, J. B., Gery, R. W., and Golinelli, D. "Experiencing Interpersonal Violence: Perspectives of Sexually Active, Substance-using Women Living in Shelters and Low-income Housing." *Violence against Women* 11, no. 10 (2005): 1319–1340.

Tutty, L., Bidgood, B., and Rothery, M. "Support Groups for Battered Women: Research on Their Efficacy." *Journal of Family Violence* 8 (1993): 325–343.

Tutty, L., Bidgood, B., and Rothery, M. (1996) "Evaluating the Effect of Group Process and Client Variables in Support Groups for Battered Women." *Research on Social Work Practice* 6 (1996): 308–324.

Wright, N. M., Tompkins, C. N., and Sheard, L. "Is Peer Injection a Form of Intimate Partner Abuse? A Qualitative Study of the Experiences of Women Drug Users." *Health and Social Care in the Community* 15, no. 5 (2007): 417–42

CASE STUDY OF A TRAUMA-INFORMED CONCURRENT DISORDER GROUP
Rachael Pascoe

According to a survey by Health Canada (2014), most Canadians (78.4%) report consuming alcohol throughout the year, and 18.6 percent of Canadian drinkers report exceeding the Canadian guidelines for low-risk alcohol consumption. The survey found that approximately 21.6 percent of Canadians met the criteria for a substance use disorder throughout their lifetime, and 4.4 percent met the criteria within the past year (Pearson, Janz, & Ali, 2013). Past research has consistently demonstrated the harmful impact of substance use not only for the individual but also for society. It is becoming increasingly apparent that in order to fully address substance use in Canada, it is important to reduce the harms of such substances through education, prevention, and effective intervention. Unfortunately, funding remains disproportionately allotted, with 73 percent of funds being channeled into enforcement and 20 percent into intervention, prevention, and harm reduction (DeBeck, Wood, Montaner, & Kerr, 2009). Due to high need, underfunding, and inaccessibility, private intervention centers or public-private partnerships have become an avenue for individuals to receive help (Mental Health Commission of Canada, 2012).

What compounds this problem further is that most individuals who are diagnosed with an addiction also meet the criteria for a concurrent mental health issue. Research shows that more than 50 percent of those seeking help for an addiction also have a mental illness (Canadian Centre on Substance Abuse, 2009). Many concurrent disorders reported are trauma-related, and between 25 and 90 percent of individuals in intervention for substance use report concurrent trauma (MacKenzie, 1990). Additionally, of those diagnosed with post traumatic stress disorder (PTSD), 25.5 percent reported a concurrent substance use disorder, compared to 7.2 percent of individuals without PTSD (Van Ameringen, Mancini, Patterson, & Boyle, 2008). Therefore, more addiction intervention centers are becoming "trauma informed" in order to ensure that programming meets the needs of this clinical population (Jean Tweed Centre, 2013). This can create an intervention context where individuals seeking addiction intervention can have their needs met in an environment that fosters a sense of safety. This translates into an intervention experience that can benefit a variety of groups of individuals, including those who present with concurrent disorders and those who do not.

Organizational and Community Context

Bellwood Health Services in Toronto serves individuals across Canada coping with addictions, eating disorders, trauma, and concurrent disorders. The residential program is fee for service, but has roughly 20 percent of beds allocated to a twenty-one-day Ministry of Health funded program for individuals addicted to alcohol. The agency also offers withdrawal management services, aftercare, family programming, and outpatient groups. Many of the consumers at Bellwood Health Services receive funding for intervention by their Employee Assistance Program, the Department of National Defense, Veterans Affairs Canada, their home province, or their workplace. There are multiple programming options for consumers, including: a core addiction program; a process addiction stream for consumers who are engaging in problem gambling or who have a sex addiction; an eating disorder stream; and a concurrent addiction and post traumatic stress disorder (PTSD) program for individuals who have sustained occupational trauma (for military personnel and first responders).

Group Purpose and Goals

Group therapy is considered an integral aspect of the Bellwood approach, and all consumers, regardless of stream, attend such sessions. The open-ended process groups provide members the opportunity to explore the origin and impact of their addictions and develop adaptive coping mechanisms for their stressors. In their first group therapy sessions, group members develop a narrative of their history, their addiction, the impact of their behaviors, and the origins of their addictions. Through the mutual aid of the group (Steinberg, 2014), members learn that they are not alone with their narratives when they are provided a safe and therapeutic environment in which to share experiences and feelings. Often consumers develop concrete action plans, practice problem solving, rehearse new behaviors, and develop a new vocabulary to talk about important issues. Members work through conflict that arises in the group in order to reach a resolution. This is often a new skill for members who have used their addictions to avoid healthy resolution of interpersonal conflicts. Developing a sense of safety in the group is fundamental, and meditation and grounding exercises are taught throughout sessions.

Group Membership

While individuals with process addictions, eating disorders, and PTSD receive group therapy sessions specific to their "special stream," all consumers receive group therapy three times per week in the core program. During these sessions, group composition is somewhat heterogeneous, as group membership consists of all consumers currently attending residential intervention at the agency. The agency attempts to keep group composition between eight and ten consumers, and the mix of age and gender must be appropriate within the group. A concerted effort is made to ensure that membership is conducive to establishing safety and meaningful group work. The prevalence of concurrent disorders and the need for integrated intervention are evident in the therapy groups, where many members describe how they are coping with concurrent depression, anxiety, trauma, suicidal ideation, early psychosis, traumatic brain injuries, and problems in cognitive functioning.

The consumer population served by the agency is made up mostly of men (86.2% for military members and 59.4% for civilian consumers) and is predominantly Caucasian. The average age of group members is forty-two for nonmilitary members and thirty-eight for military consumers. Group membership varies greatly in respect to education and socioeconomic status, with roughly one third of consumers having completed high school. Although secure housing is a condition of admission, there are consumers who have a history of homelessness. Furthermore, because the agency is a preferred provider of care to the Canadian Forces and Veterans Affairs Canada, about 30 percent of the group are active members of the Department of Defense or Veterans Affairs Canada. Thus, connections and cohesion must be created in groups with members who have a broad range of socioeconomic privilege, occupations, and trauma histories. Trauma-informed care is necessary in group therapy, as the narratives shared in group vary from early childhood trauma, such as abuse and neglect, to occupational trauma from military service engagements.

Group Structure

New members enter the group therapy program on the basis of "rolling recruitment." The procedure starts with new consumers entering the center and receiving one week of orientation programming. After this introductory work, they join the group therapy sessions that are already in process with several experienced members who have been in the program for several weeks. New members are brought into the group each Monday. After their course of intervention is complete, members graduate on Fridays when they are discharged from the facility. Consumers are expected to attend the two-hour groups three times a week for the full period of their stay at the center. Residential stays can vary from three to twelve weeks, with most consumers staying between twenty-one and forty-five days. Therapy sessions are open-ended process groups that continue throughout a consumer's time in residential intervention. The number of group therapy sessions a member attends therefore depends on program length. The minimum number of group therapy sessions a consumer would receive is nine (or three weeks' worth), and the maximum number is thirty-six (or twelve weeks' worth). Therefore, group membership is constantly in flux in terms of experience in the group and length of stay. Group members with more experience offer a seasoned voice for the more apprehensive newcomers.

Group therapy sessions generally begin with a mindfulness or grounding exercise so that members are encouraged to bring their full attention to the group process. This is followed by a check-in where members tell how they are feeling and report any important events or issues that have happened since the last group session. During the group, discussions arise from the members on any topics that they want to discuss. There is a break in the middle of the two-hour session, and the group ends with checkout, where members report how they are feeling, their experience of the group, and any inspirational moments or insights they gained. Groups are facilitated by one worker, to whom consumers are assigned and with whom they remain for the duration of their intervention. At any one time, five to six group therapy sessions are active within the intervention facility. Topics raised by members include interpersonal issues in the consumer community or in their lives outside of the agency, questions about learning points shared in psychoeducational sessions, or the sharing of taboo subjects such as trauma or shame. The role of the worker is to facilitate the group discussion by referring back to group norms or rules and redirecting the group discussion when needed. The group norms include strict confidentiality so that the members do not talk about the group events or other members outside of group meetings. Safety is paramount to the group process and is a topic often raised both by members and the facilitator. The worker encourages the use of the personal pronoun "I," and advice giving is discouraged. Mutual respect and appropriate language is expected, and acting out aggressively is strictly prohibited. Thus the worker creates a semi-structured and safe environment that facilitates the empowerment of group members to share narratives, feedback, insights, and questions.

The worker encourages members to share and use the group as a forum to voice their thoughts and feelings. When interpersonal conflict arises between members of the group, the worker identifies what is happening amongst the members. Members are asked to discuss the conflict and are supported to find a safe resolution. The group creates a stage upon which members recreate the conflicts in their lives. These conflicts are often a consequence of ongoing interpersonal styles, emotional histories, and patterns that members have outside of the program. By identifying the conflicts and helping members verbalize their experience of each other, the worker helps the group become a place to explore these patterns. Members learn ways to resolve conflict effectively and gain insight into how their behavior affects others in their lives. This process is powerful for many members, and they learn ways to confront conflict with effective strategies and not escape through addictive behaviors.

Group Activities

Although group format is generally dependent on the worker's preference and consumer need, general content of sessions is universal across group cultures and therapists. During the first group session of every week, the worker provides group members with an overview of the purpose of group therapy, group norms, and rules of confidentiality. Group members who are new to therapy during the first group of the week are asked to introduce themselves by telling their story, stating how they came to attend group, and describing aspects of their childhood and their addiction history. This allows members to establish their unique narrative, identify relational patterns from their youth, and name topics that may be important for them to work on while they are in group. Other group members offer feedback or ask questions concerning the new group members' sharing and provide examples as to how they may relate to the story.

Throughout the week, new group members have one individual session, a psychosocial assessment with the worker that is intended to identify goals and themes that they can bring to group. Throughout the week, members may bring issues or topics to group to discuss. Each group begins with a three-minute mindfulness exercise, which may be silent breathing, guided meditation or imagery, or a grounding exercise, intended to offer healthy detachment from anxiety or trauma symptoms (Najavits, 2002). These exercises may also be offered as needed throughout the group session.

Although most groups are a place for discussion, a number of activities may be offered within the group context. Activities may involve: role plays, with all members providing their input; self-care exercises in the form of art therapy; and creation of an addiction timeline to offer greater insight into members' past use. These exercises help members to share their insights and learn that there are aspects of each other's stories to which they relate. This is in contrast to their initial assumptions that they are all different or that no one understands them. Therefore, an important component of the work is creating cohesion, despite the members' perceptions of being alone and isolated in their experiences.

During the last group session of the week, graduating members are offered final feedback from the other group members, along with any observations about their personal growth or change. Members express their hopes or concerns for the future of the graduate and describe the impact that group member may have had on them. This offers graduating members an appreciation of the changes that they have made, a sense of closure, and a direction for future group or individual therapy sessions.

Use of Diversity over Time

The first group for consumers entering group therapy is often an intimidating experience, with many members reporting feeling apprehensive and anxious about sharing. During their first group, they are asked to share their story, important experiences from their childhood, and any relevant factors that contributed to their addiction. For many members, this is an anxiety-provoking process at first. However, members often report a sense of relief after having shared with the group. Furthermore, this process connects them to the group and facilitates group cohesion. However, not all members are able to share early in their intervention, especially those who do not feel safe.

Safety is emphasized as the first stage of healing in Judith Herman's stages of trauma intervention, in which trauma survivors develop the skills necessary to keep them safe from their trauma symptoms (Herman, 1997). The second stage in trauma intervention is remembrance and mourning, in which the trauma survivor creates a narrative of his or her trauma, processing the grief of their experiences, exploring the impact that trauma had on their lives, and sharing memories to lessen their emotional intensity. In the third stage of trauma intervention, reconnection, the survivor creates a future for himself or herself and works on interpersonal relationships, learning how they have been affected by their trauma, and how they can develop new relationships. This model is important for understanding why it is difficult for some members with a history of trauma to share in the group.

Many of the consumers entering group therapy have achieved a sense of safety because the agency offers a secure environment where they cannot engage in their addiction. All their basic needs are met and they are in an environment where people are motivated to work on their recovery. However, sharing a history of trauma is often intimidating early in intervention, because it evokes intense feelings without usual coping mechanisms (i.e., addictive substances or behaviors) (Najavits, 2004). Therefore, at the outset of a consumer's group therapy session they are given the *choice* to share rather than the instruction to do so. This facilitates their empowerment. Many members who have reported fears about sharing are encouraged by senior members who recall their own fears. They are able to identify how they have benefited from the process. This encourages a sense of mutual aid and allows new members to feel that they are in control of their stories, an important experience for individuals who have felt helpless because of their trauma and addiction.

However, issues of diversity arise when the narratives of new members are perceived as more "intense" or legitimate than those of other members. For example, if a member shares a history of interpersonal trauma and social exclusion, other members with a history of economic privilege and no identified trauma story may feel that their narrative is invalidated. Although the story elicits empathetic responses and supportive feedback to the member sharing it, it has the potential to shut down other members who perceive their story as less serious, important, or valid. The worker can identify the issue, and this opens up the possibility of deeper work. For example, the comparisons and judgments members make about themselves and others can result in isolation from the group and a rejection of the support that is available to them. When handled well by the facilitator and group members, this scenario may ultimately result in greater cohesion and deeper sharing, because members have had the opportunity to identify patterns and develop insight. However, the risk in this scenario is that if the issue is not identified it can result in feelings of shame and social isolation.

As intervention progresses, members may explore issues related to their trauma in greater detail. However, this can result in triggering other members of the group who are coping with similar traumas. The group leader needs to be vigilant to the reactions of the other group members, as details that are shared can be triggering. For instance, members of the military who served on deployment missions are asked not to provide details of their combat stories so that they do not trigger other members with similar traumas and symptoms of PTSD. This helps to maintain the safety of the group and to guide the group in identifying coping strategies. The use of grounding exercises that focus participants on the moment and physical sensations in the environment are very helpful. For example, the leader might direct members to feel their feet on the floor, look at the color of the walls, or experience the sensations of their breathing to help members self-regulate. Stories of interpersonal and early childhood trauma may be treated in the same way, with the facilitator focusing on the sharing member, while maintaining an awareness of how other group members are reacting. At times, it may be necessary for the facilitator to interrupt the sharing and ask the member to check in with himself or herself (i.e., "What is happening to your body as you tell your story?"). It is important to address the experience of the group as well ("Just checking in, how are people feeling as they hear this?"). This fosters safety in the group by demonstrating that the leader is aware of the group process and has the skill to help members manage their feelings of being triggered.

Differences in group members' capacity to process aspects of their history can affect their ability to do deeper work. Some members may struggle to develop insight because of differences in their ability to assess affect, their cognitive functioning, or the presence of a dual diagnosis or concurrent disorder. Such a member may be challenged by the group and encouraged to probe more deeply. The group may express frustration when the member is unable to do so. Group members may distance themselves and even resent the member's presence. However, if the leader is aware of this process, it can offer a valuable opportunity for group members to examine their own expectations and refocus their energy on their own recovery goals. For the member who is unable to respond to probing, this group exercise may provide them with validation of their level of ability to engage in the group and a redefinition of how they can use the group to reach their goals.

Minority group members who face social exclusion in society may offer the group an alternative perspective on certain issues. For example, voices that have been powerful in group therapy come from consumers who identify as members of the LGBTQ community, racialized groups, or women. By sharing a different perspective that challenges privilege and entitlement, these members provide teachable moments in which the group can learn about the impact of social exclusion. However, it is important in such instances that the facilitator be aware of any tokenism that may be occurring, as it is very important that the member does not feel pushed into being the sole representative of all members of their minority status.

At the end of their stay, members often report feeling more confident. They have processed a number of their goals in the group, and often report feeling ready to leave residential intervention. Individuals with PTSD may have experienced relief from many of their trauma symptoms, have a greater understanding of their addiction, and feel ready for the next stage of intervention. The voicing of these feelings is very beneficial to incoming consumers who are at a different stage in their intervention. It can provide them with hope that they will recover as well. Graduating consumers often recall their early experiences and feelings to the group and detail their improvement over time as they progressed in intervention. They offer hope, peer support, and mutual aid, and act as a role model to incoming group members.

Critical Incidents

Critical incidents in group can occur when members with acute PTSD or trauma symptoms are in a group with individuals who have moderate to no trauma issues. For instance, group members who are experiencing anxiety or dissociation symptoms report having difficulty feeling safe in group and sharing. Early in group they may be visibly shaking or dissociating. Military members with PTSD often request seats in which they can see the doors and windows, and report not wanting to be obstructed by columns or protrusions in the walls. As these members progress in their intervention, they may begin to report feeling safer in group and take risks in sharing their stories. However, these members often report feeling highly triggered and express anger and frustration as a way to deal with symptoms they perceive as unmanageable.

To protect the confidentiality of specific consumers, the following incidents are based on aggregated experiences of multiple therapists working at the addiction service. Joe, a former soldier with the Canadian military, was attending treatment for an addiction to alcohol and combat-related PTSD. Joe had difficulty feeling safe in group, and shared very little when he initially entered the group. He felt that group therapy was not going to be helpful to him. Joe stated that he did not feel that the group therapy model worked for him and that he could not relate to the other members because of his traumatic experiences. Initially, the group members validated Joe's anxiety but eventually they became frustrated when he continued to resist sharing. As Joe progressed in treatment, and learned grounding skills, he began to open up more in group. The other members encouraged him and continued to offer affirmations about his service and trauma. Joe reported feeling uncomfortable with this appraisal, given his mixed feelings towards his actions while on tour, but thanked the members for their encouragement. Joe continued to experience symptoms of dissociation, in which he would "tune out" of group therapy. The other members of the group reported feeling concerned for Joe's well-being, but stated that seeing the symptoms of PTSD provided them with a greater understanding and appreciation of its effects.

Often Joe reported feeling triggered by sounds, intrusive thoughts, or flashbacks he experienced during group. In these instances, the group members and facilitator would provide a safe space for Joe to discuss these symptoms and to ground from them. At times, Joe had combat-related flashbacks and acted out the experiences in a dissociated state. In order to maintain the safety of the group, the facilitator would send the other group members out of the room and ground Joe by verbally reinforcing his safety and whereabouts, asking him to provide the name of the agency, the date, and city. At times, a part of Joe heard this and responded, eventually returning from the flashback and requiring further grounding. At this point, the group members might be brought back to debrief and participate in the grounding together.

As new members entered the group with similar acute symptoms as Joe, the group would discuss the symptoms with familiarity and ask the new members what would be helpful to them in times of stress. At times, Joe expressed anger and volatility. The facilitator would provide him with opportunities to self-soothe, such as leaving the room or performing breathing exercises. When Joe reported that he felt ready to process these moments, the group provided feedback on the feelings his anger brought up for them and devised coping mechanisms for him during times of hyper-arousal. These exercises were helpful for members who experienced similar symptoms as well.

In groups in which this diversity is present, group facilitators often employ psychoeducation about PTSD and empathetic responses to the transference issues that may arise for members witnessing acute symptoms in other members. Towards the end of Joe's intervention, Joe reported feeling stronger and stated his PTSD symptoms were more manageable. Members were able to provide positive feedback about Joe's change and stated that his apparent well-being gave them hope for their recoveries as well.

Evaluation and Outcomes

In measures of consumer experience, group therapy is continuously rated as a highly satisfactory experience and is considered the most valuable aspect of treatment. Group therapist feedback is frequently positive, and graduating consumers frequently express their gratitude to the facilitator and members of the group. Members are asked to rate their group therapy experience on a five-point Likert scale ranging from one (poor) to five (excellent). In 2014, program evaluations consistently demonstrated that group therapy was rated as either four (very good) (30.4% of respondents) to five (excellent) (58.2%). Group therapy tends to be the highest rated part of intervention after medical care. For military members who complete the program, 97 percent state they will recommend the program, and 93 percent rate the intervention programs as very good or excellent. For consumers in the PTSD program, 98 percent rate the program as good and excellent, and 98 percent state they would recommend the intervention. Furthermore, at six-month follow up, 75 percent of former PTSD consumers reported being drug-free.

Implications for Practice

Given the importance of trauma-informed care in the addiction field, discussing the diversity issues that mixed membership groups have is important. The research literature has demonstrated that consumers in addiction settings with histories of trauma are more likely to drop out of intervention if the trauma is not concurrently addressed (Brown, Harris, & Fallot, 2013). Therefore, having trauma competency is important for group facilitators in order to foster a group environment that is perceived as safe and secure for the trauma survivor. Due to the complexity of many consumers' narratives, emphasizing their autonomy and going at their pace are important practices. Group acts as an instrumental means of healing from the shame and pain associated with trauma and a source of personal growth for consumers with acute symptoms. These healing narratives are inspiring to incoming members who are also survivors of trauma.

FURTHER READING

Brown, V. B., Harris, M., and Fallot, R. "Moving toward Trauma Informed Practice in Addiction Treatment: A Collaborative Model of Agency Assessment." *Journal of Psychoactive Drugs* 45, no. 5 (2013): 386–393.

DeBeck, K., Wood, E., Montaner, J., and Kerr, T. "Canada's New Federal 'National Anti-Drug Strategy': An Informal Audit of Reported Funding Allocation." *International Journal of Drug Policy* 20, no. 2 (2009): 188–191.

Health Canada. *Canadian Alcohol and Drug Use Monitoring Survey,* http://www.hc-sc.gc.ca/hc-ps/drugs-drogues/stat/_2012/summary-sommaire-eng.php#s7 (accessed April 2008).

Herman, J. *Trauma and Recovery: The Aftermath of Violence—from Domestic Abuse to Political Terror.* New York, NY: Basic Books, 1997.

Jean Tweed Centre. *Trauma Matters: Guidelines for Trauma-informed Practices in Women's Substance Use Services.* Toronto, ON: Jean Tweed Centre, 2013, http://www.google.ca/url?sa=t&rct=j&q=&esrc=s&source=web&cd=1& ved=0CCwQFjAA&url=http%3A%2F%2Fwww.jeantweed.com%2FLink Click.aspx%3Ffileticket%3D3-jaLM6hb8Y%253D%26tabid%3D107%26 mid%3D514&ei=mhguU5ylEPP7yAGE-YCADg&usg=AFQjCNFcszpR-SBBJi6H6PEwnaWBqY6HFg&sig2.

MacKenzie, K. R. *Introduction to Time-limited Group Psychotherapy.* Washington, DC: American Psychiatric Publishing, 1990.

Mental Health Commission of Canada. *Changing Directions, Changing Lives: The Mental Health Strategy for Canada.* Calgary, AB: Mental Health Commission of Canada, 2012, strategy.mentalhealthcommission.ca/pdf/strategy-text-en.pdf.

Najavits, L. M. *Seeking Safety: A Treatment Manual for PTSD and Substance Abuse.* New York, NY: Guilford Press, 2002.

Najavits, L. M. "Treatment of Posttraumatic Stress Disorder and Substance Abuse." *Alcoholism Treatment Quarterly* 22, no. 1 (2004): 43–62.

Pearson, C., Janz, T., and Ali, J. *Mental and Substance Use Disorders in Canada.* Ottawa, ON: Statistics Canada, 2013.

Steinberg, D. M. *A Mutual-aid Model for Social Work with Groups* (3rd ed.). New York, NY: Routledge, 2014.

Van Ameringen, M., Mancini, C., Patterson, B., and Boyle, M. H. "Post-traumatic Stress Disorder in Canada." *CNS Neuroscience and Therapeutics* 14, no. 3 (2008): 171–181.

CHAPTER 15

GROUPS ACROSS THE LIFESPAN

CHILDREN'S EXPERIENTIAL THERAPY GROUP IN AN ELEMENTARY SCHOOL
Julie Anne Laser-Maira

Needs of the Population Served by the Group

The group discussed in this section was formed to promote friendship and to help children gain a better understanding of themselves and each other. Each of the group members was referred to the school social worker due to their difficulty making friends or sustaining friendships. Many of the teachers who had referred the children to the group had witnessed them being relegated to outsiders or loners in the school hierarchy. They were the children who often ate alone at lunch, played alone at recess, or were often the last chosen for teamwork.

The children had parents who were involved and interested in their lives but were often required to be at work rather than facilitating play dates and after school activities for their children. Hence many of the group members were not given opportunities for play outside of school recess or gym class. Because the school day had lengthened, lunch recess time had shortened, and gym was only offered once a week, many of the group members were "starved" for playtime, especially active play. Play is a wonderful way for children from diverse backgrounds to learn about each other and to become more supportive and cohesive as a group.

Many of the group members had deficits in their communication skills, either because English was not their first language or they had not learned well how to get their needs met while also being aware, concerned, and accepting of other people's needs. All of the group members had at least average intelligence, were at their grade level academically, and had no physical limitations.

Organizational and Community Context

The school was located in a medium-sized city in the mountain region of the United States. The school was an elementary school serving grades kindergarten through fourth. The school had a large playground and a good-sized gymnasium. The students of the school generally came from middle class families who were stable financially but were not affluent.

The group goals were:

- to increase the self-esteem and self-concept of group members by providing opportunities for self-discovery and self-awareness
- to give group members opportunities to leave their comfort zone.

Group Membership

There were six group members. Friendship, not diversity, was the primary focus of the group, though they were a very diverse group. The names used are pseudonyms, so that their identities are protected. They were:

Luisa. She was a nine-year-old Latina who was being raised in a single parent family. Her mother was a teacher in a nearby school district. Luisa was very introverted. She was often hard to hear because she spoke quietly. She had a very hard time vocalizing her needs or wishes. Because she was so quiet, she was often overlooked by her classmates.

Octavio. He was a seven-year-old Latino. He was being raised in a single parent family. His mother was a nurse. Octavio had been diagnosed with ADHD. His mother did not want him to be put on medication and preferred to try behavioral interventions first. Due to his impulsivity, and his not always following the rules, many of the other children stayed away from him.

Chantal. She was an eight-year-old African refugee from the Ivory Coast. Her father and brother had died in the conflict. Chantal witnessed many atrocities during the conflict, followed by a period of near starvation until Chantal and her mother were able to get to a refugee camp. Chantal suffered from PTSD and grief and loss issues due to the loss of her father and brother. She and her mother had immigrated to the United States four years previously. Her mother had since remarried. Her new stepfather was kindly and accepting of Chantal. Chantal's first language was not English; thus she sometimes felt that she did not have the words to express herself, though her English was very good. Chantal shared that she felt that she looked physically different from the other children at her school and often felt that she did not fit in.

Shaunte. She was an eight-year-old African American girl. Shaunte came from a single parent family. Her mother was a policewoman. Shaunte presented as tough and streetwise. She enjoyed playing active games with boys and did not enjoy sedentary play. She tended to be very bossy with the other girls in her class and thus many stayed away from her.

Thomas. He was a seven-year-old Caucasian boy. He came from a two-parent professional family. Thomas was very verbal and always had an opinion. He tended to have a difficult time finding merit in other students' points of view. Due to the lack of validation he gave his classmates, they often excluded him from recess play.

Nico. He was a bicultural nine-year-old boy. Nico's mom's family had immigrated from India; she was the first generation born in the United States. Nico's dad was Caucasian. Nico came from a two-parent professional family. He was very bright and had mastered many levels of video games. In gym class, he was very uncoordinated and often refused to try new activities. Thus, out at recess, he did not freely enter into play with the other boys, nor did they seek him out to include him in play.

Group Structure

This was an ongoing group throughout one school year. There were no additions or changes to the six members of the group after it began. Most sessions lasted for one hour on Friday afternoons. The school social worker's role was to facilitate experiential activities and foster an atmosphere for debriefing the activities. The activities highlighted mutual respect and comfort, and modeled good listening and effective communication skills.

Group Activities

The group was created to support students from diverse backgrounds to come together, to learn from each other, and to become a source of support and friendship. The vehicle for moving students from individuals to supportive group members was experiential therapy. Experiential therapy focuses on experiences that push the students out of their comfort zone and into a place of self-discovery, confidence building, and self-awareness. The experience can be a game, an activity, a mental puzzle to work out as a group, time in nature, or a physical challenge. Experiential therapy puts students in novel situations; thus, to be successful, they need to be engaged and trust their team members. The results of experiential therapy are often team-building, team member appreciation, and awareness and valuing of others' skills and attributes.

Challenge by choice is the overarching philosophy of experiential therapy (Carlson & Evans, 2001; Nicotera & Laser-Maira, 2016). Challenge by choice has three core values. The first value is to allow participants to set their own goals for the activity (Carlson & Evans, 2001; Nicotera & Laser-Maira, 2016). Before the activity begins, each student is asked his or her own goal for the activity. Is their goal merely to watch the activity, enter in the activity, fully participate in the activity, or successfully complete the activity? There is never any coercion or demand to fully participate. The second value of challenge by choice is to determine the student's own ending point (Carlson & Evans, 2001; Nicotera & Laser-Maira, 2016). Allowing each participant to decide when he or she is finished with the activity maintains the sense that he/she has not given his/her power away or had it usurped. The third value of challenge by choice is for every participant to make informed choices (Carlson & Evans, 2001; Nicotera & Laser-Maira, 2016). How can the student set a goal for the activity and an endpoint if they do not understand the activity? So sharing the purpose and the objectives of the activity, as well as the directions of the activity, is critical. With fidelity to challenge by choice, experiential activities can be amazing growth opportunities for both individuals and groups.

How the Group Worked with Diversity over Time

To demonstrate the development of the group, three experiential activities are highlighted: one used at the inception of the group, one used mid group, and one used as a closing activity for the group. They are written in the experiential activity format, whereby the reader can use the activity in her/his own practice.

Inception of Group Experiential Activity: All My Neighbors

Purpose/objective: The purpose of the activity is to recognize individual strengths and capabilities and to support individual differences and commonalities in the group.

Equipment/materials needed: Enough paper plates for every participant, minus one.

Framing: What makes us unique? How are we similar to the rest of the group? Directions for activity:

1. Arrange plates in a circle, with one less plate than participants.
2. Explain that everyone will have a chance to be the leader. The leader will mention an experience and a way to cross the circle. For instance: "All of my neighbors who like to listen to music, move across the circle

like a sumo wrestler," or, "All of my neighbors who have visited Mexico, move across the circle in lunge steps," or, "All of my neighbors who have lived in more than four different homes in their lives move across the circle on tiptoes," or, "All of my neighbors who like to bake, cross the circle like a butterfly." Encourage creativity in finding both experiences and silly ways of crossing the circle.

3. Select the first leader and have her/him stand in the middle of the circle and introduce herself/himself. Have everyone say hello, using the leader's name. Then have the leader say, "All of my neighbors who . . . ." and mention an experience and a way of crossing the room. (The leader must have had this experience).

4. Everybody who has had this experience needs to cross the circle in the way they are instructed to move. They must find a circle that is not immediately next to them.

5. The leader quickly takes a circle along with everyone else who has had the experience.

6. The new leader is the one who is left standing without a circle and repeats the process, "All of my neighbors."

7. Play until everyone has had the opportunity to be the leader.

Debriefing questions: Did you learn new information about group members? Are you surprised you are with such an interesting and talented group? Did you realize you have more similarities to other group members than originally thought? When you were the leader, did you find yourself trying to find similar interests to other group members? Did it feel comfortable or uncomfortable to let the group know something about yourself when you were the leader?

This first activity helped the group gain some basic knowledge and comfort with each other. By walking in silly ways, it let the students' feelings of embarrassment subside into laughter. Luisa and Nico, the quietest members of the group, were as involved as the other members. Shaunte and Thomas had to take turns and allow others to speak. Octavio, because he was moving, was fully engaged in the activity, and Chantal could not stop smiling. This experiential activity was the initial icebreaker that set the tone and level of comfort among group members throughout the year. They all felt validated and valued as group members.

Mid Group Experiential Activity: A Tangled Web

Purpose/objective: This is an activity that helps members to further learn about each other.

Equipment/materials needed: Large ball of thin yarn.

Framing: By getting to know a little more about each other, we'll find we share many things in common and yet have a few things that set us apart.

Directions for activity:

1. Ask the group to sit/stand in a circle. Inform students that if they are uncomfortable answering a question, they can "pass" and give the ball of yarn back to the student who was previously holding it.
2. Ask a question such as: Where were you born? What's your favorite food? What's the last book/movie you read/saw? How long have you lived here? What's the hardest thing you've ever done? What's one thing you really like about yourself? If you could go anywhere in the world, where would you go? If you could be any kind of animal, what would it be and why? If you could be anything when you grow up, what would you be? What has been your happiest day? What has been your saddest day? When were you most proud of yourself?
3. The receiver of the ball of yarn then shares her/his information. While holding on to the yarn, they then roll or throw the ball to a different person and the process is repeated until everyone has had a chance to speak.
4. This can continue as many times as time allows. The web will get thicker and more complex the more times the ball of cord travels across the circle.
5. With everyone holding on to the cord, have them hold the web up overhead. The web should still be strong and complex. Have one person drop their cord. What happens to the web?

Debriefing questions: What did you learn about each other? What were some surprises you found out about others? What's it like to be part of a group where not everyone is the same? Did you feel sympathy/empathy (explain these terms) for other group members? Can you relate to other group members because of the activity? What happened when one student dropped their strand, and how does this relate to teamwork? We are all needed in the group to make it a success, aren't we?

As the group members became more familiar with each other, there was more sharing, more trust being built, and conflict. This activity helped Luisa find her voice because she had to speak loudly for those on the other side of the room to hear where she was throwing the yarn. It brought some conflict when Thomas did not agree with Octavio's answer and told him. But Octavio held firm to his response and thus others (Chantal, Shaunte, and Nico) also gave unique responses and were not persuaded by Thomas to conform to his answers. The facilitator supported Octavio, Chantal, and Nico to speak for themselves. This activity accelerated the movement to an "even playing field" in the group. The activity allowed the group to consider the importance of being both similar and unique and strengthened ties between members. They discussed how everyone had their own opinion and their own way of seeing the world. There was never one experience or understanding that was superior to the other experiences or understandings. There was never a right or wrong answer. All answers were correct. They discussed the concept of tolerance and how they needed to show tolerance of each other's ideas, experiences, and understandings, as long as they did not hurt other group members' feelings. Conversely, they learned that they needed to be intolerant if they heard a group member say or do something that was hurtful to another group member.

Thomas began to understand that the web was strong only when everyone held it; he could not be the only one to hold the web, just as he could not be in charge of what others said or thought. It was a turning point day for the group. The group became much more connected, more aware of each other, and more engaged with each other.

Closing Activity: Passing the Paper

Purpose/objective: To help encourage and bring positive energy into each group member's life.

Equipment/materials needed: Writing utensil and paper, one for each member of the group. The facilitator could precut the paper into shapes such as hearts or stars to add extra symbolic imagery.

Framing: What makes our group special? What have we learned from each other? What have we learned about each other? What do we value in each other?

Directions for activity:

1. Instruct each student to get a paper and a pencil/pen/marker. On the top of the paper, have them write their name.
2. Ask each student to pass their paper to the person sitting to their right. Then ask: What do you value about this person? What makes them a special group member? Each person will have two minutes to think of and write down an answer. After the time is up, pass the papers in the same direction until each member has had two minutes to write something on the paper. Each paper should eventually end up back in the original person's hands after completing a full circle around the group.

Debriefing Questions: What did it feel like to think of something positive for each group member? How did you react to reading something positive about yourself? How does it feel to know what others value in you?

This activity was done at the last session of the group. By this time, the group had really congealed and they were able to support each other and joke with each other. The papers were filled with kind words to each other that they could remember and hold close to their hearts.

Evaluation and Outcomes

At numerous times the following year, all the group members mentioned how they had loved the group and how looking at the paper that they made on the last day made them feel better when they had a bad day.

The boys frequently were seen playing together at recess and the girls had sleepovers at each other's homes on the weekends throughout the summer and the next school year. The group of outsiders and loners truly became a group of friends.

Implications for Practice

Children can be great sources of support for each other, if their best selves are encouraged to be shown. Experiential therapy provides an opportunity for group members to let their guard down, play, communicate, and grow. When children are engaged in experiential activities, they gain both a greater sense of self and knowledge of others.

FURTHER READING

Carlson, J., and Evans, K. "Whose Choice Is It? Contemplating Challenge by Choice." *Journal of Experiential Education* 24, no. 1 (2001): 58.

Nicotera, N., and Laser-Maira, J. *Innovative Skills to Support Well-being and Resiliency in Youth.* Chicago, IL: Lyceum, 2016.

A COMMUNITY-BASED COPE PARENTING GROUP WITH INDIGENOUS PARENTS
Lori Hill

This section outlines how the Community Parent Education (COPE) program was implemented within an indigenous population in the Six Nations community. Although the participants were diverse in many ways, effective strategies were used to work with their diversity and create an inclusive environment for group members to learn parenting strategies.

Colonialism: The Disruption of Parenting Practices for Indigenous People

Due to the insidious processes of assimilation and colonialism in the Canadian context, the indigenous population struggles with a multitude of socioeconomic issues that negatively affect almost every facet of their lives, including their parenting skills. Although there have been countless aggressive assimilative practices and policies waged against indigenous people in Canada, one of the most devastating ones was the residential school system (Royal Commission on Aboriginal Peoples, 1996; Sinclair, 2004; Blackstock, 2009; Baskin, 2011). Indigenous children were removed from their homes and communities and forced to reside within residential schools, where their language and culture were forcibly forbidden as a means of assimilating them into the dominant Euro-Western society. There have been disclosures from residential school survivors of sexual, emotional, and physical abuse (even some deaths) by church and state authorities who operated these schools (Fournier & Crey, 1997). Residential schools can particularly be linked to many of the struggles within indigenous communities, because, in addition to the widespread abuse of the children, the institutions led to the decline of parenting skills. Attendees were not exposed to role modeling of healthy and/or traditional parenting skills, but rather abusive and unhealthy behaviors (Fournier & Crey, 1997; Sinclair, 2004). The school survivors, therefore, brought their learned, dysfunctional parenting skills as well as their emotional distress and maladaptive coping patterns into their families and child rearing practices. Indigenous parents who never attended residential schools still suffer from the intergenerational effects and transmission of the historical trauma of past discriminatory policies. These effects are compounded by the ongoing oppression that indigenous people continue to endure in Euro-Western society (Wesley-Esquimaux & Smolewski, 2004; Muir & Bohr, 2014).

As a result of the devastating impacts of colonialism, indigenous people currently struggle with several socioeconomic issues and physical ailments, which are disproportionate to the rest of the Canadian population. Many indigenous families are led by significantly younger parents who were abused and maltreated in their childhoods (Trocme, Knoke, & Blackstock, 2004).

Organizational and Community Context

The main territory of the Six Nations reserve is located approximately twenty-five kilometers southwest of the city of Hamilton, Ontario. The Six Nations reserve has the largest population of all First Nations in Canada. According to the

Six Nations Lands Membership Department, as of December 2013, the total membership was 25,660, with 12,271 living within the Six Nations community (www.sixnation.ca/CommunityProfile.html).

The Grand River Child and Family Services (GRCFS) agency is located in the center of the Six Nations community. It offers an array of preventative and family preservation services, such as individual, couple, and family counseling as well as group counseling. The GRCFS also provides recreational and leisure programs, including seasonal special events. Its services are designated for children (0-18 years old) and their families who reside on the Six Nations reserve as well as registered Six Nation members residing off the reserve for less than one year (www.sixnations.ca/SocServDepart.html).

Purpose and Goals

COPE is a community-based parent training program. It is designed to assist parents to develop skills to strengthen their relationships with their children, increase cooperation, and solve problems. It was intended to be utilized in neighborhood schools and early childhood education settings as a means of increasing accessibility to services, reducing obstacles to attendance, and eliminating stigma that reduce parental participation in parent training (Cunningham, Bremner, & Secord-Gilbert, 1993).

Group Membership

The COPE group was held at the GRCFS. Although all of the participants were community members living on the Six Nations, there was, nevertheless, a great deal of diversity within the group.

There were fifteen participants, two of whom were men who came with their partners. Seven of the participants reported being single parents. The members ranged in age between nineteen and forty-five years old. There were five mothers under the age of twenty-one. Five group members revealed they were mandated to receive services. The participants also were diverse in terms of their mental health and psychosocial functioning. Several members identified that they were dealing with stress, depression, anxiety, and/or social isolation. Many of the participants also struggled with poverty and other socioeconomic issues. As will be highlighted, there was also diversity in the participants' acceptance or adherence to traditional indigenous parenting practices. Furthermore, there was diversity amongst the participants' children, who were all under twelve years of age. Their children's behaviors ranged from being typical of their age group to more disruptive, aggressive behaviors.

COPE Structure and Format

The COPE program is informed by principles, techniques, and goals from social learning-based programs, social cognitive psychology, family systems theory, small group interventions, and models for large groups (Cunningham, 2006). It is structured to be a closed group. This particular COPE group was composed of eight weekly sessions lasting two hours and was held in the evenings.

The sessions were structured in a manner that allowed participants to work in a large group and to break into smaller groups in order to problem solve around parenting issues (Cunningham et al., 1993; Thorell, 2009). The role of the COPE facilitator was to provide a neutral, facilitative approach to group discussions, encouraging the participants to explore potential advantages and disadvantages of alternative approaches to child management, in contrast to more didactic instructional strategies (Cunningham, 2006).

Program Activities

At the beginning, the group as a whole reviewed the preceding session's parenting strategies and then members divided into smaller subgroups (four to five participants) to discuss situations where they had successfully applied the preceding session's strategies at home. After the homework review, the group shifted into a problem-solving phase (Cunningham, 2006). In the initial part of the problem-solving phase, the COPE facilitator played a videotape depicting exaggerated errors in managing child behavior in potentially problematic situations (e.g., getting ready for bedtime). In subgroups, parents identified the mistakes that they observed on the tape and discussed potential consequences. Next, the subgroups discussed alternatives to the errors depicted in the tape. Each subgroup leader summarized his or her group's conclusions in the larger group. Following this review, the COPE facilitator summarized and integrated the feedback/suggestions of the respective subgroups and prompted a larger group discussion. This problem-solving aspect of the group created a space for diverse approaches to parenting. It also reflected a cultural way of learning for indigenous people in the sense that it followed a nondirective approach to solving problems, affording the individual autonomy and responsibility for their choices and decision making (Baskin, 2011).

Next, the group shifted to a modeling phase where the large group selected one problem and developed a detailed plan of managing it (e.g., getting ready for school) (Cunningham, 2006). The COPE facilitator summarized the plan proposed by the group, posed questions to refine the strategy, and then role played the solution with a member of the group playing the role of the child.

In closing, participants set goals to apply new strategies to specific situations at home and recorded them on a homework monitoring sheet. The COPE facilitator prompted members to contact participants who were absent that week as a means of enhancing participation, strengthening social networks, and relationship building.

How the Six Nations Group Worked with Diversity

In the planning stage of the group process, funds were allocated for a corresponding children's social skills group (ages three to twelve) and for childcare for children under the age of three years. Providing this childcare option was necessary for attending to the diverse needs of the participants; it was determined that parents who had young children might not have been able to attend the group if they lacked a social support system and/or financial resources to obtain childcare. As a means of addressing socioeconomic barriers, transportation was provided to those parents who required this service. The Six Nations reserve is a geographically vast rural territory where there is no public transportation available; several of the participants utilized this service.

Prior to each session, the diverse caregiving needs of the parents and their children were addressed as various resource materials were displayed (e.g., local individual and family counseling centers, learning supports for children, breastfeeding supports, drop-in centers, daycare centers, subsidized housing, food banks). Participants were also encouraged to share any formal and informal support information amongst themselves. This information sharing time allowed them to build and strengthen their relationships and networks with each other. Food was also a part of this informal relationship building and network period, as sharing food represents a cultural way of relating with one another for indigenous people. Agency funds were allocated for providing refreshments for each session. As a means of facilitating reciprocity, participants were also invited to bring or share any child-friendly recipes that were simple and cost-efficient to prepare.

At the beginning of the first session, the COPE facilitator, who is the author of this case study, identified the diversity that she brought to the group. Locating and identifying oneself in the helping relationship is particularly critical in indigenous communities as a means of establishing trust and credibility. She shared that, although she did not reside in the Six Nations community, she was a Mohawk member who grew up in the community and worked at the GRCFS. In addition, she informed the group that although she was not a parent, she had gathered a rich knowledge base about children, parenting skills, and human developmental and attachment theories through her extensive practice experience in working with children and ongoing professional training. She also noted that she was regularly involved with caring for her nephews. This self-disclosure assisted in building a rapport with the participants, as they stated that they appreciated the facilitator's transparency. This disclosure also effectively bridged the diversity that she brought to the group; the participants expressed that being a parent was different from working with children, but they felt that she could teach them useful parenting information. At this point, the facilitator highlighted that each of them brought diverse parenting experiences that could provide new perspectives.

Another important means of attending to issues of diversity at the beginning of the group was to establish group rules and processes. The group members collectively identified, negotiated, and agreed upon group rules that, despite members' diversity, would enable them to feel that they were respected and gain a level of comfort in sharing within the group. This aspect of trust building was particularly necessary for group members to feel safe enough to share their ideas about parenting and their experiences. Interestingly, the rules that the group members collectively constructed (confidentiality, respect, kindness, caring, sharing) reflected the communal values of the wider Six Nations community. These rules were posted in the group room at each session to remind the participants that, despite members' diversity, these values guided the process.

It became apparent that there was diversity with respect to the parents' emotional functioning and mental health. For instance, some parents shared that they felt stressed overall in their lives, as they were struggling with having limited financial resources, relationship problems, and/or balancing multiple roles, particularly the single mothers. At these points, the facilitator encouraged them to share ideas and solutions to their stressors. In addition, if they were not already in counseling, they were advised to seek such services outside of the group.

Throughout the group, participants naturally developed closer relationships and bonds to those participants with whom they shared some similarities. For instance, the younger participants tended to form a relatively close bond with one another while the two couples and some of the older members clustered in a subgroup. This dynamic allowed participants to effectively troubleshoot ideas with other members who had similar experiences and with whom they felt comfortable sharing. When the subgroups reported their ideas to the larger group, the COPE facilitator noted the different parenting solutions between the subgroups and facilitated a group discussion on how participants could potentially learn from others' experiences.

Issues of diversity emerged with regard to cultural parenting practices. This was not surprising given the vast diversity of acculturation amongst indigenous people due to assimilation practices and policies that have been imposed. For instance, in the subgroups, some of the participants suggested traditional parenting ideas that they had been taught, such as splashing a small amount of water on their children's faces in order to gain their attention. One of the participants discussed how using the traditional medicines (e.g., sage, sweet grass) in her home allowed her to stay emotionally grounded and assisted her in effectively applying some of the parenting techniques that she learned within the group. During these discussions, some parents expressed some intimidation and/or frustration with discussions about traditional parenting, as they stated that they were not "traditional" and did not employ these techniques. At this point, the facilitator reminded the participants about group rules, particularly having respect for each other's beliefs, leading to a discussion about the importance of utilizing their resources and strengths to assist in the challenging parenting role.

At other times, although participants did not specifically allude to traditional practices, they indirectly described aspects of cultural parenting, such as role modeling. For example, some of them discussed the importance of "walking the walk" and behaving in ways that modeled positive behaviors to their children. Some of them also reflected upon times when they noticed that their children calmed down when they regulated their own emotions (despite feeling overwhelmed or angry). The facilitator noted the similar ideas that the group seemed to share around role modeling and how it might be viewed as a cultural parenting technique.

At the end of the group, certificates of completion of the COPE group were awarded to each of the participants. These certificates were given to them not only to acknowledge the efforts that they put forth but also to provide documentation for the participants who were mandated to attend without singling them out.

Evaluation

Following the last group session, participants were requested to complete an evaluation of the group. A series of closed-ended questions were listed in the evaluation. The participants were asked to rate the effectiveness of the group on a scale of one to five. Overall, participants scored the group very highly. Parents reported significant improvement in the behaviors of their children in the home. Their scores also indicated that they felt much more confident in their parenting abilities. The effectiveness of this COPE group was consistent with prior studies that have evaluated this program (Cunningham, Bremner, & Boyle, 1995; Cunningham et al., 2000; Tamm et al., 2005; Thorell, 2009).

Of the fifteen participants in the COPE group, five of them missed as many as three sessions, and one stopped attending. Cunningham and others (2000) found that most families attributed nonparticipation in parenting groups to having busy personal schedules, inconvenient time of the group, and logistical difficulties.

Implications

There are some relevant practice implications that can be derived from this community-based parent training program. First, the problem-solving approach was effective in allowing a diverse group of participants to develop meaningful parenting strategies to meet their unique needs and situations.

Second, group facilitators must self-reflect and consider the diversity that *they* may bring to the group. When there is diversity between the facilitator and the group, an open discussion within the group can create an opportunity to foster relationship building and an articulation of the ways in which differences can enhance the group process and outcomes.

Third, the facilitator can potentially mediate and bridge the differences between group members by taking a neutral stance. In this parent group, there were instances in the group process when parents expressed diverse parenting views. At these points, the facilitator highlighted how members could learn from the differing views and the diversity of members' experiences, encouraging participants to express their ideas. The group was diverse in many ways, including their cultural values and practices. However, the facilitator stressed the importance of participants using their individual resources in problem solving (including their culture); the facilitator also noted the similarities between the group members' values, assisting them to work well together despite their cultural differences.

Diverse membership in a group can be used as an opportunity to facilitate a rich environment for participants to learn from each other. The parent training group with indigenous parents described in this case study demonstrates how the diversity within the group was effectively used to teach participants useful strategies to parent.

FURTHER READING

Baskin, C. *Strong Helpers' Teachings: The Value of Indigenous Knowledges in the Helping Professions*. Toronto, ON: Canadian Scholars Press, 2011.

Blackstock, C. "The Occasional Evil of Angels: Learning from the Experiences of Aboriginal People and Social Work." *First Nations Child and Family Review* 4, no. 1 (2009): 28–37.

Cunningham, C. E. "COPE Large Group Community Based, Family-centered Training Program." In *Attention Deficit Hyperactivity: A Handbook of Diagnosis and Treatment*, edited by R. A. Barkley, 480–497. New York, NY: Guilford Press, 2006.

Cunningham, C. E., and others. "Tri-ministry Study: Correlates of School-based Parenting Course Utilization." *Journal of Consulting and Clinical Psychology* 68 (2000): 928–933.

Cunningham, C. E., Bremner, R., and Boyle, M. "Large Group Community-based Programs for Families of Preschoolers at Risk for Disruptive Behaviour Disorders: Utilization, Cost effectiveness, and Outcomes." *Journal of Child Psychology and* Psychiatry 36 (1995): 1141–1159.

Cunningham, C. E., Bremner, R., and Secord, Gilbert, M. "Increasing the Availability, Accessibility, and Cost Efficacy of Services for Families of ADHD Children: A School-based Systems-oriented Parenting Course." *Canadian Journal of School Psychology* 9 (1993): 1–15.

Fournier, S., and Crey, E. *Stolen from Our Embrace: The Abduction of First Nations Children and the Restoration of Aboriginal Communities.* Vancouver, BC: Douglas and McIntyre, 1997.

Muir, N., and Bohr, Y. "Contemporary Practice of Traditional Aboriginal Child Rearing: A Review." *First Peoples Child and Family Review* 9 (2014): 66–79.

Royal Commission on Aboriginal Peoples. *Report of the Royal Commission on Aboriginal Peoples.* Ottawa, ON: Queens Printer, 1996.

Sinclair, R. "Aboriginal Social Work Education in Canada: Decolonizing Pedagogy for the Seventh Generation." *First Nations and Family Review* 1, no. 1 (2004): 49–61.

Tamm, L., and others. "Intervention for Preschoolers at Risk for Attention Deficit/Hyperactivity Disorder (ADHD): Services before Diagnosis." *Clinical Neuroscience Research* 5 (2005): 247–253.

Thorell, L. B. "The Community Parent Education Program (COPE): Treatment Effects in a Clinical and Community-based Sample." *Clinical Child Psychology and Psychiatry* 14, no. 3 (2009): 373–387.

Trocme, N., Knoke, D., and Blackstock, C. "Pathways to the Overrepresentation of Aboriginal Children in Canada's Child Welfare System." *Social Services Review* 78 (2004): 577–600.

Wesley-Esquimaux, C. C., and Smolewski, M. *Historical Trauma and Aboriginal Healing.* Prepared for the Aboriginal Healing Foundation (2004), http://www.ahf.ca/publications/research series.

EXPLORING HIP HOP GROUP THERAPY WITH HIGH-RISK YOUTH: THE STEP UP PROGRAM
Anthony T. Estreet and Paul Archibald

Needs of the Population Served by the Group

Hip hop music and culture have become major influences of youth culture, especially in many urban environments (Tyson, 2003). Once limited to urban music and dance, hip hop has become a widespread form of communication exhibited and enjoyed by young people throughout the world. Given this fact, it seems appropriate that such an influential characteristic be incorporated into various clinical interventions that are targeted at youth. Given that the hip hop culture is a way of life and is intricately woven into every aspect of young people's daily lives, its use in social work settings for individual and group work among voluntary and involuntary populations has been shown to be effective among the population (Tyson, 2003; Abdul-Adil, 2006; Alvarez, 2011). Hip hop therapy is not a new approach to working with youth; however, it is underutilized to a very large degree (Elligan, 2004). The STEP UP program is a hip hop intervention that was designed and implemented with high-risk youth populations.

Typically, high-risk youth are involuntarily referred to therapy by their parents or through mandates issued by the juvenile justice or educational system (Garland, Lau, Yeh, McCabe, Hough, & Landsverk, 2005). Research has indicated that high-risk youth have significantly lower levels of therapeutic engagement, which results in ongoing and increased symptoms (Pittman, Irby, Tolman, Yohalem, & Ferber, 2011). This lack of engagement among the high-risk population can be attributed to several factors; most notable is the lack of trust between the client and therapist due to the belief that the therapist is in alliance with other adults (parents, courts, probation officers, other practitioners). Another factor to consider is the inability of the youth to recognize their need for participation in ongoing therapy to address issues they may not see as problematic (Mishne, 1997). Last, high-risk youth may perceive a disconnect from the therapist given the vastly different lifestyles and cultures that may exist between them.

High-risk youth living in an urban environment can benefit from culturally sensitive approaches that address the immense needs that often arise from navigating these environments (violence, trauma, substance use, family conflict, grief and loss, education, poverty, etc.). Youth popular culture, more specifically hip hop culture, seems to form the schemas that organize how many youths think, feel, relate, act, understand, and interpret the world around them. An individual's culture is often shaped by their background, experiences, and environment (Elligan,

2004). Because this process is occurring most times outside of their conscious awareness, strong beliefs and assumptions are developed that can become maladaptive without appropriate exploration and processing. When these youths do not have access to appropriate exploration and processing, their perceptions and interpretations of situations become extremely egocentric, self-centered, selective, and rigid, causing an onslaught of multiple cognitive distortions. These cognitive distortions, or thought patterns, become habitual, are experienced as automatic, and are not easily identified by the youth.

With this in mind, it has been shown that it is the interpretation one places on events rather than the events themselves that determine one's emotions. Individuals tend to construct their irrational thoughts in a manner that reinforces and solidifies their negative emotions and maladaptive behaviors. However, they are also capable of reconstructing their irrational thoughts and viewing situations differently, which then leads to more positive feelings and more adaptive behaviors. Hence, this innovative and culturally responsive psychotherapy group integrated the very same youth popular culture to reform the youths' schemas. This was accomplished by incorporating familiar hip hop music, themes, and values during the group intervention to assist youth with uncovering and reexamining their negative beliefs and replacing them with more adaptive ways of viewing life events. Youth utilized the music along with the lyrics to learn self-help techniques that were effective in producing rapid symptom shifts while improving their concept of self and the world around them.

Organizational and Community Context

The STEP UP program has been ongoing within the context of a community agency situated in the Sandtown/Winchester Community located in West Baltimore. Youth residing in this community face a variety of factors that make them at higher risk for developing mental health and substance use disorders. According to a 2011 Baltimore City Health Department report, one of every four juveniles in this community was arrested between 2005 and 2009, and the neighborhood's juvenile arrest rate was 252 per 1,000 residents, nearly double the rest of the city. Moreover, nearly half of the neighborhood's high school students were listed as chronically absent in 2012. According to the Justice Policy Institute report, unemployment among those aged sixteen to sixty-four was at 52 percent in 2012 while the median household income in 2010 was $22,000. Approximately 30 percent of the families in this neighborhood were living below the federal poverty line. According to the health department, between 2005 and 2009, the neighborhood's homicide rate was more than double that of Baltimore overall;

although the crime rate had started to decline, the biggest problem remained narcotics offenses. Most of those arrested were black men.

The community agency provides ongoing services for behavioral health (mental health and substance use) disorders. Referrals are accepted from other community providers, family members, self-referral, and the criminal justice system. The agency provides services for clients of all ages and has specialized programming for youth ages ten to thirteen, fourteen to seventeen, and eighteen to twenty-four. The STEP UP program has been implemented in both residential and outpatient settings with high-risk youth who have significant Department of Juvenile Services (DJS) involvement. These youth have experienced a myriad of social issues such as mental health, substance use, academic difficulties, family conflict, criminal charges, poverty, and other related issues. Youth who have participated in this program have been diagnosed with internalizing disorders, externalizing disorders, or both.

Group Purpose and Goals

STEP UP is a hip hop psychotherapy group program based on the individual and community empowerment framework proposed by Professor Travis and Professor Bowman from Texas State University (2011). STEP UP utilizes a culturally responsive curriculum that allows facilitators to engage participants in a meaningful discussion about topics that otherwise would have been difficult to discuss. STEP UP is based on the following premises:

- During youth development, several aspects of thinking (such as all-or-nothing thinking or overgeneralization) influence the development and course of emotional and behavioral problems.

- The music associated with the hip hop culture actualizes the potential for cognitive change by facilitating progress towards emotional well-being and positive youth development.

- Millennial youth can be taught coping skills in a culturally responsive manner through the music and lyrics associated with the hip hop culture, which enables them to deal with their life problems.

The main objectives of the hip hop psychotherapy group are to: (1) teach participants how their thinking influences their behavior; (2) facilitate cognitive restructuring through the use of culturally relevant music; and (3) reduce the participants' tendencies to engage in self-serving cognitive distortions or thinking errors.

Group Membership

The STEP UP program can be utilized with a wide range of diverse ages and populations. Typically, group membership has been utilized with youth populations ranging from ages ten to twenty-one. The unique aspect about this intervention is that it can be integrated into a variety of therapeutic or educational settings as well as various age groups. The program is diverse in nature and can be utilized with most racial and ethnic groups. The one key feature of this intervention is that the binding concept is related to the hip hop culture. Individual participants and group facilitators need to be familiar with or have ongoing experiences with hip hop music and the various aspects of the culture.

In this case study, a significant portion of the high-risk youth participants (70%) were African American. This can be attributed to the organizational location within an urban environment and the high percent of African American youth that come into contact with the Department of Juvenile Services. Moreover, the group membership consisted of participants who had some experience with trauma (complex grief and loss), and had been indicated as resistant to therapy based on therapists' reports and other collateral information. Two concurrent groups were composed, consisting of youth from the ten to thirteen and the fourteen to seventeen age groups. Members from both groups were diagnosed with internalizing and externalizing disorders with a large majority having depression and conduct disorder as their primary diagnosis. Additional diagnoses included substance use disorder (primarily cannabis use disorder) and anxiety disorder, which ranged from traumatic stress to post traumatic stress disorders (PTSD). The participants for these groups were referred from the agency as likely candidates for this intervention. More specifically, those individuals who were deemed as resistant to therapy and hard to engage were selected for this program.

Group Structure

The STEP UP program had a ten-week curriculum (continuous cycle) with two group sessions per week. Each group session lasted about one and a half hours, broken down in the following way: fifteen to twenty minutes for check-in, forty minutes for a discussion regarding the "song or theme of the day," fifteen minutes for journaling time, and fifteen minutes for wrap-up and discussion. The group structure was flexible in that participants could contribute or select the song or theme of the day. This was typically an open group, given the structure of the organization, and allowed for new participants who showed an interest to self-select into the group. This structure was selected based on the understanding that youth will attract other youth to the program (the program promotes itself from participants).

Within the group structure, the role of the social worker was to assist with facilitation of the group. The worker was there to keep the discussion moving and flowing on the topic at hand, making specific connections to the selected hip hop song selected for the group. It is important to note that the social worker should have some ongoing and working knowledge of the hip hop culture and current trends among youth participants. Additionally, the social worker was responsible for bringing the necessary resources (a/v equipment, journals, pencils, and colored pencils) and three preapproved songs that were consistent with the theme or activity for the day. These songs were prescreened by the program leaders and additional staff through a structured process.

As previously mentioned, the STEP UP program can be used with diverse populations. In this case, group members were from various racial/ethnic backgrounds with the majority of participants being African American or black. A majority of the participants identified as male; however, females were encouraged and often participated in small numbers. This phenomenon of low female referral and participation is consistent with the history of the DJS youth in Baltimore City, which is made up primarily of male juveniles. Historically, across the state, approximately 27 percent of DJS intakes were females; of that number, only 40 percent were authorized for formal petition (process for juvenile court hearing). Of those juveniles, approximately 22 percent were placed on probation with 4.8 percent being committed to DJS (Department of Juvenile Services, 2015). Overall, the group make-up was fairly diverse given the overall composition of clients seen within the community-based agency.

Group Activities

There are many elements to hip hop group therapy that have a lasting impact on youth participants. Within the STEP UP program, there are specific components that highlight and help the youth to process their ongoing issues in an empowering way. The use of hip hop as a form of music therapy is significant to the intervention. Music therapy has been demonstrated to be effective among a number of populations, including youth. According to Tyson (2003), music can be used to create opportunities for nonthreatening therapeutic engagement and as a means for group members to relate to one another despite ongoing differences. The use of hip hop as a culture provides many angles for greater creative expression. For

Table 15.1 Sample of Hip Hop Song List and Themes

Artist	Song	Relevant Themes or Issues
Akon	"Locked Up"	Incarceration, changing life around, being away from family
Bone Thugs n Harmony	"Crossroads"	Grief and loss, spirituality
Common featuring Kayne West and The Last Poets	"The Corner"	Reflections of an urban environment
Eminem	"I'm Not Afraid"	Overcoming addiction, facing adversity, believing in oneself, recovery network, changing life around
Ghostface Killah	"All That I Got Is You"	Product of environment, struggling and coping with poverty, strength of a single mother, family cohesion
J. Cole	"Lost Ones"	Teenage pregnancy (female perspective)
NAS	"I Can"	Positive self-image, overcoming adversity
Nas featuring Lauren Hill	"If I Ruled the World"	Self-esteem, hope, thinking about one's (alternate) life
OutKast featuring Goodie Mob	"Git Up, Get Out"	Self-sufficiency, changing life, decision making, personal responsibility
P. Diddy	"I'll Be Missing You"	Grief and loss, remembrance
Slick Rick	"Children's Story"	Decision making, trying to fit in with peers
T.I. featuring Rihanna	"Life Your Life"	Understanding life, decision making, facing adversity, getting life back on track
T.I. featuring Chris Brown	"Get Back Up"	Staying focused, setting goals, overcoming adversity, redemption
T.I. and Justin Timberlake	"Dead and Gone"	Decision making, changing life around, grief and loss, reflecting on street life
Talib Kweli	"Get By"	Overcoming addiction, street life, personal responsibility, community responsibility, facing problems
Tupac	"Dear Mama"	Strength of a single mother, decision making, struggles and coping with poverty, family conflict
Tupac	"Keep Ya Head Up"	Facing adversity, decision making, personal responsibility
Tupac	"I Ain't Mad at Cha"	Forgiveness, understanding, changing life around, acceptance
Young Jeezy	"My President Is Black"	Hope, pride for African Americans, social awareness

example, the STEP UP program encouraged youth to rap, write and read poetry, engage in controlled graffiti (art), dance (breaking, also known as B-boy or B-girl), and journal. There were many instances where youth used hip hop to express their frustration with gangs, death and violence, poverty, drug use in the community, and, more recently, police brutality.

The STEP UP group allowed for journaling and creative expression among group members through narrative therapy to express and share their own thoughts, reactions, and self-identified connections to the hip hop theme/song of the day. This powerful approach allowed for participants to tell their own story and express emotions which may have been too difficult to do in traditional therapeutic approaches. For example, one aspect of the STEP UP group process allowed for participants to create their own lyrics (poetry or rap) or creative expressions (graffiti art) which were maintained in the participants' journals. The aspect of journaling or creative expression allowed for those who were not able to express themselves in the traditional manner to be active participants. As part of the journaling process, the social worker was encouraged to read and provide feedback (nonjudgmental and thoughtful) in the journal, which could further the youth's thought process. Although the journaling aspect was kept private between the therapist and client, participants were encouraged to discuss and share their work with the group. One of the key elements of this group that helped to create ongoing cohesion is the fact that most of the youth had similar experiences and could relate to each other's creative works.

How the Group Worked with Diversity over Time

Participants in the STEP UP program worked through diversity issues fairly well. The majority of the diversity came in the pregroup period, where group members did not know each other and did not necessarily come from the same neighborhood. This neighborhood representation was an ongoing factor during the pregroup period (East vs. West Baltimore, Baltimore City vs. County residents). These community differences and the fact that most youth did not know everyone in the group created some mild to moderate tension, which was demonstrated by some group members' reluctance to participate. It was important in the beginning of the group process to discuss in detail the purpose of the group and the need for ongoing participation. The assessment phase, which was still considered pregroup, consisted of the social worker and group members discussing why they were interested and selected to come to the program and what hip hop represented to them.

During the beginning sessions, playing brief samples of hip hop for the group helped to ease the tension, as a large majority of the participants were able to relate to the songs and overall culture. Additionally, the use of an icebreaker such as "Name that song" or "Whose line is it?" works very well to ease that initial tension with group participation. "Name that song" consists of playing a quick five-second clip of a song and having the participants guess the artist and the name of the song. "Whose line is it?" consists of playing a brief clip of the song and having participants say the next line of the song. Both of these icebreakers can be done with individuals or with small teams (important for building cohesion). Also important is the process of incentivizing participation, which helps to build buy-in and make the group fun and exciting. The use of icebreaking activities was a great way to assist with the diversity issues that often arose.

One such diversity issue that often arose within the STEP UP program was the issue of race. As previously noted, only 30 percent of participants were not African American. Within the beginning stages, some of the African American participants would question the hip hop knowledge of the white participants, making comments such as, "Don't you listen to rock 'n' roll or country music?" This ongoing stereotype threat was pervasive within the hip hop culture in that a musician who was not black would have to prove herself/himself to the larger culture. Within the STEP UP group, the icebreaker provided all participants an opportunity to even the playing field. After the white group members were able to name songs and participate in the icebreaker, the issue of race disappeared, as the focus was now on hip hop and the white members were essentially accepted among the African American participants.

As part of the beginning stages of the group process with the STEP UP program, the group facilitator guided the group members towards the development of group rules and guidelines. This process was important to create buy-in and to ensure that everyone was aware of the group rules and structure. This was also where the group facilitator inserted rules with regards to profanity, behavior, and participation, as well as addressed the importance of respecting diversity among group members. For example, only one person was allowed to speak at a time (this was reinforced with the use of a microphone; the person with the microphone had the floor). Having these established rules helped to keep the disagreements low and assisted with resolving disagreements when they arose. The STEP UP program also used motivational incentives to assist with behavior management (Dawes & Larson, 2011). Each session, group members started with five mics (a term used to rate hip hop music, with five mics being the highest) and for each rule violation, participants lost a mic. At the end of the week, those individuals with remaining mics were able to draw from a fishbowl full of prizes that ranged from a "Great Job!" certificate to a five-dollar gift card to McDonalds. The use of motivational incentives enhanced group participation as well as encouragement of other group members to participate. Group participants were able to earn back a mic by engaging in positive group behaviors and helping out peers.

As the STEP UP group progressed through the established ten-week curriculum, many topics and issues were discussed as they related to various aspects within the hip hop culture. Often these topics were discussed within the complexity of participants' diverse perspectives. For example, the topic of interacting with the police and police brutality arose. Some of the African American group members were frustrated with what was going on in the community (the recent police killing of Mr. Freddie Gray) and how they were not able to feel safe even from those sworn to protect and serve. One of the white participants was able to express his concern for what the other members were going through; however, this created some misunderstanding, as an African American participant said, "You couldn't possibly understand what we go through with all the harassment and bullying from the police." The white group member attempted to express his understanding with words, but was better able to express it through graffiti, in which he depicted his hope for black and white unity.

When provided with an opportunity to share his graffiti and explain the meaning, the white group member was able to convey and describe the emotions that some of the African American group members were feeling. That moment led to an ongoing dialogue about discrimination and a better understanding of relevant social issues from diverse perspectives. Although diversity issues arose during the group process, the ability of the group members to relate to one another around the hip hop culture allowed them to see past their differences and look towards their love of hip hop as a point of connection and therapeutic healing.

The end of the group was a highlight of the group for many of the members. Participants were provided with the opportunity to discuss how the group benefited them in addressing their issues. This included members addressing how they were better able to cope with issues and differences that arose within their environment. More to the point, every quarter, the group facilitator sets up an open mic night for friends and family of past and present group members to display a hip hop creative expression of their choosing. This open mic night provides many benefits that extend beyond the immediate group structure. It (1) showcases the talent of high-risk urban youth, (2) provides for a final culminating event for youth (completion ceremony), (3) provides hope to parents/guardians of youth, and (4) presents a positive event within the community. Additionally, this creates a quasi-support group where individuals can express themselves in an ongoing manner through hip hop. It provides a positive outlet in an environment that has many negative opportunities for the group members.

Evaluation and Outcomes

One of the main outcomes of the STEP UP program was to facilitate attitudinal and behavioral change around cognitive distortions. Some of the key evaluation indicators include:

a. Knowledge acquisition. That is, did the participants learn the ten common cognitive distortions (Burns, 1980) and were they able to demonstrate an understanding by completing five belief driven formulations (Beck, 2011)? (The ten common cognitive distortions are available at http://www.apsu.edu/sites/apsu.edu/files/counseling/COGNITIVE_0.pdf. The belief driven formulation worksheet is available at http://media.psychology.tools/worksheets/english_us/belief_driven_formulation_en-us.pdp.)

b. Skill acquisition. That is, did the participants utilize at least three out of the ten ways "to untwist your thinking" in response to situations reflected by self-report?

c. Negative automatic thought control enhancement. That is, did the participants demonstrate fewer cognitive distortions or thinking errors that lead to acting-out behaviors than they did when they began the program?

One of the evaluation tools that was used to measure changes in cognitive distortions includes the "How I Think (HIT)" questionnaire (available at: https://www.researchpress.com/books/937/hit-how-i-think-questionnaire). This tool measures four categories of self-serving cognitive distortions (thinking errors): (1) self-centered, (2) blaming others, (3) minimizing/mislabeling, and (4) assuming the worst. The HIT questionnaire is a fifty-four-item measure that can be administered in groups or with individuals. It is typically completed in five to fifteen minutes and requires only a fourth-grade reading level. The eight-page questionnaire, which includes scoring and computation instructions and forms, is useful in assessment, treatment planning, tracking therapeutic progress, and individual- or program-level outcome evaluation. A secondary objective of the program was to increase retention and engagement within the therapeutic process among high-risk youth. Retention and engagement were measured through the number of sessions attended and the number of successful completions of the ten-week curriculum. The ongoing evaluations of the STEP UP program indicate that participants showed statistically significant decreases in cognitive distortions when compared to baseline. Moreover, retention and engagement among this high-risk population increased significantly, with most youth attending at least one group per week and a completion rate of 76 percent.

Implications for Practice and Policy

The ongoing need for the continued development of culturally sensitive interventions continues to be largely unmet within the urban community. The STEP UP program is a solution to the ongoing need. In regard to practice, this intervention has demonstrated that it has the potential to engage and retain a population of high-risk youth that would otherwise not be participating in therapy. Moreover, it provides practitioners with an opportunity to better understand their clients in a way that traditional therapy may not have provided. The rawness of the hip hop provides for client expression and increases the chances of developing and maintaining the therapeutic alliance among hard-to-reach youth. As a prevailing culture within the urban population, hip hop music and culture should continue to be explored as a viable tool for which to develop interventions. According to Tyson (2003), practitioners who choose not to understand the relevance of hip hop among youth and incorporate it into treatment could be missing out on an opportunity to affect youth in a much more meaningful way.

FURTHER READING

Abdul-Adil, J. K. "Rap Music and Urban Rhapsody: Violence Prevention for Inner-city African American Male Adolescents." *Journal of Urban Youth Culture* 4, no. 1 (2006).

Alvarez III, T. T. "Beats, Rhymes, and Life: Rap Therapy in an Urban Setting." In *Therapeutic Uses of Rap and Hip-hop*, edited by S. Hadley and G. Yancy, 117–128. New York, NY: Routledge, 2011.

Beck, J. S. *Cognitive Behavior Therapy: Basics and Beyond*. New York, NY: Guilford Press, 2011.

Burns, D. D. *Feeling Good: The New Mood Therapy*. New York, NY: New American Library, 1980.

Elligan, D. *Rap Therapy: A Practical Guide for Communicating with Youth and Young Adults through Rap Music*. New York, NY: Kensington, 2004.

Dawes, N. P., and Larson, R. "How Youth Get Engaged: Grounded-theory Research on Motivational Development in Organized Youth Programs." *Developmental Psychology* 47. no. 1 (2011): 259.

Garland, A. F., Lau, A. S., Yeh, M., McCabe, K. M., Hough, R. L., and Landsverk, J. A. "Racial and Ethnic Differences in Utilization of Mental Health Services among High-risk Youths." *American Journal of Psychiatry* 167, no. 7 (2005): 1336–1343, doi: 10.1176/appi.ajp.162.7.133.

Mishne, J. "Clinical Social Work with Adolescents." In *Theory and Practice in Clinical Social Work*, edited by J. R. Brandell, 101–131. New York, NY: The Free Press, 1997.

Pittman, K. J., Irby, M., Tolman, J., Yohalem, N., and Ferber, T. "Preventing Problems, Promoting Development, Encouraging Engagement: Competing Priorities or Inseparable Goals?" *Council of Juvenile Correctional Administrators*. Washington, DC: Forum for Youth Investment, 2011.

Travis, R., and Bowman, S. W. "Negotiating Risk and Promoting Empowerment through Rap Music: Development of a Measure to Capture Risk and Empowerment Pathways to Change." *Journal of Human Behavior in the Social Environment* 21, no. 6 (2011): 654–678.

Tyson, E. H. "Rap Music in Social Work Practice with African American and Latino Youth: A Conceptual Model with Practical Applications." *Journal of Human Behavior in the Social Environment* 11, no. 3/4 (2003): 59–82.

A COGNITIVE BEHAVIORAL INTERVENTION FOR TRAUMA IN SCHOOLS (CBITS) WITH DIVERSE MINORITY AND IMMIGRANT SCHOOL CHILDREN
Abdelfettah Elkchirid

Needs of Diverse Minority and Immigrant School Children

It is estimated that 20 to 50 percent of American children have experienced trauma from their home/familial environment, their schools, and/or their communities (Finkelhor, Turner, Shattuck, & Hamby, 2013). These traumatic experiences include sexual abuse, physical abuse, and exposure to community and domestic violence (Kataoka et al., 2003; Briggs-Gowan, Carter, Clark, Augustyn, McCarthy, & Ford, 2010; National Child Traumatic Stress Network, 2015). Recent California studies have found that among eight- to eleven-year-old elementary school students, 40 percent have had a life threatening experience; in addition, 68 percent of adolescents have had at least one traumatic experience (Langley, Santiago, Rodríguez, & Zelaya, 2013).

Research also suggests that low-income minority students, as well as those from immigrant urban families, are often exposed to higher frequencies of traumatic events and secondary adversities (Osofsky, 2004; Jaycox et al., 2009; Langley et al., 2013). Immigrant families suffer exposure to violence in their country of origin, during their immigration to the United States, and/or after their arrival and settlement to a disadvantaged neighborhood (Hinson, 2015; RAND Corporation, 2015). These findings suggest an urgent need to provide mental health interventions for children in schools in order to address the impact of these traumatic experiences.

To address this phenomenon, group work following the Cognitive Behavioral Intervention for Trauma in Schools (CBITS) program was implemented for minority and immigrant students in two public schools in urban centers. The CBITS program "is a school based, group and individual intervention. It is designed to reduce symptoms of post traumatic stress disorder (PTSD), depression, and behavioral problems, and to improve functioning, grades and attendance, peer and parent support, and coping skills" (Cognitive Behavioral Intervention for Trauma in Schools, 2015, "CBITS at a Glance," para. 1).

The group work was able to answer these two practice and research questions:

1. Can clinical social workers be involved in CBITS intervention effectively to assist in student cognitive mental health?
2. Can early CBITS intervention improve student cognitive mental health and recovery from trauma and violence exposure?

This case study offers first hand, useful information to assist in future and wider range implementation of the CBITS in schools and neighborhoods.

Organizational and Community Context

The trauma counseling groups were conducted in two public schools in Jersey City, New Jersey. Jersey City is the second most populated city in New Jersey, with an estimated population of 262,146 in 2014 (U.S. Census Bureau, 2015). The public schools have students from diverse backgrounds, including minority and immigrant families with low-income backgrounds.

Group Purpose

CBITS interventions aimed to assist in improving the mental health of students who were exposed to traumatic and violent events. The CBITS interventions were designed to resolve students' psychosocial issues with diversity of their country and religious origins. Additionally, this new mental health service implementation in public school settings (U.S. Department of Education, 2008; Goodkind, Lanoue, & Milford, 2010) focused on the engagement of a clinical social worker throughout this intervention.

Group Membership

A total of five groups, each with ten to twelve participants, was selected. The student groups consisted of children from grades six and seven of a middle school, and youth participants from grade eleven of a high school. The students were identified as minority and immigrant students living in low-income families. The groups included student participants from African American, Latino American, and other minority populations with country origins of Egypt, Morocco, Columbia, and Honduras. Overall, student participants were ethnically and socio-economically representative of the diverse demographics of the school districts.

The selection method of student participants was based on teacher referrals, and potential participants were screened using the trauma exposure questionnaire and the Child PTSD Symptom Scale (CPSS). Students who were exposed to trauma or violence with post trauma and violence stress symptoms within one year and were willing to discuss their traumatic experience were selected to participate in the group intervention (Kataoka et al., 2011; Langley, Santiago, Rodríguez, & Zelaya, 2013). Eligible student participants were given consent forms with letters explaining the group's objectives to be given to their parents or legal guardians. Upon submitting the signed consent forms, students were assessed by the social worker to evaluate the students' eligibility to ensure that the qualities and standards of the groups met the design and requirements of CBITS.

Group Structure

The CBITS approach comprises four steps: pregroup preparation, screening, intervention, data collection and analysis. The steps are described as follows:

1. Pregroup Preparation
The social worker worked with the school principals and the teachers in the two schools to prepare and organize the groups' intervention design, session organization, and student selection.

2. Screening
Self-report screening through the trauma exposure questionnaire was conducted among low-income, minority, and immigrant students from grades six, seven, and eleven. The social worker further screened potential participants to determine their appropriateness to participate in this intervention.

3. Intervention
Five groups of ten to twelve students were formed. Students were randomly assigned to early intervention groups to participate in early CBITS intervention.

The CBITS group intervention was performed by the social worker, who had received CBITS training. The social worker utilized a treatment manual following the CBITS standard cognitive behavioral therapy skills, which have been conducted and proved successful in the treatment of diverse students in other public school districts (Ngo, Langley, Kataoka, Nadeem, Escudero, & Stein, 2008; Langley, Nadeem, Kataoka, Stein, & Jaycox, 2010; CBITS Program, 2015). The CBITS cognitive behavioral therapy is a group format (ten to twelve students per group) that addresses post traumatic anxiety, stress, and depression relevant to violence exposure over the course of ten group meetings. The CBITS therapy specifically targets diverse students with its core components of fidelity and flexibility of appropriate skills as well as examples and activities. The group therapy was scheduled by the school administrators in this study to arrange the intervention as one class period per week for the selected students. The intervention was scheduled during academic periods at different times per week to minimize the same academic class missing rates of the participant students.

4. Data Collection and Analysis
All student participants were evaluated by the clinical social worker for their mental health before and after the CBITS intervention upon completion of the intervention sessions. Evaluation and data collection methods included pre and post Child PTSD Symptom Scale (CPSS) (Foa, Johnson, Feeny, & Treadwell, 2001), as well as Child Depression Inventory (CDI) (Finch, Saylor, & Edwards, 1985).

Group Activities

The social worker worked closely with each of the school principals to organize, monitor and manage the groups. In group, the social worker implemented the following activities:

- Preparatory Activities: These included icebreaker games, trust-building games and activities, and team-building games and activities. As an example, one icebreaker game was "Same and different," in which students were asked to write "Same" and "Different" at the top of each paper page and then proceed to find qualities that were shared by the group as a whole. Students were given time to determine some aspects that were unique to only one member of their group. This was not only a great activity for getting to know each other, but also emphasized the shared commonalities and unique differences that made up an interesting and complete group work (Lewis, 2014).

- Psychoeducation and Relaxation Activities: Activities were chosen to educate students about common reactions to stress or trauma. These included deep breathing, stress identification, and muscle relaxation activities.

- Identifying and Combating Negative Thoughts Activities: These "fear thermometer" activities linked thoughts to feelings and actions. They helped students identify how much fear they had of a specific situation or thing. Students were asked to make a list of situations where they felt scared, and to make a fear thermometer to classify their lived situations from the least scary to the scariest. They would use the thermometer to rate their situations from zero (no fear) to ten (tons of fear).

- Trauma Exposure Activities: These games and activities helped students to express hidden trauma memory using songs, plays, drawings, or writing.

- Relapse Prevention Activities: These relapse prevention exercises helped students practice skills such as problem solving.

Group Work with Diversity

Diversity factors were considered throughout the stages of the group to encourage culturally appropriate and culturally sensitive activities and interventions. In the planning phase, the program was tailored to introduce important contextual issues specific to diverse populations. Attention was given to cultural concepts, treatment, and special language needs to increase participant engagement and clinical salience. The social worker ensured that participants were aware of the diversity purpose of the group work.

Before the CBITS group work started, meetings were scheduled between the social worker and the school principals to discuss the purpose, organization, work schedules, and relevant issues to ensure that the social worker and the schools fully understood and acknowledged the diversity group work and its implementation requirements. The social worker and the principals were in agreement on the effective completion of the group work, which was organized and processed based on the four phases as follows:

Pregroup Preparation, Phase I (one month)

The social worker worked with the principals to prepare and organize the intervention design, including session organization and student selection. Characters of different races and religious backgrounds from TV, music, graphic novels, sports, and history were used as teaching tools to help students solve problems. Other concepts, such as cultural issues, stress expression, help preferences, communication styles, family values, migration experience, and sociopolitical history, which have been confirmed important in previous research (Ngo et al., 2008), were integrated into the intervention with specific racial groups (examples are given at the end of this section). These concepts were addressed through the group interventions to be congruent with and respectful to specific racial groups. Because racial diversity sensitivity has been emphasized by CBITS in its training, consultation, and supervision, the clinical social worker had been trained about the key components in the application of cultural and contextual knowledge to effectively convey treatment concepts. This process was necessary for the social worker to be fully prepared for the roles, knowledge, and skills required for facilitating the diversity groups.

Screening, Phase II (three weeks)
In this phase, the prescreened student participants completed the self-report screening. In guiding this phase, the social worker followed exclusively the principles and guidelines learned in the CBITS training to ensure that all prescreened students were treated evenly, without bias. During this phase, students finished the questionnaires, writing down their past traumatic and violent experiences. The social worker examined all self-reports to collect data, established files and folders for data organization, and prepared student information for the next phase.

Intervention, Phase III (three months)
Thirty-two students formed three intervention groups of ten to twelve students per group from each public school. All CBITS intervention was conducted by the social worker following the CBITS intervention guideline and standards established in phase II.

To build relationships with every single student, the social worker attended to each unique cultural background in the group intervention. The discussion started with the introduction of diversity in its broader sense (i.e., we are dealing with difficulties in different ways) and included cultural sensitivity to respect family, cultural, and religious beliefs. In addition, individual needs related to endorsed symptoms and functional impairment were handled based on cultural and family context, as stated in the CBITS manual. Participants were asked to share the ways that they used to deal with similar situations, such as getting a lower mark or being late on a school project. Participants were reminded that there are no standard reactions, just individual approaches, and that everyone needs to respect other people's ways of reacting and expressing themselves.

To further explain the ways that the social worker encountered and addressed diversity over time, three examples are given to describe critical incidents when diversity events arose and how the social worker worked with them.

Example 1. Handling Diversity Group Conflict　In one of the first meetings of the CBITS groups while the group members (all African American participants) were introducing themselves, a fight broke out. When the social worker, as an Arab Muslim from North Africa, was trying to get things under control, a student said, "This is a black world and you don't know nothing about it." The group meeting was ended, as fighting was not allowed, per the school policy. Two days later, the group worker received a call from the school social worker stating that the students submitted a letter of apology. The following week, the social worker went to the group and started by exploring the student's comment. Participants were asked about the best way for the social worker to learn more about their world. One of the comments was that the social worker needed to be interested in knowing and not to be afraid of asking. The social worker took this as an opportunity to ask the participants the following question: "Well, I live in North Bergen (which is a middle class neighborhood), and I am wondering if I were a young person like you who lived in North Bergen, and who moved to 8th Street in Jersey City, how would my life be different?" Students then started talking about their neighborhoods in comparison to what they thought life was like in a middle class neighborhood. As a consequence, the social worker and the participants built a friendship, which was conducive to the successful completion of the group's work.

Example 2. Handling Misunderstanding Due to Cultural Differences　In one of the groups, which included both Latinas and Arabic participants, the male Arab participants often misinterpreted some of the Latina participants' actions. For example, smiling, getting closer, and innocent touching were considered by male Arabic participants as an expression of romantic advances. The male Arabic participants would react in response to the romantic assumption, which resulted in the Latina participants taking their distance. In order to explore this, the social worker used activities to help participants understand different cultural meanings of the same gestures. Examples included smiling, which could range from a smirk to a grin, and nodding one's head, which in some parts of the world means no but in other parts means yes. The group then discussed how one could misinterpret another person's gestures, and how these gestures would differ from one culture to another. This diversity discussion reduced misunderstanding among participants and helped the continuation of the group work.

Example 3. Handling Culture Specific Communication Styles   Communication style includes what was said, how it was said, and when it was said. Participants would misinterpret one another's statements, tones, and the timing of comments. In the beginning, participants were asked to clarify further what they wanted to say, their reasons for using a particular tone, and the reasons behind their timing. It was then explained to participants that in order for them to learn from each other, they should not make judgments too quickly, but rather ask one another about what they meant to say, or the reason that they said something in a certain way. This was challenging, as some participants considered questioning to be rude and therefore did not consider it appropriate to ask others what they meant. The difference between asking questions and questioning someone was explained. Although this strategy did not get participants to always ask for clarifications from one another, it did, to a considerable amount, lead to more positive communications between participants from different cultural groups.

Data Collection and Analysis, Phase IV (one month)

All student participants were evaluated by the clinical social worker regarding mental health before the group and one month after the CBITS intervention. The CBITS intervention results were collected as a way of assessing students' post-traumatic stress symptoms, which were measured using two different methods. (1) Method 1: The Child PTSD Symptom Scale (Foa, Johnson, Feeny, & Treadwell, 2001) is a child self-report measure, with seventeen items and ratings that range from zero to fifty-one. It has been confirmed to have high reliability, convergent and discriminant validity, and internal consistency. Student participants rated themselves about the frequencies of each symptom in different time periods such as per week or per month on a scale from zero to three. (2) Method 2: Student depression was measured by the Child Depression Inventory (Finch, Saylor, & Edwards, 1985), which is a measure with twenty-six items and ranges from zero to fifty-two, assessing students' cognitive and depressive behavioral symptoms. The measure's validity and reliability have been confirmed.

Study data results from the two measures of pre and post CPSS and CDI were collected and organized as baseline data before the intervention, and data after early intervention. The two data sets from two different time points were compared and analyzed based on student violence exposure, student and parent characteristics, and student mental health symptoms. These were standardized wherever possible.

In the study, data showed that participating students had a mean age of eleven; 54 percent of them were female; and 50 percent of them had family household incomes below $20,000. Overall, participants in this study had significant levels of violence exposure because 77 percent of them reported being direct witnesses or being victims to certain types of violence in the past year. Before intervention, the mean PTSD symptom score was twenty-three, and the mean CDI score was twenty-nine. After the CBITS group work with interventions, 75 percent of the participants reported positive outcomes on their CPSS scores, and 68 percent reported positive outcomes on their CDI scores.

Implications for Practice and Policy

Data results from the group work offer information on the effectiveness of this school-based group intervention in addressing the mental health impact from exposure to violence and trauma. These data support the continued application of this group intervention with diverse students from middle school and high school settings because 75 percent of participating students had improved CPSS scores, and 68 percent of them had improved CDI scores. In addition, the school-based intervention plays a critical role in improving diverse student mental health and assisting the district management to fill the public health gap of violence exposed students, particularly those minority and immigrant students from low-income families.

The most important impact from this group work is the proof that clinical social workers can effectively conduct CBITS interventions to assist in the improvement of students with diverse backgrounds, including different minority race groups and multiple religions, as well as cognitive mental health post violent and traumatic exposure. The CBITS intervention protocol and examples in this research can be adopted and applied to CBITS interventions in other middle and high school settings to support and improve mental conditions of trauma in diverse student populations. The group interventions have significant impact on district management of relevant strategy implementation to reduce the need of clinical therapists, reduce budgets in public school management, and, most important, assist in the mental health well-being of diverse students from minority and low-income families with various country origins and religions.

FURTHER READING

Briggs-Gowan, M. J., Carter, A. S., Clark, R., Augustyn, M., McCarthy, K. J., and Ford, J. D. "Exposure to Potentially Traumatic Events in Early Childhood: Differential Links to Emergent Psychopathology." *Journal of Child Psychology and Psychiatry* 51, no. 10 (2010): 1132–1140.

CBITS Program. *Success Stories*, 2015, http://cbitsprogram.org/succcess-stories.

Finkelhor, D., Turner, H. A., Shattuck, A, and Hamby, S. L. "Violence, Crime, and Abuse Exposure in a National Sample of Children and Youth: An Update." *JAMA Pediatrics* 167, no. 7 (2013): 614–621

Goodkind, J. R., Lanoue, M. D., and Milford, J. "Adaptation and Implementation of Cognitive Behavioral Intervention for Trauma in Schools with American Indian Youth." *Journal of Clinical Child and Adolescent Psychology* 39, no. 6 (2010): 858–872.

Hinson, J. *The Treatment of Trauma in Immigrant Youth: Final Paper, CBITS*, 2015, http://globalmigration.web.unc.edu/files/2013/09/Treatment-of-Trauma-in-Immigrant-Youth.pdf.

Jaycox, L. H., Langley, A. K., Stein, B. D., Wong, M., Sharma, P., Scott, M., and Schonlau, M. "Support for Students Exposed to Trauma: A Pilot Study." *School Mental Health* 1, no. 2 (2009): 49–60.

Kataoka, S., Jaycox, L. H., Wong, M., Nadeem, E., Langley, A., Tang, L., and Stein, B. D. "Effects on School Outcomes in Low-income Minority Youth: Preliminary Findings from a Community-partnered Study of a School-based Trauma Intervention." *Ethnicity and Disease* 21, no. 3, Suppl. 1 (2011): S1-71–S1-7.

Kataoka, S., Stein, B. D., Jaycox, L. H., Wong, M., Escudero, P., Tu, W., Zaragoza, C. and Fink, A. "A School-based Mental Health Program for Traum   Latino Immigrant Children." *Journal of American Child and Adol   o. 3 (2003): 311–318.

Langley   H., Stein, B. D., and Jaycox, L. H. "P   Programs in Schools: Barriers and   mentation." *School Mental Health* 2,

La   ríguez, A., and Zelaya, J. "Improving   lealth Services for Trauma in Multicultural   holder Perspectives on Parent and Educator Engageme   *Behavioral Health Services and Research* 40, no. 3 (2013): 247–

Lewis, B. *Same and Different Ice Breaker Game for Back to School*, 2014, http://k6educators.about.com/od/icebreakers/qt/ibsamedifft.htm.

National Child Traumatic Stress Network. *Psychological Impact of the Recent Shooting*, 2015, http://www.nctsn.org/sites/default/files/assets/pdfs/psychological_information_sheet_two_pager.pdf.

Ngo, V., Langley, A., Kataoka, S. H., Nadeem, E., Escudero, P., and Stein, B. D. "Providing Evidence Based Practice to Ethnically Diverse Youth: Examples from the Cognitive Behavioral Intervention for Trauma in Schools (CBITS) Program." *Journal of the American Academy of Child and Adolescent Psychiatry* 47, no. 8 (2008): 858–862.

Osofsky, J. D. "Community Outreach for Children Exposed to Violence." *Infant Mental Health Journal* 25, no. 5 (2004): 478–487.

RAND Corporation. *Helping Children Cope with Violence and Trauma: A School-based Program that Works*, 2015, http://www.rand.org/content/dam/rand/pubs/research_briefs/2011/RAND_RB4557-2.pdf.

ENGAGING ACROSS THE AGES: THE VALUE OF A COMMUNITY INTERGENERATIONAL DIALOGUE GROUP PROCESS

Paul Archibald, Anthony Estreet, and Kevin Daniels

Needs of the Population Served

Intergenerational relationships in the urban environment are essential to the transactions by which people of different generations interrelate with one another to disseminate their experiences (Waites, 2008). Bengtson (2001) identifies several factors that point to the importance of intergenerational relationships: (1) generations interacting for longer periods of time; (2) the increased role of grandparenting and intergenerational kin (uncles and aunts) in fulfilling family functions; and (3) the intergenerational solidarity that is expressed over time. Strauss and Howe (1991) describe the intergenerational process as generations possessing their own generational personality with which they enter each life stage. The authors challenge the notion that there is a universal life cycle, pointing to the shaping of generational peer personalities, which develop from the collective behaviors and events that were experienced during each generation's formative years.

Researchers and practitioners generally used the term "intergenerational" to refer to relationships between two vulnerable populations—children and the elderly (Kuehne, 1999; Rosenbrook & Larkin, 2002). However, Gambone (2002) identified six generational cohorts in the United States based on the intergenerational dialogues that he developed and conducted during his extensive field experiences: (1) Civic or G.I. Generation (born 1931 or before). These were active participants in World War II. They came out of an agricultural economy and lived as young adults through the Depression. (2) Adaptive or Mediating Generation (1932–1944). Some were actively involved in the Korean War and transitioned personal work ethics to organizational work ethics by being loyal to employers and moving towards building careers. (3) Baby Boom Generation (1945-1963). This is considered the most famous of the generations due to the increased number of college attendees who were raised in a prosperous culture highly influenced by television. (4) Diversity or Gen X Generation (1964-1981). They have been influenced by increasing rates of divorce, suicide by young people, and chronic diseases like AIDS. They have maneuvered through a very multicultural, multiracial society. (5) Millennial Generation (1982-2002). This generation has been influenced by a very advanced technological society. (6) Digital Generation (2003 to present). Although it is too early to make full predictions about this generation, they are influenced by even more advanced technological society, the first black President, and the new face of racial tensions. When two or more of these generations come together to collaborate in an effort to nurture and support one another, intergenerationality is formed.

People have a propensity to gather in groups for mutually beneficial purposes. It is through the elements of group process that persons relate simultaneously to each other while innovative and productive goals are accomplished. It has been argued that a person's ability to function appropriately in groups determines their level of self-efficacy (Yalom, 1985). The functionality in generational groups is personified over time by the informal social contract expressed through the reciprocal interactions between generations and also between generations and community/society (Cornman & Kingson, 1999). This social contract is currently being challenged by the growth in the number of generations coupled with the inequality in society. This has the potential for increased intergenerational conflict and barriers as members of generations attempt to combat this inequality in society by trying to figure out how to efficiently use these inadequate resources (Wisesale, 2003). Intergenerational community-based groups are designed to remove the perceived intergenerational conflict and barriers in a community by engaging in activities and interactions that share the resources of each generation. Through this process, a mutual appreciation of commonality and generativity is recognized by each generation; moving away from an antagonistic framework to a more reciprocal mentor/learner framework (Mistry, Rosansky, McGuire, McDermott, & Jarvik, 2001).

Organizational and Community Context

In an effort to move their community forward, five generations of the Sandtown/Winchester community in Baltimore, Maryland, utilized an intergenerational

community-based group process to address the issues of gang violence. Sandtown/
Winchester is a seventy-two-square-block community in West Baltimore, known
by the over 10,300 residents as "Sandtown." This community is considered the
highest incarcerated community in Maryland, accounting for $75 million of the
state's spending on corrections. There are 458 people from Sandtown behind bars,
accounting for an incarceration rate of 3,074 per 100,000 persons compared to the
national incarceration rate of 455 per 100,000. The juvenile arrest rate is 211 per
100,000 persons compared to the national juvenile arrest rate of 39.4 per 100,000
persons. More than half of residents age sixteen to sixty-four are unemployed;
there is a median household income of $24,000; and a quarter of the residents
receive public assistance. Nineteen out of every 1,000 people in the area die
between the ages of fifteen and twenty-four, and life expectancy caps off at age
sixty-eight. The rate of elevated blood lead levels (7.4%) is three times that of the
rest of Baltimore. Fewer than 40 percent of those living in the neighborhood have
a high school diploma, likely because almost half of all students (49.3%) are
chronically absent (Prison Policy Initiative, 2015).

This community is plagued with higher poverty, crime, and substance use,
making it a breeding ground for gang recruitment, activities, and violence.
Although Sandtown/Winchester's unique demographics and characteristics seem
to impede successful alliances between different generations living in the community, intergenerational dialogues were utilized as a way to allow members of
each generation to present unique and valuable perspectives on the gang issues.
The purpose of the intergenerational dialogues was to allow the five generations
of the Sandtown/Winchester community to come together to create an action plan
to address the gang issues. Representatives from each of the generations evaluated the benefits and challenges of their community differently, although each
equally contributed to the planning, brainstorming, discussing, and creating a plan
of action to address the gang prevention needs of the community. All represented
age groups of the community were involved in the group process to develop a
planned action towards solution commitment in reference to gang prevention.

Group Purpose and Goals

The Gang Prevention Intergenerational Dialogue Program was a ten-week program that utilized Schwartz's (1971) four task group stages and integrated
Gambone's intergenerational dialogues (Gambone, 2002) with African American
intergenerationality (Waites, 2008), bringing together five generations who par-

ticipated in several dialogues: (1) adaptive (1932 to 1944); (2) baby boomers (1945 to 1963); (3) gen X (1964 to 1981); (4) millennials (1982-2002); and (5) digital (2003 to present). The main objectives of the intergenerational dialogues were to: (1) provide an opportunity for several generations of African Americans in an urban environment to engage in a face-to-face dialogue with each other on several themes in reference to gang issues that they identified; (2) exchange perspectives and recommendations from each other on the themes and to address the concerns and issues presented; and (3) agree on some key proposals and make recommendations on the main themes identified. There were five elements of the intergenerational dialogues: (1) generational circles: joining of participants in circles based on age categories; (2) scenarios: open-ended stories of interest to the five generations, describing the gang issues in the community; (3) generational groups: large groups formed from representatives from each of the five generations; (4) intergenerational groups: small groups formed from all the participants consisting of an even distribution of all the generations represented; and (5) group recommendations: intergenerationally created recommendations for actions that the community planned to use to resolve the gang issues presented. Participants said that the sessions broke down barriers between the generations by encouraging them to listen intentionally to the values of each generation, then work together intergenerationally to come up with action steps that moved them toward common goals.

Tuning In Phase

Group Membership
The members for the group were recruited with help from the neighborhood associations and a faith-based organization. A group planning committee composed of three members (ages ten to ninety) from each generation, two social workers, and four social work interns was formed and developed the initial intergenerational dialogue group event. The members consisted of students from elementary schools, middle schools, high schools, four-year and community colleges and trade schools, parents, business owners, gang members, members of faith-based organizations, and correctional officers (see table 15.2).

The facilitators made preparation for the commencement of the group utilizing rapport building skills (i.e., finding links between mutual common experiences, showing empathy) as a strategy to learn about the language, verbal and nonverbal cues, and life experiences of the participants; this allowed for the development of stronger cohesion during group process.

Table 15.2 Gang Prevention Intergenerational Dialogue Planning Committee Composition

Adaptive 1932–1944	Baby Boomers 1945–1963	Gen X 1964–1981	Millennials 1982–2002	Digital 2003–present
Female retiree	Female correctional officer	Female single parent	Male high school student and gang member	Male elementary school student
Male grandfather	Male business owner	Female community college student	Male college student	Male elementary school student
Female grandmother	Male unemployed father	Male trade school student	Female nurse's aide worker	Female middle school student

Beginning and Middle Phases

Group Structure

During the first four weeks, the intergenerational dialogue process was focused on the intergenerational planning committee. By the fourth week, all persons were recruited for the Gang Prevention Intergenerational Dialogue Program (see table 15.3).

The planning committee's first task was to brainstorm and select an issue that had an impact on all the generations within the community. The social work facilitators assisted with probing the participants in an effort to allow them to select a high priority issue that affected all generations and one where group efficacy could be achieved. It took some time but the group decided to address the negative gang activities in their community. After the topic for the intergenerational dialogue was selected, the planning committee determined other community members who would be representing each generation from within their community to participate in the group process.

The group met on Tuesday evenings from 7:30 p.m. to 9:00 p.m. in a faith-based organization known for its advocacy work in the community. The social workers spent some time explaining fully the purpose and goals of an intergenerational dialogue. The group sat in chairs in a circular format. An affirmation was read before every group and at the end of every group. A different generational member was responsible for choosing the affirmation. After the affirmation was read, the social workers began to discuss the expectations of the members of the planning committee as well as distributed responsibilities among each generation

Table 15.3 Gang Prevention Intergenerational Dialogue Final Composition

Adaptive 1932–1944	Baby Boomers 1945–1963	Gen X 1964–1981	Millennials 1982–2002	Digital 2003–present
Female retiree	Female correctional officer	Female single parent with ninth-grade education	Male high school student and gang member	Male elementary school student
Male grandfather	Male business owner	Female community college student	Male college student	Male elementary school student
Female grandmother	Male unemployed father with tenth-grade education	Male trade school student	Female nurse's aide worker	Female middle school student
Female grandmother	Male living in transition home	Male college student and gang member	Female returning citizen and unemployed with GED	Male elementary school student
Male deacon in faith-based organization	Male college student and nonprofit owner	Female single parent with eighth-grade education	Female college student	Female middle school student
Male retired veteran	Female MTA bus driver	Male returning citizen and unemployed with eleventh-grade education	Transgender woman with high school diploma	Female elementary school student

within the planning committee so that all members contributed equally and felt that they were included.

During the fifth week, when all group members had been selected, the format changed. During this session, the participants were asked to participate in a generational circle. During the generational circle, they were each given a note card and asked to write one word that described their generation. They assembled in a circle from oldest to youngest. Each person shared their name, age, and word while the others listened. This activity served as both an icebreaker and a glimpse inside the perspectives of each generation present.

During the sixth week, all thirty members met together in theater style seating; a table with five chairs was set up for the panel (five members representing each of the generations), and a projector and microphone for the social work facilitators. During this session, the social work facilitators were able to gain some insight from all the generations in reference to their views of the gang activity in their community and its effect on the community. Each generation was given an opportunity to discuss their perspectives of the gang issues in the community while listening to the views of the other generations. The information gathered was utilized to create several scenarios highlighting the varied perspectives from the generations in a nonthreatening manner. The scenarios developed were written out in a few paragraphs and described a fictional gang event in the community. The social workers prepared the scenarios to be read during the intergenerational dialogue group sessions in an effort to focus the group discussions. A set of questions based on the scenarios was also developed for each generation to answer during the group process.

During the seventh through the ninth weeks, all thirty members met together in theater style seating for the reading of the scenario. The person reading the scenario read the scenario out loud from a place where they could not be seen to eliminate the possibility of bias. The social work facilitators guaranteed that all participants heard the scenario clearly.

Critical Incidents

There were several episodes of conflict throughout the intergenerational dialogue sessions that led to change in the group process and an increase in cohesion. For example, members of the planning committee expressed their frustration surrounding their inability to recruit more participants from the community to engage in the process. Initially, members from the millennial generation said that they were working harder than members of other generations. Other members felt that the millennials had addressed the group inappropriately. Members from the baby boomer generation reported that their work and family responsibilities were making it difficult to fulfill their requirements to the group process. Other members became agitated and felt that the baby boomers were being insensitive to the fact that all members had other responsibilities separate from the intergenerational dialogue process. At this point, the process was becoming chaotic and the efforts to address the selected issue (gang activities) were in jeopardy. The social work facilitators reminded the participants that each generation's perspective was important to the process and reiterated the intergenerational dialogue principles (Gambone, 2002): (1) respect, which allows participants to treat others the way they would like to be treated; (2) caring, which creates a positive, safe, and honest environment where all can learn; and (3) cooperation, which breaks down the barriers between generations so they can work together. This reminder seemed to have an effect on the group and shifted the momentum of the group process. Group members were all asked to talk about what respect, caring, and cooperation meant to them. For instance, according to Kwame Jackson (name changed for anonymity), a member of the digital generation, (personal communication, August 13, 2013):

> Sometimes I just want older people to just listen, you feel me? Stop thinking we don't have feelings, like we don't have problems, like we don't matter. We are no different when it comes to wanting to be heard. I know I shouldn't be acting like I do but then I just do it and it makes me feel bad. I thought it would help coming to this group and being around people who might know how I'm feeling and might could help with what's happening out there.

The sentiments of his statements were supported by the other two members of the digital generation present. Ginnifer Johnson (name changed for anonymity), member of the baby boomer generation, (personal communication, August 13, 2013), responded by stating:

> I never looked at it that way. I guess I have always been taught that a child needs to stay in a child's place so that's just the way I have always carried it. You have to admit that sometimes you guys can be very disrespectful but I guess I was at times too. I really didn't realize that we were coming across like that. I really do value you young folks' opinions but I must keep it 100 that I don't always show that. I guess I need to get to know you guys better.

The social work facilitator used this as an opportunity to emphasize the need to accomplish the goals set forth by the group by summarizing and integrating the group experiences thus far (e.g., "So far I've heard some suggestions to enhance our group goals. One is for members of each generations to openly, honestly, and respectfully share the experiences that you have had with members of other generations, and the other, which Kwame just mentioned, is to listen to each other and support one another as we attempt to develop some solutions to the gang issues in the community; especially when it comes to feeling hurt, sad, angry, worried, or guilty"). This allowed all participants to uncover the differences that each generation was contributing to the process, which in turn de-escalated the negative interactions.

Another conflictual episode occurred when the gang scenario was presented. Initially, there were some verbally aggressive statements made as the different generations presented their perspectives about gangs in the community. According to Frank Jackson (name changed for anonymity), a member of the millennial generation, (personal communication, September 7, 2013):

> You guys always {expletive} thinking that a {expletive} can't do nothing good in a gang. Ya'll just don't really know how it is. It's real out here and sometimes a {expletive} has to do what a {expletive} has to do. It ain't like ya'll got no job for a {expletive}. Homies don't only want to do {expletive} stuff. You just do what you got to do to eat. It's a dog eat dog eat world out here and sometimes you just got to get them before they get you.

That response stimulated many responses from the group, which at times had to be redirected by the social work facilitators. Ms. Johnson (name changed for anonymity), member of the adaptive generation, responded (personal communication, September 7, 2013):

> What I try to understand is why you guys have to cuss so much. Ya'll don't seem to have no respect for the elderly anymore. The gangs in the community do what they do right in front of the elderly with no regards for how we feel. I don't mind helping anybody but when I don't feel respected, I feel like I can't help. I have to really admit that I am afraid of the young people in my neighborhood. I don't feel safe coming outside at all. I feel like a prisoner in my own home in my own community. How would you like to feel like that? Just think about this, it's the elderly that worked hard and took the abuse to get us where we are now. We used to look out for one another but no more. I want ya'll to have jobs. I want ya'll to have what ya'll need to survive. I want to help you, son, but I can't help you if I'm afraid of you.

It was shown that group members had a clear understanding of their task and a general feel for who they were as a group. They exhibited confidence by addressing some of the issues surrounding the group. The more dominant of the group members began to emerge. The less confrontational members continued to suppress their feelings although they asked clarification questions about the group process. For the remainder of this session, members from the different generations noted that they really wanted the same things for their families and community but utilized different skills:

1. The adaptive generation focused on activities that involved the shared responsibility and interdependency of the members of the community in creating and maintaining the good in the community (collaborative and collectivistic skills).
2. The baby boomers focused on activities that involved the socialization process, including the values that affirmed and strengthened the family and culture of the community (social organizational skills).
3. Gen X focused on activities that involved understanding the art and process of gaining, maintaining, and using the power associated with the political process (political organizational skills).
4. Millennials focused on activities that involved the characteristics and achievements of the members of the community that distinguished them from others (entrepreneurial skills).
5. The digital generation focused on activities that involved the creative aspects of the community that were reflective of the community members' life experiences and aspirations (artistic skills).

As these skills were processed and explained by the members of the group, a mutual respect was developed.

Group Activities

After the scenario was read, each member participant transitioned to one of the five tables (representing their generation) for their group sessions. During their generational group sessions, each participant was asked to respond to a set of questions presented by the social work facilitators. The questions were designed to gain insight into each generation's unique perspective on the gang issues in the community while highlighting the unique perspectives of each generation present. Each set of generational questions had the same theme but had different specifics for each generation (based on results of the generational circles) and focused on specific attributes of the generation. For example, when soliciting from participants how the gang issues were viewed in the community, the question was asked the following ways:

1. Adaptive: Your generation has witnessed a lot of changes in society over time; how do you think members of your generation view the gang issues in the community?
2. Baby boomers: With there being so many baby boomers in the community raising grandchildren who are involved in gang activities, how do you think members of your generation view the gang issues in the community?

3. Gen X: With the political influence of the hip hop culture during your period, how do you think members of your generation view the gang issues in the community?

4. Millennials: With all this attention to technology and social media during your period, how do you think members of your generation view the gang issues in the community?

5. Digital: As you are hanging out in your neighborhood or at school with friends who are in your age group, how do you guys feel about the gang issues in the community?

After all members had an opportunity to respond to the questions, they returned to the theater style seating, remained silent, and listened to each generation's responses before asking questions if clarity was needed. After all generations had a chance to answer and ask questions of one another in regard to the scenario, the social work facilitators created new groups consisting of at least one member from each generation. These newly formed intergenerational groups then moved back to the five tables and spent time brainstorming a list of solutions to the gang issue described in the scenario, keeping in mind the perspectives shared from each generation. Each intergenerational group then selected their top solutions to share with the entire group. The solutions from each intergenerational group were then posted publicly for each individual to vote upon and were considered the intergenerational recommendations for action. Each member then voted on the solutions that were determined most workable for solving the problem. The participants were allowed to cast more than one vote per solution if they wished and could vote for or against the solutions that their intergenerational group created. All votes were tallied by the social work facilitators and the top solution was announced.

Evaluation and Outcomes

During the tenth week, the social work facilitators helped the intergenerational group to organize an action plan based on the solution that was selected after the processing of the scenarios read during the last session. The social work facilitators helped the group organize an action plan based on the selected solution. The solution was the development of plans to build a community center, to be called the Franklin Entrepreneurial and Apprenticeship Center (FEAC). The intergenerational group organized a strategy to create a 501(c)(3) nonprofit organization and developed plans to build the community center in West Baltimore through a joint venture of a faith-based organization and a nonprofit community-based organization. The plans to develop the center were taken from the intergenerational recommendations formed at the end of the dialogue sessions and is currently being made a reality. FEAC is scheduled to be a state of the art training facility for youth and adults alike. The current building located at 2128 Madison Avenue will undergo an extensive renovation that will employ the latest "green building" technologies and construction methods. The 10,000-square-foot facility will comprise classrooms, a computer lab, office space, a conference room, two multipurpose rooms, a commercial kitchen for a café and culinary training programs, a meditation garden, a rooftop deck, and a greenhouse. The entrepreneurial and apprenticeship training programs will target youth and unskilled individuals in building trades and business development to encourage self-empowerment and sufficiency, thus serving as an inoculation to gang activities. The program design will take a methodical three-pronged approach to address social and economic issues that affect the local residents as well as provide opportunities for others in the metropolitan Baltimore area. The program approaches include entrepreneurship training, academic enhancement, and construction skills trades training. Members of all generational groups were encouraged to attend future meetings in order for progress to continue and for each perspective to be shared. Evaluations of the intergenerational dialogues were conducted, and concluding remarks were made before the group was dismissed.

Use of Diversity over Time

This intergenerational community group process helped to define some of the variations within these generations and the differences between the generations' approaches to the negative gang activities in their community. These unique characteristics proved to be useful when attempting to manage the diversity within the group process because the participants began to understand their own biases and assumptions. When addressing the gang issues in this particular community, each generation evaluated the issue through their generational lens, formulating several themes. For instance, members of the adaptive generation based their assumptions about the gang issue on the following themes: dedication, sacrifice, hard work, conformity, respect for authority, and duty before pleasure. The themes that surfaced for the baby boomers were: optimism, personal gratification, personal growth, health and wellness, and involvement. The gen X themes were: balance, fun, self-reliance, and diversity. The millennials' themes surrounded: civic duty, social media, technology, confidence, achievement, street smarts, and diversity. The digital generation's themes focused on: youth, fun, informality, techno-literacy, and sociability.

These differences in themes played out in a very productive way for the group throughout the group process. The differences became conflictual only when they shifted from the group's differences about the topical issue (gang activities in the community) and strayed back into negative generational stereotypes. These negative stereotypes made the communication difficult and slowed down the productivity and movement of the group. For instance, when the baby boomers saw the gen Xs' initial lack of interest in the community's gang issue, they concluded that the gen X participants were apathetic and had an increased appetite for instant gratification. The following is a sample of the dialogue:

Baby boomer: Well, I just don't believe that you guys (gen X members) are really interested in helping this community. You guys are never in things for the long haul.

Social work facilitator: I'd like for us to not use judging sarcasm and words like "always" and "never." If you remember, we discussed and contracted in our initial group meeting that we would focus on self-reports and not use indirect messages that discredit or judge another person.

Gen Xer: I hear you but what she mean? Ya'll think you are the only ones that know how to work hard. We just don't depend on others to keep us going. We do for self. That's how we get it done.

Social work facilitator: Can you rephrase that statement by starting out with the pronoun "I"? This time identify your feelings, or what you want or need.

Gen Xer: I get really angry and hurt when you don't consider how hard we work too. I want you to understand that we feel that we can help our community within our community. We don't have to go begging help from outsiders.

Baby boomer: How do you think you can really help your community if you don't rely on others? That's you being selfish, only willing to do things if it benefits you. My bad, I know. I know that was judging and labeling. I just want you to think about how we can do things within the community and we can also benefit from help from others outside of the community, people like these social workers here who are not from this community.

Gen Xer: I feel you but we are not selfish. We are just self-reliant. We want our community to be free of this gang {expletive} too.

The social work facilitator capitalized on this moment to focus the group's attention on what was occurring. The specific behaviors along with the progression of the events that had just transpired were processed with the group. This allowed for the group to focus on the issue presented and problem solve a resolution. As the problem-solving process progressed, the participants were able to present a different view of themselves and why they expressed their behaviors the way that they did. The group was then able to return to discussing their differences about the gang issue in the community rather than their specific generational differences.

Implications for Practice

Heterogeneous groups consist of individuals who differ in diagnostic and demographic characteristics, such as persons from different generations. Such groups offer more diverse and multidirectional processes than homogeneous groups. Heterogeneous groups are valuable for positively altering symptoms and character structures by modifying perceptual distortions about others, although this process may occur more slowly than with homogeneous groups (Frances, Clarkin, & Marachi, 1980). During the heterogeneous group process, cohesiveness takes longer to occur, and interactive problems and intragroup conflicts are increased (Furst, 1952; Rosenthal, 1985). However, there is some benefit to conflict in the group process, as it increases members' tolerance for interpersonal interactions with persons different from themselves as long as the conflict does not exceed the members' tolerance for it (Harrison & Lubin, 1965; Yalom, 1985).

This heterogeneous, intergenerational, community-based group offers an opportunity for practitioners to allow group members to understand generational diversity around group tasks and responsibilities while addressing an issue in their community. This type of group process allows for conflict to manifest itself into a product that benefits not just individual group members but a whole community. The activities in the group allow for cross-generational bonds to be developed, which in turn reduces generational isolation, alienation, and separation, stimulated by the competence and preparation of group facilitators (Yalom, 1985).

The group is facilitated in a way that creates a platform for each generation to identify intrapersonal and interpersonal strengths as a means of bridging the generational gaps that may have been developed over time. The self-efficacy that is developed in this group process provides the participants an opportunity to expand their psychosocial boundaries through the structure and theoretical framework of the intergenerational dialogues, based on the synergy of all generations represented. This synergistic interaction that is created during the group process creates a sense of an intergenerational community that is generalizable to the participants' everyday lives, as well as to the community as a whole.

FURTHER READING

Bengtson, V. L. "Beyond the Nuclear Family: The Increasing Importance of Multigenerational Relationships in American Society." *Journal of Marriage and the Family* 63, no. 1 (2001): 1–16.

Cornman, J. M., and Kingson, E. R. "Yes, John, There Is a Social Compact." *Generations* 22, no. 4 (1999): 10–14.

Frances, A., Clarkin, J., and Marachi, J. "Selection Criteria for Group Therapy." In *Controversy in Psychiatry*, edited by J. Brady and H. K. Brody, 679–702. Philadelphia: W. B. Saunders, 1980.

Furst, W. "Homogeneous and Heterogeneous Groups." *International Journal of Group Psychotherapy* 2 (1952): 120–123.

Gambone, J. V. *Together for Tomorrow: Building community through Intergenerational Dialogue*. Crystal Bay, MN: Elder Eye Press, 2002.

Harrison, R., and Lubin, B. "Personal Style, Group Composition, and Learning." *Journal of Applied Behavioural Science* 1 (1965): 286–301.

Kuehne, V. S. "Building Intergenerational Communities through Research and Evaluation." *Generations* 22, no. 4 (1999): 82–87.

Mistry, R., Rosansky, J., McGuire, J., McDermott, C., & Jarvik, L. "Social Isolation Predicts Re-hospitalization in a Group of Older American Veterans Enrolled in the UPBEAT Program." *International Journal of Geriatric Psychiatry* 16 (2001): 950–959.

Rosenbrook, V., and Larkin, E. "Introducing Standards and Guidelines: A Rationale for Defining the Knowledge, Skills, and Dispositions of Intergenerational Practice." *Journal of Intergenerational Relationships* 1 (2002): 133–144.

Rosenthal, L. "A Modern Analytic Approach to Group Resistance." *Modern Psychoanalysis* 10 (1985): 165–182.

Schwartz, W. "On the Use of Group in Social Work Practice." In *The Practice of Group Work*, edited by W. Schwartz and S. Zalba, 13–18. New York, NY: Columbia University Press, 1971.

Strauss, W., and Howe, N. *Generations: The History of America's Future, 1584 to 2069*, New York, NY: William Morrow, 1991.

Waites, C. *Social Work Practice with African-American Families: An Intergenerational Perspective*. New York, NY: Routledge, 2008.

Wisesale, S. K. "Global Aging and Intergenerational Equity." *Journal of Intergenerational Relationships* 1 (2003): 29–47.

Yalom, I. *The Theory and Practice of Group Psychotherapy* (4th ed.). New York, NY: Basic Books, 1995.

CHAPTER 16

SUPPORTIVE GROUPS

EDMONTON'S BIPOLAR SUPPORT GROUP
Samantha Pekh

Individuals who have been affected by bipolar disorder often feel quite hopeless in their prospects of being able to successfully live life in spite of the bipolar disorder, and struggle in managing its symptoms. Those attending the support group are often in various stages of awareness and stability, including people who have had recent diagnoses and/or are questioning if they have bipolar disorder, people who have known about their diagnosis for several years and/or are now interested in managing/supporting it better, and people who are quite informed but want to connect with others affected by bipolar disorder. As a result, the format and process of each group can differ depending on the needs of the members attending and their knowledge of bipolar disorder.

The intent of this group is to support individuals who suspect they have bipolar disorder, those who have been diagnosed with bipolar disorder, and their loved ones. Although it may first appear to be difficult to include loved ones in a support group, members have found the inclusion of both those with bipolar disorder and supporters to be very beneficial to group discussions, adding an extra dimension with their personal learning and insights. This experience aligns with general knowledge that the involvement of supportive loved ones and having a strong support system is a key contributor to the success of managing mental illness.

Specifically, group members are taught about different strategies that can be used to help manage symptoms, with the aim to reduce the frequency and intensity of symptoms. This information is shared primarily through a psychoeducational format and group discussion, and supplemented by at-home assignments. Topics are regularly personalized by encouraging members to share their own experiences, what has worked for them, and what has not worked for them. One topic that is often of great benefit for members is the management of suicidal ideation and/or attempts. By leading discussions on this topic and other important topics, members are supported in the development of collaborative and proactive self-management plans.

Organizational and Community Context

Currently this group is being run in Edmonton, Alberta, a growing city with a population of 877,926 (City of Edmonton, 2015). According to the 2011 national census, Edmonton's total census metropolitan area population was 1,159,869 (Statistics Canada, 2012), making it one of the largest metropolitan areas of Canada. Statistics indicate that about 2.6 percent of the United States population has bipolar disorder (Kessler, Chiu, Demler, & Walters, 2005, as cited by the National Institute of Mental Health, 2015), with some studies suggesting that the prevalence is actually closer to being between 5 to 6 percent of the United States population (Akiskal, Bourgeois, et al., 2000, as cited by Fast & Preston, 2006). If the 2.6 percent estimate is applied to the population of Edmonton and its greater area, this would mean that 22,826 to 30,156 Edmontonians have been diagnosed with bipolar disorder. Taking the more recent estimate of 5 to 6 percent of the population, approximately 43,896 to 57,993 Edmontonians have been diagnosed with bipolar disorder, or if put another way, approximately one in every fifteen to twenty people. Either way, these estimates do not even take into account all the people who have not yet been diagnosed or all the people who are affected by bipolar disorder, either directly or indirectly. When considering this sphere of impact, it becomes clear that a support group that addresses this topic is needed, a need that the growing membership of this group demonstrates.

Fortunately, this need was recognized and, through the extensive support of Edmonton's Momentum Walk-in Counselling (http://www.momentumcounselling.org/) and funding provided by the Wellness Network of Edmonton (http://wellnessnetworkedmonton.com/), the Bipolar Support Group of Edmonton was initiated in 2013. The role of the facilitator, who is the author of this case study and an independent registered psychologist, is supported by the assistance of two to three WICSOE (Walk-in Counselling Society of Edmonton) volunteer cofacilitators. Although not a primary goal of the support group, an added benefit of the cofacilitation roles of volunteers is that volunteer students have been provided the opportunity to gain in-depth understanding about bipolar disorder, while also learning about the dynamics of group process and individual support. As a result, the support group has also contributed to the professional development of emerging mental health professionals within the community.

Group Purpose and Goals

The main goal of the group, aside from providing a supportive community, is to assist all group members in the creation of a personalized self-management plan. After it has been completed, this plan can be used to help reduce the severity and intensity of symptoms. The creation of this plan also helps ensure that supporters know what is expected from them and what they can do for their loved one that is actually helpful. Supporters may attend to learn more about bipolar disorder, but they also have the opportunity to learn how the strategies taught in group can be used to reduce their own levels of stress, depression, and/or anxiety.

Group Membership

As this is an open group and bipolar disorder does not discriminate when it comes to whom it affects, membership has been highly diverse and has included individuals from different socioeconomic statuses, ethnic backgrounds, ages, and genders. As mentioned earlier, membership includes individuals who have bipolar disorder and individuals wanting to learn how to be a more effective support person. All members arrive with different levels of support in place, with some members coming from minimal support and understanding from their families to members who have been graced with large support systems and/or professional help already established. There is also diversity in the level of acceptance among members themselves, with some members struggling with their diagnosis and self-perception and other members who feel the need to become an advocate and help educate the public.

There is often diversity among members in their knowledge and understanding about bipolar disorder. It is not uncommon for individuals to attend who have only a basic understanding of bipolar disorder. Therefore, the initial weeks of group meetings usually focus on providing an overview of bipolar disorder, common symptoms, and basic strategies. It is also, however, not uncommon to have members who have known about their bipolar disorder for several years and are already quite knowledgeable about bipolar disorder. The knowledge and experience of these members is regularly used to help contribute to discussions on how bipolar disorder has personally affected them, what they have found helpful, and what they have not found helpful. This last topic is usually of great benefit for not only those with bipolar disorder but for supporters struggling to know what they can do that is truly supportive. By assisting members to share their own experiences and relate them to the topics at hand, the material taught during group becomes less academic or theoretical and instead more meaningful and applicable.

Group Structure

The open drop-in structure of this group presents some interesting challenges, as new members can arrive over the course of the group and therefore are at a disadvantage of having missed important information. This difficulty has been managed by ensuring that new members have access to the volunteer cofacilitators between group meetings for individual no-cost catch-up sessions. These individual sessions are held at the Momentum Counselling Centre and are supervised by licensed mental health professionals who are either employed by or volunteer their time at Momentum. To further address the need of acclimatizing new members, each meeting begins with a standard check-in. During this check-in, members are encouraged to share their names and explain whether they are attending the group because they have bipolar disorder, are interested in learning more about bipolar disorder, or because they are a support person. There is also the opportunity to share personal updates. Sharing this basic information helps each member become aware of the composition and diversity within the group.

The group runs for eight weeks in total, with each session lasting for one and a half hours. To date, each group has collectively opted out of having a bathroom break, indicating instead their preference to remain in attendance for the entire hour and a half. During the first two to three weeks, the group leaders play a primary role by leading group topics, facilitating discussions, and presenting educational information. As members become more comfortable, they begin to contribute and share more, and topics are adjusted according to members' feedback and their current needs. During each group meeting, members are encouraged to integrate the information by participating in group and individual exercises, with the primary goal being that each member leaves the group with a completed self-management plan in place. Between group sessions, members are provided with additional resources and handouts through the weekly group e-newsletter.

Group Activities

As discussed above, one of the primary goals of the group is to assist each member in developing a personalized self-management plan. This goal applies to all members, whether they have bipolar disorder or are attending as a support person and could benefit from learning how to manage their own life stressors. Therefore, weekly topics are covered and exercises are completed that assist with this goal.

Topics include but are not limited to: knowing your symptoms, managing triggers, understanding and applying appropriate boundaries with others, addressing misconceptions, identifying life changes that may need to be made, and the importance of medications. Activities primarily revolve around developing action plans for depression, hypo/mania, stress, anxiety, anger, paranoia, and so on. Collectively, these action plans become the self-management plan. The topic of managing suicidal ideation and/or attempts is also covered and often a full meeting is dedicated to the development of a proactive personalized suicide prevention plan.

Following the resource manuals provided by the Centre for Clinical Interventions (2008) and the work of Julie Fast and John Preston (2006, 2012, 2015), the action plans include identifying the common symptoms or clues that a particular concern is arising (i.e., depression, stress, etc.), what the individual can do to address this concern (i.e., go for a walk), and what their support people can do to be helpful (i.e., "stay close and just watch a movie with me"). This last category often initiates a lot of conversation among members as they discuss what support they have previously found helpful or not. Finally, group discussions are facilitated by viewing short videos on various coping strategies and personal stories of people affected by bipolar disorder. At the end of each group meeting, members are encouraged to apply what they have learned by completing various homework exercises.

How the Group Worked with Diversity over Time

One of the diversity issues that this group must manage is the wide age range of group members. To date, members have ranged in age from eighteen years to approximately seventy years. As one can assume, such a wide age range can bring very different experiences and perceptions on mental health, and more specifically, bipolar disorder. Although not true for all of the younger members, it has been this group's experience that younger members are more accepting of mental health difficulties and interested in helping people understand what bipolar disorder is and what it is not. Older members are very interested in learning more about bipolar disorder, but they sometimes have to "unlearn" some long-held beliefs or misconceptions. The process of "unlearning" and "relearning" is facilitated by attending the group and by posing questions, sometimes questions that have remained unanswered for a long time. At times, however, when members have asked questions that highlighted their lack of understanding about mental health issues or their misconceptions of bipolar disorder, some members (although they have remained polite) have become upset or annoyed. If not managed properly by the group leaders, this can lead to a situation where upset members begin to shut down, become adversarial, or split among each other within the group. This can then lead to a situation in which members no longer feel safe to ask questions and, thus, become limited in their ability to address their misconceptions, to learn from their group members, and to receive the support the large membership so clearly highlights is needed.

To date, this has been handled by encouraging members to view seemingly "ignorant" comments or questions posed by other members as opportunities to address misconceptions and to share their perspectives in a nonthreatening and open manner. Group members are then encouraged to use the same approach with people they interact with outside the group. By approaching questions in this manner, members begin to understand that how they react and respond to the questions they receive can help shape and contribute to their community's (i.e., family, social network, work, school, etc.) increased knowledge of bipolar and mental health in general, and in their own small way, help to reduce the stigma that is often attached to mental health difficulties.

A second diversity issue that must be managed is the fact that group members often find themselves in different stages of change and levels of acceptance. It will be helpful to highlight the stages of change so that readers have some context to understand this process and how it affects group membership. According to Prochaska, Norcross, and DiClemente (1994), there are six stages of change: precontemplation, contemplation, preparation, action, maintenance, and relapse. Precontemplation is the stage that involves lack of awareness or recognition that there is a problem to address. As people begin to enter the stage of contemplation, they are becoming aware that a problem exists and may even begin thinking about making some changes. In the preparation stage, people are usually beginning to make at least small steps towards change. After someone is actively taking steps towards change and the goals they have chosen, they have entered the action stage. As they continue with their new behaviors and begin to tweak the strategies they have in place or add new ones to their repertoire, they are entering the maintenance stage. Finally, the relapse stage occurs when people find themselves returning to old behaviors or experiencing a return of symptoms. Although this stage can be discouraging for those who experience it, this stage also offers lots of information that can be used to strengthen future efforts, such as identifying and understanding what circumstances or factors led to the return of symptoms. It should be noted at this point that the process of change is not necessarily a linear process that involves stages of equal time length. Instead, individuals may find themselves staying in one stage longer than another and moving between the stages in a different order than their peers. For example, one individual may move from contemplation to preparation, then back to contemplation, over several years, whereas another individual may move from contemplation, to preparation, to action, and then to relapse, only to quickly return to action again within the course of a year.

In the bipolar group under study here, few participants have been in the precontemplation stage, but there have been several members in the contemplation and preparation stages, as well as the action stage. Some members, mainly those who have been aware of their diagnosis for several years, have been in the beginning stages of the maintenance stage. Managing this variability in readiness for change and adjusting strategies to meet the needs of members in different stages have proved to be beneficial for the group. Through this variability, members have had opportunities to witness other members who are more ready to take charge of their symptoms and make difficult albeit necessary life changes. This has helped to create a sense of hope and has helped some members begin to move forward in their own personal intervention plans and self-care. Conversely, members further along in the process of change have had the opportunity to share their knowledge and experiences with members who have only just learned about their diagnosis or are beginning to make changes in their life to address their symptoms.

Ensuring that some consistency and structure are maintained across groups throughout the year can be difficult due to the unique composition of each group and its particular collective "personality." For example, some groups are composed of members who engage easily and desire more processing time than educational time. Other groups have been composed mostly of quiet members wanting to absorb and listen to information rather than engage in conversation. Furthermore, the needs of each group usually differ somewhat, in addition to the specific topics in which members are interested. Therefore, although there is some structure to the information and topics that are covered within this support group, the order of topics, the length of processing time versus instruction time, and the amount of engagement required from group leaders change from group to group. Although this can create extra demands for the group leaders and increase the time required to prepare, it is the flexible and adaptive nature of this group that has contributed to its success and its ability to grow in such a short time frame (from one pilot study to three groups per year in just under two years of operation).

Evaluation and Outcomes

To date, feedback has primarily been collected verbally or through the use of anonymous qualitative questionnaires administered at the end of each group meeting. Overall, the feedback from members has been quite positive, with many members indicating that they have learned something new and helpful each week and that they find the diversity of membership beneficial. Risk is monitored by having members indicate if they would like to receive extra support through individual sessions. If this is the case for a particular member, then they are required to share their name so that group leaders have a means of contacting them to set up individual appointments.

When constructive feedback is received, it is regularly used to revise the group and information covered. For example, it has become clear that outside of brief overviews, members are generally not very interested in hearing a lot about the statistics of bipolar disorder, such as prevalence, or in covering highly detailed information, such as specific diagnostic criteria as used in the *Diagnostic and Statistical Manual of Mental Disorders* (American Psychiatric Association, 2013). The interest level in discussing medication and its impact has varied across groups as well. Because this is a very important topic when learning how to manage bipolar disorder, addressing the importance of medication has been met by facilitating group discussions on members' personal experiences with medications and then providing handouts/resources that members can read or access on their own if they are interested.

As a result of the ongoing feedback, the support group has been able to secure additional funding and has now expanded from a pilot study to three eight-week groups being run throughout the year. Group members have also shared their interest in having follow-up groups or "level two" groups available for the members who have already attended this support group one or two times.

Implications for Practice and Policy

The rapid growth of this group (in as little as two years) and the increase of membership (sometimes more than twenty members per group) illustrate the level of need the community has for support in managing bipolar disorder. Experience with this group highlights the importance of incorporating flexibility within the group structure in order for the group to meet member needs effectively. At times this can be difficult for facilitators due to program requirements or, perhaps, to leaders' own uncertainties of covering information that may appear not as important as what was originally included in their outline. From the experience of this group, however, these adjustments have helped ensure that members feel supported, which has also helped increase their level of commitment. If attendance and commitment to a group can be increased, then the likelihood that needed information and support required by members will be received is also increased.

It is also important for facilitators or group leaders to be familiar with the stages of change and to recognize that some of their members may arrive for meetings with little homework being completed. This can be a frustrating experience for facilitators, as it can create difficulties in following through with intended topics or group exercises. Members sometimes attend groups, however, when they are not ready to actively apply what they are hearing. Instead, the value they pull from attendance is to simply listen to information and absorb it, perhaps holding onto it until they are ready to make some steps towards change. This is one of the main reasons that this support group provides so many handouts and has initiated an e-newsletter. With these tangible resources in hand, members have the ability to review materials and information covered when needed, even long after the group has ended and they finally feel ready to start making some steps towards health.

The success of integrating members with bipolar and their supportive loved ones has been a highlight and main contributor to the success of this group, even when members have attended the group without their respective others. For example, each group has usually consisted of a few supporters arriving without their family members who have bipolar disorder. By attending, they have been able to learn strategies that they can apply for their own self-management plans. They can also share this information when their loved ones are ready to begin learning how to manage their symptoms.

FURTHER READING

Akiskal, H. S., and Bourgeois, M. L., et al. "Re-evaluating the Prevalence of and Diagnostic Composition within the Broad Clinical Spectrum of Bipolar Disorders." *Journal of Affective Disorders* 59 (2000): Suppl. S5–530.

American Psychiatric Association. *Diagnostic and Statistical Manual of Mental Disorders* (5th ed.). Washington, DC: American Psychiatric Association, 2013.

Centre for Clinical Interventions. *Keeping Your Balance: Coping with Bipolar Disorder Infopax.* Department of Health, 2008, www.cci.health.wa.gov.au/resources/infopax.cfm?InfoID=38.

Fast, J. *The Health Cards System for Bipolar Disorder: A Revolutionary Three-step Program for the Management of Bipolar Disorder*, 2015, www.bipolar happens.com/health-cards/.

Fast, J., and Preston, J. D. *Take Charge of Bipolar Disorder: A Four-step Plan for You and Your Loved Ones to Manage the Illness and Create Lasting Stability.* New York, NY: Grand Central Life and Style, 2006.

Fast, J., and Preston, J. D. *Loving Someone with Bipolar Disorder: Understanding and Helping Your Partner* (2nd ed.). Oakland, CA: New Harbinger, 2012.

Kessler, R. C., Chiu, W. T., Demler, O., and Walters, E. E. "Prevalence, Severity, and Comorbidity of Twelve-month DSM-IV Disorders in the National Comorbidity Survey Replication (NCS-R)." *Archives of General Psychiatry* 62, no. 6 (2005): 617–627.

Prochaska, J. O., Norcross, J. C., and DiClemente, C. C. *Changing for Good: The Revolutionary Program that Explains the Six Stages of Change and Teaches You How to Free Yourself from Bad Habits.* New York, NY: William Morrow, 1994.

THE EXOTIC DANCER POWER PROGRAM
Rachael Crowder

Exotic dancers are a marginalized population who are highly stigmatized because of the work they do, and often feel that they cannot access the usual community services that most people rely on to protect their safety, health, and economic security. Dancers are often conflated with prostitutes, and many deny or distance themselves from that association. Most exotic dancers are female and identify as women, and therefore experience the gendered oppression and risk of male-perpetrated violence that is a reality for all women. Their profession puts them at further risk of exploitation by both club managers and their mostly male consumers because of the mistaken assumption that dancers are automatically consenting to these males' physical, aggressive, sexualized behaviors (Holsopple, 1999). Dancers who have a history of sexual assault and violence in their past are at further risk of exacerbated post traumatic stress symptoms.

Exotic dancers in Canada and the United States are racially and ethnically diverse, including Caucasian, indigenous, African, and immigrant women from Asia, the Caribbean, Africa, and Europe. Socioeconomic status ranges across the spectrum from otherwise unemployed to women working other full-time day jobs, including healthcare professionals. Exotic dancers experience extremely poor and dangerous working conditions that frequently contradict public health and safety standards, and are financially exploited by club managers and DJs. Strip club owners derive profit from stripping by demanding payment from both customers and dancers; most dancers are not paid a wage and usually have to turn over up to half of their income from tips. Debt is a method strip club owners use to control dancers: a minimum shift quota is set and if a woman does not earn the quota, due to a slow night, she owes the club money and must pay it back in following shifts. Most have a real need to create/supplement income and/or pay down debt (e.g. student loans), and some dance for a variety of other reasons particular to each woman, including exhibitionism or a momentary sense of mastery over her audience and environment. These women are vulnerable to exploitation in the workplace due to their economic need, and some have past experience with violence and subsequent post traumatic stress reactions, making it difficult for them to take a stand and voice their rights. Strip club owners do not meet the minimum municipal standards of health and safety because many law officers turn a blind eye to working conditions in these clubs. Owners extort dancers with outrageous fees with impunity because no dancer has successfully filed a human rights complaint. This highly stigmatized population tends not to seek help because they have not had much success in doing so collectively in the past, and, as many individuals have experienced sexual exploitation and violence in their pasts, they also have had negative experiences with help seeking as children, adolescents, and young adults.

Organizational and Community Context

Samantha Smythe, a woman in her late twenties and founder of the Dancers' Equal Rights Association (DERA), approached the staff at the Ottawa Rape Crisis Centre (ORCC) in 2003 with the proposal to initiate a support and advocacy group for exotic dancers. Samantha, a former stripper, had danced for more than seven years to support herself while going to university. She formed DERA in 2000 as a reaction to a Supreme Court ruling that allowed customers to touch dancers, thus exposing them to further exploitation and harm. In addition to the safety of dancers, Samantha was concerned with the health and working conditions at the various clubs in the city; she was organizing dancers into labor unions, pressuring the city to enforce health and safety bylaws, and collaborating with the city Health and Sexuality and Risk Reduction Program. The ORCC agreed to host the pilot program, and the ORCC coordinator for the Sex Worker Outreach Project was asked to cofacilitate the group with Samantha, who recruited group members through outreach to dancers working in local strip clubs. (The author made considerable effort to locate Samantha Smythe to offer her coauthorship of this case study, but was not successful. The author wishes to acknowledge the contributions of Smythe to this project, and the invaluable resource her final report had on the creation of this case study.)

Samantha originally conceived this as a "support" program, recognizing the level of violence, abuse, and exploitation dancers were experiencing, but soon realized that the dancers were more interested in an "empowerment program" than a "support group." The soon to be named Exotic Dancer Power Program was advertised as participant-driven to make access to a feminist organization like the ORCC more palatable to the dancers. This was a deliberate choice, as the facilitators recognized the challenges of offering "feminist" services to women in the sex industry. Samantha put it this way:

> The best analyses and most intense accountings of the sex industry are presented by women with the most exposure to it. These women must be involved in discussions and decision making concerning problems and solutions because our experience is not just a point of view, it is knowledge. Women from the sex industry think that we should be the recognized forces of explanation regarding the sex industry and our experiences in it. We also think, however, that as women who have experienced the sex industry, we have to support and promote each other and ourselves in this endeavor.

Group Purpose and Goals

The Exotic Dancer Power Program was advertised as providing skills that would be useful "as an exotic dancer or in other employment," thus nonjudgmentally conveying that this was not about helping women stay in or quit stripping. The facilitators focused on providing a group for those who wanted to accept responsibility and thus gain power over their lives, accept who they were, and develop their true potential. The approach was strengths-based, respectful, collaborative, and flexible. The facilitators were well aware that by providing this kind of safe structure and relaxed atmosphere, they would likely create an environment for support and referral when other issues arose, like violence in the home and/or workplace.

Group Membership

Although this was an open group, there was a core of about eight women, with others who came when it was convenient or there was a topic in which they were particularly interested. The core participants were the women that the facilitators got to know well. They were all cis-female (assigned female gender at birth), most had current or past male partners, and two women were new mothers. They ranged in age from early twenties to late thirties. All were Caucasian except for one Aboriginal woman (although there were many racialized women working in the clubs who were likely afraid to be exposed to deportation if they attended the group). Being in the nation's capital, some participants were bilingual, including one woman whose first language was French. Women's education and economic class also varied, from basic grade school to university, from working poor to professional. Some women had altered their bodies surgically or with tattooing and piercing, others had not. Some women were strictly against being touched while dancing, and others were willing to perform private dances and other "services" in VIP rooms at strip clubs to make more money. These were all distinctions, politics, and choices that could divide women and/or bring them together during group discussions.

Group Structure

The open group ran for eight weeks during the fall on Monday evenings from 6:30 to 9:00. The winter group was extended to 9:30 at the request of the dancers for more time for check-out, and the overall attendance from the fall to the winter group more than doubled, from nineteen to thirty-two women. The format and environment were friendly and relaxed, which assisted in the comfort level of the women who participated. Subjects were general, and the participants led the discussions around the subjects. The eight themes, one for each session, were: empowerment; time management; the power of positive thinking; resume writing and skill building; communication skills and conflict resolution; money management; community resources; and the International Women's Day celebration. Because the group was an open format, the first twenty to thirty minutes of each evening included: time for group facilitators to briefly introduce themselves, the group, and the agency; a review of group guidelines and ground rules; housekeeping (washrooms, smoking policy, etc.); and then group member introductions and check-in. That was followed by discussion of the evening's topic, which lasted about ninety minutes (sometimes with a guest presenter from the community) with a health break in the middle. The last hour was dedicated to some type of self-care activity (e.g. yoga, guided visualization, meditation) and a check-out.

Samantha usually took the lead at the beginning of each evening, as she recruited and knew all the participants. The cofacilitator's role was to provide therapeutic counseling, referral, and other support should it be needed, offer knowledge and advice about group process to Samantha when asked, and act as "gatekeeper" for the agency because she was an ORCC employee. The three-hour format might seem overly long, but the original two and a half hours proved to be too short according to feedback from the first run of the group. Because of the flexible nature of the group, the women were allowed to use the time and the discussion to suit their needs, although the facilitators kept a close eye on boundaries and containment. They used the theme structure as a container, and when the discussion wandered too broadly or resulted in interpersonal conflict, the facilitators were usually able to use those times (especially when the discussion got heated) as a teachable moment about the theme at hand. So although the container looked like "self-help" education and skills building, the interaction was sometimes more therapeutic in nature.

Group Activities

Samantha felt that it was important, as a gesture of respect to each woman and to give the program a "professional feel," to provide each participant with a binder that contained general information about the group, including the program themes and schedule, and dividers for weekly material. This practice also acted as an enticement for women to return each week, as they would get only part of the materials if they did not show up. The binder materials included readings about the theme that ranged from academic to inspirational, worksheets, and often a creative, arts-based activity. Some of these materials were read and completed during group time, and some were for home use. There was no "homework" per se, but there were many useful materials, such as the budgeting and time management sheets that had practical personal use and were meant to help women organize their money and time to give themselves and their families more options. Simple activities, such as mapping out how each woman spent her time, were quite revealing to each woman individually and also in the context of the group. How one gets to use one's time is often a clear indicator of how much privilege or money one has and whether one has other resources and relationships to lend a hand with childcare and other household tasks; this fact generated a great deal of discussion amongst the group members.

One of the aspects of this group that made it different and more challenging than other groups was that the participants were often in contact outside of group time. Some women were working in the same club. Sometimes that experience brought them together and friendships were created. But sometimes the experience resulted in conflict, as the work culture was competitive and club owners often intentionally pitted women against each other in order to create tension and chaos and maintain control over the dancers. These relationships of friendship and conflict followed the women into group, and as with all complex human beings, there was not always a clear division of camps. Despite divisive feelings, the women could set aside their differences and be empathic and concerned for the well-being of others when they did not show up for group when expected and perhaps had not been seen at work for some time either. It was not uncommon during group check-in for the women who were present to speculate and worry about those who were absent, and it was a time when their hypervigilance became understandably heightened. Many of the dancers had friends or coworkers who had gone missing or wound up dead, or they had at least seen the newspaper stories about women associated with the sex trade going missing or found murdered in their city as well as in other cities.

As a therapist, the ORCC cofacilitator was aware of the presence of post traumatic stress symptoms during these moments but unable to address them directly. Early in the group process Samantha had broached the subject of workplace harassment, and was immediately rebuffed by group members with dismissing comments about how it was "part of the job" and that it was to be expected. Whenever the facilitators brought the subject up again, it was met with similar statements and resistance. One explanation for this pushback is that when you are questioning or are perceived to be threatening an individual's perceived means of survival, if you use the theoretical framework of Maslow's hierarchy of needs, you cannot address higher levels of needs like human flourishing until the more basic needs are secured. The facilitators proceeded very carefully around this topic, and it was really the ultimate reason why they decided to focus on skills for empowerment to create change and choices in the women's lives rather than directly addressing the traumatic impacts of working (and in some cases living) with violent and abusive predators. The Holsopple study (1998) related the experiences of eighteen exotic dancers who all reported being subjected to physical abuse by customers who "spit on women, spray beer, and flick cigarettes at them. Strippers are pelted with ice, coins, trash, condoms, room keys, pornography and golf balls. . . . Women are commonly bitten, licked, slapped, punched and pinched" (p. 8). According to Briere and Scott (2015), ensuring safety, both physical and psychological, is a central principle in trauma intervention, and providing psychological safety is often the most challenging, as "the client must be able to perceive it. . . . [E]ven a safe therapeutic environment may appear unsafe" (p. 105) and when working with clients who have experienced multiple traumas it can take a very long time to establish this sense of safety. It is therefore important for therapists to be able to "determine the client's relative *experience* of therapeutic safety, because many clinical interventions involve activation and processing of upsetting memory material" (p. 105). One of the key topics to enhancing participants' sense of safety in the group was "the power of positive thinking." This topic focused on psychoeducation: the basics of cognitive behavioral therapy and positive psychology, that is, how people construct and perceive the world and themselves and how their thoughts, moods, environment, and behaviors arise. The group discussed the importance of supportive and positive relationships with others, and how positive behaviors that lead to successful changes increase motivation to do more. They also discussed the importance of a positive relationship to self, and the facilitators used a guided visualization that illuminated the resources each woman has within. This visualization began with simply paying attention to the breath, followed by an invitation to each woman to embark on a path leading to a mountain where she was greeted by a personal climbing coach with an important message to help her complete her climb to the summit. At the end of the visualization, the women were invited to remember this important message from their coach and to imagine putting the message in a secure place so they could access it at any time when they needed encouragement in their daily life. This activity was one the women really loved, and subsequent feedback the week following was that they found that this was a positive oasis in their minds where they could go to find some peace and strength. The facilitators were encouraged to repeat guided visualizations on a regular basis, suspecting that these were rare times for these woman to experience some reduction of stress and affect regulation. Giving women the tools to gain some level of psychological homeostasis (and therefore a sense of psychological safety) is essential before some aspects of trauma therapy can be initiated.

The group that was focused on communication skills and conflict resolution was an important follow up to shoring up the sense of safety within the group. As mentioned, many of the dancers had contentious relationships with each other outside of group, as they competed for tips in their mutual places of work. For example, some were strictly "no-contact" dancers and looked down on "contact" dancers (women who performed lap dances or private dances in the VIP areas of the strip clubs for extra money) as morally inferior and compromising efforts to make the strip clubs safer work environments for all dancers. Strip club owners and DJs exacerbated tensions by creating a culture of debt where many women, especially those who relied solely on dancing for survival, became so desperate they could not see the systemic oppression they experienced, only the closest perceived threat to their livelihood (i.e., the other dancers). So within the "container" of assertive communication and conflict resolution it became clearer to women that although it was useful and important to be respectfully assertive with each other (and they could agree to disagree) their anger was better directed at the real source of their poverty, violence, and desperation: the legal structures that were selectively enforced (e.g., health, labor, and safety laws) to the advantage of white, patriarchal capitalism.

Part of providing safety is also ensuring that members are relatively free of danger outside of group. Samantha continued to be a presence in the clubs by doing outreach to dancers, inviting and encouraging them to come to the power program, and also organizing for social change in the community. Because dancers were considered independent contractors, they did not receive a minimum wage or have access to benefits such as employment insurance and parental leave. Stripping is work, and workers are entitled to basic rights and benefits. Samantha formed DERA to organize dancers to pressure for changes to federal labor laws as well as for city enforcement of health and safety laws. In the interim she also arranged for registered nurses to visit clubs regularly to talk about sexually transmitted diseases, provide hepatitis B shots, do HIV testing, and provide needle exchange.

Group members further discussed their personal and professional levels of danger, and assisted in safety planning (for themselves and their children if applicable), using a handout commonly used in domestic violence shelters, a matrix of risk and assets assessment that builds towards a strategy for tapping into the women's individual, relational, and community resources. Towards the end of the group, women were requesting personal counseling and, in two cases, accompaniment to court, which the facilitators took as signs of increased perceived safety with them as counselors and towards the agency as well.

Evaluation and Outcomes

Samantha was responsible for maintaining statistics regarding her outreach work, as well as group attendance and participants' feedback, and created the project's final report (Smythe, 2004). The outreach was directly related to the success of the group, as that is where participant recruitment as well as between-group support happened. Samantha reported that she encountered expected resistance from strip club owners, who were "untrusting and skeptical about outreach workers entering the club" (p. 1), as they suspected Samantha of trying to start a union. In her report, she noted that she had made seven presentations in the fall, resulting in nineteen participants for the fall group. During the winter run of the program, the owner of one of the clubs prohibited Samantha's entrance to the club after the publication of an article about Samantha in a local magazine, and she was not able to re-establish a relationship with this owner to regain access. However, during the six weeks she did have access she was able to make fourteen visits to the club and increased participation to thirty-two dancers in the winter group. As mentioned, the facilitators changed the name from "support group" to "power group" at the suggestion of the fall group participants, and they believed that this helped to increase numbers. Other feedback included a desire for stricter time limits on check-ins and check-outs as well as enforcement of guidelines around not interrupting the speaker who had the floor. The facilitators took this advice. To limit interruptions while someone was speaking, they implemented a token economy; they gave each woman an angel card at the beginning of the group, and any time someone was interrupted they received a card from the interrupter; at the end of the evening the person with the most cards received a prize purchased from the dollar store. It was a light-hearted approach that worked very well.

Samantha's outreach and research with the dancers created other recommendations. She concluded that the community outreach in the local strip clubs was essential and should continue at an increased level, and that there was important work to be done to cultivate trust among the club owners. She had no direct recommendations about how to do that other than to ask the question, "How will an outreach worker entering the strip club benefit the owner and the business?" Samantha noted that there was definitely potential for the group to become an ongoing program at the ORCC, and that required obtaining funding. Participants said they would like the group to be increased from eight to twelve weeks, to have the group held three times per year, and to establish drop-in hours for dancers to access counseling at the ORCC.

Implications for Practice and Policy

There can be a tendency for feminist social workers, advocates, and academics to claim authority on the subject of the sex industry and claim to represent sex workers, including exotic dancers, and their interests. It is important that people not let polarized, abstract discourses blind them to the impact their politics may have on women in the sex industry. Reducing women to victims and club owners to villains does not clarify the complex negotiations around power in strip clubs. This complexity was acknowledged by Samantha in her evaluation of the exotic dancer outreach project when she asked how owners could also benefit from having outreach happen in the clubs. Embracing this complexity and letting go of political agendas and specific outcomes offers the best hope for keeping women's subjectivity and humanity foremost in people's minds when offering social services.

On a structural level, as previously noted, workers deserve basic rights like a living wage, benefits like employment insurance, parental and compassionate leave, and pensions; and laws must be evenly enforced to protect workers' health and safety. Traditional labor unions may not offer the best strategy for organizing dancers; the real solutions are most possible through individual and collective strategies of resistance. As Bruckert (2002) notes, "A worker who can effectively manage social relations, earn acceptance and maintain positive work relations with her colleagues positions herself not only to survive this volatile labor environment but to become an active participant in the creation of collective meanings" (p. 101). Providing a supportive, nonjudgmental environment for each woman to build individual and community capacity and create more strengths and skills to respond to her life as it is in each moment will better equip her to create more options and opportunities for herself and her family now and in the future, however she imagines it.

FURTHER READING

Briere, J., and Scott, C. *Principles of Trauma Therapy: A Guide to Symptoms, Evaluation, and Treatment* (2nd ed.). Thousand Oaks, CA: Sage, 2015.

Bruckert, C. *Taking It Off, Putting It On: Women in the Strip Trade*, 2002, http://ezproxy.lib.ucalgary.ca:2048/login?url=http://site.ebrary.com/lib/ucalgary/Doc?id=10191707.

Holsopple, K. *Strip Club Testimony*. Minneapolis, MN: Freedom and Justice Center for Prostitution Resources, 1998.

Holsopple, K. "Stripclubs According to Strippers." In *Making the Harm Visible: Global Sexual Exploitation of Women and Girls*, edited by D. M. Hughes and C. M. Roche. Kingston, RI: Coalition against Trafficking in Women, 1999.

Smythe, S. *Exotic Dancer Outreach Project*. Ottawa, ON: Ottawa Rape Crisis Centre, 2004.

WOMEN'S INTERCULTURAL RELATIONSHIP ONLINE SUPPORT GROUP
Kristy Stewart

Needs of the Population Served by the Group

This online Facebook group is a psychoeducational asynchronous support group, designed for women in current or past relationships with men from a specific Arab country (country name withheld due to confidentiality). The group arose out of the perceived need for an online venue to connect and share stories with others in a similar situation, due to the challenges of finding understanding and supportive people familiar with this specific culture, country, and circumstances. Many members felt isolated due to geographical, situational, or language barrier issues. Therefore, the members of this group and others have turned to the Internet in order to search for therapeutic information and supportive groups that would be relevant and helpful.

According to Gary and Remolino (2000), online support groups provide several benefits to those seeking solace from an online community. One major benefit is access. Internet access is readily available in many places in the world, and the Internet has become one of the first places people turn when seeking help or looking for information. This group in particular was designed for relatively easy access; the group name and description can be found via a simple Internet search. Many of the group's members reported finding it through this method. Second, the format is amenable to the geographical time zones and circumstances of the members. Members can post, comment, and read other members' responses twenty-four hours a day, which provides a continual flow of activity at all times. This is helpful for women who reside in different countries and time zones, as members are located all over the world, with a variety of personal circumstances and work schedules. With such widely differing availability and time zones, an online twenty-four hour format is a viable arrangement for an online group. A further benefit is that the main group worker holds a master's degree in counseling. Although this is an informal, nontraditional group, the group worker utilizes professional helping skills by guiding the group in helpful directions, monitoring member interactions, and mediating in conflict. The group worker also provides referrals to counseling resources, counseling centers, women's shelters, and social justice organizations. Sometimes members come to the group worker privately for further support, so occasional individual work transpires in addition to the group.

Privacy is another benefit specific to an online group setting. Members are not required to use real names, which helps members feel more at ease in sharing confidential information. This is of critical importance in this support group, as women's partners come from a conservative Arab background. Arab cultures are group oriented and value reputation and saving face; personal matters are kept within the family. The family is the core structure in Arab culture, and preserving the status and honor of the family within society is an important priority (Nydell, 1987). The women in this group are often aware of this dynamic and are careful in disclosing sensitive information. A strict privacy rule of no sharing group information outside of the group is in place to protect confidentiality. The Facebook group privacy settings are set to allow only members to view group content, and potential members must be personally admitted by the group worker.

Finally, despite the group's nontraditional, online format, Yalom's (1995) therapeutic factors common to group counseling are still present in an online context (Gary and Remolino, 2000). Members benefit greatly from the increased feeling of optimism and hope. They realize they are not alone by sharing their story with others and hearing from others in similar situations. Women in the group also give and receive helpful information that helps them transform their situation. They gain confidence and feel valued by altruistically sharing the knowledge they have with others, and develop a sense of belonging and self-worth. The group environment also provides members with interpersonal learning, socializing techniques, and personal growth through interactions with others in different life situations, age groups, socioeconomic status, religious affiliation, and cultural contexts. Finally, members are exposed to different stages of romantic involvement other than their own. For those in new relationships or struggling through relationship conflicts, it helps bring a sense of realism and understanding of relationship stages and how to overcome challenges. Those who have endured and/or left difficult and sometimes traumatic relationships learn from and appreciate the happy and successful relationships of other members. Exposure to successful experiences, particularly for women with difficult relationships, helps to combat stereotyping and generalizations about men from this country. The women also benefit from therapeutic cathartic release by sharing difficult, painful, and frustrating circumstances, and by gaining empathy and compassion from other members. This sharing provides an invaluable awareness to members and assists them in coping with their various struggles (Yalom, 1995).

Group Purpose and Goals

The purpose of this group is to provide educational and emotional support for women who are involved with men from a specific Arab country and are looking for support and more information about the culture and country. Women must be involved with a man from this country in some way, through either a past, current, or potential relationship. The group is specifically for women who are not natives of that country. The group also has specific goals that it strives to fulfill. The goals of the group are to do the following:

- Provide a safe and supportive environment for all members.
- Offer helpful resources such as culture- and relationship-related blogs, documentaries, articles, websites, and books.
- Maintain a positive and encouraging group atmosphere.
- Work proactively through conflicts to promote member retention.
- Uphold good conduct toward one another through respect, encouragement, sensitive and appropriate advice, and avoidance of personal attacks or insults.

Members are made aware of the goals during the screening process and in other places in the group space. The group also has rules that are clearly visible at all times, which serve as a constant reminder of the expected code of conduct and help keep discussions respectful and productive.

Group Membership

The group consists of approximately 200 members from nearly every continent. All are English speakers, although some speak English as a foreign language. All members are women. The women and their partners reside either in the Arab country or abroad. Although all group discussions take place in English, many women speak Arabic fluently or are in the process of learning Arabic. The majority of the women are converts to Islam, but a sizeable minority adheres to other faiths, particularly Christianity. A handful of members are of mixed parentage; one parent is from the Arab country and another parent is from a different country. Women's relationship statuses range from dating, married, separated, widowed, divorced, and remarried. The age ranges from eighteen to sixty years old. The educational level of the group is high; nearly all women have or are working toward college degrees.

Diversity is a common and ever-present theme of the group; women come from many cultural, religious, linguistic, and generational backgrounds and hold a wide variety of perspectives. The main topic of the group—intercultural relationships with men from the Arab country—is in itself founded on diversity; interactions among members center on one or more aspects of diversity. Not only do these women encounter the intercultural challenges that naturally arise in a mixed-culture relationship, they also face many country-specific obstacles, such as the unwieldy and complex marriage permission process for that country, obtaining a visa for permanent residence, family refusal of a foreign wife, women's rights, concerns about the quality of education for children, and legal issues and societal mores that stem from a highly conservative population.

Group Structure

It is important to note that this is an informal support group that aims to provide educational and emotional support. Therapeutic work is not its main goal; members requiring therapeutic intervention are referred to the appropriate counseling resource. Another nontraditional aspect of the group is that it is open-ended with no specific end date. Members regularly trickle in as they come across the group in their online searches or are referred to join by a friend in the group. As a result, members have their own individual start dates. End dates are experienced individually as well, as members occasionally leave for various reasons: lack of time for the group, ending of their relationship, or conflict with another member. Because there is a regular flow of new members coming in and the occasional member leaving, the dynamic and flow of the group shift slightly from time to time. Although this is a large group, not all members are active participants. There are around twenty members in the core group of regular participants; the rest comment occasionally.

The group is run by one main group worker and two assistant group workers who strive to ensure the group runs smoothly and is monitored at all times. All group workers are unpaid volunteers; their motivation stems from their own personal interest and a desire to help others in a similar situation. Although the assistant group workers have no training in counseling or group work, they were selected for their ability to skillfully manage and diffuse conflict, their knowledge of and experience with the culture, and their geographical locations. One resides in the Middle East full time and the other part time, which ensures that the group is monitored overnight. All group workers are Americans and have had personal involvement with men from the Arab country. The two assistant group workers are currently married with children, and the main group worker has both personal and professional experience: she was formerly married to a man from that country, and also teaches university students from that country.

Group Activities

Due to the nature of this group, activities take the form of posts that all members can see and respond to. Posts are nearly always related to some aspect of diversity and are of several different types: introduction posts by new members; calls for help or advice on a specific situation or incident; stories of challenge, celebration, or humor; questions about relationships, culture, legal matters, or religion; and links to helpful resources. Members are free to share contact information in the group or in a private message, which makes it possible to connect with other members living nearby. Many of the women organize get-togethers and meet-ups and form friendships outside of the group. Although these activities are not monitored by group workers, these events help contribute to the overall rapport and closeness the women report feeling in the group, and help to provide connections with people in distant locations.

Use of Diversity over Time

Diversity is present throughout all stages of the group. During the pregroup stage, prior to joining the group space, members are taken through a screening process in which they are apprised of the diverse nature of the group and the need for sensitivity, understanding, and respect for others. New members are also directed to the cultural resources located in the group page, which provide detailed explanations on the culture and religion of the country and advice on navigating intercultural relationships. In the beginning stage, a new member is asked to introduce herself so that other members can have a chance to get to know her, form connections, offer advice and support, and be made aware of the presence of a new member. In this stage, the new member will have the opportunity to get culturally sensitive feedback on her specific situation and to meet other women from diverse backgrounds in a similar situation. After introductions are made, the new member joins ongoing or recent discussions and moves into the working stage of the group with the rest of the members. In this stage, women hear from the experiences of others and offer and receive feedback. Diversity is abundantly present at this time, as women regularly provide explanations of cultural norms and frameworks, and point out cultural or religious aspects to other members who may lack awareness or understanding. All members benefit from their interactions with one another and the mutual aid that is ever present. Due to the culturally diverse nature of the Arab country, even seasoned women in lengthy relationships are not always aware of the other subcultures in that country, and can benefit from the cultural facts shared about different regions of the country. Diversity is a core element of the group, as all members are not natives of their partner's country, so all the discussions revolve around a culture that is different from their own.

Critical Incidents

This support group usually operates in the middle, working stage of the group process but occasionally shifts into the transition stage (Corey and Corey, 2006). This can be triggered by new, outspoken members or by issues brought to the group that emotionally trigger some members. Sometimes an emotionally distraught member brings a difficult issue to the group, which can cause a variety of reactions. Further, a member's situation may include aspects of diversity that not all other members understand. The group flow is generally productive and stable, and group cohesion is strong, but occasionally intense emotions, disagreement, and even conflict can arise.

One noteworthy diversity-related incident centered on one member's cultural adjustment over a period of several months. This woman, Sarah, was happily married in the United States with two children, but was now faced with her husband's decision to move his family to his home country to help care for his aging parents. Because neither Sarah nor her children had been to the country before, she had many questions for the group about their experiences living in that country. Further, just prior to the move, a crisis arose, as her visa had mistakenly been canceled. Several members offered their experiences and suggestions, which ultimately led to resolution of the situation. When the time came for the move, the family found themselves in a foreign country in the middle of the scorching hot, desert summer. Due to the lack of summer activities for children, restricted freedom of movement for women, and the language barrier, Sarah and her children were resigned to stay inside the majority of the time. This transition period was an intensely difficult time for Sarah and her children. Sarah reported falling into a deep depression that was beginning to affect her marriage. She was having trouble fitting in with her in-laws, as there was a language and cultural barrier. She had also been asked to remain fully covered in the house at all times due to the presence of male family members. Although a Muslim who normally wore a head scarf outside of the house, she was unaccustomed to being fully covered at all times inside the house. The clothing her in-laws gave her to wear in the house was too large and at one point caused her to fall down the stairs and injure herself. Her children were affected as well and were having difficulty fitting in with their relatives and making friends. Several of the members reached out to Sarah, giving her advice about activities in her area, sharing their own frustrations with lack of mobility and difficulty adjusting, discussing the conservative nature of her in-laws and ways to navigate their expectations, and offering support and encouragement. A significant turning point occurred when one member realized she lived near Sarah and began to arrange get-togethers so that Sarah and her children could get out of the house and experience a more relaxed environment. Other members in the area began reaching out and helping her get out to explore the area and feel more connected. Although Sarah still struggled with depression, the occasional outings helped keep her sanity and prevented her from giving up and returning to her home country.

After school started, new problems emerged as her non-Arabic-speaking children were thrown into a foreign, unfamiliar environment. Although hesitant and shy at first, the youngest child began to warm up and started to pick up the language and make friends. The oldest child encountered more difficulty; normally outgoing and quick to make friends, he became withdrawn and quiet, and cried frequently at school and home. Sarah reported that he often begged to go back "home" to the United States, and they had difficulty getting him to wake up for school in the mornings. After members in the area were alerted to his situation, a concerted effort was made to help him get in a school that was more welcoming and had a program for non-Arabic speakers. The semester was already under way, but members with personal connections to the school were able to get her son enrolled. Sarah was overwhelmed by the support and grateful for their help, and came back later to report that her son was doing better: he was starting to pick up the language and was no longer crying or asking to go back to the United States. Through the intervention of the group, a distraught member whose family was in crisis was able to find a path through difficulty and move into a better situation and healthier emotional state.

Another diversity-related incident involving cultural and religious differences occurred when a young member encountered difficulty with her fiancé's family. Although this particular situation was met with support, encouragement, and advice, it also sparked some debate and hurt feelings due to conflicting religious views. This member, Nikki, and her fiancé were young college students who had recently been religiously married with family approval. It is a common custom for couples in this Arab country to contract a religious marriage during the engagement period in order to spend time together without violating Islamic religious principles. However, a crisis had emerged when her fiancé discussed marriage plans with his family. His father reportedly thought his son was not serious about marrying a foreign wife. Thus, the father gave his permission in jest; he was in fact adamantly against the marriage. Several emotionally charged disputes took place between the fiancé and his family. Threats were made of disowning him, and blame was placed on him for the health problems of the parents. This greatly upset Nikki, as she could not understand why his father gave his permission in jest, and why she was so negatively looked down upon. The group rushed to provide support and empathy, and many shared their own similar stories of backlash from their husbands' families. Others helped to explain that this type of reaction is not uncommon in this culture, and the best approach is to be patient and wait for the family to settle down. Nikki was concerned by her fiancé being at odds with his family and urged him to continue to contact them in order to resolve the problem. However, this caused the conflict to worsen, and more disparaging remarks were made about Nikki's character, value, and perceived sexual immorality. At this point, the main group worker intervened and suggested that Nikki let her fiancé approach his family in the way he believed was best, and refrain from asking about the details of discussions in order to avoid affecting her ability to build relationships with them in the future. Other members followed up with advice to allow the family the time to work through their intense emotions, which seemed to help Nikki calm down and see the situation more clearly.

By this time some disagreement had begun to arise over the nature of Nikki's marriage. Different types of marriages exist in all sects of Islam, and Nikki's specific type of marriage is practiced solely by Shia Muslims. Shia Muslims are a minority in this Arab country and are often subjected to negative stereotypes, misunderstandings, and societal and governmental discrimination (see www.human rightswatch.org for more information on discrimination against Shia Muslims in the Middle East); sometimes these attitudes are transferred to the foreign wives. In this instance, a few members expressed doubt over the legitimacy of her marriage and argued that it was impermissible in Islam and that to engage in it was committing premarital sex. The main group worker stepped in to remind members of the group diversity and inclusion policy and the fact that all sects of Islam, religions, and beliefs were welcome and supported in this group. Although this immediately diffused the conflict, one member instead began to privately message Nikki, outside of the group workers' view. Nikki later reported the exchange but indicated that they had resolved the conflict.

Evaluation and Outcomes

Overall, the online support group has provided numerous benefits to members. There have been some incidents of conflict, but the group was able to work through them, with the assistance and occasional intervention of group workers. However, the online venue has some limitations and obstacles (Gary and Remolino, 2000), which should be explored by further analysis and research. One concern is the risk of a privacy breach. Members may go against the privacy rule and share information with others outside of the group, or someone's account could be hacked or accidentally left open. Occasionally, some women have partners who check their Facebook accounts, and other people could access the group by creating a fake account and providing false information during the screening process. Another limitation is the lack of nonverbal language and tone of voice (Galinsky et al., 1996). An online setting is usually restricted to communication through text only, and is devoid of any nonverbal or tonal context. As a result, it is common for misunderstandings to arise and conflict to erupt. Emoticons are helpful in conveying emotion, but not everyone uses them in the same way or with the same frequency. Also, the use of silence as a communication tool is less effective: without any context, a person may feel ignored or dismissed. Immediacy is another obstacle common to online groups. Because people join discussions at varying times, a member in a critical situation does not always receive immediate responses. Further, group workers might not notice a heated discussion occurring until after the most critical point has already passed and preventable damage has occurred.

Finally, dual/unethical relationships between group workers and members can be a concern in an online context such as Facebook. People who are Facebook friends can like and comment on each other's personal pages and form a personal relationship both online and in regular life. However, this can create a conflict of interest if a dispute within the group involves the friend, which can cause hurt feelings, misunderstanding, and even damage to the friendship. The group worker may also hesitate to intervene in a conflict involving a friend and may not utilize the appropriate intervention strategy.

Online groups are becoming increasingly popular due to ever-advancing technology and ease of Internet access in many places in the world. Such groups provide an instant way to connect with people in similar situations from diverse backgrounds who are unlikely to cross paths in regular life. Online groups are an excellent way to find solace and comfort in knowing that one is not alone, and members can benefit from the support, advice, and friendships found within groups. Finally, due to its ease of access, capacity for anonymity, and free cost, an online group can alleviate some of the fear, distrust, and other common concerns of a traditional therapeutic setting and provide an outlet for those who would otherwise not seek out counseling (Gary and Remolino, 2000). Further considerations should be made for the drawbacks of online groups, but its benefits are many, and it is a therapeutic modality that is likely to continue to grow and gain popularity in the future.

FURTHER READING

Corey, M., and Corey, G. "Transition Stage of a Group." In *Groups: Process and Practice* (7th ed.). Belmont, CA: Brooks/Cole, 2006.

Galinsky, M., Schopler, J., and Abell, M. "Connecting Group Members through Telephone and Computer Groups." *Social Work with Groups* 19, no. 3/4 (1996): 21–39.

Gary, J. M., and Remolino, L. *Online Support Groups: Nuts and Bolts, Benefits, Limitations and Future Directions*. Greensboro, NC: ERIC Counseling and Student Services Clearinghouse, 2000.

Nydell, M. *Understanding Arabs: A Guide for Westerners*, Yarmouth, ME: Intercultural Press, 1987.

CHAPTER 17

AN ORGANIZATIONAL GROUP

THE KAHKIYAW PROGRAM:
A UNIQUE APPROACH TO CHILD INTERVENTION SERVICES
Julie Mann-Johnson

The views and opinions expressed in this case study are strictly those of the author and do not necessarily reflect those of the government of Alberta.

Kahkiyaw ayisiyinowak ka wahkoot, a Cree phrase meaning "all people, especially traditional peoples, are related," identifies the inclusive and collaborative perspective of the Kahkiyaw program's unique approach to child intervention services (Diebel & Whiskeyjack, 2012). The Kahkiyaw program started in April 2012 to provide services to Aboriginal children, youth, and families within the central neighborhood in Edmonton, Alberta, Canada. Aboriginal children and youth are overrepresented in the child intervention system. In September 2014, 69 percent of children living in the care of the director of the Child, Youth, and Family Enhancement Act in Alberta were of Aboriginal descent (Human Services, 2014). Yet, only 6.2 percent of Alberta's population identifies themselves as Aboriginal (Government of Canada, 2011). The disproportionate number of children in care suggests Aboriginal families experience child welfare services differently than non-Aboriginal families in the province of Alberta.

There is a long history of trauma within government services for Aboriginal families. This started with the forcible removal of children aged five to fifteen from their families to the residential schools in the 1870s. At the height of their operations in the 1940s, approximately 8,900 children attended these residential schools. John Milloy describes these children as being placed in residential schools "with a goal of assimilating them under the guise of Christian education objectives" (cited in Blackstock, 2011, p. 188). Assimilation practices within these institutions attempted to isolate Aboriginal children from their culture, language, and communities. Many of these institutions were fraught with physical, emotional, sexual, and spiritual abuse. High rates of death due to preventable causes, such as disease and negligence, were also common in these facilities. Future generations were also affected, as the children placed in residential schools did not encounter "healthy parental role models and, as adults, frequently had diminished capacity to care for their own children" (Trocme et al., 2004, p. 578).

The Aboriginal community continues to feel these effects, as the last of these schools was closed as recently as 1996, even though the federal government started to close these institutions in the 1950s. Even so, the legacy of Aboriginal children and youth being removed from their families and communities continued into the 1960s with the "sixties scoop." This refers to the high numbers of Aboriginal children who were apprehended and placed with non-Aboriginal families who, in most cases, eventually adopted them. This practice led to another generation of First Nation children who were not raised with their families or communities and thus became further colonized.

The child intervention system has started to recognize how to meet the needs of the Aboriginal population more inclusively. Efforts have been under way to empower and engage the Aboriginal community in child intervention service delivery as a means to ensure culturally appropriate and relevant services are provided.

Organization and Community Context

Kahkiyaw operates under the provincial Outcomes Based Service Delivery (OBSD) initiative. OBSD started as a practice initiative for child intervention in Alberta in 2008 and represents a new relationship between government, agencies, children, and families. OBSD sites around the province have piloted or phased in this approach in different ways. The province has allowed for flexibility in the implementation to recognize uniqueness and diversity in each community. At implementation, Kahkiyaw focused its service delivery towards Aboriginal children, youth, and families in the central area of Edmonton, Alberta.

The initiative includes three main components. These are: flexibility in service delivery, focus on data about the outcomes of services provided, and collaborative practice. The component of collaborative practice has been described by child intervention and agency staff as the component with the greatest impact.

Group Purpose and Goals

Alberta's child intervention system has five identified outcomes that drive all OBSD initiatives, including Kahkiyaw. These include:

1. Vulnerable children have the support they need to live successfully in their communities.

2. Children in temporary care are quickly reunited with their families.
3. Children in permanent care are quickly placed in permanency homes.
4. Youth make successful transitions to adulthood.
5. Aboriginal children live in culturally appropriate homes in which their unique cultural identities are respected and fostered. (Alberta Human Services, 2016)

Kahkiyaw identifies the ultimate goal as individual and collective family wellness that results when the four national outcome matrix domains (safety, well-being, permanence, and family and community supports) and the four medicine wheel tenets (know our truth, respect our truth, feel our truth, and see our truth) are fulfilled and in balance (Diebel & Whiskeyjack, 2012). This perspective creates an integrated and inclusive approach to the purpose and goals for the group.

Group Membership

Kahkiyaw represents a tripartite partnership among (1) Edmonton and Area Child and Family Services (specifically the central neighborhood center), (2) Bent Arrow Traditional Healing Society (Bent Arrow), and (3) Boyle Street Community Services.

Beyond these three partners, however, there are many other partnerships and stakeholders that have contributed to the success of this inclusive approach to child intervention. Partnerships with other community agencies and professional service providers play a role in service delivery. For example, a recent policy change that shifted the focus of service delivery beyond Aboriginal-only consumers led the partners to create further links with services such as the Mennonite Centre for Newcomers and Multi-Cultural Health Brokers.

In this program, children, youth, and families become team members in service delivery, and decision making is shared. The program operates by including many partners in this shared decision making: families, natural supports, professionals, and members of the official partnership. It is this process of "widening the circle" that makes this group inclusive.

Group Structure

Shared practice and shared decision making are integral parts of OBSD, and for Kahkiyaw shared responsibility is a stated value. "Kahkiyaw takes these relationships to the next level in a unique tripartite partnership that seeks to reduce the number of Aboriginal children and youth in care in Alberta. All decision making is shared by the three parties" (Kahkiyaw, 2014).

Kahkiyaw developed a comprehensive model that acknowledged that good work was occurring by all members of the tripartite partnership prior to this initiative but that it was happening in a "piecemeal manner." By bringing these three agencies together, their good work and approaches became more efficient and effective, began to fill existing gaps in service delivery, and changed the nature of service delivery altogether (Kahkiyaw, 2014).

Bent Arrow and Boyle Street are members of Align Association of Community Services (Align). Align functions to strengthen member agencies and promote attitudes, practices, and conditions that contribute to quality services for vulnerable children and families. Through these functions, Align has become a significant stakeholder for OBSD initiatives throughout Alberta and has been a supporter of Kahkiyaw. Early in the partnership, a memorandum of understanding (MOU) was created between Bent Arrow and Boyle Street to provide clarity within the agency partnership. The MOU has been revisited regularly with the support of Align.

Group Activities

At implementation in 2012, new child intervention files were referred to Kahkiyaw after an assessment determined that there was a need for child intervention. This "net-new" approach meant that existing open files would continue receiving traditional, non-OBSD child intervention services. For the new files referred to Kahkiyaw, family wellness services were provided through agency staff. These services included cultural connection, lodge keeping, family wellness circles, family wellness plans, family success plans, strengths-based family assessments, referrals to community resources, advocacy, mediation, cultural services, kin and significant other searches, and life skills (Kahkiyaw, 2014). This model continues to guide Kahkiyaw services. Services are provided to the family until it is determined by the team that they are no longer required. In this situation, the team includes children, youth, families, agency staff, and a caseworker.

In addition to direct service delivery, agency and Child and Family Services staff involved in Kahkiyaw meet on a regular basis to discuss the case. Leadership (supervisors and managers from both Child and Family Services and the agencies) met six times per week at the outset of the project. They continue to meet regularly, including a weekly breakfast meeting. In addition, caseworkers and agency delivery staff, known as family wellness workers, meet regularly to discuss case events, progress, and planning.

A significant process with OBSD and Kahkiyaw is the inclusion of family in case planning. Shared decision making and case planning include the family and, at Kahkiyaw, this process is often facilitated through family wellness circles where all parties involved with the case plan are present. This circle process facilitated by the agency staff ensures all participants have an equal voice in the process.

The Kahkiyaw model states:

> Under Kahkiyaw, children, youth, and families requiring support and empowerment are not passive recipients of services. Instead, they are active members of a family wellness team consisting of their community—kin, elders, role models, neighbors, schools, professionals, and community agencies. The team uses a continuum of innovative Western and traditional cultural approaches in efforts to achieve the individual, family, and community balance needed for family reunification and/or safe, healthy permanent care. These approaches are called family wellness services. (Kahkiyaw, 2014)

Bent Arrow describes culture playing a very large role in their structure and in their practice. Their belief is that "practice is culture" and this approach has permeated through the partnership. Culture and culturally connected services are particularly important and central to the delivery of services in Kahkiyaw (Whiskeyjack, C., personal communication, 2014).

How the Group Worked with Diversity over Time

In many ways, work began fifteen years ago to start building this collaborative partnership and approach to service delivery. In the summer of 1998, one small unit of caseworkers from Child and Family Services in Edmonton started a collaborative pilot project with support workers from Bent Arrow. The intent was to serve three difficult-to-serve Aboriginal families through a partnership with agency support staff. Agency staff would have ongoing face-to-face contact with the families, while there was weekly contact between the caseworkers and agency staff. The anecdotal impacts from this new approach were that families were less resistant, further empowered, and able to address necessary issues after child and family services were one step removed from service delivery.

In this process, close relationships between agency staff and caseworkers were being built. Caseworkers were learning valuable lessons about Aboriginal culture, ways of helping, and the Aboriginal community. Relationships were built by spending time with agency staff at the agency office, soup and bannock days, and staff retreats. Caseworkers started to spend time with agency staff at the agency, as opposed to meeting in government offices. This was a significant shift.

By 2004, this relationship had continued to develop, and a unit of caseworkers was colocated at the Bent Arrow agency. Initially this was a unit of caseworkers delivering services to voluntary staff through a family enhancement approach and within the geographical area surrounding the Bent Arrow agency. Consumers reported feeling more comfortable in going to see their worker at the agency compared to a government office.

However, over time colocating alone was not nurturing the relationship component necessary to a true and inclusive partnership in delivery services. The caseworkers were, in effect, leasing office space, and the collaborative manner of delivering services was missed (C. Whiskeyjack, personal communication, 2014). At the same time, another colocation endeavor was occurring with another unit of caseworkers and Boyle Street Community Services. Although colocation does not necessarily represent collaborative practice, it was an important step towards inclusive service delivery and formed partnerships that eventually led to Kahkiyaw.

The development of Kahkiyaw went beyond colocating and renewed a focus on the importance of relationship within this group. The beginning of the formal partnership was initiated by attending a traditional sweat together and making offerings for the partnership and guidance (Diebel & Whiskeyjack, 2012). The executive director of Bent Arrow stresses the importance of making time to build and nurture these relationships, and all leaders involved in the partnership support and honor this as being important. Staff and group members make an effort to connect with each other on a human level, including cooking together, eating together, and just being together. Relationship building has been and continues to be a crucial component of the partnership and the ability to work inclusively.

This new opportunity for shared decision making in the child intervention system involved a steep learning curve for all partners in the beginning. It was important to "slow down" and ensure decisions were made with everyone at the table, and that everyone at the table had a shared understanding (C. Whiskeyjack, personal communication, 2014). Many difficult and uncomfortable conversations where partners were challenged on practice or decisions were held. But those involved report a sense of growth and enhanced practice. Partners at the table gained opportunities for reflective and challenging practice, and definite professional growth arose out of this challenge.

Complicating the partnership is the issue of delegation. Caseworkers with child and family services are delegated under the Child, Youth, and Family Enhancement Act of Alberta by the director. Ultimately, the director is responsible for the caseworker, case planning, and other services provided to children. Duties and powers are delegated to caseworkers. This means caseworkers are primarily responsible for the active role of child intervention. This creates a number of formal lines of accountability, responsibility, and authority. In order to honor the inclusive process of shared decision making, caseworkers have had to keep their delegation in their back pockets. Although delegation is still exercised, it can be done in a manner that is not overbearing. Relationship and trust building has played a key role in their ability to do so. This came through many meetings and conversations where all perspectives were opened up and laid out on the table. Seeing successful outcomes from new and different processes was also beneficial for all members at the table. Thus it has allowed for a willingness to trust this new process.

There have been various situations where disagreement has been complex and consensus cannot be reached. Partners may disagree with a direction in a case, an approach taken with a family, or the manner in which services are provided. Strong relationships continue to be the basis of consensus building, but conflict resolution is required at times. Attempts are made to resolve the conflict through discussion at the level that it occurred initially. As an example, if a conflict arises between front line workers, attempts to resolve it at that level are made. If that is not possible, then an escalation to supervisors and then corresponding managers, if required, occurs to seek resolution.

The Kahkiyaw model and principles of practice identified in the partnerships and the MOU also serve as a basis and grounding element for conflict. Any conflict is discussed within the context of the principles. For example, if there was a conflict regarding the level of involvement of a family in decision making, the team would refer to the model for direction. In this case the model states, "Children, youth, and families requiring support and empowerment are not passive recipients of services. Instead, they are active members of a Family Wellness Team." Or additionally, the principles of the child intervention practice framework recognize the rights of parents to share in decision making (Alberta Human Services, 2014). These agreed upon principles of practice help create clarity in times of conflict.

Evaluation and Outcomes

Ongoing evaluation occurs in Kahkiyaw formally and informally. Staff and leadership identify "learning as we go" and are regularly assessing informally what is working well and what needs shifting.

More formally, the tracking of data to measure outcomes is one of the three areas of focus in Outcomes Based Services Delivery (OBSD). For Kahkiyaw, data are tracked through electronic information systems by both government and agencies. These data measure the four domains of the national outcomes measures, which are: (1) family and community support, (2) permanence, (3) child development and well-being, and (4) safety. Additional tools and documents, such as healing plans, critical incident reports, family assessment forms, and ages and stages assessments, also inform the measures.

Further to these OBSD standards and measures, Kahkiyaw measures consumer engagement through face to face interviews, consumer evaluations following intervention, and statistics on placement needs, types, breakdowns, school moves, and so on.

Kahkiyaw has been working on a research partnership with the University of Calgary since its inception. This project, known as the knowing-doing project, asks the question: "How do service users and service providers perceive the benefits of involvement working with the Kahkiyaw project?" This research is not yet completed; however, it is anticipated that the findings will be able to further inform the development of this inclusive, shared practice approach.

Implications for Practice and Policy

Alberta's child intervention system has learned a lot from the Kahkiyaw OBSD initiative. More OBSD initiatives are starting up throughout the province of Alberta with the Edmonton region going all in with the OBSD model of practice and partnership. Shared practice and decision making, with agency partners and families as meaningful participants, are now recognized as best practices within child intervention in Alberta (Maygard, 2013).

This grassroots practice shift has created a need for policy, training, hiring, and continuous improvement processes within government to reflect concepts of shared and inclusive practice. Decisions and case plans are no longer made or created in isolation, and this new practice must be supported organizationally. Work is under way for this to be realized.

This work is primarily supported through the creation of a provincial child intervention practice framework with a set of identified guiding principles for added clarity for partners working together to provide child intervention services. Collaboration is one of the six guiding principles and is further described in the following manner:

> We are child-focused and family-centered. We collaborate with families, community agencies, and other stakeholders in building positive, respectful partnerships across integrated multidisciplinary teams and providing individualized, flexible and timely services to support these efforts. (Alberta Human Services, 2014).

The Kahkiyaw partnership has shown this principle in practice, and has been an example of truly inclusive practice and service delivery within child intervention.

FURTHER READING

Alberta Human Services. *Child Intervention Practice Framework*, 2014, http://humanservices.alberta.ca/abuse-bullying/17242.html.

Alberta Human Services. *What Is Outcomes Based Service Delivery?* 2016, http://humanservices.alberta.ca/abuse-bullying/17242.html.

Blackstock, C. "The Canadian Human Rights Tribunal on First Nations Child Welfare: Why If Canada Wins, Equality and Justice Lose." *Children and Youth Services Review* 33, no. 1 (2011): 187–194.

Diebel, C., and Whiskeyjack, C. "Kahkiyaw Ayisiyinowak Ka Wahkohot: The First Aboriginal OBSD Phase-in Site." *Outcome Based Service Delivery (OBSD) Update*, 6 (2012), http://www.aascf.com/aascf-initiatives/obsd-newsletter?view=docman.

Government of Canada. *National Household Survey (NHS): Aboriginal People in Canada: First Nations, Métis and Inuit,* 2011, http://www.12statcan.gc.ca.nhs-enm/2011/as.sa.

Human Services. *Child Intervention Information and Statistics Summary*, 2014, http://humanservices.alberta.ca/documents/child-intervention-info-stats-summary-2014-15-q2.pdf.

Kahkiyaw. *An Outcomes-based Service Delivery Model*, 2014, http://bentarrow.ca/wp-content/uploads/2012/04/Kahkiyaw-Two-Pager-08-Jun-2012.pdf.

Maygard, S. "The Evolving Nature of OBSD." *OBSD Joint Newsletter* 1, no. 1 (2013), http://www.aascf.com/aascf-initiatives/obsd-newsletter?view=docman.

IMAGINING A WORLD OF INCLUSIVE PRACTICE

LEARNING OBJECTIVES

At the end of this chapter you will be able to:
- **Appraise inclusive practice as a group work approach.**
- **Recognize and describe how inclusive group work practice can affect society.**
- **Identify ways in which the inclusive approach can empower group members.**

In a globalized world, North American society now encompasses many different people—people whose unique perspectives, worldviews, and life experiences contribute to the richness of society. Social workers now more than ever recognize the importance of the diversity present in the relationships and the lives of those with whom they work. This is evident by the attention they give to practices and approaches that embrace diversity and the way that they recognize its impact on the lives of the people they serve. Indeed, diversity is omnipresent and provides the potential to enrich the world. Unfortunately, throughout history, diversity has not been recognized this way. For many years, diversity has been something that is tolerated but not necessarily accepted or embraced. Differences have been used as a way to alienate, disenfranchise, and oppress others who did not fit into dominant societal norms. If you watch the news, there are daily, numerous examples of how people who are different are discriminated against merely because they are not the same. It is social workers' ethical responsibility and imperative to promote a just society. Imagine a world where being unique was truly embraced, a world where others welcomed you for who you were as an individual and not based on societal "acceptable" characteristics, traits, or qualifications. Picture a world that embraces diversity and its contributions to a rich and progressive society. Given current social reality, a world such as this sounds like a dream. However, this dream can become a reality through a conscious and concerted effort.

Yalom and Leszcz (2005) introduced the notion that groups are a social micro-cosm of the society in which they are embedded. That is, group members and the interactions in group can reflect the strengths and deficiencies present in the larger society. Well, what if the change in group was reflective of the change that could occur in society—a glimpse of the conditions needed to make effective change toward a more inclusive world?

All professional social work group experiences attempt to provide the group's members with opportunities to have a productive interpersonal journey. The hope and expectation is that using the in-group experience, members will grow and develop and further contribute to the communities in which they live. This book provides the tools for social workers, working with groups, to redefine how soci-ety approaches diversity from something that is exclusionary to something that is a strength and inclusive. By including this approach in their group work practice, social workers can empower their group members, one group at a time, to do the same and effect change in their communities.

This book has offered a new way of looking at diversity. In keeping with the principles of inclusive practice, the book has moved far beyond what is comfort-able discourse to address diversity directly and pragmatically. It has also moved beyond the prevailing norms in social work literature, which largely focus on rais-ing awareness about various diverse populations, to offer a new conceptualization of diversity and strategies that are aimed at harnessing the benefits that arise with diversity in groups. In this way, the book offers a fundamental turn in the litera-ture and discourse relating to diversity.

One of the book's most important contributions is founded in its redefinition of diversity as a relational concept, in that it has shifted the locus of diversity from that of an attribute or characteristic possessed by an often marginalized other, to a state that exists in relationships between people. The book's focus moves away from the traditional discourse relating to how to work with those who are differ-ent or diverse to how to promote productive relationships between group members.

By embracing this approach and integrating inclusive group work practice, a worker and group members can begin to acknowledge, respect, and embrace the diversity that is present in the group and hopefully in any social situation. Thus, group members can recognize that individual identity is complex and, in order for all members to be treated equally, their individuality must be accepted and respected. Through an inclusive approach, the worker can encourage mutual respect and foster a sense of belonging by recognizing that all members have com-mon needs, but how these needs are met is unique to the individual. By promot-ing and accepting individuality, this approach engages all members to challenge issues of discrimination and inequity, particularly those that arise due to differences among individuals. If group members can inculcate this understanding and respect for diversity in their daily lives, as they do other concepts learned in group, group members will become catalysts for change for an inclusive society.

Beyond shifting the conceptualization of diversity, this book has also offered a new understanding of the role that diversity plays in bringing about change. The book's basic proposition is that change is dependent upon the presence of diversity. Although it may seem self-evident, it's important to stress that it is only through arousal of diverse ideas and behaviors that change can occur. For this reason, the book challenges the prevailing overemphasis on homogeneity as the most important factor in the development of effective social work groups. Regardless of whether one is speaking of intervention groups, where a diversity of strategies gives rise to new, more effective social functioning, or task groups, where a diversity of knowledge and skills is vital for the successful completion of assigned tasks, diversity is an essential resource that brings about change. Furthermore, when one closely examines most models of group development, it is often the infusion of diversity that heralds the shifting from one phase of development to another.

The hope is that readers of this book will take away an understanding of how to work with this complex topic in groups. In inclusive practice, diversity plays a vital role in helping the group process achieve its purpose. This is aided by what are often described as effective group work practice principles and skills. This book has provided conceptual and practice-ready tools for working with a variety of people and their concerns. To this end, the book incorporates the contemporary work of practitioners to highlight how group workers have served people. The authors identify the methods that are useful when working with diverse populations. All identify the importance of the group worker nurturing the group through its difficulties, challenges, and growth.

The book has addressed numerous topics and questions related to inclusive group work practice. It has offered a social work definition of group work—a definition that appreciates the power of group to bring about change. It has also introduced readers to the various types and the vast array of applications of group work as well as to the ethics and value base of social work with groups. Readers will have been introduced to a number of specialized skills used in task and intervention groups and will take away some new tools to assess group development and functioning.

A central concept for practice is empowerment through mutual aid. Group members work together to understand their concerns and move to resolve them through the group's interdependence. As group members learn to live their individual lives and yet utilize support offered within the group, it is hoped that they will be able to apply the newly formed interpersonal skills outside of the group.

Diversity in group work will present challenges to the group worker. Attention must be provided to the needs of populations, group processes, and relationships in groups. For example, persons from different cultural groups may enter a group not expecting to openly share intimate details of their lives. All interventions must be smartly and specifically designed for the group. The group's activities must meet the needs of the members, not simply satisfy the group worker's needs to have a successful group. Research of group practice needs to elaborate more than simple measures of outcomes. It is also important to research the group processes to uncover what happens in groups when dealing with diversity and inclusiveness.

There is a very real risk that members will become uncomfortable with the varieties of differences experienced in a group, and a group worker will have to be vigilant to a member's rejection or withdrawal due to discomfort. A general objective is to encourage all group members to be open and accepting of their fellow human beings.

The group worker must guard against marginalization of any member in the group by exhibiting hope and openness when beginning group discussions on issues of individuality, distinctiveness, and social oppression. The group worker must relate to members of dissimilar groups with a considerate and equal approach. When challenging oppressive attitudes and beliefs in the group, the group worker will need to remind group members that groups can be most effective when diverse points of view are included in problem-solving efforts.

It is important for the group worker to acknowledge that the likenesses and divergence evident in group serve to augment relationships among the individual group members. The group worker must recognize that there will be differentness among members of the group and that no one can be allowed to chastise or castigate others because of this differentness. In this way, group members will appreciate that they can express their distinctive and genuine selves.

Individual members' personal and sociocultural diversity can provide significant learning for the entire group. The hope is that by finding out about one another, group members will be able to transfer this group learning to their everyday lives. In doing this, they share and spread new understandings by interacting with significant others outside of the group. Overall, the objectives of group work are to empower group members to seek their individual self-sufficiency and at the same time recognize their ultimate reliance on the relationships with others to accomplish tasks and goals.

THE GROUP WORKER'S RESPONSIBILITY

Group workers are encouraged to examine their own biases, attitudes, and beliefs about persons who are different from themselves. This means that they develop and show increasing awareness and sensitivity to the great variety of differences found in practice. These include visible difference, such as racial distinctness, and not-readily-seen differences, such as sexual orientations or life experiences.

An individual group worker's awareness of his or her cultural background and identity will facilitate the work to be done. Becoming aware of one's acculturation and socialization process leads a group worker to an understanding of how this powerful influence mediates social responses with others. The schema of one's own pathway in social living provides a blueprint for uncovering other's schemas, and this can be useful in group.

Group workers affirm members' helping and healing practices as found in their communities, such as those of indigenous people. Group workers must become aware of barriers in communities and societal institutions that prevent full participation of all community members. This includes discriminatory practices in society and within the community.

A skilled group worker utilizes both verbal and nonverbal channels of human communication. The unearthing of interpersonal differences provides opportunities for learning in a group. At the same time, group workers must identify any judgmental points of view when these surface in a group at either the verbal or nonverbal levels. Yalom identified the potential of such data in a group. "I never cease to be awed by the rich, subterranean load of data that exists in every group and in every meeting. Beneath each sentiment expressed, there are layers of invisible, unvoiced ones" (Yalom, 1985, p. 154). The group worker must identify and ask for clarification of veiled or indirect messages within the group so that all members might feel some level of safety. Safety is a necessary ingredient for group maintenance and mutual aid to develop. The exploration of both positive and negative potential is necessary when working with diversity in groups.

Group workers can prepare themselves to deliver more empathic responses. The key is to recognize group members' different feelings and their difficulties in expressing emotions. The group worker needs to accept the members' worldviews and the experiences that helped to shape those views. The group worker can also improve understandings of the members' issues by acquiring more sophisticated knowledge of the problems and concerns faced by group members.

At the core, group workers need to self-examine their own sociocultural backgrounds in order to begin to develop cultural competencies. These competencies include awareness of their own personal assumptions and responses to those who present differently from their ethnocultural familiarity.

Contemporary groups are planned for a wide variety of members' needs related to interpersonal change and personal growth. A flexible plan for the group experience can provide a potential for that change to occur and for members to develop a sense of hope and well-being. It is important for group workers to work with the group members' statements of what is needed. The group worker's ideology and preferred theory for practice need to be examined in order to provide inclusive practice. Group workers can expect to make many midcourse corrections as they attempt to provide services in inclusive group practice. They may be expected to deal with anticipated and unexpected issues raised in the group. A group worker may have to make a few diversions or alternate plans to better meet the needs of a group.

AN INVITATION FOR CRITICAL REFLECTION AND EXPRESSION OF DIVERSE PERSPECTIVES

This book offers guiding principles and pathways for improving inclusive group work practice. Critical self-reflection and curiosity are essential for inclusive practice. Inclusive practice also eschews the making of assumptions about others and the correctness of one's own worldview. The authors believe that group workers will have to stretch and adapt their practice to accommodate the emerging needs of people in this evolving and diverse society. In sum, it is the authors' hope that readers will take from this book a new appreciation of the value of diversity and how to harness it in service of group goals.

It is regrettable that a concept such as diversity that has been the focus of so much commentary in group work has received such modest attention in terms of research. Although the authors continue to conduct research into harnessing the potential of diversity in groups, they invite other researchers to examine diversity from different perspectives and in various situations. They believe that additional research relating to group processes that uncovers what happens in groups when dealing with diversity and inclusiveness is needed. In this way, diversity will continue to promote deeper learning and understanding.

A World of Inclusive Practice

Some problems presented by group members may not be solved in the group. Groups are a way that a community can offer support to its members who are disenfranchised, removed, or disengaged. Empowering group members may be only one element needed to start a process of improving their situations. In keeping with the legacy of the settlement house movement, groups can identify and respond to societal issues that may not otherwise receive much press coverage. Sometimes it is necessary to engage in micro and macro interventions. Change may be needed outside of the group experience. Single intervention strategies may not be effective without calling attention to the gravity of a situation faced by others. By paying attention to group members' needs as well as community and organizational elements, the group will attend to the profession's core value of social justice.

Many of the principles of inclusive group work practice offer a way forward in helping not only group workers but human service practitioners working in nearly all practice settings. When one thinks about diversity as a relational concept, one realizes that it is present in all human relationships. In this way, practitioners working with individuals, families, organizations, and communities may benefit from these principles. Moreover, just as a family may be viewed as a group, group work is also a critical facet of effective practice with organizations and communities.

In a world of increasing strife over religious, cultural, and racial diversity, it is to be hoped that these principles and the ensuing discourse relating to inclusive practice will support progress for humankind to realize the potential benefits offered by diversity.

The authors wish to encourage others to critically reflect upon what is presented in this book. They encourage discourse and further investigation into what has been presented here. They invite practitioners to apply these principles in their practice and to share their insights about working with diversity. They ask readers to explore this question: Are there some situations where these principles are most helpful and others where they are not?

APPENDIX A:
SAMPLE PERMISSION SLIP

Month, Year

Dear Parent or Guardian:

Starting **DATE**, we will be hosting a **TYPE of GROUP/GROUP NAME** at **AGENCY/LOCATION** and we would like to provide your child the opportunity to participate. The purpose of the group is to **GROUP PURPOSE**. Group participation can result in many benefits to a child, including **POTENTIAL BENEFITS OF YOUR GROUP**.

Attached you will find more information about the group, including the time frame, group rules, and planned activities so that you can determine whether or not your child would benefit from participating in this group.

If you have any questions/concerns, please contact **INDIVIDUAL** at **CONTACT INFORMATION**.

Completed permission forms are due to AGENY/LOCATION on DATE.

*****Please detach and return lower portion of the page to LOCATION.*****

My child, _____, has my permission to participate in the **GROUP TITLE** group.

Parent's/Guardian's Printed Name: _____

Parent's/Guardian's Email: _____

Parent's/Guardian's Phone Number: _____

Parent/Guardian Signature: _____

Date: _____

I, _____, would like to participate in **GROUP TITLE**

Child's name

_____ Date: _____

Child's signature

APPENDIX B:
GROUP PLANNING CHECKLIST

Check items that you have completed when planning a group.

Key One: Needs Assessment

_____ Read journal articles and books about the topic and similar groups
_____ Checked agency mission statement to see if aligns with the group's purpose
_____ Communicated with consumers about interests and needs
_____ Communicated with agency/community to secure data validating need and approval

Key Two: Purpose

_____ Developed a purpose statement
_____ Developed goals and objectives for the group
_____ Named the group (name aligns with the group purpose)

Key Three: Coworker

_____ Planned and coordinated with a coworker if appropriate

Key Four: Structure

_____ Size of group
_____ Open or closed
_____ Number of sessions
_____ Duration of session
_____ Allowed time for processing
_____ Developed activities for each session
_____ Established rules

Key Five: Location, Time, and Accommodations

_____ Found location that is private, accessible, safe, and comfortable
_____ Arranged a time that is convenient for members
_____ Arranged for accommodations
      _____ accessible for members' disabilities
      _____ refreshments or meals
      _____ childcare
      _____ transportation
      _____ incentives

Key Six: Recruitment, Pre-engagement, and Selection of Members

_____ Created and posted flyers
_____ Advertised the group with colleagues
_____ Advertised in diverse venues
_____ Contacted media
_____ Contacted potential members in person or by telephone
_____ Prescreened members and made referrals if inappropriate
_____ Selected diverse members

Task Group Member Recruitment and Selection

_____ Recruited and selected task group members with knowledge of the task
_____ Recruited and selected task group members with motivation
_____ Recruited and selected task group members with political power
_____ Recruited and selected diverse task group members with expertise

Key Seven: Content and Activities

_____ Read current journal articles and books about the topic
_____ Read current journal articles and books about similar groups
_____ Discussed ideas for the group with experienced professionals
_____ Explored theories that will be utilized and evidence-based practices
_____ Established content for the group's sessions
_____ Established activities for sessions
_____ Educated self regarding cultures of group members

Key Eight: Evaluation

_____ Developed an evaluation design
_____ Researched instruments for the evaluation
_____ Arranged for the evaluation
_____ Validated that evaluation is congruent with the group's purpose/objectives

Key Nine: Budget and Budget Narrative

_____ Created a budget considering all group expenses
_____ Wrote a budget narrative explaining budget items and costs

Key Ten: Written Group Proposal

_____ Wrote a draft of a group proposal incorporating all appropriate planning keys
_____ Created a timeline for the group proposal
_____ Submitted the proposal for agency approval or for grant funding

APPENDIX C: ICEBREAKERS FOR THE BEGINNING STAGE

- Give your name and a word that describes you with the first letter of your name. For example: I am Nancy and a word that describes me is "nice" or I am Jeffrey and a word that describes me is "just."

- Put numbers one through eight in a hat. Each participant draws a number and must tell that number of bits of information about themselves. For example, if they pick the number three, they must tell three things about themselves.

- Tell two truths and one lie about yourself. Have the members guess which one of the statements is a lie. For example: My name is Solomon. I love to fish. I have four children. I was born in El Salvador. Which is the lie?

- For a children's group, break into pairs and draw a picture with your favorite thing to do, your favorite food, and your favorite subject in school. Talk to each other about your pictures. What do you have that is similar in your pictures? What is different?

- For an older adult group, tell your country of origin, how long you've lived in this country, what you miss about your country of origin, and what you like about living in this country.

- After training members to do an ecomap of themselves, have the members show their ecomap and explain either who is in their family or what systems affect their lives.

- Give your name and your favorite activity to do.

- Tell your name and one of the goals you hope to accomplish in this group.

- Tell your name and one hope you have for your future.

- Tell your name and what brings you to this group.

- Bring in your favorite song. Play an excerpt for the group and tell them the reasons you like the song. Find out how group members feel about your selection.

APPENDIX D: SAMPLE CONTRACT

Parent Education and Support Group Contract

1. I understand the purpose of the Parent Education and Support Group, which is to learn and share effective parenting methods, techniques and resources that will improve parenting of children.

2. As a member of the Parent Education Support Group I agree to the following:

   a. Attend and be prompt for all ten sessions. If I am going to be absent I will notify the group worker by telephone at _____ or email at _____ prior to the group meeting and give an acceptable reason, such as illness, for not being able to attend. I am aware that attendance will be reported to my Children's Social Worker (CSW). I also understand that I may be removed from the group if I have two or more absences.

   b. My goals are:
      - To attend all sessions as measured by my attendance record
      - To contribute to each session by asking questions and sharing ideas with other members as measured by my self-report of participation during the processing of each meeting
      - To improve my knowledge and behaviors regarding parenting of my child or children as evidenced by my answers on evaluation measures and the report of my CSW.

3. I will keep information shared in the group by other group members confidential and private. I expect that my information will be kept confidential by the group worker, with the exception of reporting harm to myself or others, my attendance, and willingness to participate.

4. I understand that the group worker's role is to facilitate the meeting in a prepared and respectful manner.

5. I agree to act in a respectful way to the group worker and all group members.

6. The group worker will:

   a. Facilitate each session of the group, arriving on time and prepared.

   b. Take attendance and report attendance to the CSW.

I will adhere to this contract to the best of my ability, and I am willing to be in this group.

Group member (print and sign name and date)

Print Name _____

Sign Name: _____

Date: _____

Group worker (print and sign name and date)

Print Name _____

Sign Name: _____

Date: _____

APPENDIX E: CHECKLIST FOR THE BEGINNING STAGE

Check If These Beginning Stage Tasks and Skills of the Group Worker Have Been Accomplished

_____ Set up room environment prior to group in a comfortable way—in a circle, refreshments, name tags, etc.

_____ Welcomed participants to the group

_____ Discussed the purpose of the group

_____ Related the mission of the agency or group sponsor

_____ Encouraged involuntary members to express feelings and thoughts about being in the group

_____ Held a discussion of group rules and norms, including confidentiality and its limits

_____ Introduced the group worker, sharing credentials and experience

_____ Used an icebreaker to introduce members and/or to further cohesion in the group

_____ Group worker modeled how members were to introduce themselves or others

_____ Engaged members in the group

_____ Noticed nonverbal communication

_____ Used eye contact or attention skills with each participant

_____ Asked the members what they hoped to get from the group

_____ Linked members' commonalities to support relationship building

_____ Oriented group members to group's structure, expectations, member roles, group worker roles, etc.

_____ Discussed group goals

_____ Brainstormed ideas and goals in a task group

_____ Discussed participants' obstacles

_____ Set individual goals in a personal group

_____ Discussed diversity of group members

_____ Discussed group ethics and standards—confidentiality, respect for everyone, democratic decision making, social justice

_____ Gave information

_____ Discussed any reporting or consequences (if applicable) (i.e., attendance in a mandatory group, participation in a parenting group, consequence of not attending might be serving jail time)

_____ Empowered group members

_____ Processed the beginning sessions with the members

_____ Used the skills of organizing, attending, expressing, responding, clarifying, giving information, linking, summarizing, scanning, directing, processing, supporting, demanding work, focusing, reaching for thoughts, feelings, and behaviors, sharing information, fostering mutual aid, being friendly, etc.

_____ Began the evaluation process

_____ For an existing group but new to the group worker: researched the group, dealt with feelings of separation, and took things slowly while engaging members

_____ Identified theories used in group sessions

_____ If a coworker, discussed strategies, theories, processing of group with other coworker after meetings

_____ Wrote a group and individual record

_____ Planned for next meetings

_____ Broke the group into dyads or smaller groups

_____ Contracted with members

_____ Reached out to indigenous leaders

REFERENCES

Abdul-Adil, J. K. (2006). Rap music and urban rhapsody: Violence prevention for inner-city African American male adolescents. *Journal of Urban Youth Culture, 4*(1).

Abels, P. (2012). History of the standards for social work practice with groups: A partial view. *Social Work with Groups, 36,* 259–269.

Abernethy, A. (2002). The power of metaphors for exploring cultural differences in groups. *Group, 26*(3), 219–231.

Akiskal, H. S., Bourgeois, M. L., et al. (2000). Re-evaluating the prevalence of and diagnostic composition within the broad clinical spectrum of bipolar disorders. *Journal of Affective Disorders, 59,* Suppl. S5-530.

Alberta Human Services. (2014). *Child intervention practice framework.* Retrieved from http://humanservices.alberta.ca/abuse-bullying/17242.html.

Alberta Human Services. (2016). *What is outcomes based service delivery?* Retrieved from http://humanservices.alberta.ca/abuse-bullying/17242.html.

Alcoholics Anonymous. (2001). *Alcoholics Anonymous* (4th ed.). New York, NY: A. A. World Services.

Alissi, A. (2008). Group work history—United States. In A. Gitterman & R. Salmon (Eds.), *Encyclopedia of social work with groups.* Florence, KY: Routledge.

Alvarez, A., & Cabbil, L. (2001). The MELD program: Promoting personal change and social justice through a year-long multicultural group experience. *Social Work with Groups, 24*(1), 3–20.

Alvarez III, T. T. (2011). Beats, rhymes, and life: Rap therapy in an urban setting. In S. Hadley & G. Yancy (Eds.), *Therapeutic uses of rap and hip-hop* (pp. 117–128). New York, NY: Routledge.

American Psychiatric Association. (2013). *Diagnostic and statistical manual of mental disorders* (5th ed.). Washington, DC: American Psychiatric Association.

Anderson, D. (2007). Multicultural group work: A force for developing and healing. *Journal for Specialists in Group Work, 32*(3), 224–244.

Anderson, J. (1997). *Social work with groups: A process model.* New York, NY: Longman.

Asch, S. (1955). Opinions and social pressures. *Scientific American, 193*(5), 31–35.

Attala, J. M., Hudson, W. W., & McSweeney, M. (1994). A partial validation of two short form partner abuse scales. *Women's Health, 21*(2/3), 12–39.

Avgar, A. C., & Neuman, E. J. (2015). Seeing conflict: A study of conflict accuracy in work teams. *Negotiation and Conflict Management Research, 2*(8), 19.

Bales, R. (1950). *Interaction process analysis.* Cambridge, MA: Addison Wesley.

Balgopal, P. R., & Vassil, T. V. (1983). *Groups in social work: An ecological approach.* New York, NY: Macmillan.

Bang, H., & Park, J. G. (2015). The double-edged sword of task conflict: Its impact on team performance. *Social Behaviour and Personality, 5*(43), 13.

Barker, R. (Ed.) (2003). *The social work dictionary* (5th ed.). Washington, DC: NASW Press.

Basescu, S. (1990). Tools of the trade: The use of self in psychotherapy. *Group, 14*(3), 156–165.

Baskin, C. (2011). *Strong helpers' teachings: The value of indigenous knowledges in the helping professions.* Toronto, ON: Canadian Scholars Press.

Basso, R., Pelech, W., & Wickham, E. (2014). Harnessing the promise of diversity in group work practice. In C. D. Lee (Ed.), *Social group work: We are all in the same boat: Proceedings of the International Association of Social Work with Groups, Long Beach, California.* London, England: Whiting and Birch.

Beck, J. S. (2011). *Cognitive behaviour therapy: Basics and beyond.* New York, NY: Guilford Press.

Bednar, R., & Kaul, T. (1994). Experiential group research: Can the canon fire? In A. E. Bergin & S. L. Garfield (Eds.), *Handbook of psychotherapy and behavior change* (4th ed.). New York, NY: Wiley.

Bemak, F., & Chung, R. C. (2004). Teaching multicultural group counseling: Perspectives for a new era. *Journal for Specialists in Group Work, 29*(1), 31–41.

Bengtson, V. L. (2001). Beyond the nuclear family: The increasing importance of multigenerational relationships in American society. *Journal of Marriage and the Family, 63*(1), 1–16.

Bennett, L., & O'Brien, P. (2007). Effects of coordinated services for drug-abusing women who are victims of intimate partner violence. *Violence against Women, 13*(4), 395–411.

Bernard, H. S., & MacKenzie, R. (1994). *Basics of group psychotherapy*. New York, NY: Guilford Press.

Bieschke, K. J., Gehlert, K. M., Wilson, D., Matthews, C. R., & Wade, J. (2003). Qualitative analysis of multicultural awareness in training groups. *Journal for Specialists in Group Work, 28*(4), 325–338.

Blackstock, C. (2009). The occasional evil of angels: Learning from the experiences of Aboriginal people and social work. *First Nations Child and Family Review, 4*(1), 28–37.

Blackstock, C. (2011). The Canadian human rights tribunal on First Nations child welfare: Why if Canada wins, equality and justice lose. *Children and Youth Services Review, 33*(1), 187–194.

Blundo, R., & Greene, R. R. (2008). Social construction. In R. R. Greene (Ed.), *Human behavior and social work practice* (pp. 237–264). Piscataway: NJ: Transaction Publishers.

Brabender, V., Fallon, A., & Smolar, A. (2004). *Essentials of group therapy*. Hoboken, NJ: Wiley.

Breton, M. (2004). An empowerment perspective. In C. Garvin, L. Gutierrez, & M. J. Galinsky (Eds.), *Handbook of social work with groups* (pp. 58–75). New York, NY: Guilford Press.

Briere, J., & Scott, C. (2015). *Principles of trauma therapy: A guide to symptoms, evaluation, and treatment* (2nd ed.). Thousand Oaks, CA: Sage.

Briggs-Gowan, M. J., Carter, A. S., Clark, R., Augustyn, M., McCarthy, K. J., & Ford, J. D. (2010). Exposure to potentially traumatic events in early childhood: Differential links to emergent psychopathology. *Journal of Child Psychology and Psychiatry, 51*(10), 1132–1140.

Brown, A., & Mistry, T. (2005). Group work with mixed membership groups: Issues of race and gender. *Social Work with Groups, 28*(3/4), 133–148.

Brown, V., Harris, M., & Fallot, R. (2013). Moving toward trauma informed practice in addiction treatment: A collaborative model of agency assessment. *Journal of Psychoactive Drugs, 45*(5), 386–393.

Brown, V., Mechoir, L. A., Panter, A. T., Slaughter, R., & Huba, G. J. (2000). Women's steps of change and entry into drug abuse treatment: A multidimensional stages of change model. *Journal of Substance Abuse Treatment, 18*, 231–240.

Bruckert, C. (2002). *Taking it off, putting it on: Women in the strip trade*. Retrieved from http://ezproxy.lib.ucalgary.ca:2048/login?url=http://site.ebrary.com/lib/ucalgary/Doc?id=10191707.

Burlingame, G. M., Fuhriman, A., & Johnson, J. E. (2002). Psychotherapy relationships that work: Therapist contributions and responsiveness to patients. In J. Norcross (Ed.), *Cohesion in group psychotherapy* (pp. 71–87). New York, NY: Oxford University Press.

Burlingame, G. M., Strauss, B., Joyce, A. S., MacNair-Semands, R. R., MacKenzie, K. R., Ogrodniczuk, J., & Taylor, S. (2006). *Core battery-revised: An assessment tool kit for promoting optimal group selection, process and outcome.* New York, NY: American Group Psychotherapy Association.

Burnes, T. R., & Ross, K. L. (2010). Applying social justice to oppression and marginalization in group process: Interventions and strategies for group counselors. *Journal for Specialists in Group Work, 35*(2), 169–176.

Burns, D. D. (1980). *Feeling good: The new mood therapy.* New York, NY: New American Library.

Camacho, S. F. (2001). Addressing conflict rooted in diversity: The role of the facilitator. *Social Work with Groups, 26*(3/4), 135–152.

Canadian Association of Social Workers (CASW) (2005). *Code of ethics.* Retrieved from http://www.casw-acts.ca/en/what-social-work/casw-code-ethics.

Canadian Centre on Substance Abuse. (2009). *Substance abuse in Canada: Concurrent disorders.* Ottawa, ON: Canadian Centre on Substance Abuse.

Caplan, T., & Thomas, H. (2002). The forgotten moment: Therapeutic resiliency and its promotion in social work with groups. *Social Work with Groups, 22*(2), 5–26.

Caplan, T., & Thomas, H. (2004a). If this is week three, we must be doing "feelings": An essay on the importance of client-paced group work. *Social Work with Groups, 26*(3), 5–15.

Caplan, T., & Thomas, H. (2004b). If we are all in the same canoe, why are we using different paddles? The effective use of common themes in diverse group situations. *Social Work with Groups, 27*(1), 53–73.

Carlson, J., & Evans, K. (2001). Whose choice is it? Contemplating challenge by choice. *Journal of Experiential Education, 24*(1), 58.

CBITS Program. (2015). *Success stories.* Retrieved from http://cbitsprogram .org/success-stories.

Centre for Clinical Interventions. (2008). *Keeping your balance: Coping with bipolar disorder infopax.* Department of Health. Retrieved from www.cci.health.wa.gov.au/resources/infopax.cfm?Info ID=38.

Cheng, W. D., Chae, M., & Gunn, R. W. (1998). Splitting and projective identification in multicultural group counseling. *Journal for Specialists in Group Work, 23*(4), 372–387.

City of Edmonton. (2015). *Municipal Census 2014: Population history.* Retrieved from http://www.edmonton.ca/city_government/facts_figures/population-history.aspx.

Cohen, C. S., Phillips, M. H., & Hanson, M. (2009). *Think group: Strength and diversity through group work.* London, England: Whiting and Birch.

Cohen, C. S., Macgowan, M. J., Garvin, C., & Muskat, B. (2013) From the guest editors. *Social Work with Groups, 36*(2/3), 106–110. Retrieved from doi: 10.1080/01609513.2012.762490.

Coker, A. L., et al. (2002). Physical and mental health effects of intimate partner violence for men and women. *American Journal of Preventive Medicine, 23*, 260–268.

Conflict (2015). Retrieved from http://www.merriam-webster.com/dictionary/conflict.

Constantine, M. G., Hage, S. M., Kindaichi, M. M., & Bryant, R. M. (2007). Social justice and multicultural issues: Implications for the practice and training of counselors and counseling psychologists. *Journal of Counseling and Development, 85*(1), 24–29.

Cooley, C. H. (1909). *Social organization.* New York, NY: Scribner.

Corey, M., & Corey, G. (2006). Transition stage of a group. In *Groups: Process and practice* (7th ed.). Belmont, CA: Brooks/Cole.

Corey, M., Corey, G., & Corey, C. (2013). *Groups: Process and practice* (9th ed.). Belmont CA: Brooks/Cole.

Corey, M., Corey, G., & Corey, C. (2010). *Groups: Process and practice* (8th ed.). Belmont, CA: Brooks/Cole.

Cornman, J. M., & Kingson, E. R. (1999). Yes, John, there is a social compact. *Generations, 22*(4), 10–14.

Corsini, R., & Rosenberg, B. (1955). Mechanisms of group psychotherapy: Processes and dynamics. *Journal of Abnormal and Social Psychology, 51*, 406–411.

Covington, S. (2008). Women and addiction: A trauma-informed approach. *Journal of Psychoactive Drugs, 40* (SARC Suppl. 5), 377–385.

Coyle, G. (1948). *Group work with American youth.* New York, NY: Harper.

Cunningham, C. E. (2006). COPE large group community based, family-centered training program. In R. A. Barkley (Ed.), *Attention deficit hyperactivity: A handbook of diagnosis and treatment* (pp. 480–497). New York, NY: Guilford Press.

Cunningham, C. E., Bremner, R., & Boyle, M. (1995). Large group community-based programs for families of preschoolers at risk for disruptive behaviour disorders: Utilization, cost effectiveness, and outcomes. *Journal of Child Psychology and Psychiatry, 36,* 1141–1159.

Cunningham, C. E., Bremner, R., & Secord, Gilbert, M. (1993). Increasing the availability, accessibility, and cost efficacy of services for families of ADHD children: A school-based systems-oriented parenting course. *Canadian Journal of School Psychology, 9,* 1–15.

Cunningham, C. E., et al. (2000). Tri-ministry study: Correlates of school-based parenting course utilization. *Journal of Consulting and Clinical Psychology, 68,* 928–933.

Davis, L., Galinsky, M., & Schopler, J. (1995). RAP: A framework for leadership of multiracial groups. *Social Work with Groups, 40*(2), 155–165.

Davis, W. (2008). The worldwide web of belief and ritual. Retrieved from https://www.ted.com/talks/wade_davis_on_the_worldwide_web_of_belief_and_ritual?language=en.

Dawes, N. P., & Larson, R. (2011). How youth get engaged: Grounded-theory research on motivational development in organized youth programs. *Developmental Psychology, 47*(1), 259.

DeBeck, K., Wood, E., Montaner, J., & Kerr, T. (2009). Canada's new federal "national anti-drug strategy": An informal audit of reported funding allocation. *International Journal of Drug Policy, 20*(2), 188–191.

Debiak, D. (2007). Attending to diversity in group psychotherapy: An ethical imperative. *International Journal of Group Psychotherapy, 57*(1), 1–12.

DeLois, K., & Cohen, M. B. (2000). A queer idea: Using group work principles to strengthen learning in a sexual minorities seminar. *Social Work with Groups, 23*(3), 53–67.

Delucia-Waack, J., & Donigian, J. (2004). *The practice of multicultural group work.* Belmont, CA: Brooks/Cole.

Department of Juvenile Services. (2015). *Data resource guide: Fiscal year 2014.* Retrieved from http://www.djs.state.md.us/drg/Full_2014_DRG.pdf.

Diebel, C., & Whiskeyjack, C. (2012). Kahkiyaw ayisiyinowak ka wahkohot: The first Aboriginal OBSD phase-in site. *Outcome Based Service Delivery (OBSD) Update, 6*. Retrieved from http://www.aascf.com/aascf-initiatives/obsd-newsletter?view=docman.

Dion, K. L. (2000). Group cohesion: From "field of forces" to multidimensional construct. *Group Dynamics: Theory, Research, and Practice, 4*, 19.

Diversity. (n.d.). *Merriam Webster online dictionary*. Springfield, MA: Merriam-Webster.

Dobash, R. E., & Dobash, R. P. (1992). The therapeutic society. In *Women, violence, and social change* (pp. 242–250). New York, NY: Routledge.

Doyle, R., & George, U. (2008). Achieving and measuring diversity: An organizational change approach. *Social Work Education, 27*(1), 97–110.

Elligan, D. (2004). *Rap therapy: A practical guide for communicating with youth and young adults through rap music*. New York, NY: Kensington.

Elliot, D. E., Gjelajac, P., Fallot, R. D., Markoff, L. S., & Glover Reed, B. (2005). Trauma-informed or trauma-denied: Principles and implementation of trauma-informed services for women. *Journal of Community Psychology, 33*(4), 461–477.

Epstein, L. (1992). *Brief treatment and a new look at the task centred approach*. New York, NY: Macmillan.

Epston, D., & White, M. (1990). *Narrative means to therapeutic ends*. New York, NY: Norton.

Este, D. (1999). Social work and cultural competency. In G. Y. Lie & D. Este (Eds.), *Professional social service delivery in a multicultural world* (pp. 27–45). Toronto, ON: Canadian Scholars Press.

Eubank, E. (1932). *The concepts of sociology*. Boston, MA: D. C. Heath.

Family violence in Canada: A statistical profile (2000, 14th ed.). Ottawa, ON: Statistics Canada.

Fast, J. (2015). The health cards system for bipolar disorder: A revolutionary three-step program for the management of bipolar disorder. Retrieved from www.bipolarhappens.com/health-cards/.

Fast, J., & Preston, J. D. (2006). *Take charge of bipolar disorder: A four-step plan for you and your loved ones to manage the illness and create lasting stability*. New York, NY: Grand Central Life and Style.

Fast, J., & Preston, J. D. (2012). Loving someone with bipolar disorder: Understanding and helping your partner. (2nd ed.). Oakland, CA: New Harbinger.

Fatout, M., & Rose, S. (1995). *Task groups in social services.* Thousand Oaks, CA: Sage.

Fellin, P. (2000). Revisiting multiculturalism in social work. *Journal of Social Work Education, 36*(2), 261–278.

Finch, A. J., Saylor, C. F., & Edwards, G. L. (1985). Children's depression inventory: Sex and grade norms for normal children. *Journal of Consulting and Clinical Psychology, 53,* 424–425.

Finkelhor, D., Turner, H. A., Shattuck, A., & Hamby, S. L. (2013). Violence, crime, and abuse exposure in a national sample of children and youth: An update. *JAMA Pediatrics, 167*(7), 614–621.

Fischer, J., & Corcoran, K. (2013). *Measures for clinical practice and research: A sourcebook* (5th ed.). New York, NY: Oxford University Press.

Fluhr, T. (2005). Transcending differences: Using concrete subject-matter in heterogeneous groups. *Social Work with Groups, 27*(2), 35–54.

Foa, E. B., Johnson, K. M., Feeny, N. C., & Treadwell, K. R. (2001). The Child PTSD Symptom Scale (CPSS): A preliminary examination of its psychometric properties. *Journal of Clinical Child Psychology, 30*(3), 376–384.

Fournier, S., & Crey, E. (1997). *Stolen from our embrace: The abduction of First Nations children and the restoration of Aboriginal communities.* Vancouver, BC: Douglas and McIntyre.

Frances, A., Clarkin, J., & Marachi, J. (1980). Selection criteria for group therapy. In J. Brady & H. K. Brody (Eds.), *Controversy in psychiatry* (pp. 679–702). Philadelphia, PA: W. B. Saunders.

Furhman, R. D. (2009). *An experiential approach to group work.* Chicago, IL: Lyceum.

Furman, R., Bender, K., & Rowan, D. (2014). *An experiential approach to group work* (2nd ed.). Chicago, IL: Lyceum.

Furst, W. (1952). Homogeneous and heterogeneous groups. *International Journal of Group Psychotherapy, 2,* 120–123.

Galinsky, M., & Schopler, J. (1989). The social work group. In J. Shaffer & D. Galinsky (Eds.), *Models of group therapy* (2nd ed., pp. 18–32). Upper Saddle River, NJ: Prentice Hall.

Galinsky, M., Schopler, J., & Abell, M. (1996). Connecting group members through telephone and computer groups. *Social Work with Groups, 19*(3/4), 21–39.

Gambone, J. V. (2002). *Together for tomorrow: Building community through intergenerational dialogue.* Crystal Bay, MN: Elder Eye Press.

Gambrill, E. (2000). Honest brokering of knowledge and ignorance. *Journal of Social Work Education, 36*(3), 387–397.

Garland, A. F., Lau, A. S., Yeh, M., McCabe, K. M., Hough, R. L., & Landsverk, J. A. (2005). Racial and ethnic differences in utilization of mental health services among high-risk youths. *American Journal of Psychiatry, 162*(7), 1336–1343. Retrieved from doi: 10.1176/appi.ajp.162.7.133.

Garland, J., Jones, H., & Kolodny, R. L. (1965). A model for stages of development in social work groups. In S. Berntein (Ed.), *Explorations in group work* (pp. 17–71). Boston, MA: Milford House.

Garvin, C. (1997). *Contemporary group work* (3rd ed.). Boston, MA: Allyn and Bacon.

Garvin, C., Reid, W., & Epstein, L. (1976). A task-centered approach. In R. W. Roberts & H. Northen (Eds.), *Theories of social work with groups* (pp. 238–267). New York, NY: Columbia University Press.

Gary, J. M., & Remolino, L. (2000). *Online support groups: Nuts and bolts, benefits, limitations and future directions.* Greensboro, NC: ERIC Counseling and Student Services Clearinghouse.

Gearing, R. E. (2002). Gender diversity: A powerful tool for enriching group experience. In S. Henry, J. East, & C. L. Schmitz (Eds.), *Social work with groups: Mining the gold.* New York, NY: Haworth Press.

Gitterman, A. (2005). Group formation. In A. Gitterman & L. Shulman (Eds.), *Mutual aid groups, vulnerable and resilient populations, and the life cycle* (3rd ed., pp. 73–110). New York, NY: Columbia University Press.

Gitterman, A., & Germain, C. B. (2008). *The life model of social work practice.* New York, NY: Columbia University Press.

Gitterman, A., & Shulman, L. (2005). *Mutual aid groups, vulnerable populations, and the life cycle* (3rd ed.). New York, NY: Columbia University Press.

Goldberg, C. (1983). The function of the therapist's affect in therapeutic conflict in groups. *Group, 7*(1), 3–18.

Goldberg Wood, G., & Roche, S. E. (2001). Representing selves, reconstructing lives: Feminist group work with women survivors of male violence. *Social Work with Groups, 23*(4), 5–23.

Goodkind, J. R., Lanoue, M. D., & Milford, J. (2010). Adaptation and implementation of cognitive behavioral intervention for trauma in schools with American Indian youth. *Journal of Clinical Child and Adolescent Psychology, 39*(6), 858–872.

Goodman, M., & Fallon, B. (1995) *Pattern changing for abused women: An educational program.* Thousand Oaks, CA: Sage.

Government of Canada. (2011). *National household survey: Aboriginal people in Canada: First Nations, Métis and Inuit.* Retrieved from http://www.12 statcan.gc.ca.nhs-enm/2011/as.sa.

Gramsci, A. (2011). *Prison notebooks: Volume 1.* New York, NY: Columbia University Press.

Green, Z., & Stiers, M. J. (2002). Multiculturalism and group therapy in the United States: A social constructionist perspective. *Group, 26*(3), 233–246.

Greene, B. (2004). African American lesbians and other culturally diverse people in psychodynamic psychotherapies: Useful paradigms or oxymoron? *Journal of Lesbian Studies, 8*(1/2), 57–77.

Haley-Banez, L., Brown, S., Molina, B., D'Andrea, M., Arrendondo, P., Merchant, N., & Wathen, S. (1999). Association for specialists in group work principles for diversity-competent group workers. *Journal for Specialists in Group Work, 24*(1), 7–14.

Harrison, R., & Lubin, B. (1965). Personal style, group composition, and learning. *Journal of Applied Behavioral Science, 1,* 286–301.

Hartford, M. E. (1971). *Groups in social work.* New York, NY: Columbia University Press.

Health Canada. (2014). *Canadian alcohol and drug use monitoring survey.* Retrieved from http://www.hc-sc.gc.ca/hc-ps/drugs-drogues/stat/_2012/ summary-sommaire-eng.php#s7.

Henry, S. (1992). *Group skills in social work: A four-dimensional approach.* Pacific Grove, CA: Brooks/Cole.

Herman, J. (1997). *Trauma and recovery: The aftermath of violence—from domestic abuse to political terror.* New York, NY: Basic Books.

Hinson, J. (2015). *The treatment of trauma in immigrant youth: Final paper, CBITS.* Retrieved from http://globalmigration.web.unc.edu/files/2013/09/ Treatment-of-Trauma-in-Immigrant-Youth.pdf.

Holsopple, K. (1998). *Strip club testimony.* Minneapolis, MN: Freedom and Justice Center for Prostitution Resources.

Holsopple, K. (1999). Stripclubs according to strippers. In D. M. Hughes & C. M. Roche (Eds.), *Making the harm visible: Global sexual exploitation of women and girls*. Kingston, RI: Coalition against Trafficking in Women.

Human Services. (2014). *Child intervention information and statistics summary*. Retrieved from http://humanservices.alberta.ca/documents/child-intervention-info-stats-summary-2014-15-q2.pdf.

Ibrahim, F. A. (2010). Social justice and cultural responsiveness: Innovative teaching strategies for group work. *Journal for Specialists in Group Work, 35*(3), 271–280.

International Association of Social Work with Groups (IASWG) (2010). *Standards for social work practice with groups.* Retrieved from IASWG.org.

International Federation of Social Workers (IFSW) (2012). *Statement of ethical principles*. Retrieved from http://ifsw.org/policies/statement-of-ethical-principles.

Ivey, A. E., Pedersen, P. B., & Ivey, M. B. (2007). *Group microskills: Culture-centered group process and strategies*. Hanover, MA: MicroTraining Associates.

Jackson, S. E., Stone, V., & Alvarez, E. (1992). Socialization amidst diversity: The impact of demographics on work oldtimers and newcomers. In B. Staw & L. Cummings (Eds.), *Research in organizational behavior* (Vol. 15, pp. 45–109).

Jacobs, E., Harvill, R., & Schimmel, C. (2009). *Group counseling: Strategies and skills* (7th ed.). New York, NY: Brooks/Cole.

Janis, I. (1972). *Victims of groupthink*. Boston MA: Houghton Mifflin.

Janssen, O., Van de Vliert, E., & Veenstra, C. (1999). How task and person conflict shape the role of positive interdependence in management teams. *Journal of Management, 2*(25), 25.

Jaycox, L. H., Langley, A. K., Stein, B. D., Wong, M., Sharma, P., Scott, M., & Schonlau, M. (2009). Support for students exposed to trauma: A pilot study. *School Mental Health, 1*(2), 49–60.

Jean Tweed Centre. (2013). *Trauma matters: Guidelines for trauma-informed practices in women's substance use services*. Retrieved from http://www.google.ca/url?sa=t&rct=j&q=&esrc=s&source=web&cd=1&ved=0CCw QFjAA&url=http%3A%2F%2Fwww.jeantweed.com%2FLinkClick.aspx %3Ffileticket%3D3-jaLM6hb8Y%253D%26tabid%3D107%26mid% 3D514&ei=mhguU5ylEPP7yAGE-YCADg&usg=AFQjCNFcszpR-SBBJi6H6PEwnaWBqY6HFg&sig2.

Jehn, K. A., Northcraft, G. B., & Neale, M. A. (1999). Why differences make a difference: A field study of diversity, conflict, and performance in workgroups. *Administrative Science Quarterly, 44*, 741–763.

Kahkiyaw (2014). *An outcomes-based service delivery model.* Retrieved from http://bentarrow.ca/wp-content/uploads/2012/04/Kahkiyaw-Two-Pager-08-Jun-2012.pdf.

Kahn, E. (1996). Coleadership gender issues in group psychotherapy. In B. DeChant (Ed.), *Women and group psychotherapy* (pp. 442–461). New York, NY: Guilford Press.

Kataoka, S., Jaycox, L. H., Wong, M., Nadeem, E., Langley, A., Tang, L., & Stein, B. D. (2011). Effects on school outcomes in low-income minority youth: Preliminary findings from a community-partnered study of a school-based trauma intervention. *Ethnicity and Disease, 21*(3 Suppl. 1), S1-71–S1-7.

Kataoka, S., Stein, B. D., Jaycox, L. H., Wong, M., Escudero, P., Tu, W., Zaragoza, C., & Fink, A. (2003). A school-based mental health program for traumatized Latino immigrant children. *Journal of the American Academy of Child and Adolescent Psychiatry, 42*(3), 311–318.

Kelly, L. (1988). What's in a name? Defining child sexual abuse. *Feminist Review, 28*, 65–73.

Kessler, R. C., Chiu, W. T., Demler, O., & Walters, E. E. (2005). Prevalence, severity, and comorbidity of twelve-month DSM-IV disorders in the National Comorbidity Survey Replication (NCS-R). *Archives of General Psychiatry, 62*(6), 617–627.

Kieffer, C. H. (1984). Citizen empowerment: A developmental perspective. In P. Raffoul & C. A. McNeece (Eds.), *Future issues for social work practice* (pp. 229–239). Boston, MA: Allyn & Bacon.

Kiyoshk, R. (2001). *Family violence in Aboriginal communities: A review.* Ottawa, ON: The Aboriginal Nurses Association of Canada and Royal Canadian Mounted Police.

Kiyoshk, R. (2003). Integrating spirituality and domestic violence treatment: Treatment of Aboriginal men. *Journal of Aggression Maltreatment and Trauma, 7*(1–2), 237–256.

Klein, A., (1972). *Effective groupwork.* New York, NY: Associated Press.

Kropotkin, P. (1902). *Mutual aid: A factor in evolution.* London, England: Robert Heinemann.

Kuehne, V. S. (1999). Building intergenerational communities through research and evaluation. *Generations, 22*(4), 82–87.

Kulkarni, S., Bell, H., & McDaniel Rhodes, D. (2012). Back to basics: Essential qualities of services for survivors of intimate partner violence. *Violence against* Women, *18*(1), 85–101.

Kurland, R. (2008). Planning: The neglected component of group development. *Social Work with Groups, 28*(3/4), 9–16.

Kurland, R., & Salmon, R. (1998a). Purpose: A misunderstood and misused keystone of group work practice. *Social Work with Groups, 21*(3), 5–17.

Kurland, R., & Salmon, R. (1998b). *Teaching a methods course in social work with groups.* Alexandria, VA: Council on Social Work Education.

LaFromboise, T. D., Coleman, H. L. K., & Hernandez, A. (1991). *Professional psychology: Research and practice, 22*(380). Retrieved from doi: 10.1037/ 0735-7028.22.5.380.

Lakin, M. (1988). *Ethical issues in the psychotherapies.* New York, NY: Oxford Press.

Lang, N. C. (1972). A broad-range model of practice in the social work group. *Social Service Review, 46*(1), 76–89. Retrieved from doi: 10.2307/30021870.

Lang, N. C. (1979). A comparative examination of therapeutic uses of groups in social work and in adjacent human services professions: The literature from 1969-1978. *Social Work with Groups, 2*(3), 197–220.

Lang, N. C. (1987). Social work practice in small social forms. *Social Work with Groups, 9*(4), 7–32.

Lang, N. C. (1994). Integrating the data processing of qualitative research and social work practice to advance the practitioner as knowledge builder: Tools for knowing and doing. In E. Sherman & W. Reid (Eds.), *Qualitative research in social work* (pp. 265–278). New York, NY: Columbia University Press.

Lang, N. C. (2010). *Group work practice to advance social competence.* New York, NY: Columbia University Press.

Lang, N. C. (2011). *Group work practice to advance social competence: A specialized methodology for social work.* New York, NY: Columbia University Press.

Langley, A., Nadeem, E., Kataoka, S. H., Stein, B. D., & Jaycox, L. H. (2010). Evidence-based mental health programs in schools: Barriers and facilitators of successful implementation. *School Mental Health, 2*(3), 105–113.

Langley, A., Santiago, C. D., Rodríguez, A., & Zelaya, J. (2013). Improving implementation of mental health services for trauma in multicultural elementary schools: Stakeholder perspectives on parent and educator engagement. *Journal of Behavioural Health Services and Research, 40*(3), 247–262.

LeBon, G. (1910). *The crowd: A study of the popular mind*. London, England: George Allen and Unwin.

Lee, C. (1997). Eight keys to passing parent education legislation. *Family and Conciliation Courts Review, 35*, 470–483.

Lee, J. A. B., & Hudson, R. (2011). Empowerment approach to social work practice. In F. J. Turner (Ed.), *Social work treatment: Interlocking approaches* (5th ed., pp. 157–177). New York, NY: Oxford.

Lejarraga, T., Lejarraga, J., & Gonzales, C. (2014). Decisions from experience: How groups and individuals adapt to change. *Memory and Cognition, 42*(8), 1384–1397.

Lewin, K. (1997). *Resolving social conflicts: Field theory in social science*. Washington, DC: American Psychological Association.

Lewis, B. (2014). *Same and different ice breaker game for back to School*. Retrieved from http://k6educators.about.com/od/icebreakers/qt/ ibsamedifft.htm.

Lewis, E. (1992). Regaining promise: feminist perspectives for social group work practice. *Social Work with Groups, 15*(2/3), 271–284. Retrieved from http://ezproxy.lib.ucalgary.ca/login?url=http://search.ebscohost.com/login .aspx?direct=true&db=swh&AN=60523&site=ehost-live.

Lieberman, M., Yalom, I., & Miles. (1973). *Encounter groups: First facts*. New York, NY: Basic Books.

Liu, S., Morrison-Dore, M., & Amrani-Cohen, I. (2013). Treating the effects of interpersonal violence: A comparison of two group models. *Social Work with Groups, 36*, 59–72.

Macgowan, M. J. (1997). A measure of engagement for social work group: The groupwork engagement measure (GEM). *Journal of Social Service Research, 23*(2), 17. Retrieved from doi: 10.1300/j079v23n02_02.

Macgowan, M. J. (2012). *A standards-based inventory of foundation competencies in social work with groups, 22*(5), 578–589. Retrieved from doi: 10.1177/1049731512443288.

MacKenzie, K. R. (1990). *Introduction to time-limited group psychotherapy*. Washington, DC: American Psychiatric Publishing.

Malekoff, A. (2004). *Group work with children and adolescents*. New York, NY: Guilford Press.

Malekoff, A., & Laser, M. (1999). Addressing difference in group work with children and young adolescents. *Social Work with Groups, 21*(4), 23–34.

Marbley, A. F. (2004). His eye is on the sparrow: A counselor of color's perception of facilitating groups with predominantly white members. *Journal for Specialists in Group Work, 29*(3), 247–258.

Marrs Fuchsel, C. L. (2014) Exploratory evaluation of Sí, Yo Puedo: A culturally competent empowerment program for immigrant Latina women in group settings. *Social Work with Groups, 37*, 279–296.

Marsiglia, F. F., & Kulis, S. (2009). *Diversity, oppression and change*. Chicago, IL: Lyceum.

Maygard, S. (2013). The evolving nature of OBSD. *OBSD Joint Newsletter, 1*(1). Retrieved from http://www.aascf.com/aascf-initiatives/obsd-newsletter?view=docman.

McDougall, W. (1920). *The group mind*. New York, NY: Putnam.

Mead, G. H. (1934). *Mind, self and society*. Chicago, IL: University of Chicago Press.

Mental Health Commission of Canada. (2012). *Changing directions, changing lives: The mental health strategy for Canada*. Calgary, AB: Mental Health Commission of Canada. Retrieved from strategy.mentalhealthcommission.ca/pdf/strategy-text-en.pdf.

Middleman, R. (1982). *The non-verbal in working with groups: The use of activities in teaching, counseling and therapy*. Hebron, CT: Practitioners Press.

Middleman, R., & Goldberg Wood, G. (1990a). From social group work to social work with groups. *Social Work with Groups, 13*(3), 3–20.

Middleman, R., & Goldberg Wood, G. (1990b). *Skills for direct practice in social work*. New York, NY: Columbia University Press.

Miller, J., Donner, S., & Fraser, E. (2004). Talking when talking is tough: Taking on conversations about race, sexual orientation, gender, class and other aspects of social identity. *Smith College Studies in Social Work, 74*(2), 377–392.

Milliken, F., Barel, C., & Kurtzberg, T. (2003). Diversity and creativity in work groups. In P. Paulus & B. Nijstad (Eds.), *Group creativity: Innovation through collaboration* (pp. 32–62). New York, NY: Oxford University Press.

Mindell, A. (2014). *Sitting in the fire: Large group transformation using conflict and diversity*. Florence, OR: Deep Democracy Exchange.

Mishne, J. (1997). Clinical social work with adolescents. In J. R. Brandell (Ed.), *Theory and practice in clinical social work* (pp. 101–131). New York, NY: Free Press.

Mistry, R., Rosansky, J., McGuire, J., McDermott, C., & Jarvik, L. (2001). Social isolation predicts re-hospitalization in a group of older American veterans enrolled in the UPBEAT program. *International Journal of Geriatric Psychiatry, 16,* 950–959.

Mizhari, T., & Lombe, M. (2006). Perspectives from women organizers: Views on gender, race, class, and sexual orientation. *Journal of Community Practice, 14*(3), 93–118. Retrieved from doi: 10.1300/J125v14n03-06.

Morton, S. (2013). *Cuan Saor strategic review*. Cuan Saor: Clonmel, Co Tipperary, Ireland.

Morton, S. (2014). *Cuan Saor pattern change program: Report on the support and outcomes for participants*. Cuan Saor: Clonmel, Co Tipperary, Ireland.

Moyer, S. (1992). Race, gender, and homicide: Comparisons between Aboriginals and other Canadians. *Canadian Journal of Criminology, 34*(1), 15–34.

Muir, N., & Bohr, Y. (2014). Contemporary practice of traditional Aboriginal child rearing: A review. *First Peoples Child and Family Review, 9,* 66–79.

Nadan, Y., Weinberg-Kurnik, G., & Ben-Ari, A. (2015). Bringing context and power relations to the fore: Intergroup dialogue as a tool in social work education. *British Journal of Social Work, 45*(1), 260–277. Retrieved from doi: 10.1093/bjsw/bct116.

Nagai, C. (2012). Disaster relief volunteer work: Great east Japan earthquake and tsunami. *Reflections, 18*(1), 41–52.

Nagda, B. A., Spearmon, M. L., Holley, L. C., Harding, S., Balasson, M. L., Motse-Swanson, D., & De Mello, S. (1999). Intergroup dialogues: An innovative approach to teaching about diversity and justice in social work programs. *Journal of Social Work Education, 35*(3), 433–449.

Najavits, L. M. (2002). *Seeking safety: A treatment manual for PTSD and substance abuse*. New York, NY: Guilford Press.

Najavits, L. M. (2004). Treatment of posttraumatic stress disorder and substance abuse. *Alcoholism Treatment Quarterly, 22*(1), 43–62.

National Association of Social Workers (NASW). (2008). Retrieved from http://socialhttp://socialworkers.org/pubs/code/code.asp?print=1&.

National Child Traumatic Stress Network. (2015). *Psychological impact of the recent shooting.* Retrieved from http://www.nctsn.org/sites/default/files/assets/pdfs/psychological_information_sheet_two_pager.pdf.

National Institute of Mental Health. (n.d.). *Bipolar disorder among adults.* Retrieved from http://www.nimh.nih.gov/health/statistics/prevalence/bipolar-disorder-among-adults.shtml.

Ngo, V., Langley, A., Kataoka, S. H., Nadeem, E., Escudero, P., & Stein, B. D. (2008). Providing evidence based practice to ethnically diverse youth: Examples from the Cognitive Behavioral Intervention for Trauma in Schools (CBITS) program. *Journal of the American Academy of Child and Adolescent Psychiatry, 47*(8), 858–862.

Nicotera, N., & Laser-Maira, J. (2016). *Innovative skills to support well-being and resiliency in youth.* Chicago, IL: Lyceum.

Northen, H. (1988). *Social work with groups* (3rd ed.). New York, NY: Columbia University Press.

Northen, H. (2003). I hate conflict, but. . . . *Social Work with Groups, 25*(1/2), 5.

Northen, H. (2004). Ethics and values in group work. In C. Garvin, L. Gutierrez, & M. J. Galinsky (Eds.), *Handbook of social work with groups* (pp. 76–89). New York, NY: Guilford Press.

Northen, H., & Kurland, R. (2001). *Social work with groups* (3rd ed.). New York, NY: Columbia University Press.

Northen, H., & Kurland, R. (2005). *Social work with groups* (4th ed.). New York, NY: Columbia University Press.

Nydell, M. (1987). *Understanding Arabs: A guide for Westerners.* Yarmouth, ME: Intercultural Press.

Olivier, C. (2009). Enhancing confidentiality within small groups: The experiences of AIDS service organizations. *Social Work with Groups, 32*(4), 13.

O'Reilly, C., Caldwell, D., & Barnett, W. (1989). Work group demography, social integration and turnover. *Administrative Science Quarterly, 34*, 21–37.

Ortega, R. M., & Faller, K. C. (2011). Training child welfare workers from an intersectional cultural humility perspective: A paradigm shift. *Child Welfare Journal, 90*(5), 27–49.

Osofsky, J. D. (2004). Community outreach for children exposed to violence. *Infant Mental Health Journal, 25*(5), 478–487.

Papell, C., & Rothman, B. (1966). Social group work models: Possession and heritage. *Journal of Education for Social Work, 2*(2), 66–77. Retrieved from doi: 10.2307/41350397.

Papell, C., & Rothman, B. (1980). Relating the mainstream model of social work with groups to group psychotherapy and the structured group approach. *Social Work with Groups, 3*(2), 5–23.

Parrott, L. (2009). Constructive marginality: Conflicts and dilemmas in cultural competence and anti-oppressive practice. *Social Work Education, 28*(6), 617–630.

Pearson, C., Janz, T., & Ali, J. (2013). *Mental and substance use disorders in Canada.* Ottawa, ON: Statistics Canada.

Pedersen, P. B. (2008). A response to "Social privilege, social justice, and group counseling: An inquiry": Inclusive cultural empathy and the search for social justice. *Journal for Specialists in Group Work, 33*(4), 370–376.

Pelled, L. H., Eisenhardt, K. M., & Xin, K. R. (1999). Exploring the black box: An analysis of work group diversity, conflict, and performance. *Administrative Science Quarterly, 44*(1), 1–28.

Perrault, S. (2011). *Education groups for men who batter: The Duluth model.* New York, NY: Spring Publishing.

Phillips, H. (1957). *Essentials of social group work skill.* New York, NY: Association Press.

Pittman, K. J., Irby, M., Tolman, J., Yohalem, N., & Ferber, T. (2011). Preventing problems, promoting development, encouraging engagement: Competing priorities or inseparable goals. *Council of Juvenile Correctional Administrators.* Washington, DC: Forum for Youth Investment.

Polzer, J., Milton, L., & Swann, W. (2002). Capitalizing on diversity: Interpersonal congruence in small work groups. *Administrative Science Quarterly, 47,* 296–324.

Pottick, K. J. (1989). Jane Addams revisited. *Social Work with Groups, 11*(4), 11–26.

Prison Policy Initiative. (2015). *The right investment? Corrections spending in Baltimore City.* Washington, DC: Justice Policy Institute. Retrieved from http://www.prisonpolicy.org/origin/md/report.html.

Prochaska, J. O., Norcross, J. C., & DiClemente, C. C. (1994). *Changing for good: The revolutionary program that explains the six stages of change and teaches you how to free yourself from bad habits.* New York, NY: William Morrow.

Qureshi, A. (2005). Dialogical relationship and cultural imagination: A hermeneutic approach to intercultural psychotherapy. *American Journal of Psychotherapy, 59*(2), 119–135.

Ramsbotham, O., Woodhouse, T., & Miall, H. (2011). *Contemporary conflict resolution* (3rd ed.). Malden, MA: Polity Press.

RAND Corporation. (2015). *Helping children cope with violence and trauma: A school-based program that works.* Retrieved from http://www.rand.org/content/dam/rand/pubs/research_briefs/2011/RAND_RB4557-2.pdf.

Ratts, M. J., Anthony, L., & Santos, K. (2010). The dimensions of social justice model: Transforming traditional group work into a socially just framework. *Journal for Specialists in Group Work, 35*(2), 160–168.

Raven, B. H. (2008). The bases of power and the power/interaction model of interpersonal influence. *Analyses of Social Issues and Public Policy, 8*(1), 1–22. Retrieved from doi: 10.1111/j.1530-2415.2008.00159.x.

Reid, K. E. (1991). *Social work practice with groups: A clinical perspective.* Pacific Grove, CA: Brooks/Cole.

Richards, T. (1974). *Problem solving through creative analysis.* New York, NY: Wiley.

Ringel, S. (2005). Group work with Asian-American immigrants: A cross cultural perspective. In G. Grief & P. Ephross (Eds.), *Group work with populations at risk.* New York, NY: Oxford University Press.

Roberts, T. L., & Smith, L. A. (2002). The illusion of inclusion: An analysis of approaches to diversity within predominantly white schools of social work. *Journal of Teaching in Social Work, 22*(3/4), 189–211.

Rosenbrook, V., & Larkin, E. (2002). Introducing standards and guidelines: A rationale for defining the knowledge, skills, and dispositions of intergenerational practice. *Journal of Intergenerational Relationships, 1*, 133–144.

Rosenthal, L. (1985). A modern analytic approach to group resistance. *Modern Psychoanalysis, 10*, 165–182.

Royal Commission on Aboriginal Peoples. (1996). *Report of the Royal Commission on Aboriginal Peoples.* Ottawa, ON: Queens Printer.

Roysircar, G. (2008). A response to "Social privilege, social justice, and group counseling: An inquiry": Social privilege: Counselors' competence with systemically determined inequalities. *Journal for Specialists in Group Work, 33*(4), 377–384.

Russell, M., & Gockel, A. (2005). Recovery processes in a treatment program for women. *Journal of Social Work Practice in the Addictions, 54*(4), 27–46.

Saino, M. (2003). A new language for groups: Multilingual and multiethnic group work. *Social Work with Groups, 26*(1), 69–82.

Schiller, L. Y. (2007). Not for women only: Applying the relational model of group development with vulnerable populations. *Social Work with Groups,* *30*(2), 11–26

Schopler, J. H., & Galinsky, M. J. (1990). Can open-ended groups move beyond beginnings? *Small Group Research, 21*(4), 435–449.

Schopler, J. H., Galinsky, M. J., Davis, L. E., & Despard, M. (1996). The RAP model: Assessing a framework for leading multiracial groups. *Social Work with Groups, 19*(3/4), 21–39.

Schwartz, W. (1969). Private troubles and public issues: One social work job or two? In T. Berman-Ross (Ed.), *The collected works of William Schwartz* (pp. 377–394). Itasca, IL: Peacock.

Schwartz, W. (1971). On the use of group in social work practice. In. W. Schwartz & S. Zalba (Eds.), *The practice of group work* (pp. 13–18). New York, NY: Columbia University Press.

Schwartz, W. (1976). Between client and system: The mediating function. In R. W. Roberts & H. Northen (Eds.), *Theories of social work with groups* (pp. 171–198). New York, NY: Free Press.

Schwartz, W. (1994). Private troubles and public issues: One social work job or two? In T. Berman-Ross (Ed.), *Social work: The collected writings of William Schwartz* (pp. 377–394). Itasca, IL: Peacock.

Schwartz, W. (2006). The group work tradition and social work practice. *Social Work with Groups, 28*(3/4), 69–89. Retrieved from doi: 10.1300/ J009v28n03_06.

Schwartz, W., & Zalba, S. (1971). *The practice of group work.* New York, NY: Columbia University Press.

Sciarra, D. (1999). *Multiculturalism in counseling.* Itasca, IL: Peacock.

Shapiro, E. L., & Ginzberg, R. (2002). Parting gifts: Termination rituals in group therapy. *International Journal of Group Psychotherapy, 52,* 17.

Shulman, L. (1986). The dynamics of mutual aid. *Social Work with Groups, 8*(4), 51–60.

Shulman, L. (2011). *Dynamics and skills of group counseling.* Belmont, CA: Brooks/Cole.

Shulman, L. (2015). *The skills of helping individuals, families, groups and communities* (8th ed.). Belmont, CA: Brooks/Cole.

Sinclair, R. (2004). Aboriginal social work education in Canada: Decolonizing pedagogy for the seventh generation. *First Nations and Family Review, 1*(1), 49–61.

Singh, A. A., & Salazar, C. F. (2010). Six considerations for social justice group work. *Journal for Specialists in Group Work, 35*(3), 308–319.

Smith, L. C., & Shin, R. Q. (2008). Social privilege, social justice, and group counseling: An inquiry. *Journal for Specialists in Group Work, 33*(4), 351–366.

Smythe, S. (2004). *Exotic dancer outreach projec*t. Ottawa, ON: Ottawa Rape Crisis Centre.

Statistics Canada. (2012). *Edmonton, AB (Code 835) & Alberta (Code 48) census profile, 2011 census*. Retrieved from http://www12.statcan.gc.ca/census-recensement/2011/dp-pd/prof/index.cfm?Lang=E.

Steinberg, D. M. (2014). *A mutual-aid model for social work with groups* (3rd ed.). New York, NY: Routledge.

Strauss, W., & Howe, N. (1991). *Generations: The history of America's future, 1584 to 2069*. New York, NY: William Morrow.

Sullivan, N. (2004). Conflict as an expression of difference: A desirable group dynamic in anti-oppressive social work practice. In C. Carson, A. Fritz, E. Lewis, J. Ramey, & D. Suguichi (Eds.), *Growth and development through group work* (pp. 75–89). New York, NY: Haworth Press.

Tamm, L., et al. (2005). Intervention for preschoolers at risk for Attention deficit/hyperactivity disorder (ADHD): Services before diagnosis. *Clinical Neuroscience Research, 5*, 247–253.

Theodorson, G., & Theodorson, A. (1969). *A modern dictionary of sociology*. New York, NY: Crowell.

Thorell, L. B. (2009). The Community Parent Education Program (COPE): Treatment effects in a clinical and community-based sample. *Clinical Child Psychology and Psychiatry, 14*(3), 373–387.

Tjosvold, D., Poon, M., & Zi-You, Y. (2005). Team effectiveness in China: Cooperative conflict for relationship building. *Human Relations, 3*(58), 26.

Topor, D. R., Grosso, D., Burt, J., & Falcon, T. (2013). Skills for recovery: A recovery-oriented dual diagnosis group for veterans with serious mental illness and substance abuse. *Social Work with Groups, 36*, 222–235.

Toseland, R., & Horton, H. (2008). Group work. In T. Mizrahi & H. Horton (Eds.), *Encyclopedia of social work*. Washington, DC: National Association of Social Workers.

Toseland, R., & Rivas, R. F. (2005). *An introduction to group work practice* (5th ed.). Boston, MA: Allyn and Bacon.

Toseland, R., & Rivas, R. F. (2011). *An introduction to group work practice* (7th ed.). Boston, MA: Pearson.

Toseland, R., Jones, L., & Gellis, Z. (2004). Group dynamics. In C. Garvin, L. Guitierrez, & M. Galinsky (Eds.), *Handbook of social work with groups* (pp. 13–31). New York, NY: Guilford Press.

Travis, R., & Bowman, S. W. (2011). Negotiating risk and promoting empowerment through rap music: Development of a measure to capture risk and empowerment pathways to change. *Journal of Human Behavior in the Social Environment, 21*(6), 654–678.

Trecker, H. (1972). *Social group work*. New York, NY: Association Press.

Trocme, N., Knoke, D., & Blackstock, C. (2004). Pathways to the overrepresentation of Aboriginal children in Canada's child welfare system. *Social Services Review, 78*, 577–600.

Tucker, J. S., Wenzel, S. L., Straus, J. B., Gery, R. W., & Golinelli, D. (2005). Experiencing interpersonal violence: Perspectives of sexually active, substance-using women living in shelters and low-income housing. *Violence against Women, 11*(10), 1319–1340.

Tuckman, B. (1963). Developmental sequence in small groups. *Psychological Bulletin, 63*, 384–399.

Tuckman, B., & Jensen, K. (1977). Stages of group development revisited. *Journal of Group and Organizational Studies, 2*(4), 419–427.

Tutty, L., Bidgood, B., & Rothery, M. (1993) Support groups for battered women: Research on their efficacy. *Journal of Family Violence, 8*, 325–343.

Tutty, L., Bidgood, B., & Rothery, M. (1996) Evaluating the effect of group process and client variables in support groups for battered women. *Research on Social Work Practice, 6*, 308–324.

Tyson, E. H. (2003). Rap music in social work practice with African American and Latino youth: A conceptual model with practical applications. *Journal of Human Behavior in the Social Environment, 11*(3/4), 59–82.

United States Department of Education. (2008). *Psychological first aid (PFA) for students and teachers: Listen, protect, connect—model and teach.* Retrieved from http://rems.ed.gov/docs/HH_Vol3Issue3.pdf.

Van Ameringen, M., Mancini, C., Patterson, B., & Boyle, M. H. (2008). Post-traumatic stress disorder in Canada. *CNS Neuroscience & Therapeutics, 14*(3), 171–181.

Van Knippenberg, D., & Schippers, M. C. (2007). Work group diversity. *The Annual Review of Psychology, 58*, 515–541.

Vinter, R. (1974). The essential components of social group work practice. In P. Glasser, R. Sarri, & R. Vinter (Eds.), *Individual change through small groups* (pp. 9–33). New York, NY: Free Press.

Von Glinow, M. A., Shapiro, D. L., & Brett, J. M. (2004). Can we talk, and should we? Managing emotional conflict in multicultural teams. *Academy of Management Review, 29*(4), 578–592. Retrieved from http://www.jstor.org/stable/20159072.

Waites, C. (2008). *Social work practice with African-American families: An intergenerational perspective.* New York, NY: Routledge.

Watson, D., & Parsons, S. (2005) *Domestic abuse of women and men in Ireland: Report on the National Study of Domestic Abuse.* National Crime Council: Dublin, Ireland.

Wesley-Esquimaux, C. C., & Smolewski, M. (2004). *Historical trauma and Aboriginal healing.* Prepared for the Aboriginal Healing Foundation. Retrieved from http://www.ahf.ca/publications/research series.

Wheelan, S. (2005). *Creating effective teams: A guide for members and leaders* (2nd ed.). Thousand Oaks, CA: Sage.

Wickham, E., Pelech, W., & Basso, R. (2009). *Group work practice.* Toronto, ON: Thompson Educational.

Wilson, F. R., Rapin, L. S., & Haley-Banez, L. (2004). How teaching group work can be guided by foundational documents: Best practice guidelines, diversity principles, training standards. *Journal for Specialists in Group Work, 29*(1), 19–29.

Wilson, G. (1976). From practice to theory. In R. W. Roberts & H. Northen (Eds.), *Theories of social work with groups* (pp. 1–44). New York, NY: Columbia University Press.

Wilson, G., & Ryland, G. (1949). *Social group work practice.* Cambridge MA: Houghton Mifflin.

Wisesale, S. K. (2003). Global aging and intergenerational equity. *Journal of Intergenerational Relationships, 1*, 29–47.

Wright, N. M., Tompkins, C. N., & Sheard, L. (2007) Is peer injection a form of intimate partner abuse? A qualitative study of the experiences of women drug users. *Health and Social Care in the Community, 15*(5), 417–425.

Yalom, I. (1970). *The theory and practice of group psychotherapy.* New York, NY: Basic Books.

Yalom, I. (1985). *The theory and practice of group psychotherapy* (3rd ed.). New York, NY: Basic Books.

Yalom, I. (1995). *The theory and practice of group psychotherapy* (4th ed.). New York, NY: Basic Books.

Yalom, I., & Leszcz, M. (2005). *The theory and practice of group psychotherapy.* New York, NY: Basic Books.

Yuval-Davis, N. (2006). Intersectionality and feminist politics. *European Journal of Women's Studies, 13*(3), 193–209. Retrieved from doi: 10.1177/1350506806065752.

INDEX

ABOUT THE EDITORS

William Pelech, PhD, currently holds an appointment as full professor and associate dean in the Faculty of Social Work at the University of Calgary. He has practiced and taught group work for over twenty years. His doctoral dissertation focused on patterns of nonverbal behavior in interventive groups. Pelech currently holds a major national tricouncil grant, which focuses on how practitioners utilize diversity in their group work practice. He has been a coprincipal investigator on a major nation grant relating to intergenerational trauma among First Nations people and a national research project, which developed a virtual community of practice for practitioners and caregivers for individuals who experience fetal alcohol spectrum disorder. Pelech also pioneered the BSW Virtual Learning Circle, a blended BSW program, and was presented the prestigious Killam Award for Innovation in Education for this work. He has served on the board of directors and as cochair of the 36th Annual Symposium of the International Association for Social Work with Groups, as well as being a member of the editorial board of *Groupwork*.

Robert Basso, MSW, ACSW, PhD, currently holds an appointment as associate professor in the Faculty of Social Work at Wilfrid Laurier University in Waterloo, Ontario. He currently is associate dean of a BSW program and is chair of the University Research Ethics Board. He has been a practicing group worker for over three decades, working with men who have been abused as children and coronary care patients and in a variety of hospital-based group work programs. He has been involved in research focusing on practice in medical social work and practice with children and adolescents. He has published many research-based group practice articles and a book relating to group work practice.

Cheryl D. Lee, MSW, PhD, is professor at the School of Social Work, California State University, Long Beach. She has taught social work with groups for sixteen years. She has been very active in the International Association of Social Work with Groups (IASWG), serving as Southern California chapter chair, international board member, chair of the 2011 International Symposium on the *Queen Mary* in Long Beach, California, and editor of the Long Beach Symposium Proceedings. In addition, she initiated a long-standing student group work club. She has published and made numerous presentations about group work and also serves on the editorial board of *Groupwork*. She has facilitated intervention, task, and legislative groups and believes strongly in this social work method of helping people and society progress. She received her social work education at Arizona State University where she also taught. Her undergraduate degree is in sociology from George Washington University.

Maria Gandarilla, BSW, MSW, currently works as a hospice social worker in Orange County, California. In this position, she is one of the social workers responsible for establishing support groups for families receiving services and the community. Gandarilla has facilitated or cofacilitated several groups throughout her career, including teen parenting support groups, anger management groups, parent advocacy groups, and talking circles with elementary-aged children. Gandarilla has served and participated on several task-oriented groups, including the board of managers for the YMCA of Greater Long Beach Community Development Branch, the International Association of Social Work with Groups (IASWG) international board, and the Social Work Alumni Group of California State University, Long Beach, to name a few. Gandarilla serves as an elected board member with the IASWG Southern California chapter and has held multiple leadership positions, currently holding the position of cochair.

CPSIA information can be obtained
at www.ICGtesting.com
Printed in the USA
BVOW08s0207161217
502851BV00004B/9/P